BEAR, MAN, and GOD:

Seven Approaches to William Faulkner's

THE BEAR

BEAR, MAN, & GOD

Seven Approaches to

William Faulkner's

The Bear

Edited by

FRANCIS LEE UTLEY
Ohio State University

LYNN Z. BLOOM
Western Reserve University

ARTHUR F. KINNEY
University of Massachusetts

Random House New York

Design by Tere LoPrete

To the memory of William Faulkner

ACKNOWLEDGMENTS

To work with the prose of William Faulkner can be a thrilling and satisfying experience. Many have helped us in this endeavor, and to that extent share in its rewards. But we should like to extend our gratitude publicly to Professors Richard Altick, Arthur J. Carr, Joe Lee Davis, Hubert M. English, Claude Simpson, and Mark Spilka for their professional counsel; to Charles Pettee of Charles Scribner's Sons, who first suggested the present collaboration; to Philip Lee Utley, who taught one of us how much *The Bear* could mean to an undergraduate; to the staffs of the University of Michigan, Ohio State University, and Clements Libraries for their kind and patient assistance with our research; and to the staff of the University of Michigan Audio-Visual Education Center for their aid. We all owe special thanks to Jane P. Alles of Random House, who has combined the roles of wise advisor, good friend, and communications center.

For the three of us, second only to working with *The Bear* has been the joy of working as colleagues. We have had the discovery of new insights and experienced the meeting of minds which bridges varied backgrounds—two of the reasons men read and write at all. We hope some of our readers may discover such pleasures as well.

CONTENTS

WILLIAM FAULKNER'S *THE BEAR*

Introduction   3

The Bear   5

SEVEN APPROACHES TO *THE BEAR*

Introduction   115

The Role of Personal Experience in Faulkner's Work   121

MICHAEL MILLGATE, William Faulkner: A Bio-
graphical Sketch   121

Anecdotes and Other Stories About Old Ben   129

CYNTHIA GRENIER, The Art of Fiction: An Inter-
view with William Faulkner—September, 1955   129

JOHN B. CULLEN in collaboration with FLOYD C.
WATKINS, From *Old Times in the Faulkner
Country*   130

WILLIAM FAULKNER, Lion: A Story   132

WILLIAM FAULKNER, *The Bear* (*Saturday Evening
Post* version)   149

***The Bear* in Relation to Faulkner's Other Works**   165

MILLAR MacLURE, The Historic Ages of Yok-
napatawpha County   165

ROBERT PENN WARREN, Tradition, Moral Con-
fusion, the Negro: Themes in Faulkner's Work   166

WILLIAM FAULKNER, Speech of Acceptance upon the Award of the Nobel Prize for Literature 170

MALCOLM COWLEY, On Method and Theme in Faulkner 171

WILLIAM FAULKNER, From *The Hamlet* 172

WILLIAM FAULKNER, Sam Fathers 172

WILLIAM FAULKNER, From "Was" 173

WILLIAM FAULKNER, The Blood Ritual of Isaac McCaslin 174

WILLIAM FAULKNER, Race at Morning 180

WILLIAM FAULKNER, Boon Hogganbeck 181

The Cultural Roots of *The Bear* 185

FRANK G. SPECK and JESSE MOSES, How to Catch Bears (Twenyucis's Dream) 185

A. IRVING HALLOWELL, From *Bear Ceremonialism in the Northern Hemisphere* 187

MIRCEA ELIADE, The Pattern of Initiation 190

A. C. FLETCHER and F. LaFLESCHE, An Indian Boy's Initiation into Manhood in the Omaha Tribe 193

AUDREY I. RICHARDS, A Girls' Initiation Ceremony Among the Bemba of Northern Rhodesia 196

W. J. CASH, From *The Mind of the South* 198

THOMAS BANGS THORPE, The Big Bear of Arkansas 208

SAMUEL L. CLEMENS, You Can't Pray a Lie 223

KENNETH LaBUDDE, Cultural Primitivism in William Faulkner's *The Bear* 226

FRANCIS LEE UTLEY, Pride and Humility: The Cultural Roots of Ike McCaslin 233

Critical Interpretations of *The Bear* 261

THOMAS C. WERTENBAKER, JR., Faulkner's Point of View and The Chronicle of Ike McCaslin 261

DALE G. BREADEN, William Faulkner and the Land 273

HARRY MODEAN CAMPBELL and RUEL E. FOSTER, Primitivism and *The Bear* 279

JOHN LYDENBERG, Nature Myth in Faulkner's *The Bear* 280

WALTER F. TAYLOR, JR., Let My People Go: The White Man's Heritage in *Go Down, Moses* 290

HERBERT A. PERLUCK, The Heart's Driving Complexity: An Unromantic Reading of Faulkner's *The Bear* 301

IRVING MALIN, Ike McCaslin's Covenants 303

R. W. B. LEWIS, The Hero in the New World: William Faulkner's *The Bear* 306

OLGA W. VICKERY, God's Moral Order and the Problem of Ike's Redemption 323

DAVID H. STEWART, The Purpose of Faulkner's Ike 327

The Relation of Style and Meaning in Faulkner's Work 337

FREDERICK J. HOFFMAN, Faulkner's Concepts of Time 337

WILLIAM VAN O'CONNOR, Rhetoric in Southern Writing: Faulkner 342

HARRY MODEAN CAMPBELL and RUEL E. FOSTER, Faulkner's Uses of Imagery and Humor 347

IRVING HOWE, The Relationship Between Part IV and the Rest of *The Bear* 349

Sean O'Faolain, Faulkner's Stylistic Failings   352

Martha Bennett Stiles, The Saxon Beauty and
   the Three Black Bears   355

**The Relationship Between "Delta Autumn" and *The
Bear***   361

William Faulkner, "Delta Autumn"   361
Arthur F. Kinney, "Delta Autumn": Postlude to
   The Bear   384

APPENDIXES   397

Ward L. Miner, From *The World of William
   Faulkner*   399
Michael Millgate, Descendants of L. Q. C. Mc-
   Caslin   401
Book of Genesis, The Sacrifice of Isaac   402
The Immediate Critical Reception of *Go Down,
   Moses*   404
Questions for Discussion and Writing   407
Bibliography   417
William Faulkner's Canon   428

William Faulkner's
THE BEAR

Introduction

Despite the central position *The Bear* holds today in the works of William Faulkner and of twentieth-century America, the story remained relatively unknown for several years. Parts of *The Bear* first appeared as magazine stories—one in 1935 and another the day after the final version was published in book form as one of the seven parts of *Go Down, Moses*. The book (Random House, 1942) was concerned with the white McCaslin and the Negro Beauchamp descendants of Lucius Quintus McCaslin. Since that time, *The Bear* has come to take its place with the best works of American fiction.

The Bear is comparable in length to *Old Man* and *Spotted Horses*. It is part of the saga of Faulkner's own imaginative Yoknapatawpha County, which Ward Miner, among others, has contended is the fictional counterpart of present-day Lafayette County in Mississippi. The work is divided into five parts. Parts one, two, three, and five form the central story of the boy Isaac's search for Old Ben and its aftermath; it is one of the great hunting stories in the English language, and it is in Faulkner's simplest and most energetic style. Part four is more difficult; it is Faulkner's attempt to give the other four parts an explanation through Isaac's quest into the past, and significance by showing what the events mean to Ike and what the quest does to his future. This section is Faulkner's comprehensive attempt to express ideas about God, nature, and man coupled with his interpretation of the history of the South; and he has put it into one sentence. Malcolm Cowley (in *The Portable Faulkner*) has pointed out that this sentence runs to sixteen hundred words, each placed rhythmically yet precisely between one capital letter and one period—one of the longest sentences in all literature. Within it, notes Cowley, roam other sentences up to six pages long and, near the center, a parenthesis which extends for two pages. But if the style is unusually challenging for Faulkner readers, this section contains much of what Faulkner spent a lifetime writing about.

The Bear

The events of The Bear *occur in the northwestern corner of Yok-napatawpha County, well north of Jefferson, its capital city, in a woods along the Tallahatchie River bottom. The land, formerly belonging to a large plantation of a hundred square miles, owned by Thomas Sutpen, was taken over by Major Cassius de Spain through foreclosures. The Major turned a poor white's shack on the land into a hunting cabin and shortly after, each November, began two-week hunting parties into the woods with his old friends General Compson, McCaslin Edmonds, and finally young Isaac McCaslin, the boy of this story. After Major de Spain discovered Old Ben, the bear which was ravaging the countryside, the Major, his friends, and his servants—the Indian guide Sam Fathers, the part-Indian Boon, and the Negro cook Ash—made him the principal quarry of their hunting parties.*

1.

There was a man and a dog too this time. Two beasts, counting Old Ben, the bear, and two men, counting Boon Hogganbeck, in whom some of the same blood ran which ran in Sam Fathers, even though Boon's was a plebeian strain of it and only Sam and Old Ben and the mongrel Lion were taintless and incorruptible.

FROM *Go Down, Moses* (New York: Random House, 1942), pp. 191-331. Reprinted by permission of Random House, Inc. Copyright 1942 by the Curtis Publishing Co., Copyright 1942 by William Faulkner.

He was sixteen. For six years now he had been a man's hunter.
For six years now he had heard the best of all talking. It was of
the wilderness, the big woods, bigger and older than any recorded
document:—of white man fatuous enough to believe he had
bought any fragment of it, of Indian ruthless enough to pretend
that any fragment of it had been his to convey; bigger than Major
de Spain and the scrap he pretended to, knowing better; older than
old Thomas Sutpen of whom Major de Spain had had it and who
knew better; older even than old Ikkemotubbe, the Chickasaw
chief, of whom old Sutpen had had it and who knew better in his
turn. It was of the men, not white nor black nor red but men,
hunters, with the will and hardihood to endure and the humility
and skill to survive, and the dogs and the bear and deer juxtaposed
and reliefed against it, ordered and compelled by and within the
wilderness in the ancient and unremitting contest according to the
ancient and immitigable rules which voided all regrets and brooked
no quarter;—the best game of all, the best of all breathing and
forever the best of all listening, the voices quiet and weighty and
deliberate for retrospection and recollection and exactitude among
the concrete trophies—the racked guns and the heads and skins—
in the libraries of town houses or the offices of plantation houses
or (and best of all) in the camps themselves where the intact and
still-warm meat yet hung, the men who had slain it sitting before
the burning logs on hearths when there were houses and hearths or
about the smoky blazing of piled wood in front of stretched tarpaulins when there were not. There was always a bottle present,
so that it would seem to him that those fine fierce instants of heart
and brain and courage and wiliness and speed were concentrated
and distilled into that brown liquor which not women, not boys and
children, but only hunters drank, drinking not of the blood they
spilled but some condensation of the wild immortal spirit, drinking it moderately, humbly even, not with the pagan's base and
baseless hope of acquiring thereby the virtues of cunning and
strength and speed but in salute to them. Thus it seemed to him on
this December morning not only natural but actually fitting that
this should have begun with whisky.

He realised later that it had begun long before that. It had
already begun on that day when he first wrote his age in two

ciphers and his cousin McCaslin brought him for the first time to
the camp, the big woods, to earn for himself from the wilderness
the name and state of hunter provided he in his turn were humble
and enduring enough. He had already inherited then, without ever
having seen it, the big old bear with one trap-ruined foot that in
an area almost a hundred miles square had earned for himself a
name, a definite designation like a living man:—the long legend of
corn-cribs broken down and rifled, of shoats and grown pigs and
even calves carried bodily into the woods and devoured and traps
and deadfalls overthrown and dogs mangled and slain and shotgun
and even rifle shots delivered at point-blank range yet with no
more effect than so many peas blown through a tube by a child—
a corridor of wreckage and destruction beginning back before the
boy was born, through which sped, not fast but rather with the
ruthless and irresistible deliberation of a locomotive, the shaggy
tremendous shape. It ran in his knowledge before he ever saw it.
It loomed and towered in his dreams before he even saw the unaxed woods where it left its crooked print, shaggy, tremendous,
red-eyed, not malevolent but just big, too big for the dogs which
tried to bay it, for the horses which tried to ride it down, for the
men and the bullets they fired into it; too big for the very country
which was its constricting scope. It was as if the boy had already
divined what his senses and intellect had not encompassed yet:
that doomed wilderness whose edges were being constantly and
punily gnawed at by men with plows and axes who feared it because it was wilderness, men myriad and nameless even to one
another in the land where the old bear had earned a name, and
through which ran not even a mortal beast but an anachronism
indomitable and invincible out of an old dead time, a phantom,
epitome and apotheosis of the old wild life which the little puny
humans swarmed and hacked at in a fury of abhorrence and fear
like pygmies about the ankles of a drowsing elephant;—the old
bear, solitary, indomitable, and alone; widowered childless and
absolved of mortality—old Priam reft of his old wife and outlived
all his sons.

    Still a child, with three years then two years then one year yet
before he too could make one of them, each November he would
watch the wagon containing the dogs and the bedding and food and

guns and his cousin McCaslin and Tennie's Jim and Sam Fathers too until Sam moved to the camp to live, depart for the Big Bottom, the big woods. To him, they were going not to hunt bear and deer but to keep yearly rendezvous with the bear which they did not even intend to kill. Two weeks later they would return, with no trophy, no skin. He had not expected it. He had not even feared that it might be in the wagon this time with the other skins and heads. He did not even tell himself that in three years or two years or one year more he would be present and that it might even be his gun. He believed that only after he had served his apprenticeship in the woods which would prove him worthy to be a hunter, would he even be permitted to distinguish the crooked print, and that even then for two November weeks he would merely make another minor one, along with his cousin and Major de Spain and General Compson and Walter Ewell and Boon and the dogs which feared to bay it and the shotguns and rifles which failed even to bleed it, in the yearly pageant-rite of the old bear's furious immortality.

His day came at last. In the surrey with his cousin and Major de Spain and General Compson he saw the wilderness through a slow drizzle of November rain just above the ice point as it seemed to him later he always saw it or at least always remembered it— the tall and endless wall of dense November woods under the dissolving afternoon and the year's death, sombre, impenetrable (he could not even discern yet how, at what point they could possibly hope to enter it even though he knew that Sam Fathers was waiting there with the wagon), the surrey moving through the skeleton stalks of cotton and corn in the last of open country, the last trace of man's puny gnawing at the immemorial flank, until, dwarfed by that perspective into an almost ridiculous diminishment, the surrey itself seemed to have ceased to move (this too to be completed later, years later, after he had grown to a man and had seen the sea) as a solitary small boat hangs in lonely immobility, merely tossing up and down, in the infinite waste of the ocean while the water and then the apparently impenetrable land which it nears without appreciable progress, swings slowly and opens the widening inlet which is the anchorage. He entered it. Sam was waiting, wrapped in a quilt on the wagon seat behind

the patient and steaming mules. He entered his novitiate to the
true wilderness with Sam beside him as he had begun his apprenticeship in miniature to manhood after the rabbits and such with
Sam beside him, the two of them wrapped in the damp, warm,
negro-rank quilt while the wilderness closed behind his entrance
as it had opened momentarily to accept him, opening before his
advancement as it closed behind his progress, no fixed path the
wagon followed but a channel nonexistent ten yards ahead of it
and ceasing to exist ten yards after it had passed, the wagon pro-
gressing not by its own volition but by attrition of their intact yet
fluid circumambience, drowsing, earless, almost lightless.

It seemed to him that at the age of ten he was witnessing his
own birth. It was not even strange to him. He had experienced it
all before, and not merely in dreams. He saw the camp—a paintless six-room bungalow set on piles above the spring high-water—
and he knew already how it was going to look. He helped in the
rapid orderly disorder of their establishment in it and even his
motions were familiar to him, foreknown. Then for two weeks he
ate the coarse, rapid food—the shapeless sour bread, the wild
strange meat, venison and bear and turkey and coon which he had
never tasted before—which men ate, cooked by men who were
hunters first and cooks afterward; he slept in harsh sheetless blankets as hunters slept. Each morning the gray of dawn found him
and Sam Fathers on the stand, the crossing, which had been allotted him. It was the poorest one, the most barren. He had expected that; he had not dared yet to hope even to himself that he
would even hear the running dogs this first time. But he did hear
them. It was on the third morning—a murmur, sourceless, almost
indistinguishable, yet he knew what it was although he had never
before heard that many dogs running at once, the murmur swelling
into separate and distinct voices until he could call the five dogs
which his cousin owned from among the others. "Now," Sam said,
"slant your gun up a little and draw back the hammers and then
stand still."

But it was not for him, not yet. The humility was there; he had
learned that. And he could learn the patience. He was only ten,
only one week. The instant had passed. It seemed to him that he
could actually see the deer, the buck, smoke-colored, elongated

with speed, vanished, the woods, the gray solitude still ringing even when the voices of the dogs had died away; from far away across the sombre woods and the gray half-liquid morning there came two shots. "Now let your hammers down," Sam said.

He did so. "You knew it too," he said.

"Yes," Sam said. "I want you to learn how to do when you didn't shoot. It's after the chance for the bear or the deer has done already come and gone that men and dogs get killed."

"Anyway, it wasn't him," the boy said. "It wasn't even a bear. It was just a deer."

"Yes," Sam said, "it was just a deer."

Then one morning, it was in the second week, he heard the dogs again. This time before Sam even spoke he readied the too-long, too-heavy, man-size gun as Sam had taught him, even though this time he knew the dogs and the deer were coming less close than ever, hardly within hearing even. They didn't sound like any running dogs he had ever heard before even. Then he found that Sam, who had taught him first of all to cock the gun and take position where he could see best in all directions and then never to move again, had himself moved up beside him. "There," he said. "Listen." The boy listened, to no ringing chorus strong and fast on a free scent but a moiling yapping an octave too high and with something more than indecision and even abjectness in it which he could not yet recognise, reluctant, not even moving very fast, taking a long time to pass out of hearing, leaving even then in the air that echo of thin and almost human hysteria, abject, almost humanly grieving, with this time nothing ahead of it, no sense of a fleeing unseen smoke-colored shape. He could hear Sam breathing at his shoulder. He saw the arched curve of the old man's inhaling nostrils.

"It's Old Ben!" he cried, whispering.

Sam didn't move save for the slow gradual turning of his head as the voices faded on and the faint steady rapid arch and collapse of his nostrils. "Hah," he said. "Not even running. Walking."

"But up here!" the boy cried. "Way up here!"

"He do it every year," Sam said. "Once. Ash and Boon say he comes up here to run the other little bears away. Tell them to get

to hell out of here and stay out until the hunters are gone. Maybe."
The boy no longer heard anything at all, yet still Sam's head continued to turn gradually and steadily until the back of it was toward him. Then it turned back and looked down at him—the same face, grave, familiar, expressionless until it smiled, the same old man's eyes from which as he watched there faded slowly a quality darkly and fiercely lambent, passionate and proud. "He dont care no more for bears than he does for dogs or men neither. He come to see who's here, who's new in camp this year, whether he can shoot or not, can stay or not. Whether we got the dog yet that can bay and hold him until a man gets there with a gun. Because he's the head bear. He's the man." It faded, was gone; again they were the eyes as he had known them all his life. "He'll let them follow him to the river. Then he'll send them home. We might as well go too; see how they look when they get back to camp."

The dogs were there first, ten of them huddled back under the kitchen, himself and Sam squatting to peer back into the obscurity where they crouched, quiet, the eyes rolling and luminous, vanishing, and no sound, only that effluvium which the boy could not quite place yet, of something more than dog, stronger than dog and not just animal, just beast even. Because there had been nothing in front of the abject and painful yapping except the solitude, the wilderness, so that when the eleventh hound got back about mid-afternoon and he and Tennie's Jim held the passive and still trembling bitch while Sam daubed her tattered ear and raked shoulder with turpentine and axle grease, it was still no living creature but only the wilderness which, leaning for a moment, had patted lightly once her temerity. "Just like a man," Sam said. "Just like folks. Put off as long as she could having to be brave, knowing all the time that sooner or later she would have to be brave once so she could keep on calling herself a dog, and knowing beforehand what was going to happen when she done it."

He did not know just when Sam left. He only knew that he was gone. For the next three mornings he rose and ate breakfast and Sam was not waiting for him. He went to his stand alone; he found it without help now and stood on it as Sam had taught him. On the third morning he heard the dogs again, running strong and free on a true scent again, and he readied the gun as he had learned to do and heard the hunt sweep past on since he was not ready yet, had not deserved other yet in just one short period of two weeks as compared to all the long life which he had already dedicated to the wilderness with patience and humility; he heard the shot again, one shot, the single clapping report of Walter Ewell's rifle. By now he could not only find his stand and then return to camp without guidance, by using the compass his cousin had given him he reached Walter waiting beside the buck and the moiling of dogs over the cast entrails before any of the others except Major de Spain and Tennie's Jim on the horses, even before Uncle Ash arrived with the one-eyed wagon-mule which did not mind the smell of blood or even, so they said, of bear.

It was not Uncle Ash on the mule. It was Sam, returned. And Sam was waiting when he finished his dinner and, himself on the one-eyed mule and Sam on the other one of the wagon team, they rode for more than three hours through the rapid shortening sunless afternoon, following no path, no trail even that he could discern, into a section of country he had never seen before. Then he understood why Sam had made him ride the one-eyed mule which would not spook at the smell of blood, of wild animals. The other one, the sound one, stopped short and tried to whirl and bolt even as Sam got down, jerking and wrenching at the rein while Sam held it, coaxing it forward with his voice since he did not dare risk hitching it, drawing it forward while the boy dismounted from the marred one which would stand. Then, standing beside Sam in the thick great gloom of ancient woods and the winter's dying afternoon, he looked quietly down at the rotted log scored and gutted with claw-marks and, in the wet earth beside it, the print of the enormous warped two-toed foot. Now he knew what he had heard in the hounds' voices in the woods that morning and what he had smelled when he peered under the kitchen where they huddled. It was in him too, a little different because they were brute beasts and he was not, but only a little different—an eagerness, passive; an abjectness, a sense of his own fragility and impotence against the timeless woods, yet without doubt or dread; a flavor like brass in the sudden run of saliva in his mouth, a hard sharp constriction either in his brain or his stomach, he could not tell

which and it did not matter; he knew only that for the first time
he realised that the bear which had run in his listening and loomed
in his dreams since before he could remember and which therefore must have existed in the listening and the dreams of his
cousin and Major de Spain and even old General Compson before
they began to remember in their turn, was a mortal animal and
that they had departed for the camp each November with no
actual intention of slaying it, not because it could not be slain
but because so far they had no actual hope of being able to. "It
will be tomorrow," he said.

"You mean we will try tomorrow," Sam said. "We aint got the
dog yet."

"We've got eleven," he said. "They ran him Monday."

"And you heard them," Sam said. "Saw them too. We aint got
the dog yet. It wont take but one. But he aint there. Maybe he
aint nowhere. The only other way will be for him to run by accident over somebody that had a gun and knowed how to shoot it."

"That wouldn't be me," the boy said. "It would be Walter or
Major or ——"

"It might," Sam said. "You watch close tomorrow. Because
he's smart. That's how come he has lived this long. If he gets
hemmed up and has got to pick out somebody to run over, he
will pick out you."

"How?" he said. "How will he know. . . ." He ceased. "You
mean he already knows me, that I aint never been to the big bottom before, aint had time to find out yet whether I . . ." He
ceased again, staring at Sam; he said humbly, not even amazed:
"It was me he was watching. I dont reckon he did need to come
but once."

"You watch tomorrow," Sam said. "I reckon we better start
back. It'll be long after dark now before we get to camp."

The next morning they started three hours earlier than they
had ever done. Even Uncle Ash went, the cook, who called himself by profession a camp cook and who did little else save cook
for Major de Spain's hunting and camping parties, yet who had
been marked by the wilderness from simple juxtaposition to it
until he responded as they all did, even the boy who until two
weeks ago had never even seen the wilderness, to a hound's ripped

ear and shoulder and the print of a crooked foot in a patch of wet earth. They rode. It was too far to walk: the boy and Sam and Uncle Ash in the wagon with the dogs, his cousin and Major de Spain and General Compson and Boon and Walter and Tennie's Jim riding double on the horses; again the first gray light found him, as on that first morning two weeks ago, on the stand where Sam had placed and left him. With the gun which was too big for him, the breech-loader which did not even belong to him but to Major de Spain and which he had fired only once, at a stump on the first day to learn the recoil and how to reload it with the paper shells, he stood against a big gum tree beside a little bayou whose black still water crept without motion out of a cane-brake, across a small clearing and into the cane again, where, invisible, a bird, the big woodpecker called Lord-to-God by negroes, clattered at a dead trunk. It was a stand like any other stand, dissimilar only in incidentals to the one where he had stood each morning for two weeks; a territory new to him yet no less familiar than that other one which after two weeks he had come to believe he knew a little—the same solitude, the same loneliness through which frail and timorous man had merely passed without altering it, leaving no mark nor scar, which looked exactly as it must have looked when the first ancestor of Sam Fathers' Chickasaw predecessors crept into it and looked about him, club or stone axe or bone arrow drawn and ready, different only because, squatting at the edge of the kitchen, he had smelled the dogs huddled and cringing beneath it and saw the raked ear and side of the bitch that, as Sam had said, had to be brave once in order to keep on calling herself a dog, and saw yesterday in the earth beside the gutted log, the print of the living foot. He heard no dogs at all. He never did certainly hear them. He only heard the drumming of the woodpecker stop short off, and knew that the bear was looking at him. He never saw it. He did not know whether it was facing him from the cane or behind him. He did not move, holding the useless gun which he knew now he would never fire at it, now or ever, tasting in his saliva that taint of brass which he had smelled in the huddled dogs when he peered under the kitchen.

Then it was gone. As abruptly as it had stopped, the woodpecker's dry hammering set up again, and after a while he believed he even heard the dogs—a murmur, scarce a sound even, which he had probably been hearing for a time, perhaps a minute or two, before he remarked it, drifting into hearing and then out again, dying away. They came nowhere near him. If it was dogs he heard, he could not have sworn to it; if it was a bear they ran, it was another bear. It was Sam himself who emerged from the cane and crossed the bayou, the injured bitch following at heel as a bird dog is taught to walk. She came and crouched against his leg, trembling. "I didn't see him," he said. "I didn't, Sam."

"I know it," Sam said. "He done the looking. You didn't hear him neither, did you?"

"No," the boy said. "I ——"

"He's smart," Sam said. "Too smart." Again the boy saw in his eyes that quality of dark and brooding lambence as Sam looked down at the bitch trembling faintly and steadily against the boy's leg. From her raked shoulder a few drops of fresh blood clung like bright berries. "Too big. We aint got the dog yet. But maybe some day."

Because there would be a next time, after and after. He was only ten. It seemed to him that he could see them, the two of them, shadowy in the limbo from which time emerged and became time: the old bear absolved of mortality and himself who shared a little of it. Because he recognised now what he had smelled in the huddled dogs and tasted in his own saliva, recognised fear as a boy, a youth, recognises the existence of love and passion and experience which is his heritage but not yet his patrimony, from entering by chance the presence or perhaps even merely the bedroom of a woman who has loved and been loved by many men. *So I will have to see him,* he thought, without dread or even hope. *I will have to look at him.* So it was in June of the next summer. They were at the camp again, celebrating Major de Spain's and General Compson's birthdays. Although the one had been born in September and the other in the depth of winter and almost thirty years earlier, each June the two of them and McCaslin and Boon and Walter Ewell (and the boy too from now on) spent two weeks at the camp, fishing and shooting squirrels and turkey and running coons and wildcats with the dogs at night. That is, Boon and the negroes (and the boy too now) fished and shot squirrels and ran the coons and cats, because the proven hunters, not only Major de Spain and old General Compson (who spent those two weeks sitting in a rocking chair before a tremendous iron pot of Brunswick stew, stirring and tasting, with Uncle Ash to quarrel with about how he was making it and Tennie's Jim to pour whisky into the tin dipper from which he drank it) but even McCaslin and Walter Ewell who were still young enough, scorned such other than shooting the wild gobblers with pistols for wagers or to test their marksmanship.

That is, his cousin McCaslin and the others thought he was hunting squirrels. Until the third evening he believed that Sam Fathers thought so too. Each morning he would leave the camp right after breakfast. He had his own gun now, a new breech-loader, a Christmas gift; he would own and shoot it for almost seventy years, through two new pairs of barrels and locks and one new stock, until all that remained of the original gun was the silver-inlaid trigger-guard with his and McCaslin's engraved names and the date in 1878. He found the tree beside the little bayou where he had stood that morning. Using the compass he ranged from that point; he was teaching himself to be better than a fair woodsman without even knowing he was doing it. On the third day he even found the gutted log where he had first seen the print. It was almost completely crumbled now, healing with unbelievable speed, a passionate and almost visible relinquishment, back into the earth from which the tree had grown. He ranged the summer woods now, green with gloom, if anything actually dimmer than they had been in November's gray dissolution, where even at noon the sun fell only in windless dappling upon the earth which never completely dried and which crawled with snakes—moccasins and watersnakes and rattlers, themselves the color of the dappled gloom so that he would not always see them until they moved; returning to camp later and later and later, first day, second day, passing in the twilight of the third evening the little log pen en-closing the log barn where Sam was putting up the stock for the night. "You aint looked right yet," Sam said.

He stopped. For a moment he didn't answer. Then he said peacefully, in a peaceful rushing burst, as when a boy's miniature dam in a little brook gives way: "All right. Yes. But how? I went to the bayou. I even found that log again. I ——"

"I reckon that was all right. Likely he's been watching you. You never saw his foot?"

"I . . ." the boy said. "I didn't . . . I never thought . . ."

"It's the gun," Sam said. He stood beside the fence, motionless, the old man, son of a negro slave and a Chickasaw chief, in the battered and faded overalls and the frayed five-cent straw hat which had been the badge of the negro's slavery and was now the regalia of his freedom. The camp—the clearing, the house, the barn and its tiny lot with which Major de Spain in his turn had scratched punily and evanescently at the wilderness—faded in the dusk, back into the immemorial darkness of the woods. *The gun,* the boy thought. *The gun.* "You will have to choose," Sam said.

He left the next morning before light, without breakfast, long before Uncle Ash would wake in his quilts on the kitchen floor and start the fire. He had only the compass and a stick for the snakes. He could go almost a mile before he would need to see the compass. He sat on a log, the invisible compass in his hand, while the secret night-sounds which had ceased at his movements, scurried again and then fell still for good and the owls ceased and gave over to the waking day birds and there was light in the gray wet woods and he could see the compass. He went fast yet still quietly, becoming steadily better and better as a woodsman without yet having time to realise it; he jumped a doe and a fawn, walked them out of the bed, close enough to see them—the crash of undergrowth, the white scut, the fawn scudding along behind her, faster than he had known it could have run. He was hunting right, upwind, as Sam had taught him, but that didn't matter now. He had left the gun; by his own will and relinquishment he had accepted not a gambit, not a choice, but a condition in which not only the bear's heretofore inviolable anonymity but all the ancient rules and balances of hunter and hunted had been abrogated. He would not even be afraid, not even in the moment when the fear would take him completely: blood, skin, bowels, bones, memory from the long time before it even became his memory—all save that thin clear quenchless lucidity which alone differed him from

this bear and from all the other bears and bucks he would follow
during almost seventy years, to which Sam had said: "Be scared.
You cant help that. But dont be afraid. Aint nothing in the woods
going to hurt you if you dont corner it or it dont smell that you
are afraid. A bear or a deer has got to be scared of a coward the
same as a brave man has got to be."

By noon he was far beyond the crossing on the little bayou,
farther into the new and alien country than he had ever been,
travelling now not only by the compass but by the old, heavy,
biscuit-thick silver watch which had been his father's. He had left
the camp nine hours ago; nine hours from now, dark would already have been an hour old. He stopped, for the first time since
he had risen from the log when he could see the compass face at
last, and looked about, mopping his sweating face on his sleeve.
He had already relinquished, of his will, because of his need, in
humility and peace and without regret, yet apparently that had
not been enough, the leaving of the gun was not enough. He stood
for a moment—a child, alien and lost in the green and soaring
gloom of the markless wilderness. Then he relinquished completely
to it. It was the watch and the compass. He was still tainted. He
removed the linked chain of the one and the looped thong of the
other from his overalls and hung them on a bush and leaned the
stick beside them and entered it.

When he realised he was lost, he did as Sam had coached and
drilled him: made a cast to cross his backtrack. He had not been
going very fast for the last two or three hours, and he had gone
even less fast since he left the compass and watch on the bush.
So he went slower still now, since the tree could not be very far;
in fact, he found it before he really expected to and turned and
went to it. But there was no bush beneath it, no compass nor
watch, so he did next as Sam had coached and drilled him: made
this next circle in the opposite direction and much larger, so that
the pattern of the two of them would bisect his track somewhere,
but crossing no trace nor mark anywhere of his feet or any feet,
and now he was going faster though still not panicked, his heart
beating a little more rapidly but strong and steady enough, and
this time it was not even the tree because there was a down log
beside it which he had never seen before and beyond the log a

little swamp, a seepage of moisture somewhere between earth and water, and he did what Sam had coached and drilled him as the next and the last, seeing as he sat down on the log the crooked print, the warped indentation in the wet ground which while he looked at it continued to fill with water until it was level full and the water began to overflow and the sides of the print began to dissolve away. Even as he looked up he saw the next one, and, moving, the one beyond it; moving, not hurrying, running, but merely keeping pace with them as they appeared before him as though they were being shaped out of thin air just one constant pace short of where he would lose them forever and be lost forever himself, tireless, eager, without doubt or dread, panting a little above the strong rapid little hammer of his heart, emerging suddenly into a little glade and the wilderness coalesced. It rushed, soundless, and solidified—the tree, the bush, the compass and the watch glinting where a ray of sunlight touched them. Then he saw the bear. It did not emerge, appear: it was just there, immobile, fixed in the green and windless noon's hot dappling, not as big as he had dreamed it but as big as he had expected, bigger, dimensionless against the dappled obscurity, looking at him. Then it moved. It crossed the glade without haste, walking for an instant into the sun's full glare and out of it, and stopped again and looked back at him across one shoulder. Then it was gone. It didn't walk into the woods. It faded, sank back into the wilderness without motion as he had watched a fish, a huge old bass, sink back into the dark depths of its pool and vanish without even any movement of its fins.

2.

So he should have hated and feared Lion. He was thirteen then. He had killed his buck and Sam Fathers had marked his face with the hot blood, and in the next November he killed a bear. But before that accolade he had become as competent in the woods as many grown men with the same experience. By now he was a better woodsman than most grown men with more. There was no territory within twenty-five miles of the camp that he did not know—bayou, ridge, landmark trees and path; he could have led anyone direct to any spot in it and brought him back. He knew game trails that even Sam Fathers had never seen; in the third fall he found a buck's bedding-place by himself and unbeknown to his cousin he borrowed Walter Ewell's rifle and lay in wait for the buck at dawn and killed it when it walked back to the bed as Sam had told him how the old Chickasaw fathers did.

By now he knew the old bear's footprint better than he did his own, and not only the crooked one. He could see any one of the three sound prints and distinguish it at once from any other, and not only because of its size. There were other bears within that fifty miles which left tracks almost as large, or at least so near that the one would have appeared larger only by juxtaposition. It was more than that. If Sam Fathers had been his mentor and the back-yard rabbits and squirrels his kindergarten, then the wilderness the old bear ran was his college and the old male bear itself, so long unwifed and childless as to have become its own ungendered progenitor, was his alma mater.

He could find the crooked print now whenever he wished, ten miles or five miles or sometimes closer than that, to the camp. Twice while on stand during the next three years he heard the dogs strike its trail and once even jump it by chance, the voices high, abject, almost human in their hysteria. Once, still-hunting with Walter Ewell's rifle, he saw it cross a long corridor of down timber where a tornado had passed. It rushed through rather than across the tangle of trunks and branches as a locomotive would, faster than he had ever believed it could have moved, almost as fast as a deer even because the deer would have spent most of that distance in the air; he realised then why it would take a dog not only of abnormal courage but size and speed too ever to bring it to bay. He had a little dog at home, a mongrel, of the sort called fyce by negroes, a ratter, itself not much bigger than a rat and possessing that sort of courage which had long since stopped being bravery and had become foolhardiness. He brought it with him one June and, timing them as if they were meeting an ap-pointment with another human being, himself carrying the fyce with a sack over its head and Sam Fathers with a brace of the hounds on a rope leash, they lay downwind of the trail and actually ambushed the bear. They were so close that it turned at bay although he realised later this might have been from surprise and amazement at the shrill and frantic uproar of the fyce. It turned at bay against the trunk of a big cypress, on its hind feet; it seemed to the boy that it would never stop rising, taller and taller, and even the two hounds seemed to have taken a kind of desperate and despairing courage from the fyce. Then he realised that the fyce was actually not going to stop. He flung the gun down and ran. When he overtook and grasped the shrill, frantically pinwheeling little dog, it seemed to him that he was directly under the bear. He could smell it, strong and hot and rank. Sprawling, he looked up where it loomed and towered over him like a thunderclap. It was quite familiar, until he remembered: this was the way he had used to dream about it.

Then it was gone. He didn't see it go. He knelt, holding the frantic fyce with both hands, hearing the abased wailing of the two hounds drawing further and further away, until Sam came up, carrying the gun. He laid it quietly down beside the boy and stood looking down at him. "You've done seed him twice now, with a gun in your hands," he said. "This time you couldn't have missed him."

The boy rose. He still held the fyce. Even in his arms it continued to yap frantically, surging and straining toward the fading sound of the hounds like a collection of live-wire springs. The boy was panting a little. "Neither could you," he said. "You had the gun. Why didn't you shoot him?"

Sam didn't seem to have heard. He put out his hand and touched the little dog in the boy's arms which still yapped and strained even though the two hounds were out of hearing now. "He's done gone," Sam said. "You can slack off and rest now, until next time." He stroked the little dog until it began to grow quiet under his hand. "You's almost the one we wants," he said. "You just aint big enough. We aint got that one yet. He will need to be just a little bigger than smart, and a little braver than either." He withdrew his hand from the fyce's head and stood looking into the woods where the bear and the hounds had vanished. "Somebody is going to, some day."

"I know it," the boy said. "That's why it must be one of us. So it wont be until the last day. When even he dont want it to last any longer."

So he should have hated and feared Lion. It was in the fourth summer, the fourth time he had made one in the celebration of Major de Spain's and General Compson's birthday. In the early spring Major de Spain's mare had foaled a horse colt. One evening when Sam brought the horses and mules up to stable them for the night, the colt was missing and it was all he could do to get the frantic mare into the lot. He had thought at first to let the mare lead him back to where she had become separated from the foal. But she would not do it. She would not even feint toward any particular part of the woods or even in any particular direction. She merely ran, as if she couldn't see, still frantic with terror. She whirled and ran at Sam once, as if to attack him in some ultimate desperation, as if she could not for the moment realise that he was a man and a long-familiar one. He got her into the lot at last. It was too dark by that time to back-track her, to unravel the erratic course she had doubtless pursued.

He came to the house and told Major de Spain. It was an animal, of course, a big one, and the colt was dead now, wherever it was. They all knew that. "It's a panther," General Compson said at once. "The same one. That doe and fawn last March." Sam had sent Major de Spain word of it when Boon Hogganbeck came to the camp on a routine visit to see how the stock had wintered—the doe's throat torn out, and the beast had run down the helpless fawn and killed it too.

"Sam never did say that was a panther," Major de Spain said. Sam said nothing now, standing behind Major de Spain where they sat at supper, inscrutable, as if he were just waiting for them to stop talking so he could go home. He didn't even seem to be looking at anything. "A panther might jump a doe, and he wouldn't have much trouble catching the fawn afterward. But no panther would have jumped that colt with the dam right there with it. It was Old Ben," Major de Spain said. "I'm disappointed in him. He has broken the rules. I didn't think he would have done that. He has killed mine and McCaslin's dogs, but that was all right. We gambled the dogs against him; we gave each other warning. But now he has come into my house and destroyed my property, out of season too. He broke the rules. It was Old Ben, Sam." Still Sam said nothing, standing there until Major de Spain should stop talking. "We'll back-track her tomorrow and see," Major de Spain said.

Sam departed. He would not live in the camp; he had built himself a little hut something like Joe Baker's, only stouter, tighter, on the bayou a quarter-mile away, and a stout log crib where he stored a little corn for the shoat he raised each year. The next morning he was waiting when they waked. He had already found the colt. They did not even wait for breakfast. It was not far, not five hundred yards from the stable—the three-months' colt lying on its side, its throat torn out and the entrails and one ham partly eaten. It lay not as if it had been dropped but as if it had been struck and hurled, and no cat-mark, no claw-mark where a panther would have gripped it while finding its throat. They read the tracks where the frantic mare had circled and at last rushed in with that same ultimate desperation with which she had whirled on Sam Fathers yesterday evening, and the long tracks of dead and terrified running and those of the beast which had not even rushed at her when she advanced but had merely walked three or four paces toward her until she broke, and General Compson said, "Good God, what a wolf!"

Still Sam said nothing. The boy watched him while the men knelt, measuring the tracks. There was something in Sam's face now. It was neither exultation nor joy nor hope. Later, a man, the boy realised what it had been, and that Sam had known all the time what had made the tracks and what had torn the throat out of the doe in the spring and killed the fawn. It had been fore-knowledge in Sam's face that morning. *And he was glad,* he told himself. *He was old. He had no children, no people, none of his blood anywhere above earth that he would ever meet again. And even if he were to, he could not have touched it, spoken to it, because for seventy years now he had had to be a negro. It was almost over now and he was glad.*

They returned to camp and had breakfast and came back with guns and the hounds. Afterward the boy realised that they also should have known then what killed the colt as well as Sam Fathers did. But that was neither the first nor the last time he had seen men rationalise from and even act upon their misconceptions. After Boon, standing astride the colt, had whipped the dogs away from it with his belt, they snuffed at the tracks. One of them, a young dog hound without judgment yet, bayed once, and they ran for a few feet on what seemed to be a trail. Then they stopped, looking back at the men, eager enough, not baffled, merely questioning, as if they were asking "Now what?" Then they rushed back to the colt, where Boon, still astride it, slashed at them with the belt.

"I never knew a trail to get cold that quick," General Compson said.

"Maybe a single wolf big enough to kill a colt with the dam right there beside it dont leave scent," Major de Spain said.

"Maybe it was a hant," Walter Ewell said. He looked at Tennie's Jim. "Hah, Jim?"

Because the hounds would not run it, Major de Spain had Sam hunt out and find the tracks a hundred yards farther on and they put the dogs on it again and again the young one bayed and not one of them realised then that the hound was not baying like a dog striking game but was merely bellowing like a country dog whose yard has been invaded. General Compson spoke to the boy and Boon and Tennie's Jim: to the squirrel hunters. "You boys keep the dogs with you this morning. He's probably hanging around somewhere, waiting to get his breakfast off the colt. You might strike him."

But they did not. The boy remembered how Sam stood watching them as they went into the woods with the leashed hounds— the Indian face in which he had never seen anything until it smiled, except that faint arching of the nostrils on that first morning when the hounds had found Old Ben. They took the hounds with them on the next day, though when they reached the place where they hoped to strike a fresh trail, the carcass of the colt was gone. Then on the third morning Sam was waiting again, this time until they had finished breakfast. He said, "Come." He led them to his house, his little hut, to the corn-crib beyond it. He had removed the corn and had made a deadfall of the door, baiting it with the colt's carcass; peering between the logs, they saw an

animal almost the color of a gun or pistol barrel, what little time
they had to examine its color or shape. It was not crouched nor
even standing. It was in motion, in the air, coming toward them
—a heavy body crashing with tremendous force against the door
so that the thick door jumped and clattered in its frame, the animal, whatever it was, hurling itself against the door again seemingly before it could have touched the floor and got a new purchase to spring from. "Come away," Sam said, "fore he break his
neck." Even when they retreated the heavy and measured crashes
continued, the stout door jumping and clattering each time, and
still no sound from the beast itself—no snarl, no cry.

"What in hell's name is it?" Major de Spain said.

"It's a dog," Sam said, his nostrils arching and collapsing
faintly and steadily and that faint, fierce milkiness in his eyes
again as on that first morning when the hounds had struck the
old bear. "It's the dog."

"*The* dog?" Major de Spain said.

"That's gonter hold Old Ben."

"Dog the devil," Major de Spain said. "I'd rather have Old
Ben himself in my pack than that brute. Shoot him."

"No," Sam said.

"You'll never tame him. How do you ever expect to make an
animal like that afraid of you?"

"I dont want him tame," Sam said; again the boy watched his
nostrils and the fierce milky light in his eyes. "But I almost rather
he be tame than scared, of me or any man or any thing. But he
wont be neither, of nothing."

"Then what are you going to do with it?"

"You can watch," Sam said.

Each morning through the second week they would go to Sam's
crib. He had removed a few shingles from the roof and had put
a rope on the colt's carcass and had drawn it out when the trap
fell. Each morning they would watch him lower a pail of water
into the crib while the dog hurled itself tirelessly against the door
and dropped back and leaped again. It never made any sound
and there was nothing frenzied in the act but only a cold and grim
indomitable determination. Toward the end of the week it stopped
jumping at the door. Yet it had not weakened appreciably and it

was not as if it had rationalised the fact that the door was not
going to give. It was as if for that time it simply disdained to
jump any longer. It was not down. None of them had ever seen
it down. It stood, and they could see it now—part mastiff, something of Airedale and something of a dozen other strains probably, better than thirty inches at the shoulders and weighing as
they guessed almost ninety pounds, with cold yellow eyes and a
tremendous chest and over all that strange color like a blued
gun-barrel.

Then the two weeks were up. They prepared to break camp.
The boy begged to remain and his cousin let him. He moved into
the little hut with Sam Fathers. Each morning he watched Sam
lower the pail of water into the crib. By the end of that week the
dog was down. It would rise and half stagger, half crawl to the
water and drink and collapse again. One morning it could not
even reach the water, could not raise its forequarters even from
the floor. Sam took a short stick and prepared to enter the crib.
"Wait," the boy said. "Let me get the gun ——"

"No," Sam said. "He cant move now." Nor could it. It lay on
its side while Sam touched it, its head and the gaunted body, the
dog lying motionless, the yellow eyes open. They were not fierce
and there was nothing of petty malevolence in them, but a cold
and almost impersonal malignance like some natural force. It was
not even looking at Sam nor at the boy peering at it between the
logs.

Sam began to feed it again. The first time he had to raise its
head so it could lap the broth. That night he left a bowl of broth
containing lumps of meat where the dog could reach it. The next
morning the bowl was empty and the dog was lying on its belly,
its head up, the cold yellow eyes watching the door as Sam entered, no change whatever in the cold yellow eyes and still no
sound from it even when it sprang, its aim and co-ordination
still bad from weakness so that Sam had time to strike it down
with the stick and leap from the crib and slam the door as the
dog, still without having had time to get its feet under it to jump
again seemingly, hurled itself against the door as if the two weeks
of starving had never been.

At noon that day someone came whooping through the woods

from the direction of the camp. It was Boon. He came and looked
for a while between the logs, at the tremendous dog lying again
on its belly, its head up, the yellow eyes blinking sleepily at nothing: the indomitable and unbroken spirit. "What we better do,"
Boon said, "is to let that son of a bitch go and catch Old Ben
and run him on the dog." He turned to the boy his weather-red-
dened and beetling face. "Get your traps together. Cass says for
you to come on home. You been in here fooling with that horse-
eating varmint long enough."

Boon had a borrowed mule at the camp; the buggy was waiting
at the edge of the bottom. He was at home that night. He told
McCaslin about it. "Sam's going to starve him again until he can
go in and touch him. Then he will feed him again. Then he will
starve him again, if he has to."

"But why?" McCaslin said. "What for? Even Sam will never
tame that brute."

"We dont want him tame. We want him like he is. We just
want him to find out at last that the only way he can get out of
that crib and stay out of it is to do what Sam or somebody tells
him to do. He's the dog that's going to stop Old Ben and hold
him. We've already named him. His name is Lion."

Then November came at last. They returned to the camp. With
General Compson and Major de Spain and his cousin and Walter
and Boon he stood in the yard among the guns and bedding and
boxes of food and watched Sam Fathers and Lion come up the
lane from the lot—the Indian, the old man in battered overalls
and rubber boots and a worn sheepskin coat and a hat which had
belonged to the boy's father; the tremendous dog pacing gravely
beside him. The hounds rushed out to meet them and stopped,
except the young one which still had but little of judgment. It
ran up to Lion, fawning. Lion didn't snap at it. He didn't even
pause. He struck it rolling and yelping for five or six feet with a
blow of one paw as a bear would have done and came on into
the yard and stood, blinking sleepily at nothing, looking at no
one, while Boon said, "Jesus. Jesus.—Will he let me touch him?"

"You can touch him," Sam said. "He dont care. He dont care
about nothing or nobody."

The boy watched that too. He watched it for the next two years

from that moment when Boon touched Lion's head and then knelt
beside him, feeling the bones and muscles, the power. It was as
if Lion were a woman—or perhaps Boon was the woman. That
was more like it—the big, grave, sleepy-seeming dog which, as
Sam Fathers said, cared about no man and no thing; and the
violent, insensitive, hard-faced man with his touch of remote Indian blood and the mind almost of a child. He watched Boon
take over Lion's feeding from Sam and Uncle Ash both. He would
see Boon squatting in the cold rain beside the kitchen while Lion
ate. Because Lion neither slept nor ate with the other dogs though
none of them knew where he did sleep until in the second November, thinking until then that Lion slept in his kennel beside
Sam Fathers' hut, when the boy's cousin McCaslin said something
about it to Sam by sheer chance and Sam told him. And that
night the boy and Major de Spain and McCaslin with a lamp
entered the back room where Boon slept—the little, tight, airless
room rank with the smell of Boon's unwashed body and his wet
hunting-clothes—where Boon, snoring on his back, choked and
waked and Lion raised his head beside him and looked back at
them from his cold, slumbrous yellow eyes.

"Damn it, Boon," McCaslin said. "Get that dog out of here.
He's got to run Old Ben tomorrow morning. How in hell do you
expect him to smell anything fainter than a skunk after breathing
you all night?"

"The way I smell aint hurt my nose none that I ever noticed,"
Boon said.

"It wouldn't matter if it had," Major de Spain said. "We're not
depending on you to trail a bear. Put him outside. Put him under
the house with the other dogs."

Boon began to get up. "He'll kill the first one that happens to
yawn or sneeze in his face or touches him."

"I reckon not," Major de Spain said. "None of them are going
to risk yawning in his face or touching him either, even asleep.
Put him outside. I want his nose right tomorrow. Old Ben fooled
him last year. I dont think he will do it again."

Boon put on his shoes without lacing them; in his long soiled
underwear, his hair still tousled from sleep, he and Lion went out.
The others returned to the front room and the poker game where

McCaslin's and Major de Spain's hands waited for them on the table. After a while McCaslin said, "Do you want me to go back and look again?"

"No," Major de Spain said. "I call," he said to Walter Ewell. He spoke to McCaslin again. "If you do, dont tell me. I am beginning to see the first sign of my increasing age: I dont like to know that my orders have been disobeyed, even when I knew when I gave them that they would be.—A small pair," he said to Walter Ewell.

"How small?" Walter said.

"Very small," Major de Spain said.

And the boy, lying beneath his piled quilts and blankets waiting for sleep, knew likewise that Lion was already back in Boon's bed, for the rest of that night and the next one and during all the nights of the next November and the next one. He thought then: *I wonder what Sam thinks. He could have Lion with him, even if Boon is a white man. He could ask Major or McCaslin either. And more than that. It was Sam's hand that touched Lion first and Lion knows it.* Then he became a man and he knew that too. It had been all right. That was the way it should have been. Sam was the chief, the prince; Boon, the plebeian, was his huntsman. Boon should have nursed the dogs.

On the first morning that Lion led the pack after Old Ben, seven strangers appeared in the camp. They were swampers: gaunt, malaria-ridden men appearing from nowhere, who ran trap-lines for coons or perhaps farmed little patches of cotton and corn along the edge of the bottom, in clothes but little better than Sam Fathers' and nowhere near as good as Tennie's Jim's, with worn shotguns and rifles, already squatting patiently in the cold drizzle in the side yard when day broke. They had a spokesman; afterward Sam Fathers told Major de Spain how all during the past summer and fall they had drifted into the camp singly or in pairs and threes, to look quietly at Lion for a while and then go away: "Mawnin, Major. We heerd you was aimin to put that ere blue dawg on that old two-toed bear this mawnin. We figgered we'd come up and watch, if you dont mind. We wont do no shooting, lessen he runs over us."

"You are welcome," Major de Spain said. "You are welcome to shoot. He's more your bear than ours."

"I reckon that aint no lie. I done fed him enough cawn to have a sheer in him. Not to mention a shoat three years ago."

"I reckon I got a sheer too," another said. "Only it aint in the bear." Major de Spain looked at him. He was chewing tobacco. He spat. "Hit was a heifer calf. Nice un too. Last year. When I finally found her, I reckon she looked about like that colt of yourn looked last June."

"Oh," Major de Spain said. "Be welcome. If you see game in front of my dogs, shoot it."

Nobody shot Old Ben that day. No man saw him. The dogs jumped him within a hundred yards of the glade where the boy had seen him that day in the summer of his eleventh year. The boy was less than a quarter-mile away. He heard the jump but he could distinguish no voice among the dogs that he did not know and therefore would be Lion's, and he thought, believed, that Lion was not among them. Even the fact that they were going much faster than he had ever heard them run behind Old Ben before and that the high thin note of hysteria was missing now from their voices was not enough to disabuse him. He didn't comprehend until that night, when Sam told him that Lion would never cry on a trail. "He gonter growl when he catches Old Ben's throat," Sam said. "But he aint gonter never holler, no more than he ever done when he was jumping at that two-inch door. It's that blue dog in him. What you call it?"

"Airedale," the boy said.

Lion was there; the jump was just too close to the river. When Boon returned with Lion about eleven that night, he swore that Lion had stopped Old Ben once but that the hounds would not go in and Old Ben broke away and took to the river and swam for miles down it and he and Lion went down one bank for about ten miles and crossed and came up the other but it had begun to get dark before they struck any trail where Old Ben had come up out of the water, unless he was still in the water when he passed the ford where they crossed. Then he fell to cursing the hounds and ate the supper Uncle Ash had saved for him and went off to bed and after a while the boy opened the door of the little stale room thunderous with snoring and the great grave dog raised its head from Boon's pillow and blinked at him for a moment and lowered its head again.

When the next November came and the last day, the day on which it was now becoming traditional to save for Old Ben, there were more than a dozen strangers waiting. They were not all swampers this time. Some of them were townsmen, from other county seats like Jefferson, who had heard about Lion and Old Ben and had come to watch the great blue dog keep his yearly rendezvous with the old two-toed bear. Some of them didn't even have guns and the hunting-clothes and boots they wore had been on a store shelf yesterday.

This time Lion jumped Old Ben more than five miles from the river and bayed and held him and this time the hounds went in, in a sort of desperate emulation. The boy heard them; he was that near. He heard Boon whooping; he heard the two shots when General Compson delivered both barrels, one containing five buckshot, the other a single ball, into the bear from as close as he could force his almost unmanageable horse. He heard the dogs when the bear broke free again. He was running now; panting, stumbling, his lungs bursting, he reached the place where General Compson had fired and where Old Ben had killed two of the hounds. He saw the blood from General Compson's shots, but he could go no further. He stopped, leaning against a tree for his breathing to ease and his heart to slow, hearing the sound of the dogs as it faded on and died away.

In camp that night—they had as guests five of the still terrified strangers in new hunting coats and boots who had been lost all day until Sam Fathers went out and got them—he heard the rest of it: how Lion had stopped and held the bear again but only the one-eyed mule which did not mind the smell of wild blood would approach and Boon was riding the mule and Boon had never been known to hit anything. He shot at the bear five times with his pump gun, touching nothing, and Old Ben killed another hound and broke free once more and reached the river and was gone. Again Boon and Lion hunted as far down one bank as they dared. Too far; they crossed in the first of dusk and dark overtook them within a mile. And this time Lion found the broken trail, the blood perhaps, in the darkness where Old Ben had come up out of the water, but Boon had him on a rope, luckily, and he got down from the mule and fought Lion hand-to-hand until he got him back to camp. This time Boon didn't even curse. He stood in the door, muddy, spent, his huge gargoyle's face tragic and still amazed. "I missed him," he said. "I was in twenty-five feet of him and I missed him five times."

"But we have drawn blood," Major de Spain said. "General Compson drew blood. We have never done that before."

"But I missed him," Boon said. "I missed him five times. With Lion looking right at me."

"Never mind," Major de Spain said. "It was a damned fine race. And we drew blood. Next year we'll let General Compson or Walter ride Katie, and we'll get him."

Then McCaslin said, "Where is Lion, Boon?"

"I left him at Sam's," Boon said. He was already turning away. "I aint fit to sleep with him."

So he should have hated and feared Lion. Yet he did not. It seemed to him that there was a fatality in it. It seemed to him that something, he didn't know what, was beginning; had already begun. It was like the last act on a set stage. It was the beginning of the end of something, he didn't know what except that he would not grieve. He would be humble and proud that he had been found worthy to be a part of it too or even just to see it too.

3.

It was December. It was the coldest December he had ever remembered. They had been in camp four days over two weeks, waiting for the weather to soften so that Lion and Old Ben could run their yearly race. Then they would break camp and go home. Because of these unforeseen additional days which they had had to pass waiting on the weather, with nothing to do but play poker, the whisky had given out and he and Boon were being sent to Memphis with a suitcase and a note from Major de Spain to Mr Semmes, the distiller, to get more. That is, Major de Spain and McCaslin were sending Boon to get the whisky and sending him to see that Boon got back with it or most of it or at least some of it.

Tennie's Jim waked him at three. He dressed rapidly, shivering, not so much from the cold because a fresh fire already boomed and roared on the hearth, but in that dead winter hour when the blood and the heart are slow and sleep is incomplete. He crossed the gap between house and kitchen, the gap of iron earth beneath the brilliant and rigid night where dawn would not begin for three hours yet, tasting, tongue palate and to the very bottom of his lungs the searing dark, and entered the kitchen, the lamplit warmth where the stove glowed, fogging the windows, and where Boon already sat at the table at breakfast, hunched over his plate, almost in his plate, his working jaws blue with stubble and his face innocent of water and his coarse, horse-mane hair innocent of comb—the quarter Indian, grandson of a Chickasaw squaw, who on occasion resented with his hard and furious fists the intimation of one single drop of alien blood and on others, usually after whisky, affirmed with the same fists and the same fury that his father had been the full-blood Chickasaw and even a chief and that even his mother had been only half white. He was four inches over six feet; he had the mind of a child, the heart of a horse, and little hard shoe-button eyes without depth or meanness or generosity or viciousness or gentleness or anything else, in the ugliest face the boy had ever seen. It looked like somebody had found a walnut a little larger than a football and with a machinist's hammer had shaped features into it and then painted it, mostly red; not Indian red but a fine bright ruddy color which whisky might have had something to do with but which was mostly just happy and violent out-of-doors, the wrinkles in it not the residue of the forty years it had survived but from squinting into the sun or into the gloom of cane-brakes where game had run, baked into it by the camp fires before which he had lain trying to sleep on the cold November or December ground while waiting for daylight so he could rise and hunt again, as though time were merely something he walked through as he did through air, aging him no more than air did. He was brave, faithful, improvident and unreliable; he had neither profession job nor trade and owned one vice and one virtue: whisky, and that absolute and unquestioning fidelity to Major de Spain and the boy's cousin McCaslin. "Sometimes I'd call them both virtues," Major de Spain said once. "Or both vices," McCaslin said.

He ate his breakfast, hearing the dogs under the kitchen, wakened by the smell of frying meat or perhaps by the feet overhead. He heard Lion once, short and peremptory, as the best hunter in any camp has only to speak once to all save the fools, and none other of Major de Spain's and McCaslin's dogs were Lion's equal in size and strength and perhaps even in courage, but they were not fools; Old Ben had killed the last fool among them last year.

Tennie's Jim came in as they finished. The wagon was outside. Ash decided he would drive them over to the log-line where they would flag the outbound log-train and let Tennie's Jim wash the dishes. The boy knew why. It would not be the first time he had listened to old Ash badgering Boon.

It was cold. The wagon wheels banged and clattered on the frozen ground; the sky was fixed and brilliant. He was not shivering, he was shaking, slow and steady and hard, the food he had just eaten still warm and solid inside him while his outside shook slow and steady around it as though his stomach floated loose. "They wont run this morning," he said. "No dog will have any nose today."

"Cep Lion," Ash said. "Lion dont need no nose. All he need is a bear." He had wrapped his feet in towsacks and he had a quilt from his pallet bed on the kitchen floor drawn over his head and wrapped around him until in the thin brilliant starlight he looked like nothing at all that the boy had ever seen before. "He run a bear through a thousand-acre ice-house. Catch him too. Them other dogs dont matter because they aint going to keep up with Lion nohow, long as he got a bear in front of him."

"What's wrong with the other dogs?" Boon said. "What the hell do you know about it anyway? This is the first time you've had your tail out of that kitchen since we got here except to chop a little wood."

"Aint nothing wrong with them," Ash said. "And long as it's left up to them, aint nothing going to be. I just wish I had knowed all my life how to take care of my health good as them hounds knows."

"Well, they aint going to run this morning," Boon said. His voice was harsh and positive. "Major promised they wouldn't until me and Ike get back."

"Weather gonter break today. Gonter soft up. Rain by night." Then Ash laughed, chuckled, somewhere inside the quilt which concealed even his face. "Hum up here, mules!" he said, jerking the reins so that the mules leaped forward and snatched the lurching and banging wagon for several feet before they slowed again into their quick, short-paced, rapid plodding. "Sides, I like to know why Major need to wait on you. It's Lion he aiming to use. I aint never heard tell of you bringing no bear nor no other kind of meat into this camp."

Now Boon's going to curse Ash or maybe even hit him, the boy thought. But Boon never did, never had; the boy knew he never would even though four years ago Boon had shot five times with a borrowed pistol at a negro on the street in Jefferson, with the same result as when he had shot five times at Old Ben last fall. "By God," Boon said, "he aint going to put Lion or no other dog on nothing until I get back tonight. Because he promised me. Whip up them mules and keep them whipped up. Do you want me to freeze to death?"

They reached the log-line and built a fire. After a while the log-train came up out of the woods under the paling east and Boon flagged it. Then in the warm caboose the boy slept again while Boon and the conductor and brakeman talked about Lion and Old Ben as people later would talk about Sullivan and Kilrain and, later still, about Dempsey and Tunney. Dozing, swaying as the springless caboose lurched and clattered, he would hear them still talking, about the shoats and calves Old Ben had killed and the cribs he had rifled and the traps and deadfalls he had wrecked and the lead he probably carried under his hide—Old Ben, the two-toed bear in a land where bears with trap-ruined feet had been called Two-Toe or Three-Toe or Cripple-Foot for fifty years, only Old Ben was an extra bear (the head bear, General Compson called him) and so had earned a name such as a human man could have worn and not been sorry.

They reached Hoke's at sunup. They emerged from the warm caboose in their hunting clothes, the muddy boots and stained khaki and Boon's blue unshaven jowls. But that was all right. Hoke's was a sawmill and commissary and two stores and a loading-chute on a sidetrack from the main line, and all the men in it wore boots and khaki too. Presently the Memphis train came. Boon bought three packages of popcorn-and-molasses and a bottle of beer from the news butch and the boy went to sleep again to the sound of his chewing.

But in Memphis it was not all right. It was as if the high buildings and the hard pavements, the fine carriages and the horse cars and the men in starched collars and neckties made their boots and khaki look a little rougher and a little muddier and made Boon's beard look worse and more unshaven and his face look more and more like he should never have brought it out of the woods at all or at least out of reach of Major de Spain or McCaslin or someone who knew it and could have said, "Dont be afraid. He wont hurt you." He walked through the station, on the slick floor, his face moving as he worked the popcorn out of his teeth with his tongue, his legs spraddled and stiff in the hips as if he were walking on buttered glass, and that blue stubble on his face like the filings from a new gun-barrel. They passed the first saloon. Even through the closed doors the boy could seem to smell the sawdust and the reek of old drink. Boon began to cough. He coughed for something less than a minute. "Damn this cold," he said. "I'd sure like to know where I got it."

"Back there in the station," the boy said.

Boon had started to cough again. He stopped. He looked at the boy. "What?" he said.

"You never had it when we left camp nor on the train either." Boon looked at him, blinking. Then he stopped blinking. He didn't cough again. He said quietly:

"Lend me a dollar. Come on. You've got it. If you ever had one, you've still got it. I dont mean you are tight with your money because you aint. You just dont never seem to ever think of nothing you want. When I was sixteen a dollar bill melted off of me before I even had time to read the name of the bank that issued it." He said quietly: "Let me have a dollar, Ike."

"You promised Major. You promised McCaslin. Not till we get back to camp."

"All right," Boon said in that quiet and patient voice. "What can I do on just one dollar? You aint going to lend me another."

"You're damn right I aint," the boy said, his voice quiet too, cold with rage which was not at Boon, remembering: Boon snoring in a hard chair in the kitchen so he could watch the clock and wake him and McCaslin and drive them the seventeen miles in to Jefferson to catch the train to Memphis; the wild, never-bridled Texas paint pony which he had persuaded McCaslin to let him buy and which he and Boon had bought at auction for four dollars and seventy-five cents and fetched home wired between two gentle old mares with pieces of barbed wire and which had never even seen shelled corn before and didn't even know what it was unless the grains were bugs maybe and at last (he was ten and Boon had been ten all his life) Boon said the pony was gentled and with a towsack over its head and four negroes to hold it they backed it into an old two-wheeled cart and hooked up the gear and he and Boon got up and Boon said, "All right, boys. Let him go" and one of the negroes—it was Tennie's Jim—snatched the towsack off and leaped for his life and they lost the first wheel against a post of the open gate only at that moment Boon caught him by the scruff of the neck and flung him into the roadside ditch so he only saw the rest of it in fragments: the other wheel as it slammed through the side gate and crossed the back yard and leaped up onto the gallery and scraps of the cart here and there along the road and Boon vanishing rapidly on his stomach in the leaping and spurting dust and still holding the reins until they broke too and two days later they finally caught the pony seven miles away still wearing the hames and the headstall of the bridle around its neck like a duchess with two necklaces at one time. He gave Boon the dollar.

"All right," Boon said. "Come on in out of the cold."

"I aint cold," he said.

"You can have some lemonade."

"I dont want any lemonade."

The door closed behind him. The sun was well up now. It was a brilliant day, though Ash had said it would rain before night. Already it was warmer; they could run tomorrow. He felt the old lift of the heart, as pristine as ever, as on the first day; he would never lose it, no matter how old in hunting and pursuit: the best, the best of all breathing, the humility and the pride. He must stop thinking about it. Already it seemed to him that he was running, back to the station, to the tracks themselves: the first train going south; he must stop thinking about it. The street was busy. He watched the big Norman draft horses, the Percherons; the trim carriages from which the men in the fine overcoats and the ladies rosy in furs descended and entered the station. (They were still next door to it but one.) Twenty years ago his father had ridden into Memphis as a member of Colonel Sartoris' horse in Forrest's command, up Main street and (the tale told) into the lobby of the Gayoso Hotel where the Yankee officers sat in the leather chairs spitting into the tall bright cuspidors and then out again, scot-free ——

The door opened behind him. Boon was wiping his mouth on the back of his hand. "All right," he said. "Let's go tend to it and get the hell out of here."

They went and had the suitcase packed. He never knew where or when Boon got the other bottle. Doubtless Mr Semmes gave it to him. When they reached Hoke's again at sundown, it was empty. They could get a return train to Hoke's in two hours; they went straight back to the station as Major de Spain and then McCaslin had told Boon to do and then ordered him to do and had sent the boy along to see that he did. Boon took the first drink from his bottle in the wash room. A man in a uniform cap came to tell him he couldn't drink there and looked at Boon's face once and said nothing. The next time he was pouring into his water glass beneath the edge of a table in the restaurant when the manager (she was a woman) did tell him he couldn't drink there and he went back to the wash-room. He had been telling the negro waiter and all the other people in the restaurant who couldn't help but hear him and who had never heard of Lion and didn't want to, about Lion and Old Ben. Then he happened to think of the zoo. He had found out that there was another train to Hoke's at three oclock and so they would spend the time at the zoo and take the three oclock train until he came back from the washroom for the third time. Then they would take the

first train back to camp, get Lion and come back to the zoo where,
he said, the bears were fed on ice cream and lady fingers and he
would match Lion against them all.

So they missed the first train, the one they were supposed to
take, but he got Boon onto the three oclock train and they were
all right again, with Boon not even going to the wash-room now
but drinking in the aisle and talking about Lion and the men he
buttonholed no more daring to tell Boon he couldn't drink there
than the man in the station had dared.

When they reached Hoke's at sundown, Boon was asleep. The
boy waked him at last and got him and the suitcase off the train
and he even persuaded him to eat some supper at the sawmill
commissary. So he was all right when they got in the caboose of
the log-train to go back into the woods, with the sun going down
red and the sky already overcast and the ground would not freeze
tonight. It was the boy who slept now, sitting behind the ruby
stove while the springless caboose jumped and clattered and Boon
and the brakeman and the conductor talked about Lion and Old
Ben because they knew what Boon was talking about because this
was home. "Overcast and already thawing," Boon said. "Lion
will get him tomorrow."

It would have to be Lion, or somebody. It would not be Boon.
He had never hit anything bigger than a squirrel that anybody
ever knew, except the negro woman that day when he was shooting at the negro man. He was a big negro and not ten feet away
but Boon shot five times with the pistol he had borrowed from
Major de Spain's negro coachman and the negro he was shooting
at outed with a dollar-and-a-half mail-order pistol and would have
burned Boon down with it only it never went off, it just went
snicksnicksnicksnicksnick five times and Boon still blasting away
and he broke a plate-glass window that cost McCaslin forty-five
dollars and hit a negro woman who happened to be passing in
the leg only Major de Spain paid for that; he and McCaslin cut
cards, the plate-glass window against the negro woman's leg. And
the first day on stand this year, the first morning in camp, the
buck ran right over Boon; he heard Boon's old pump gun go
whow. whow. whow. whow. whow. and then his voice: "God

damn, here he comes! Head him! Head him!" and when he got
there the buck's tracks and the five exploded shells were not
twenty paces apart.

There were five guests in camp that night, from Jefferson: Mr
Bayard Sartoris and his son and General Compson's son and two
others. And the next morning he looked out the window, into
the gray thin drizzle of daybreak which Ash had predicted, and
there they were, standing and squatting beneath the thin rain,
almost two dozen of them who had fed Old Ben corn and shoats
and even calves for ten years, in their worn hats and hunting coats
and overalls which any town negro would have thrown away or
burned and only the rubber boots strong and sound, and the worn
and blueless guns and some even without guns. While they ate
breakfast a dozen more arrived, mounted and on foot: loggers
from the camp thirteen miles below and sawmill men from Hoke's
and the only gun among them that one which the log-train conductor carried: so that when they went into the woods this morning Major de Spain led a party almost as strong, excepting that
some of them were not armed, as some he had led in the last
darkening days of '64 and '65. The little yard would not hold
them. They overflowed it, into the lane where Major de Spain sat
his mare while Ash in his dirty apron thrust the greasy cartridges
into his carbine and passed it up to him and the great grave blue
dog stood at his stirrup not as a dog stands but as a horse stands,
blinking his sleepy topaz eyes at nothing, deaf even to the yelling
of the hounds which Boon and Tennie's Jim held on leash.

"We'll put General Compson on Katie this morning," Major
de Spain said. "He drew blood last year; if he'd had a mule then
that would have stood, he would have ———"

"No," General Compson said. "I'm too old to go helling through
the woods on a mule or a horse or anything else any more. Besides, I had my chance last year and missed it. I'm going on a
stand this morning. I'm going to let that boy ride Katie."

"No, wait," McCaslin said. "Ike's got the rest of his life to hunt
bears in. Let somebody else ———"

"No," General Compson said. "I want Ike to ride Katie. He's
already a better woodsman than you or me either and in another
ten years he'll be as good as Walter."

At first he couldn't believe it, not until Major de Spain spoke to him. Then he was up, on the one-eyed mule which would not spook at wild blood, looking down at the dog motionless at Major de Spain's stirrup, looking in the gray streaming light bigger than a calf, bigger than he knew it actually was—the big head, the chest almost as big as his own, the blue hide beneath which the muscles flinched or quivered to no touch since the heart which drove blood to them loved no man and no thing, standing as a horse stands yet different from a horse which infers only weight and speed while Lion inferred not only courage and all else that went to make up the will and desire to pursue and kill, but endurance, the will and desire to endure beyond all imaginable limits of flesh in order to overtake and slay. Then the dog looked at him. It moved its head and looked at him across the trivial uproar of the hounds, out of the yellow eyes as depthless as Boon's, as free as Boon's of meanness or generosity or gentleness or viciousness. They were just cold and sleepy. Then it blinked, and he knew it was not looking at him and never had been, without even bothering to turn its head away.

That morning he heard the first cry. Lion had already vanished while Sam and Tennie's Jim were putting saddles on the mule and horse which had drawn the wagon and he watched the hounds as they crossed and cast, snuffing and whimpering, until they too disappeared. Then he and Major de Spain and Sam and Tennie's Jim rode after them and heard the first cry out of the wet and thawing woods not two hundred yards ahead, high, with that abject, almost human quality he had come to know, and the other hounds joining in until the gloomed woods rang and clamored. They rode then. It seemed to him that he could actually see the big blue dog boring on, silent, and the bear too: the thick, locomotive-like shape which he had seen that day four years ago crossing the blow-down, crashing on ahead of the dogs faster than he had believed it could have moved, drawing away even from the running mules. He heard a shotgun, once. The woods had opened, they were going fast, the clamor faint and fading on ahead; they passed the man who had fired—a swamper, a pointing arm, a gaunt face, the small black orifice of his yelling studded with rotten teeth.

He heard the changed note in the hounds' uproar and two
hundred yards ahead he saw them. The bear had turned. He saw
Lion drive in without pausing and saw the bear strike him aside
and lunge into the yelling hounds and kill one of them almost in its
tracks and whirl and run again. Then they were in a streaming tide
of dogs. He heard Major de Spain and Tennie's Jim shouting and
the pistol sound of Tennie's Jim's leather thong as he tried to turn
them. Then he and Sam Fathers were riding alone. One of the
hounds had kept on with Lion though. He recognised its voice. It
was the young hound which even a year ago had had no judgment
and which, by the lights of the other hounds anyway, still had
none. *Maybe that's what courage is,* he thought. "Right," Sam
said behind him. "Right. We got to turn him from the river if we
can."

Now they were in cane: a brake. He knew the path through it
as well as Sam did. They came out of the undergrowth and struck
the entrance almost exactly. It would traverse the brake and come
out onto a high open ridge above the river. He heard the flat clap
of Walter Ewell's rifle, then two more. "No," Sam said. "I can
hear the hound. Go on."

They emerged from the narrow roofless tunnel of snapping and
hissing cane, still galloping, onto the open ridge below which the
thick yellow river, reflectionless in the gray and streaming light,
seemed not to move. Now he could hear the hound too. It was not
running. The cry was a high frantic yapping and Boon was running along the edge of the bluff, his old gun leaping and jouncing
against his back on its sling made of a piece of cotton plowline. He
whirled and ran up to them, wild-faced, and flung himself onto
the mule behind the boy. "That damn boat!" he cried. "It's on
the other side! He went straight across! Lion was too close to him!
That little hound too! Lion was so close I couldn't shoot! Go on!"
he cried, beating his heels into the mule's flanks. "Go on!"

They plunged down the bank, slipping and sliding in the thawed
earth, crashing through the willows and into the water. He felt no
shock, no cold, he on one side of the swimming mule, grasping
the pommel with one hand and holding his gun above the water
with the other, Boon opposite him. Sam was behind them somewhere, and then the river, the water about them, was full of dogs.

They swam faster than the mules; they were scrabbling up the bank before the mules touched bottom. Major de Spain was whooping from the bank they had just left and, looking back, he saw Tennie's Jim and the horse as they went into the water.

Now the woods ahead of them and the rain-heavy air were one uproar. It rang and clamored; it echoed and broke against the bank behind them and reformed and clamored and rang until it seemed to the boy that all the hounds which had ever bayed game in this land were yelling down at him. He got his leg over the mule as it came up out of the water. Boon didn't try to mount again. He grasped one stirrup as they went up the bank and crashed through the undergrowth which fringed the bluff and saw the bear, on its hind feet, its back against a tree while the bellowing hounds swirled around it and once more Lion drove in, leaping clear of the ground.

This time the bear didn't strike him down. It caught the dog in both arms, almost loverlike, and they both went down. He was off the mule now. He drew back both hammers of the gun but he could see nothing but moiling spotted houndbodies until the bear surged up again. Boon was yelling something, he could not tell what; he could see Lion still clinging to the bear's throat and he saw the bear, half erect, strike one of the hounds with one paw and hurl it five or six feet and then, rising and rising as though it would never stop, stand erect again and begin to rake at Lion's belly with its forepaws. Then Boon was running. The boy saw the gleam of the blade in his hand and watched him leap among the hounds, hurdling them, kicking them aside as he ran, and fling himself astride the bear as he had hurled himself onto the mule, his legs locked around the bear's belly, his left arm under the bear's throat where Lion clung, and the glint of the knife as it rose and fell.

It fell just once. For an instant they almost resembled a piece of statuary: the clinging dog, the bear, the man stride its back, working and probing the buried blade. Then they went down, pulled over backward by Boon's weight, Boon underneath. It was the bear's back which reappeared first but at once Boon was astride it again. He had never released the knife and again the boy saw the almost infinitesimal movement of his arm and shoulder as he

probed and sought; then the bear surged erect, raising with it the
man and the dog too, and turned and still carrying the man and
the dog it took two or three steps toward the woods on its hind
feet as a man would have walked and crashed down. It didn't
collapse, crumple. It fell all of a piece, as a tree falls, so that all
three of them, man dog and bear, seemed to bounce once.

He and Tennie's Jim ran forward. Boon was kneeling at the
bear's head. His left ear was shredded, his left coat sleeve was
completely gone, his right boot had been ripped from knee to in-
step; the bright blood thinned in the thin rain down his leg and
hand and arm and down the side of his face which was no longer
wild but was quite calm. Together they prized Lion's jaws from
the bear's throat. "Easy, goddamn it," Boon said. "Cant you see
his guts are all out of him?" He began to remove his coat. He
spoke to Tennie's Jim in that calm voice: "Bring the boat up. It's
about a hundred yards down the bank there. I saw it." Tennie's
Jim rose and went away. Then, and he could not remember if it
had been a call or an exclamation from Tennie's Jim or if he had
glanced up by chance, he saw Tennie's Jim stooping and saw Sam
Fathers lying motionless on his face in the trampled mud.

The mule had not thrown him. He remembered that Sam was
down too even before Boon began to run. There was no mark on
him whatever and when he and Boon turned him over, his eyes
were open and he said something in that tongue which he and
Joe Baker had used to speak together. But he couldn't move.
Tennie's Jim brought the skiff up; they could hear him shouting
to Major de Spain across the river. Boon wrapped Lion in his
hunting coat and carried him down to the skiff and they carried
Sam down and returned and hitched the bear to the one-eyed
mule's saddle-bow with Tennie's Jim's leash-thong and dragged him
down to the skiff and got him into it and left Tennie's Jim to swim
the horse and the two mules back across. Major de Spain caught
the bow of the skiff as Boon jumped out and past him before it
touched the bank. He looked at Old Ben and said quietly: "Well."
Then he walked into the water and leaned down and touched Sam
and Sam looked up at him and said something in that old tongue
he and Joe Baker spoke. "You dont know what happened?"
Major de Spain said.

"No, sir," the boy said. "It wasn't the mule. It wasn't anything. He was off the mule when Boon ran in on the bear. Then we looked up and he was lying on the ground." Boon was shouting at Tennie's Jim, still in the middle of the river.

"Come on, goddamn it!" he said. "Bring me that mule!"

"What do you want with a mule?" Major de Spain said.

Boon didn't even look at him. "I'm going to Hoke's to get the doctor," he said in that calm voice, his face quite calm beneath the steady thinning of the bright blood.

"You need a doctor yourself," Major de Spain said. "Tennie's Jim ——"

"Damn that," Boon said. He turned on Major de Spain. His face was still calm, only his voice was a pitch higher. "Cant you see his goddamn guts are all out of him?"

"Boon!" Major de Spain said. They looked at one another. Boon was a good head taller than Major de Spain; even the boy was taller now than Major de Spain.

"I've got to get the doctor," Boon said. "His goddamn guts ——"

"All right," Major de Spain said. Tennie's Jim came up out of the water. The horse and the sound mule had already scented Old Ben; they surged and plunged all the way up to the top of the bluff, dragging Tennie's Jim with them, before he could stop them and tie them and come back. Major de Spain unlooped the leather thong of his compass from his buttonhole and gave it to Tennie's Jim. "Go straight to Hoke's," he said. "Bring Doctor Crawford back with you. Tell him there are two men to be looked at. Take my mare. Can you find the road from here?"

"Yes, sir," Tennie's Jim said.

"All right," Major de Spain said. "Go on." He turned to the boy. "Take the mules and the horse and go back and get the wagon. We'll go on down the river in the boat to Coon bridge. Meet us there. Can you find it again?"

"Yes, sir," the boy said.

"All right. Get started."

He went back to the wagon. He realised then how far they had run. It was already afternoon when he put the mules into the traces and tied the horse's lead-rope to the tail-gate. He reached

Coon bridge at dusk. The skiff was already there. Before he could see it and almost before he could see the water he had to leap from the tilting wagon, still holding the reins, and work around to where he could grasp the bit and then the ear of the plunging sound mule and dig his heels and hold it until Boon came up the bank. The rope of the led horse had already snapped and it had already disappeared up the road toward camp. They turned the wagon around and took the mules out and he led the sound mule a hundred yards up the road and tied it. Boon had already brought Lion up to the wagon and Sam was sitting up in the skiff now and when they raised him he tried to walk, up the bank and to the wagon and he tried to climb into the wagon but Boon did not wait; he picked Sam up bodily and set him on the seat. Then they hitched Old Ben to the one-eyed mule's saddle again and dragged him up the bank and set two skid-poles into the open tail-gate and got him into the wagon and he went and got the sound mule and Boon fought it into the traces, striking it across its hard hollow-sounding face until it came into position and stood trembling. Then the rain came down, as though it had held off all day waiting on them.

They returned to camp through it, through the streaming and sightless dark, hearing long before they saw any light the horn and the spaced shots to guide them. When they came to Sam's dark little hut he tried to stand up. He spoke again in the tongue of the old fathers; then he said clearly: "Let me out. Let me out."

"He hasn't got any fire," Major said. "Go on!" he said sharply.

But Sam was struggling now, trying to stand up. "Let me out, master," he said. "Let me go home."

So he stopped the wagon and Boon got down and lifted Sam out. He did not wait to let Sam try to walk this time. He carried him into the hut and Major de Spain got light on a paper spill from the buried embers on the hearth and lit the lamp and Boon put Sam on his bunk and drew off his boots and Major de Spain covered him and the boy was not there, he was holding the mules, the sound one which was trying again to bolt since when the wagon stopped Old Ben's scent drifted forward again along the streaming blackness of air, but Sam's eyes were probably open

again on that profound look which saw further than them or the
hut, further than the death of a bear and the dying of a dog. Then
they went on, toward the long wailing of the horn and the shots
which seemed each to linger intact somewhere in the thick streaming air until the next spaced report joined and blended with it, to
the lighted house, the bright streaming windows, the quiet faces as
Boon entered, bloody and quite calm, carrying the bundled coat.
He laid Lion, blood coat and all, on his stale sheetless pallet bed
which not even Ash, as deft in the house as a woman, could ever
make smooth.

The sawmill doctor from Hoke's was already there. Boon would
not let the doctor touch him until he had seen to Lion. He
wouldn't risk giving Lion chloroform. He put the entrails back
and sewed him up without it while Major de Spain held his head
and Boon his feet. But he never tried to move. He lay there, the
yellow eyes open upon nothing while the quiet men in the new
hunting clothes and in the old ones crowded into the little airless
room rank with the smell of Boon's body and garments, and
watched. Then the doctor cleaned and disinfected Boon's face and
arm and leg and bandaged them and, the boy in front with a
lantern and the doctor and McCaslin and Major de Spain and
General Compson following, they went to Sam Fathers' hut. Tennie's Jim had built up the fire; he squatted before it, dozing. Sam
had not moved since Boon had put him in the bunk and Major
de Spain had covered him with the blankets, yet he opened his
eyes and looked from one to another of the faces and when Mc-
Caslin touched his shoulder and said, "Sam. The doctor wants to
look at you," he even drew his hands out of the blanket and began
to fumble at his shirt buttons until McCaslin said, "Wait. We'll do
it." They undressed him. He lay there—the copper-brown, almost
hairless body, the old man's body, the old man, the wild man not
even one generation from the woods, childless, kinless, peopleless
—motionless, his eyes open but no longer looking at any of them,
while the doctor examined him and drew the blankets up and put
the stethoscope back into his bag and snapped the bag and only
the boy knew that Sam too was going to die.

"Exhaustion," the doctor said. "Shock maybe. A man his age

swimming rivers in December. He'll be all right. Just make him
stay in bed for a day or two. Will there be somebody here with
him?"

"There will be somebody here," Major de Spain said.

They went back to the house, to the rank little room where
Boon still sat on the pallet bed with Lion's head under his hand
while the men, the ones who had hunted behind Lion and the ones
who had never seen him before today, came quietly in to look at
him and went away. Then it was dawn and they all went out into
the yard to look at Old Ben, with his eyes open too and his lips
snarled back from his worn teeth and his mutilated foot and the
little hard lumps under his skin which were the old bullets (there
were fifty-two of them, buckshot rifle and ball) and the single
almost invisible slit under his left shoulder where Boon's blade
had finally found his life. Then Ash began to beat on the bottom
of the dishpan with a heavy spoon to call them to breakfast and
it was the first time he could remember hearing no sound from
the dogs under the kitchen while they were eating. It was as if
the old bear, even dead there in the yard, was a more potent
terror still than they could face without Lion between them.

The rain had stopped during the night. By midmorning the
thin sun appeared, rapidly burning away mist and cloud, warming
the air and the earth; it would be one of those windless Mississippi
December days which are a sort of Indian summer's Indian summer. They moved Lion out to the front gallery, into the sun. It
was Boon's idea. "Goddamn it," he said, "he never did want to
stay in the house until I made him. You know that." He took a
crowbar and loosened the floor boards under his pallet bed so it
could be raised, mattress and all, without disturbing Lion's position, and they carried him out to the gallery and put him down
facing the woods.

Then he and the doctor and McCaslin and Major de Spain
went to Sam's hut. This time Sam didn't open his eyes and his
breathing was so quiet, so peaceful that they could hardly see that
he breathed. The doctor didn't even take out his stethoscope nor
even touch him. "He's all right," the doctor said. "He didn't even
catch cold. He just quit."

"Quit?" McCaslin said.

"Yes. Old people do that sometimes. Then they get a good night's sleep or maybe it's just a drink of whisky, and they change their minds."

They returned to the house. And then they began to arrive—the swamp-dwellers, the gaunt men who ran traplines and lived on quinine and coons and river water, the farmers of little corn- and cotton-patches along the bottom's edge whose fields and cribs and pig-pens the old bear had rifled, the loggers from the camp and the sawmill men from Hoke's and the town men from further away than that, whose hounds the old bear had slain and traps and deadfalls he had wrecked and whose lead he carried. They came up mounted and on foot and in wagons, to enter the yard and look at him and then go on to the front where Lion lay, filling the little yard and overflowing it until there were almost a hundred of them squatting and standing in the warm and drowsing sunlight, talking quietly of hunting, of the game and the dogs which ran it, of hounds and bear and deer and men of yesterday vanished from the earth, while from time to time the great blue dog would open his eyes, not as if he were listening to them but as though to look at the woods for a moment before closing his eyes again, to remember the woods or to see that they were still there. He died at sundown.

Major de Spain broke camp that night. They carried Lion into the woods, or Boon carried him that is, wrapped in a quilt from his bed, just as he had refused to let anyone else touch Lion yesterday until the doctor got there; Boon carrying Lion, and the boy and General Compson and Walter and still almost fifty of them following with lanterns and lighted pine-knots—men from Hoke's and even further, who would have to ride out of the bottom in the dark, and swampers and trappers who would have to walk even, scattering toward the little hidden huts where they lived. And Boon would let nobody else dig the grave either and lay Lion in it and cover him and then General Compson stood at the head of it while the blaze and smoke of the pine-knots streamed away among the winter branches and spoke as he would have spoken over a man. Then they returned to camp. Major de Spain and McCaslin and Ash had rolled and tied all the bedding. The mules were hitched to the wagon and pointed out of the bottom and the

wagon was already loaded and the stove in the kitchen was cold
and the table was set with scraps of cold food and bread and only
the coffee was hot when the boy ran into the kitchen where Major
de Spain and McCaslin had already eaten. "What?" he cried.
"What? I'm not going."

"Yes," McCaslin said, "we're going out tonight. Major wants to
get on back home."

"No!" he said. "I'm going to stay."

"You've got to be back in school Monday. You've already
missed a week more than I intended. It will take you from now
until Monday to catch up. Sam's all right. You heard Doctor
Crawford. I'm going to leave Boon and Tennie's Jim both to stay
with him until he feels like getting up."

He was panting. The others had come in. He looked rapidly
and almost frantically around at the other faces. Boon had a fresh
bottle. He upended it and started the cork by striking the bottom
of the bottle with the heel of his hand and drew the cork with his
teeth and spat it out and drank. "You're damn right you're going
back to school," Boon said. "Or I'll burn the tail off of you myself
if Cass dont, whether you are sixteen or sixty. Where in hell do
you expect to get without education? Where would Cass be?
Where in hell would I be if I hadn't never went to school?"

He looked at McCaslin again. He could feel his breath coming
shorter and shorter and shallower and shallower, as if there were
not enough air in the kitchen for that many to breathe. "This is
just Thursday. I'll come home Sunday night on one of the horses.
I'll come home Sunday, then. I'll make up the time I lost studying
Sunday night. McCaslin," he said, without even despair.

"No, I tell you," McCaslin said. "Sit down here and eat your
supper. We're going out to——"

"Hold up, Cass," General Compson said. The boy did not
know General Compson had moved until he put his hand on his
shoulder. "What is it, bud?" he said.

"I've got to stay," he said. "I've got to."

"All right," General Compson said. "You can stay. If missing
an extra week of school is going to throw you so far behind you'll
have to sweat to find out what some hired pedagogue put between
the covers of a book, you better quit altogether.—And you shut

up, Cass," he said, though McCaslin had not spoken. "You've got
one foot straddled into a farm and the other foot straddled into a
bank; you aint even got a good hand-hold where this boy was
already an old man long before you damned Sartorises and
Edmondses invented farms and banks to keep yourselves from
having to find out what this boy was born knowing and fearing
too maybe but without being afraid, that could go ten miles on a
compass because he wanted to look at a bear none of us had ever
got near enough to put a bullet in and looked at the bear and
came the ten miles back on the compass in the dark; maybe by
God that's the why and the wherefore of farms and banks.—I
reckon you still aint going to tell what it is?"

But still he could not. "I've got to stay," he said.

"All right," General Compson said. "There's plenty of grub
left. And you'll come home Sunday, like you promised McCaslin?
Not Sunday night: Sunday."

"Yes, sir," he said.

"All right," General Compson said. "Sit down and eat, boys,"
he said. "Let's get started. It's going to be cold before we get
home."

They ate. The wagon was already loaded and ready to depart;
all they had to do was to get into it. Boon would drive them out
to the road, to the farmer's stable where the surrey had been left.
He stood beside the wagon, in silhouette on the sky, turbaned like
a Paythan and taller than any there, the bottle tilted. Then he
flung the bottle from his lips without even lowering it, spinning
and glinting in the faint starlight, empty. "Them that's going," he
said, "get in the goddamn wagon. Them that aint, get out of the
goddamn way." The others got in. Boon mounted to the seat
beside General Compson and the wagon moved, on into the
obscurity until the boy could no longer see it, even the moving
density of it amid the greater night. But he could still hear it, for
a long while: the slow, deliberate banging of the wooden frame as
it lurched from rut to rut. And he could hear Boon even when he
could no longer hear the wagon. He was singing, harsh, tuneless,
loud.

That was Thursday. On Saturday morning Tennie's Jim left on
McCaslin's woods-horse which had not been out of the bottom

one time now in six years, and late that afternoon rode through
the gate on the spent horse and on to the commissary where
McCaslin was rationing the tenants and the wage-hands for the
coming week, and this time McCaslin forestalled any necessity or
risk of having to wait while Major de Spain's surrey was being
horsed and harnessed. He took their own, and with Tennie's Jim
already asleep in the back seat he drove in to Jefferson and
waited while Major de Spain changed to boots and put on his
overcoat, and they drove the thirty miles in the dark of that night
and at daybreak on Sunday morning they swapped to the waiting
mare and mule and as the sun rose they rode out of the jungle and
onto the low ridge where they had buried Lion: the low mound of
unannealed earth where Boon's spade-marks still showed and
beyond the grave the platform of freshly cut saplings bound between four posts and the blanket-wrapped bundle upon the platform and Boon and the boy squatting between the platform and
the grave until Boon, the bandage removed, ripped, from his head
so that the long scoriations of Old Ben's claws resembled crusted
tar in the sunlight, sprang up and threw down upon them with the
old gun with which he had never been known to hit anything
although McCaslin was already off the mule, kicked both feet free
of the irons and vaulted down before the mule had stopped,
walking toward Boon.

"Stand back," Boon said. "By God, you wont touch him. Stand
back, McCaslin." Still McCaslin came on, fast yet without haste.

"Cass!" Major de Spain said. Then he said "Boon! You, Boon!"
and he was down too and the boy rose too, quickly, and still Mc-
Caslin came on not fast but steady and walked up to the grave
and reached his hand steadily out, quickly yet still not fast, and
took hold the gun by the middle so that he and Boon faced one
another across Lion's grave, both holding the gun, Boon's spent
indomitable amazed and frantic face almost a head higher than
McCaslin's beneath the black scoriations of beast's claws and then
Boon's chest began to heave as though there were not enough air
in all the woods, in all the wilderness, for all of them, for him and
anyone else, even for him alone.

"Turn it loose, Boon," McCaslin said.

"You damn little spindling—" Boon said. "Dont you know I

can take it away from you? Dont you know I can tie it around your neck like a damn cravat?"

"Yes," McCaslin said. "Turn it loose, Boon."

"This is the way he wanted it. He told us. He told us exactly how to do it. And by God you aint going to move him. So we did it like he said, and I been sitting here ever since to keep the damn wildcats and varmints away from him and by God—" Then McCaslin had the gun, down-slanted while he pumped the slide, the five shells snicking out of it so fast that the last one was almost out before the first one touched the ground and McCaslin dropped the gun behind him without once having taken his eyes from Boon's.

"Did you kill him, Boon?" he said. Then Boon moved. He turned, he moved like he was still drunk and then for a moment blind too, one hand out as he blundered toward the big tree and seemed to stop walking before he reached the tree so that he plunged, fell toward it, flinging up both hands and catching himself against the tree and turning until his back was against it, backing with the tree's trunk his wild spent scoriated face and the tremendous heave and collapse of his chest, McCaslin following, facing him again, never once having moved his eyes from Boon's eyes. "Did you kill him, Boon?"

"No!" Boon said. "No!"

"Tell the truth," McCaslin said. "I would have done it if he had asked me to." Then the boy moved. He was between them, facing McCaslin; the water felt as if it had burst and sprung not from his eyes alone but from his whole face, like sweat.

"Leave him alone!" he cried. "Goddamn it! Leave him alone!"

4.

then he was twenty-one. He could say it, himself and his cousin juxtaposed not against the wilderness but against the tamed land which was to have been his heritage, the land which old Carothers McCaslin his grandfather had bought with white man's money from the wild men whose grandfathers without guns hunted it, and tamed and ordered or believed he had tamed and ordered it for the reason that the human beings he held in bondage and in the

power of life and death had removed the forest from it and in their
sweat scratched the surface of it to a depth of perhaps fourteen
inches in order to grow something out of it which had not been
there before and which could be translated back into the money
he who believed he had bought it had had to pay to get it and
hold it and a reasonable profit too: and for which reason old
Carothers McCaslin, knowing better, could raise his children, his
descendants and heirs, to believe the land was his to hold and
bequeath since the strong and ruthless man has a cynical foreknowledge of his own vanity and pride and strength and a contempt for all his get: just as, knowing better, Major de Spain and
his fragment of that wilderness which was bigger and older than
any recorded deed: just as, knowing better, old Thomas Sutpen,
from whom Major de Spain had had his fragment for money: just
as Ikkemotubbe, the Chickasaw chief, from whom Thomas Sutpen
had had the fragment for money or rum or whatever it was, knew
in his turn that not even a fragment of it had been his to relinquish
or sell

    not against the wilderness but against the land, not in pursuit
and lust but in relinquishment, and in the commissary as it should
have been, not the heart perhaps but certainly the solar-plexus of
the repudiated and relinquished: the square, galleried, wooden
building squatting like a portent above the fields whose laborers
it still held in thrall '65 or no and placarded over with advertise-
ments for snuff and cures for chills and salves and potions manufactured and sold by white men to bleach the pigment and
straighten the hair of negroes that they might resemble the very
race which for two hundred years had held them in bondage and
from which for another hundred years not even a bloody civil war
would have set them completely free

    himself and his cousin amid the old smells of cheese and salt
meat and kerosene and harness, the ranked shelves of tobacco and
overalls and bottled medicine and thread and plow-bolts, the
barrels and kegs of flour and meal and molasses and nails, the
wall pegs dependant with plowlines and plow-collars and hames
and trace-chains, and the desk and the shelf above it on which
rested the ledgers in which McCaslin recorded the slow outward
trickle of food and supplies and equipment which returned each

fall as cotton made and ginned and sold (two threads frail as
truth and impalpable as equators yet cable-strong to bind for life
them who made the cotton to the land their sweat fell on), and
the older ledgers clumsy and archaic in size and shape, on the
yellowed pages of which were recorded in the faded hand of his
father Theophilus and his uncle Amodeus during the two decades
before the Civil War, the manumission in title at least of Carothers
McCaslin's slaves:

'Relinquish,' McCaslin said. 'Relinquish. You, the direct male
descendant of him who saw the opportunity and took it, bought
the land, took the land, got the land no matter how, held it to bequeath, no matter how, out of the old grant, the first patent, when
it was a wilderness of wild beasts and wilder men, and cleared it,
translated it into something to bequeath to his children, worthy of
bequeathment for his descendants' ease and security and pride and
to perpetuate his name and accomplishments. Not only the male
descendant but the only and last descendant in the male line and
in the third generation, while I am not only four generations from
old Carothers, I derived through a woman and the very McCaslin
in my name is mine only by sufferance and courtesy and my
grandmother's pride in what that man accomplished whose legacy
and monument you think you can repudiate.' and he

'I cant repudiate it. It was never mine to repudiate. It was never
Father's and Uncle Buddy's to bequeath me to repudiate because
it was never Grandfather's to bequeath them to bequeath me to
repudiate because it was never old Ikkemotubbe's to sell to Grandfather for bequeathment and repudiation. Because it was never
Ikkemotubbe's fathers' fathers' to bequeath Ikkemotubbe to sell
to Grandfather or any man because on the instant when Ikkemotubbe discovered, realised, that he could sell it for money, on that
instant it ceased ever to have been his forever, father to father to
father, and the man who bought it bought nothing.'

'Bought nothing?' and he

'Bought nothing. Because He told in the Book how He created
the earth, made it and looked at it and said it was all right, and
then He made man. He made the earth first and peopled it with
dumb creatures, and then He created man to be His overseer on
the earth and to hold suzerainty over the earth and the animals on

it in His name, not to hold for himself and his descendants inviolable title forever, generation after generation, to the oblongs
and squares of the earth, but to hold the earth mutual and intact
in the communal anonymity of brotherhood, and all the fee He
asked was pity and humility and sufferance and endurance and
the sweat of his face for bread. And I know what you are going
to say,' he said: 'That nevertheless Grandfather—' and McCaslin

'—did own it. And not the first. Not alone and not the first
since, as your Authority states, man was dispossessed of Eden. Nor
yet the second and still not alone, on down through the tedious
and shabby chronicle of His chosen sprung from Abraham, and
of the sons of them who dispossessed Abraham, and of the five
hundred years during which half the known world and all it contained was chattel to one city as this plantation and all the life it
contained was chattel and revokeless thrall to this commissary
store and those ledgers yonder during your grandfather's life, and
the next thousand years while men fought over the fragments of
that collapse until at last even the fragments were exhausted and
men snarled over the gnawed bones of the old world's worthless
evening until an accidental egg discovered to them a new hemisphere. So let me say it: That nevertheless and notwithstanding
old Carothers did own it. Bought it, got it, no matter; kept it, held
it, no matter; bequeathed it: else why do you stand here relinquishing and repudiating? Held it, kept it for fifty years until you
could repudiate it, while He—this Arbiter, this Architect, this Um-
pire—condoned—or did He? looked down and saw—or did He?
Or at least did nothing: saw, and could not, or did not see; saw,
and would not, or perhaps He would not see—perverse, impotent,
or blind: which?' and he

'Dispossessed.' and McCaslin

'What?' and he

'Dispossessed. Not impotent: He didn't condone; not blind, because He watched it. And let me say it. Dispossessed of Eden.
Dispossessed of Canaan, and those who dispossessed him dispossessed him dispossessed, and the five hundred years of absentee
landlords in the Roman bagnios, and the thousand years of wild
men from the northern woods who dispossessed them and devoured their ravished substance ravished in turn again and then

snarled in what you call the old world's worthless twilight over the old world's gnawed bones, blasphemous in His name until He used a simple egg to discover to them a new world where a nation of people could be founded in humility and pity and sufferance and pride of one to another. And Grandfather did own the land nevertheless and notwithstanding because He permitted it, not impotent and not condoning and not blind because He ordered and watched it. He saw the land already accursed even as Ikkemotubbe and Ikkemotubbe's father old Issetibbeha and old Issetibbeha's fathers too held it, already tainted even before any white man owned it by what Grandfather and his kind, his fathers, had brought into the new land which He had vouchsafed them out of pity and sufferance, on condition of pity and humility and sufferance and endurance, from that old world's corrupt and worthless twilight as though in the sailfuls of the old world's tainted wind which drove the ships—' and McCaslin

'Ah.'

'—and no hope for the land anywhere so long as Ikkemotubbe and Ikkemotubbe's descendants held it in unbroken succession. Maybe He saw that only by voiding the land for a time of Ikkemotubbe's blood and substituting for it another blood, could He accomplish His purpose. Maybe He knew already what that other blood would be, maybe it was more than justice that only the white man's blood was available and capable to raise the white man's curse, more than vengeance when—' and McCaslin

'Ah.'

'—when He used the blood which had brought in the evil to destroy the evil as doctors use fever to burn up fever, poison to slay poison. Maybe He chose Grandfather out of all of them He might have picked. Maybe He knew that Grandfather himself would not serve His purpose because Grandfather was born too soon too, but that Grandfather would have descendants, the right descendants; maybe He had foreseen already the descendants Grandfather would have, maybe He saw already in Grandfather the seed progenitive of the three generations He saw it would take to set at least some of His lowly people free—' and McCaslin

'The sons of Ham. You who quote the Book: the sons of Ham.' and he

'There are some things He said in the Book, and some things reported of Him that He did not say. And I know what you will say now: That if truth is one thing to me and another thing to you, how will we choose which is truth? You dont need to choose. The heart already knows. He didn't have His Book written to be read by what must elect and choose, but by the heart, not by the wise of the earth because maybe they dont need it or maybe the wise no longer have any heart, but by the doomed and lowly of the earth who have nothing else to read with but the heart. Because the men who wrote his Book for Him were writing about truth and there is only one truth and it covers all things that touch the heart.' and McCaslin

'So these men who transcribed His Book for Him were sometime liars.' and he

'Yes. Because they were human men. They were trying to write down the heart's truth out of the heart's driving complexity, for all the complex and troubled hearts which would beat after them. What they were trying to tell, what He wanted said, was too simple. Those for whom they transcribed His words could not have believed them. It had to be expounded in the everyday terms which they were familiar with and could comprehend, not only those who listened but those who told it too, because if they who were that near to Him as to have been elected from among all who breathed and spoke language to transcribe and relay His words, could comprehend truth only through the complexity of passion and lust and hate and fear which drives the heart, what distance back to truth must they traverse whom truth could only reach by word-of-mouth?' and McCaslin

'I might answer that, since you have taken to proving your points and disproving mine by the same text, I dont know. But I dont say that, because you have answered yourself: No time at all if, as you say, the heart knows truth, the infallible and unerring heart. And perhaps you are right, since although you admitted three generations from old Carothers to you, there were not three. There were not even completely two. Uncle Buck and Uncle Buddy. And they not the first and not alone. A thousand other Bucks and Buddies in less than two generations and sometimes less than one in this land which so you claim God created and man himself cursed and tainted. Not to mention 1865.' and he

'Yes. More men that Father and Uncle Buddy,' not even glancing toward the shelf above the desk, nor did McCaslin. They did not need to. To him it was as though the ledgers in their scarred cracked leather bindings were being lifted down one by one in their fading sequence and spread open on the desk or perhaps upon some apocryphal Bench or even Altar or perhaps before the Throne Itself for a last perusal and contemplation and refreshment of the Allknowledgeable before the yellowed pages and the brown thin ink in which was recorded the injustice and a little at least of its amelioration and restitution faded back forever into the anonymous communal original dust

the yellowed pages scrawled in fading ink by the hand first of his grandfather and then of his father and uncle, bachelors up to and past fifty and then sixty, the one who ran the plantation and the farming of it and the other who did the housework and the cooking and continued to do it even after his twin married and the boy himself was born

the two brothers who as soon as their father was buried moved out of the tremendously-conceived, the almost barnlike edifice which he had not even completed, into a one-room log cabin which the two of them built themselves and added other rooms to while they lived in it, refusing to allow any slave to touch any timber of it other than the actual raising into place the logs which two men alone could not handle, and domiciled all the slaves in the big house some of the windows of which were still merely boarded up with odds and ends of plank or with the skins of bear and deer nailed over the empty frames: each sundown the brother who superintended the farming would parade the negroes as a first sergeant dismisses a company, and herd them willynilly, man woman and child, without question protest or recourse, into the tremendous abortive edifice scarcely yet out of embryo, as if even old Carothers McCaslin had paused aghast at the concrete indication of his own vanity's boundless conceiving: he would call his mental roll and herd them in and with a hand-wrought nail as long as a flenching-knife and suspended from a short deer-hide thong attached to the door-jamb for that purpose, he would nail to the door of that house which lacked half its windows and had no hinged back door at all, so that presently and for fifty years afterward, when the boy himself was big to hear and remember it, there was in the land a sort of folk-tale: of the countryside all night long full of skulking McCaslin slaves dodging the moonlit roads and the Patrol-riders to visit other plantations, and of the unspoken gentlemen's agreement between the two white men and the two dozen black ones that, after the white man had counted them and driven the home-made nail into the front door at sundown, neither of the white men would go around behind the house and look at the back door, provided that all the negroes were behind the front one when the brother who drove it drew out the nail again at daybreak

the twins who were identical even in their handwriting, unless you had specimens side by side to compare, and even when both hands appeared on the same page (as often happened, as if, long since past any oral intercourse, they had used the diurnally advancing pages to conduct the unavoidable business of the compulsion which had traversed all the waste wilderness of North Mississippi in 1830 and '40 and singled them out to drive) they both looked as though they had been written by the same perfectly normal ten-year-old boy, even to the spelling, except that the spelling did not improve as one by one the slaves which Carothers McCaslin had inherited and purchased—Roscius and Phoebe and Thucydides and Eunice and their descendants, and Sam Fathers and his mother for both of whom he had swapped an underbred trotting gelding to old Ikkemotubbe, the Chickasaw chief from whom he had likewise bought the land, and Tennie Beauchamp whom the twin Amodeus had won from a neighbor in a poker-game, and the anomaly calling itself Percival Brownlee which the twin Theophilus had purchased, neither he nor his brother ever knew why apparently, from Bedford Forrest while he was still only a slave-dealer and not yet a general (It was a single page, not long and covering less than a year, not seven months in fact, begun in the hand which the boy had learned to distinguish as that of his father:

Percavil Brownly 26yr Old. cleark @ Bookepper. bought from N.B.Forest at Cold Water 3 Mar 1856 $265. dolars

and beneath that, in the same hand:

5 mar 1856 No bookepper any way Cant read. Can write his Name but I already put that down My self Says he can Plough but dont look like it to Me. sent to Feild to day Mar 5 1856

and the same hand:

6 Mar 1856 Cant plough either Says he aims to be a Precher so may be he can lead live stock to Crick to Drink

and this time it was the other, the hand which he now recognised as his uncle's when he could see them both on the same page:

Mar 23th 1856 Cant do that either Except one at a Time Get shut of him

then the first again:

24 Mar 1856 Who in hell would buy him

then the second:

19th of Apr 1856 Nobody You put yourself out of Market at Cold Water two months ago I never said sell him Free him

the first:

22 Apr 1856 Ill get it out of him

the second:

Jun 13th 1856 How $1 per yr 265$ 265 yrs Wholl sign his Free paper

then the first again:

1 Oct 1856 Mule josephine Broke Leg @ shot Wrong stall wrong niger wrong everything $100. dolars

and the same:

2 Oct 1856 Freed Debit McCaslin @ McCaslin $265. dolars

then the second again:

Oct 3th Debit Theophilus McCaslin Niger 265$ Mule 100$ 365$ He hasnt gone yet Father should be here

then the first:

3 Oct 1856 Son of a bitch wont leave What would father done

the second:

29th of Oct 1856 Renamed him

the first:

31 Oct 1856 Renamed him what

the second:

Chrstms 1856 Spintrius

) took substance and even a sort of shadowy life with their passions and complexities too as page followed page and year year; all there, not only the general and condoned injustice and its slow amortization but the specific tragedy which had not been condoned and could never be amortized, the new page and the new ledger, the hand which he could now recognise at first glance as his father's:

Father dide Lucius Quintus Carothers McCaslin, Callina 1772 Missippy 1837. Dide and burid 27 June 1837
Roskus. rased by Granfather in Callina Dont know how old. Freed 27 June 1837 Dont want to leave. Dide and Burid 12 Jan 1841
Fibby Roskus Wife. bought by granfather in Callina says Fifty Freed 27 June 1837 Dont want to leave. Dide and burd 1 Aug 1849
Thucydus Roskus @ Fibby Son born in Callina 1779. Refused 10acre peace fathers Will 28 Jun 1837 Refused Cash offer $200. dolars from A.@ T. McCaslin 28 Jun 1837 Wants to stay and work it out

and beneath this and covering the next five pages and almost that
many years, the slow, day-by-day accrument of the wages allowed
him and the food and clothing—the molasses and meat and meal,
the cheap durable shirts and jeans and shoes and now and then
a coat against rain and cold—charged against the slowly yet
steadily mounting sum of balance (and it would seem to the boy
that he could actually see the black man, the slave whom his
white owner had forever manumitted by the very act from which
the black man could never be free so long as memory lasted,
entering the commissary, asking permission perhaps of the white
man's son to see the ledger-page which he could not even read,
not even asking for the white man's word, which he would have
had to accept for the reason that there was absolutely no way under the sun for him to test it, as to how the account stood, how
much longer before he could go and never return, even if only
as far as Jefferson seventeen miles away) on to the double pen-
stroke closing the final entry:

3 Nov 1841 By Cash to Thucydus McCaslin $200. dolars
Set Up blaksmith in J. Dec 1841 Dide and burid in J. 17 feb
1854
Eunice Bought by Father in New Orleans 1807 $650. dolars.
Marrid to Thucydus 1809 Drownd in Crick Cristmas Day
1832

and then the other hand appeared, the first time he had seen it
in the ledger to distinguish it as his uncle's, the cook and house-
keeper whom even McCaslin, who had known him and the boy's
father for sixteen years before the boy was born, remembered as
sitting all day long in the rocking chair from which he cooked the
food, before the kitchen fire on which he cooked it:

June 21th 1833 Drownd herself

and the first:

23 Jun 1833 Who in hell ever heard of a niger drownding
him self

and the second, unhurried, with a complete finality; the two identical entries might have been made with a rubber stamp save for the date:

Aug 13th 1833 Drownd herself

and he thought *But why? But why?* He was sixteen then. It was neither the first time he had been alone in the commissary nor the first time he had taken down the old ledgers familiar on their shelf above the desk ever since he could remember. As a child and even after nine and ten and eleven, when he had learned to read, he would look up at the scarred and cracked backs and ends but with no particular desire to open them, and though he intended to examine them someday because he realised that they probably contained a chronological and much more comprehensive though doubtless tedious record than he would ever get from any other source, not alone of his own flesh and blood but of all his people, not only the whites but the black one too, who were as much a part of his ancestry as his white progenitors, and of the land which they had all held and used in common and fed from and on and would continue to use in common without regard to color or titular ownership, it would only be on some idle day when he was old and perhaps even bored a little since what the old books contained would be after all these years fixed immutably, finished, unalterable, harmless. Then he was sixteen. He knew what he was going to find before he found it. He got the commissary key from McCaslin's room after midnight while McCaslin was asleep and with the commissary door shut and locked behind him and the forgotten lantern stinking anew the rank dead icy air, he leaned above the yellowed page and thought not Why drowned herself, but thinking what he believed his father had thought when he found his brother's first comment: Why did Uncle Buddy think she had drowned herself? finding, beginning to find on the next succeeding page what he knew he would find, only this was still not it because he already knew this:

Tomasina called Tomy Daughter of Thucydus @ Eunice Born 1810 dide in Child bed June 1833 and Burd. Yr stars fell

nor the next:

*Turl Son of Thucydus @ Eunice Tomy born Jun 1833 yr
stars fell Fathers will*

and nothing more, no tedious recording filling this page of wages
day by day and food and clothing charged against them, no entry
of his death and burial because he had outlived his white half-
brothers and the books which McCaslin kept did not include
obituaries: just *Fathers will* and he had seen that too: old Carothers' bold cramped hand far less legible than his sons' even and
not much better in spelling, who while capitalising almost every
noun and verb, made no effort to punctuate or construct whatever,
just as he made no effort either to explain or obfuscate the thou-
sand-dollar legacy to the son of an unmarried slave-girl, to be
paid only at the child's coming-of-age, bearing the consequence
of the act of which there was still no definite incontrovertible
proof that he acknowledged, not out of his own substance but
penalising his sons with it, charging them a cash forfeit on the
accident of their own paternity; not even a bribe for silence toward
his own fame since his fame would suffer only after he was no
longer present to defend it, flinging almost contemptuously, as he
might a cast-off hat or pair of shoes, the thousand dollars which
could have had no more reality to him under those conditions
than it would have to the negro, the slave who would not even
see it until he came of age, twenty-one years too late to begin to
learn what money was. *So I reckon that was cheaper than saying
My son to a nigger* he thought. *Even if My son wasn't but just
two words. But there must have been love* he thought. *Some sort
of love. Even what he would have called love: not just an afternoon's or a night's spittoon.* There was the old man, old, within
five years of his life's end, long a widower and, since his sons were
not only bachelors but were approaching middleage, lonely in the
house and doubtless even bored since his plantation was established now and functioning and there was enough money now, too
much of it probably for a man whose vices even apparently remained below his means; there was the girl, husbandless and
young, only twenty-three when the child was born: perhaps he
had sent for her at first out of loneliness, to have a young voice
and movement in the house, summoned her, bade her mother

send her each morning to sweep the floors and make the beds and the mother acquiescing since that was probably already understood, already planned: the only child of a couple who were not field hands and who held themselves something above the other slaves not alone for that reason but because the husband and his father and mother too had been inherited by the white man from his father, and the white man himself had travelled three hundred miles and better to New Orleans in a day when men travelled by horseback or steamboat, and bought the girl's mother as a wife for

and that was all. The old frail pages seemed to turn of their own accord even while he thought *His own daughter His own daughter. No No Not even him* back to that one where the white man (not even a widower then) who never went anywhere any more than his sons in their time ever did and who did not need another slave, had gone all the way to New Orleans and bought one. And Tomey's Terrel was still alive when the boy was ten years old and he knew from his own observation and memory that there had already been some white in Tomey's Terrel's blood before his father gave him the rest of it; and looking down at the yellowed page spread beneath the yellow glow of the lantern smoking and stinking in that rank chill midnight room fifty years later, he seemed to see her actually walking into the icy creek on that Christmas day six months before her daughter's and her lover's (*Her first lover's* he thought. *Her first*) child was born, solitary, inflexible, griefless, ceremonial, in formal and succinct repudiation of grief and despair who had already had to repudiate belief and hope

that was all. He would never need look at the ledgers again nor did he; the yellowed pages in their fading and implacable succession were as much a part of his consciousness and would remain so forever, as the fact of his own nativity:

Tennie Beauchamp 21yrs Won by Amodeus McCaslin from Hubert Beauchamp Esqre Possible Strait against three Treys in sigt Not called 1859 Marrid to Tomys Turl 1859

and no date of freedom because her freedom, as well as that of her first surviving child, derived not from Buck and Buddy Mc-

Caslin in the commissary but from a stranger in Washington and
no date of death and burial, not only because McCaslin kept no
obituaries in his books, but because in this year 1883 she was still
alive and would remain so to see a grandson by her last surviving
child:

*Amodeus McCaslin Beauchamp Son of tomys Turl @ Ten-
nie Beauchamp 1859 dide 1859*

then his uncle's hand entire, because his father was now a member of the cavalry command of that man whose name as a slave-
dealer he could not even spell: and not even a page and not even
a full line:

Dauter Tomes Turl and tenny 1862

and not even a line and not even a sex and no cause given though
the boy could guess it because McCaslin was thirteen then and
he remembered how there was not always enough to eat in more
places than Vicksburg:

Child of tomes Turl and Tenny 1863

and the same hand again and this one lived, as though Tennie's
perseverance and the fading and diluted ghost of old Carothers'
ruthlessness had at last conquered even starvation: and clearer,
fuller, more carefully written and spelled than the boy had yet
seen it, as if the old man, who should have been a woman to
begin with, trying to run what was left of the plantation in his
brother's absence in the intervals of cooking and caring for himself and the fourteen-year-old orphan, had taken as an omen for
renewed hope the fact that this nameless inheritor of slaves was
at least remaining alive long enough to receive a name:

*James Thucydus Beauchamp Son of Tomes Turl and Tenny
Beauchamp Born 29th december 1864 and both Well Wanted
to call him Theophilus but Tride Amodeus McCaslin and
Callina McCaslin and both dide so Disswaded Them Born
at Two clock A,m, both Well*

but no more, nothing; it would be another two years yet before
the boy, almost a man now, would return from the abortive trip

into Tennessee with the still-intact third of old Carothers' legacy
to his Negro son and his descendants, which as the three surviving children established at last one by one their apparent intention
of surviving, their white half-uncles had increased to a thousand
dollars each, conditions permitting, as they came of age, and
completed the page himself as far as it would even be completed
when that day was long passed beyond which a man born in 1864
(or 1867 either, when he himself saw light) could have expected
or himself hoped or even wanted to be still alive; his own hand
now, queerly enough resembling neither his father's nor his uncle's nor even McCaslin's, but like that of his grandfather's save
for the spelling:

*Vanished sometime on night of his twenty-first birthday Dec
29 1885. Traced by Isaac McCaslin to Jackson Tenn. and
there lost. His third of legacy $1000.00 returned to McCaslin
Edmonds Trustee this day Jan 12 1886*

but not yet: that would be two years yet, and now his father's
again, whose old commander was now quit of soldiering and
slave-trading both; once more in the ledger and then not again
and more illegible than ever, almost indecipherable at all from
the rheumatism which now crippled him and almost completely
innocent now even of any sort of spelling as well as punctuation,
as if the four years during which he had followed the sword of
the only man ever breathing who ever sold him a negro, let alone
beat him in a trade, had convinced him not only of the vanity of
faith and hope but of orthography too:

Miss sophonsiba b dtr t t @ t 1869

but not of belief and will because it was there, written, as Mc-
Caslin had told him, with the left hand, but there in the ledger
one time more and then not again, for the boy himself was a year
old, and when Lucas was born six years later, his father and uncle
had been dead inside the same twelve-months almost five years;
his own hand again, who was there and saw it, 1886, she was just
seventeen, two years younger than himself, and he was in the
commissary when McCaslin entered out of the first of dusk and
said, 'He wants to marry Fonsiba,' like that: and he looked past

McCaslin and saw the man, the stranger, taller than McCaslin and wearing better clothes than McCaslin and most of the other white men the boy knew habitually wore, who entered the room like a white man and stood in it like a white man, as though he had let McCaslin precede him into it not because McCaslin's skin was white but simply because McCaslin lived there and knew the way, and who talked like a white man too, looking at him past Mc-Caslin's shoulder rapidly and keenly once and then no more, without further interest, as a mature and contained white man not impatient but just pressed for time might have looked. 'Marry Fonsiba?' he cried. 'Marry Fonsiba?' and then no more either, just watching and listening while McCaslin and the Negro talked:

'To live in Arkansas, I believe you said.'

'Yes. I have property there. A farm.'

'Property? A farm? You own it?'

'Yes.'

'You dont say Sir, do you?'

'To my elders, yes.'

'I see. You are from the North.'

'Yes. Since a child.'

'Then your father was a slave.'

'Yes. Once.'

'Then how do you own a farm in Arkansas?'

'I have a grant. It was my father's. From the United States. For military service.'

'I see,' McCaslin said. 'The Yankee army.'

'The United States army,' the stranger said; and then himself again, crying it at McCaslin's back:

'Call aunt Tennie! I'll go get her! I'll——' But McCaslin was not even including him; the stranger did not even glance back toward his voice, the two of them speaking to one another again as if he were not even there:

'Since you seem to have it all settled,' McCaslin said, 'why have you bothered to consult my authority at all?'

'I dont,' the stranger said. 'I acknowledge your authority only so far as you admit your responsibility toward her as a female member of the family of which you are the head. I dont ask your permission. I——'

'That will do!' McCaslin said. But the stranger did not falter. It was neither as if he were ignoring McCaslin nor as if he had failed to hear him. It was as though he were making, not at all an excuse and not exactly a justification, but simply a statement which the situation absolutely required and demanded should be made in McCaslin's hearing whether McCaslin listened to it or not. It was as if he were talking to himself, for himself to hear the words spoken aloud. They faced one another, not close yet at slightly less than foils' distance, erect, their voices not raised, not impactive, just succinct:

'—I inform you, notify you in advance as chief of her family. No man of honor could do less. Besides, you have, in your way, according to your lights and upbringing ——'

'That's enough, I said,' McCaslin said. 'Be off this place by full dark. Go.' But for another moment the other did not move, contemplating McCaslin with that detached and heatless look, as if he were watching reflected in McCaslin's pupils the tiny image of the figure he was sustaining.

'Yes,' he said. 'After all, this is your house. And in your fashion you have. . . . But no matter. You are right. This is enough.' He turned back toward the door; he paused again but only for a second, already moving while he spoke: 'Be easy. I will be good to her.' Then he was gone.

'But how did she ever know him?' the boy cried. 'I never even heard of him before! And Fonsiba, that's never been off this place except to go to church since she was born ——'

'Ha,' McCaslin said. 'Even their parents dont know until too late how seventeen-year-old girls ever met the men who marry them too, if they are lucky.' And the next morning they were both gone, Fonsiba too. McCaslin never saw her again, nor did he, because the woman he found at last five months later was no one he had ever known. He carried a third of the three-thousand-dollar fund in gold in a money-belt, as when he had vainly traced Tennie's Jim into Tennessee a year ago. They—the man—had left an address of some sort with Tennie, and three months later a letter came, written by the man although McCaslin's wife Alice had taught Fonsiba to read and write too a little. But it bore a different postmark from the address the man had left with Tennie,

and he travelled by rail as far as he could and then by contracted
stage and then by a hired livery rig and then by rail again for a
distance: an experienced traveller by now and an experienced
bloodhound too and a successful one this time because he would
have to be; as the slow interminable empty muddy December
miles crawled and crawled and night followed night in hotels, in
roadside taverns of rough logs and containing little else but a bar,
and in the cabins of strangers and the hay of lonely barns, in none
of which he dared undress because of his secret golden girdle like
that of a disguised one of the Magi travelling incognito and not
even hope to draw him but only determination and desperation,
he would tell himself: *I will have to find her. I will have to. We
have already lost one of them. I will have to find her this time.*
He did. Hunched in the slow and icy rain, on a spent hired horse
splashed to the chest and higher, he saw it—a single log edifice
with a clay chimney which seemed in process of being flattened
by the rain to a nameless and valueless rubble of dissolution in
that roadless and even pathless waste of unfenced fallow and wilderness jungle—no barn, no stable, not so much as a hen-coop:
just a log cabin built by hand and no clever hand either, a meagre
pile of clumsily-cut firewood sufficient for about one day and not
even a gaunt hound to come bellowing out from under the house
when he rode up—a farm only in embryo, perhaps a good farm,
maybe even a plantation someday, but not now, not for years yet
and only then with labor, hard and enduring and unflagging work
and sacrifice; he shoved open the crazy kitchen door in its awry
frame and entered an icy gloom where not even a fire for cooking
burned and after another moment saw, crouched into the wall's
angle behind a crude table, the coffee-colored face which he had
known all his life but knew no more, the body which had been
born within a hundred yards of the room that he was born in and
in which some of his own blood ran but which was now completely inheritor of generation after generation to whom an un-
announced white man on a horse was a white man's hired Pa-
troller wearing a pistol sometimes and a blacksnake whip always;
he entered the next room, the only other room the cabin owned,
and found, sitting in a rocking chair before the hearth, the man
himself, reading—sitting there in the only chair in the house, be-

fore that miserable fire for which there was not wood sufficient to last twenty-four hours, in the same ministerial clothing in which he had entered the commissary five months ago and a pair of gold-framed spectacles which, when he looked up and then rose to his feet, the boy saw did not even contain lenses, reading a book in the midst of that desolation, that muddy waste fenceless and even pathless and without even a walled shed for stock to stand beneath: and over all, permeant, clinging to the man's very clothing and exuding from his skin itself, that rank stink of baseless and imbecile delusion, that boundless rapacity and folly, of the carpet-bagger followers of victorious armies.

'Dont you see?' he cried. 'Dont you see? This whole land, the whole South, is cursed, and all of us who derive from it, whom it ever suckled, white and black both, lie under the curse? Granted that my people brought the curse onto the land: maybe for that reason their descendants alone can—not resist it, not combat it —maybe just endure and outlast it until the curse is lifted. Then your peoples' turn will come because we have forfeited ours. But not now. Not yet. Dont you see?'

The other stood now, the unfrayed garments still ministerial even if not quite so fine, the book closed upon one finger to keep the place, the lenseless spectacles held like a music master's wand in the other workless hand while the owner of it spoke his measured and sonorous imbecility of the boundless folly and the baseless hope: 'You're wrong. The curse you whites brought into this land has been lifted. It has been voided and discharged. We are seeing a new era, an era dedicated, as our founders intended it, to freedom, liberty and equality for all, to which this country will be the new Canaan ——'

'Freedom from what? From work? Canaan?' He jerked his arm, comprehensive, almost violent: whereupon it all seemed to stand there about them, intact and complete and visible in the drafty, damp, heatless, negro-stale negro-rank sorry room—the empty fields without plow or seed to work them, fenceless against the stock which did not exist within or without the walled stable which likewise was not there. 'What corner of Canaan is this?'

'You are seeing it at a bad time. This is winter. No man farms this time of year.'

'I see. And of course her need for food and clothing will stand still while the land lies fallow.'

'I have a pension,' the other said. He said it as a man might say *I have grace* or *I own a gold mine.* 'I have my father's pension too. It will arrive on the first of the month. What day is this?'

'The eleventh,' he said. 'Twenty days more. And until then?'

'I have a few groceries in the house from my credit account with the merchant in Midnight who banks my pension check for me. I have executed to him a power of attorney to handle it for me as a matter of mutual ——'

'I see. And if the groceries dont last the twenty days?'

'I still have one more hog.'

'Where?'

'Outside,' the other said. 'It is customary in this country to allow stock to range free during the winter for food. It comes up from time to time. But no matter if it doesn't; I can probably trace its footprints when the need ——'

'Yes!' he cried. 'Because no matter: you still have the pension check. And the man in Midnight will cash it and pay himself out of it for what you have already eaten and if there is any left over, it is yours. And the hog will be eaten by then or you still cant catch it, and then what will you do?'

'It will be almost spring then,' the other said. 'I am planning in the spring ——'

'It will be January,' he said. 'And then February. And then more than half of March——' and when he stopped again in the kitchen she had not moved, she did not even seem to breathe or to be alive except her eyes watching him; when he took a step toward her it was still not movement because she could have retreated no further: only the tremendous fathomless ink-colored eyes in the narrow, thin, too thin coffee-colored face watching him without alarm, without recognition, without hope. 'Fonsiba,' he said. 'Fonsiba. Are you all right?'

'I'm free,' she said. Midnight was a tavern, a livery stable, a big store (that would be where the pension check banked itself as a matter of mutual elimination of bother and fret, he thought) and a little one, a saloon and a blacksmith shop. But there was a bank there too. The president (the owner, for all practical pur-

poses) of it was a translated Mississippian who had been one of
Forrest's men too: and his body lightened of the golden belt for
the first time since he left home eight days ago, with pencil and
paper he multiplied three dollars by twelve months and divided it
into one thousand dollars; it would stretch that way over almost
twenty-eight years and for twenty-eight years at least she would
not starve, the banker promising to send the three dollars himself
by a trusty messenger on the fifteenth of each month and put it
into her actual hand, and he returned home and that was all because in 1874 his father and his uncle were both dead and the old
ledgers never again came down from the shelf above the desk to
which his father had returned them for the last time that day in
1869. But he could have completed it:

*Lucas Quintus Carothers McCaslin Beauchamp. Last sur-
viving son and child of Tomey's Terrel and Tennie Beauchamp. March 17, 1874*

except that there was no need: not *Lucius Quintus* @c @c @c,
but *Lucas Quintus,* not refusing to be called Lucius, because he
simply eliminated that word from the name; not denying, declining the name itself, because he used three quarters of it; but simply taking the name and changing, altering it, making it no longer
the white man's but his own, by himself composed, himself self-
progenitive and nominate, by himself ancestored, as, for all the
old ledgers recorded to the contrary, old Carothers himself was
    and that was all: 1874 the boy; 1888 the man, repudiated de-
nied and free; 1895 and husband but no father, unwidowered but
without a wife, and found long since that no man is ever free and
probably could not bear it if he were; married then and living in
Jefferson in the little new jerrybuilt bungalow which his wife's
father had given them: and one morning Lucas stood suddenly in
the doorway of the room where he was reading the Memphis paper and he looked at the paper's dateline and thought *It's his
birthday. He's twenty-one today* and Lucas said: 'Whar's the rest
of that money old Carothers left? I wants it. All of it.'
    that was all: and McCaslin
    'More men than that one Buck and Buddy to fumble-heed that

Exploring history of the South as evidence for the declining plan of man

truth so mazed for them that spoke it and so confused for them that heard yet still there was 1865:' and he

'But not enough. Not enough of even Father and Uncle Buddy to fumble-heed in even three generations not even three generations fathered by Grandfather not even if there had been nowhere beneath His sight any but Grandfather and so He would not even have needed to elect and choose. But He tried and I know what you will say. That having Himself created them He could have known no more of hope than He could have pride and grief but He didn't hope He just waited because He had made them: not just because He had set them alive and in motion but because He had already worried with them so long: worried with them so long because He had seen how in individual cases they were capable of anything any height or depth remembered in mazed incomprehension out of heaven where hell was created too and so He must admit them or else admit His equal somewhere and so be no longer God and therefore must accept responsibility for what He Himself had done in order to live with Himself in His lonely and paramount heaven. And He probably knew it was vain but He had created them and knew them capable of all things because He had shaped them out of the primal Absolute which contained all and had watched them since in their individual exaltation and baseness and they themselves not knowing why nor how nor even when: until at last He saw that they were all Grandfather all of them and that even from them the elected and chosen the best the very best He could expect (not hope mind: not hope) would be Bucks and Buddies and not even enough of them and in the third generation not even Bucks and Buddies but—' and Mc-Caslin

'Ah:' and he

'Yes. If He could see Father and Uncle Buddy in Grandfather He must have seen me too.—an Isaac born into a later life than Abraham's and repudiating immolation: fatherless and therefore safe declining the altar because maybe this time the exasperated Hand might not supply the kid—' and McCaslin

'Escape:' and he

'All right. Escape.—Until one day He said what you told Fon-

siba's husband that afternoon here in this room: *This will do.
This is enough:* not in exasperation or rage or even just sick to
death as you were sick that day: just *This is enough* and looked
about for one last time, for one time more since He had created
them, upon this land this South for which He had done so much
with woods for game and streams for fish and deep rich soil for
seed and lush springs to sprout it and long summers to mature it
and serene falls to harvest it and short mild winters for men and
animals and saw no hope anywhere and looked beyond it where
hope should have been, where to East North and West lay illimitable that whole hopeful continent dedicated as a refuge and
sanctuary of liberty and freedom from what you called the old
world's worthless evening and saw the rich descendants of slavers,
females of both sexes, to whom the black they shrieked of was
another specimen another example like the Brazilian macaw
brought home in a cake by a traveller, passing resolutions about
horror and outrage in warm and air-proof halls: and the thundering cannonade of politicians earning votes and the medicine-
shows of pulpiteers earning Chautauqua fees, to whom the outrage and the injustice were as much abstractions as Tariff or
Silver or Immortality and who employed the very shackles of its
servitude and the sorry rags of its regalia as they did the other
beer and banners and mottoes redfire and brimstone and sleight-
of-hand and musical handsaws: and the whirling wheels which
manufactured for a profit the pristine replacements of the shackles
and shoddy garments as they wore out and spun the cotton and
made the gins which ginned it and the cars and ships which hauled
it, and the men who ran the wheels for that profit and established
and collected the taxes it was taxed with and the rates for hauling
it and the commissions for selling it: and He could have repudiated them since they were his creation now and forever more
throughout all their generations until not only that old world from
which He had rescued them but this new one too which He had
revealed and led them to as a sanctuary and refuge were become
the same worthless tideless rock cooling in the last crimson evening except that out of all that empty sound and bootless fury one
silence, among that loud and moiling all of them just one simple
enough to believe that horror and outrage were first and last sim-

ply horror and outrage and was crude enough to act upon that, illiterate and had no words for talking or perhaps was just busy not even bothered to inform Him in advance what he was about and had no time to, one out of them all who did not bother Him with cajolery and adjuration then pleading then threat and had so that a lesser than He might have even missed the simple act of lifting the long ancestral musket down from the deerhorns above the door, whereupon He said *My name is Brown too* and the other *So is mine* and He *Then mine or yours cant be because I am against it* and the other *So am I* and He triumphantly *Then where are you going with that gun?* and the other told him in one sentence one word and He: amazed: Who knew neither hope nor pride nor grief *But your Association, your Committee, your Officers. Where are your Minutes, your Motions, your Parliamentary Procedures?* and the other *I aint against them. They are all right I reckon for them that have the time. I am just against the weak because they are niggers being held in bondage by the strong just because they are white.* So He turned once more to this land which He still intended to save because He had done so much for it—' and McCaslin

'What?' and he

'—to these people He was still committed to because they were his creations—' and McCaslin

'Turned back to us? His face to us?' and he

'—whose wives and daughters at least made soups and jellies for them when they were sick and carried the trays through the mud and the winter too into the stinking cabins and sat in the stinking cabins and kept fires going until crises came and passed but that was not enough: and when they were very sick had them carried into the big house itself into the company room itself maybe and nursed them there which the white man would have done too for any other of his cattle that was sick but at least the man who hired one from a livery wouldn't have and still that was not enough: so that He said and not in grief either Who had made them and so could know no more of grief than He could of pride or hope: *Apparently they can learn nothing save through suffering, remember nothing save when underlined in blood*—' and McCaslin

'Ashby on an afternoon's ride, to call on some remote maiden cousins of his mother or maybe just acquaintances of hers, comes by chance upon a minor engagement of outposts and dismounts and with his crimson-lined cloak for target leads a handful of troops he never saw before against an entrenched position of backwoods-trained riflemen. Lee's battle-order, wrapped maybe about a handful of cigars and doubtless thrown away when the last cigar was smoked, found by a Yankee Intelligence officer on the floor of a saloon behind the Yankee lines after Lee had already divided his forces before Sharpsburg. Jackson on the Plank Road, already rolled up the flank which Hooker believed could not be turned and, waiting only for night to pass to continue the brutal and incessant slogging which would fling that whole wing back into Hooker's lap where he sat on a front gallery in Chancellorsville drinking rum toddies and telegraphing Lincoln that he had defeated Lee, is shot from among a whole covey of minor officers and in the blind night by one of his own patrols, leaving as next by seniority Stuart that gallant man born apparently already horsed and sabred and already knowing all there was to know about war except the slogging and brutal stupidity of it: and that same Stuart off raiding Pennsylvania hen-roosts when Lee should have known of all of Meade just where Hancock was on Cemetery Ridge: and Longstreet too at Gettysburg and that same Longstreet shot out of saddle by his own men in the dark by mistake just as Jackson was. His face to us? His face to us?' and he

'How else have made them fight? Who else but Jacksons and Stuarts and Ashbys and Morgans and Forrests?—the farmers of the central and middle-west, holding land by the acre instead of the tens or maybe even the hundreds, farming it themselves and to no single crop of cotton or tobacco or cane, owning no slaves and needing and wanting none and already looking toward the Pacific coast, not always as long as two generations there and having stopped where they did stop only through the fortuitous mischance that an ox died or a wagon-axle broke. And the New England mechanics who didn't even own land and measured all things by the weight of water and the cost of turning wheels and the narrow fringe of traders and ship-owners still looking backward across the Atlantic and attached to the continent only by their counting-houses. And those who should have had the alertness to see: the wildcat manipulators of mythical wilderness townsites; and the astuteness to rationalise: the bankers who held the mortgages on the land which the first were only waiting to abandon and on the railroads and steamboats to carry them still further west, and on the factories and the wheels and the rented tenements those who ran them lived in; and the leisure and scope to comprehend and fear in time and even anticipate: the Boston-bred (even when not born in Boston) spinster descendants of long lines of similarly-bred and likewise spinster aunts and uncles whose hands knew no callus except that of the indicting pen, to whom the wilderness itself began at the top of tide and who looked, if at anything other than Beacon Hill, only toward heaven —not to mention all the loud rabble of the camp-followers of pioneers: the bellowing of politicians, the mellifluous choiring of self-styled men of God, the—' and McCaslin

'Here, here. Wait a minute:' and he

'Let me talk now. I'm trying to explain to the head of my family something which I have got to do which I dont quite understand myself, not in justification of it but to explain it if I can. I could say I dont know why I must do it but that I do know I have got to because I have got myself to have to live with for the rest of my life and all I want is peace to do it in. But you are the head of my family. More. I knew a long time ago that I would never have to miss my father, even if you are just finding out that you have missed your son.—the drawers of bills and the shavers of notes and the schoolmasters and the self-ordained to teach and lead and all that horde of the semiliterate with a white shirt but no change for it, with one eye on themselves and watching each other with the other one. Who else could have made them fight: could have struck them so aghast with fear and dread as to turn shoulder to shoulder and face one way and even stop talking for a while and even after two years of it keep them still so wrung with terror that some among them would seriously propose moving their very capital into a foreign country lest it be ravaged and pillaged by a people whose entire white male population would have little more than filled any one of their larger cities: except

Jackson in the Valley and three separate armies trying to catch
him and none of them ever knowing whether they were just retreating from a battle or just running into one and Stuart riding
his whole command entirely around the biggest single armed
force this continent ever saw in order to see what it looked like
from behind and Morgan leading a cavalry charge against a
stranded man-of-war. Who else could have declared a war against
a power with ten times the area and a hundred times the men and
a thousand times the resources, except men who could believe
that all necessary to conduct a successful war was not acumen nor
shrewdness nor politics nor diplomacy nor money nor even in-
tegrity and simple arithmetic but just love of land and courage ——'

'And an unblemished and gallant ancestry and the ability to
ride a horse,' McCaslin said. 'Dont leave that out.' It was evening
now, the tranquil sunset of October mazy with windless wood-
smoke. The cotton was long since picked and ginned, and all day
now the wagons loaded with gathered corn moved between field
and crib, processional across the enduring land. 'Well, maybe
that's what He wanted. At least, that's what He got.' This time
there was no yellowed procession of fading and harmless ledger-
pages. This was chronicled in a harsher book and McCaslin, fourteen and fifteen and sixteen, had seen it and the boy himself had
inherited it as Noah's grandchildren had inherited the Flood although they had not been there to see the deluge: that dark corrupt and bloody time while three separate peoples had tried to
adjust not only to one another but to the new land which they
had created and inherited too and must live in for the reason that
those who had lost it were no less free to quit it than those who
had gained it were:—those upon whom freedom and equality had
been dumped overnight and without warning or preparation or
any training in how to employ it or even just endure it and who
misused it not as children would nor yet because they had been
so long in bondage and then so suddenly freed, but misused it as
human beings always misuse freedom, so that he thought *Apparently there is a wisdom beyond even that learned through suffering necessary for a man to distinguish between liberty and license;* those who had fought for four years and lost to preserve a

condition under which that franchisement was anomaly and paradox, not because they were opposed to freedom as freedom but
for the old reasons for which man (not the generals and politicians
but man) has always fought and died in wars: to preserve a status
quo or to establish a better future one to endure for his children;
and lastly, as if that were not enough for bitterness and hatred
and fear, that third race even more alien to the people whom they
resembled in pigment and in whom even the same blood ran, than
to the people whom they did not,—that race threefold in one and
alien even among themselves save for a single fierce will for rapine
and pillage, composed of the sons of middleaged Quartermaster
lieutenants and Army sutlers and contractors in military blankets
and shoes and transport mules, who followed the battles they
themselves had not fought and inherited the conquest they themselves had not helped to gain, sanctioned and protected even if
not blessed, and left their bones and in another generation would
be engaged in a fierce economic competition of small sloven farms
with the black men they were supposed to have freed and the
white descendants of fathers who had owned no slaves anyway
whom they were supposed to have disinherited and in the third
generation would be back once more in the little lost county seats
as barbers and garage mechanics and deputy sheriffs and mill-
and gin-hands and power-plant firemen, leading, first in mufti then
later in an actual formalised regalia of hooded sheets and pass-
words and fiery christian symbols, lynching mobs against the race
their ancestors had come to save: and of all that other nameless
horde of speculators in human misery, manipulators of money and
politics and land, who follow catastrophe and are their own protection as grasshoppers are and need no blessing and sweat no
plow or axe-helve and batten and vanish and leave no bones, just
as they derived apparently from no ancestry, no mortal flesh, no
act even of passion or even of lust: and the Jew who came without protection too since after two thousand years he had got out
of the habit of being or needing it, and solitary, without even the
solidarity of the locusts and in this a sort of courage since he had
come thinking not in terms of simple pillage but in terms of his
great-grandchildren, seeking yet some place to establish them to
endure even though forever alien: and unblessed: a pariah about

the face of the Western earth which twenty centuries later was
still taking revenge on him for the fairy tale with which he had
conquered it. McCaslin had actually seen it, and the boy even at
almost eighty would never be able to distinguish certainly between
what he had seen and what had been told him: a lightless and
gutted and empty land where women crouched with the huddled
children behind locked doors and men armed in sheets and masks
rode the silent roads and the bodies of white and black both,
victims not so much of hate as of desperation and despair, swung
from lonely limbs: and men shot dead in polling-booths with the
still wet pen in one hand and the unblotted ballot in the other:
and a United States marshal in Jefferson who signed his official
papers with a crude cross, an ex-slave called Sickymo, not at all
because his ex-owner was a doctor and apothecary but because,
still a slave, he would steal his master's grain alcohol and dilute
it with water and peddle it in pint bottles from a cache beneath
the roots of a big sycamore tree behind the drug store, who had
attained his high office because his half-white sister was the concubine of the Federal A.P.M.: and this time McCaslin did not
even say Look but merely lifted one hand, not even pointing, not
even specifically toward the shelf of ledgers but toward the desk,
toward the corner where it sat beside the scuffed patch on the
floor where two decades of heavy shoes had stood while the white
man at the desk added and multiplied and subtracted. And again
he did not need to look because he had seen this himself and,
twenty-three years after the Surrender and twenty-four after the
Proclamation, was still watching it: the ledgers, new ones now and
filled rapidly, succeeding one another rapidly and containing more
names than old Carothers or even his father and Uncle Buddy
had ever dreamed of; new names and new faces to go with them,
among which the old names and faces that even his father and
uncle would have recognised, were lost, vanished—Tomey's Terrel dead, and even the tragic and miscast Percival Brownlee, who
couldn't keep books and couldn't farm either, found his true niche
at last, reappeared in 1862 during the boy's father's absence and
had apparently been living on the plantation for at least a month
before his uncle found out about it, conducting impromptu revival
meetings among negroes, preaching and leading the singing also

in his high sweet true soprano voice and disappeared again on
foot and at top speed, not behind but ahead of a body of raiding
Federal horse and reappeared for the third and last time in the
entourage of a travelling Army paymaster, the two of them passing through Jefferson in a surrey at the exact moment when the
boy's father (it was 1866) also happened to be crossing the
Square, the surrey and its occupants traversing rapidly that quiet
and bucolic scene and even in that fleeting moment and to others
beside the boy's father giving an illusion of flight and illicit holiday like a man on an excursion during his wife's absence with
his wife's personal maid, until Brownlee glanced up and saw his
late co-master and gave him one defiant female glance and then
broke again, leaped from the surrey and disappeared this time
for good and it was only by chance that McCaslin, twenty years
later, heard of him again, an old man now and quite fat, as the
well-to-do proprietor of a select New Orleans brothel; and Tennie's Jim gone, nobody knew where, and Fonsiba in Arkansas
with her three dollars each month and the scholar-husband with
his lenseless spectacles and frock coat and his plans for the spring;
and only Lucas was left, the baby, the last save himself of old
Carothers' doomed and fatal blood which in the male derivation
seemed to destroy all it touched, and even he was repudiating
and at least hoping to escape it;—Lucas, the boy of fourteen
whose name would not even appear for six years yet among those
rapid pages in the bindings new and dustless too since McCaslin
lifted them down daily now to write into them the continuation
of that record which two hundred years had not been enough to
complete and another hundred would not be enough to discharge;
that chronicle which was a whole land in miniature, which multiplied and compounded was the entire South, twenty-three years
after surrender and twenty-four from emancipation—that slow
trickle of molasses and meal and meat, of shoes and straw hats
and overalls, of plowlines and collars and heel-bolts and buck-
heads and clevises, which returned each fall as cotton—the two
threads frail as truth and impalpable as equators yet cable-strong
to bind for life them who made the cotton to the land their sweat
fell on: and he

'Yes. Binding them for a while yet, a little while yet. Through

and beyond that life and maybe through and beyond the life of
that life's sons and maybe even through and beyond that of the
sons of those sons. But not always, because they will endure.
They will outlast us because they are—' it was not a pause, barely
a falter even, possibly appreciable only to himself, as if he couldn't
speak even to McCaslin, even to explain his repudiation, that
which to him too, even in the act of escaping (and maybe this
was the reality and the truth of his need to escape) was heresy:
so that even in escaping he was taking with him more of that evil
and unregenerate old man who could summon, because she was
his property, a human being because she was old enough and female, to his widower's house and get a child on her and then dis-
miss her because she was of an inferior race, and then bequeath
a thousand dollars to the infant because he would be dead then
and wouldn't have to pay it, than even he had feared. 'Yes. He
didn't want to. He had to. Because they will endure. They are
better than we are. Stronger than we are. Their vices are vices
aped from white men or that white men and bondage have taught
them: improvidence and intemperance and evasion—not laziness:
evasion: of what white men had set them to, not for their ag-
grandisement or even comfort but his own—' and McCaslin

'All right. Go on: Promiscuity. Violence. Instability and lack
of control. Inability to distinguish between mine and thine—'
and he

'How distinguish, when for two hundred years mine did not
even exist for them?' and McCaslin

'All right. Go on. And their virtues—' and he

'Yes. Their own. Endurance—' and McCaslin

'So have mules:' and he

'—and pity and tolerance and forbearance and fidelity and love
of children—' and McCaslin

'So have dogs:' and he

'—whether their own or not or black or not. And more: what
they got not only not from white people but not even despite
white people because they had it already from the old free fathers
a longer time free than us because we have never been free—'
and it was in McCaslin's eyes too, he had only to look at Mc-
Caslin's eyes and it was there, that summer twilight seven years

ago, almost a week after they had returned from the camp before
he discovered that Sam Fathers had told McCaslin: an old bear,
fierce and ruthless not just to stay alive but ruthless with the fierce
pride of liberty and freedom, jealous and proud enough of liberty
and freedom to see it threatened not with fear nor even alarm
but almost with joy, seeming deliberately to put it into jeopardy
in order to savor it and keep his old strong bones and flesh supple and quick to defend and preserve it; an old man, son of a
Negro slave and an Indian king, inheritor on the one hand of the
long chronicle of a people who had learned humility through
suffering and learned pride through the endurance which survived
the suffering, and on the other side the chronicle of a people even
longer in the land than the first, yet who now existed there only
in the solitary brotherhood of an old and childless Negro's alien
blood and the wild and invincible spirit of an old bear; a boy who
wished to learn humility and pride in order to become skillful and
worthy in the woods but found himself becoming so skillful so
fast that he feared he would never become worthy because he had
not learned humility and pride though he had tried, until one day
an old man who could not have defined either led him as though
by the hand to where an old bear and a little mongrel dog showed
him that, by possessing one thing other, he would possess them
both; and a little dog, nameless and mongrel and many-fathered,
grown yet weighing less than six pounds, who couldn't be dangerous because there was nothing anywhere much smaller, not fierce
because that would have been called just noise, not humble because it was already too near the ground to genuflect, and not
proud because it would not have been close enough for anyone
to discern what was casting that shadow and which didn't even
know it was not going to heaven since they had already decided
it had no immortal soul, so that all it could be was brave even
though they would probably call that too just noise. *'And you
didn't shoot,' McCaslin said. 'How close were you?'*

*'I dont know,' he said. 'There was a big wood tick just inside
his off hind leg. I saw that. But I didn't have the gun then.'*

*'But you didn't shoot when you had the gun,' McCaslin said.
'Why?' But McCaslin didn't wait, rising and crossing the room,
across the pelt of the bear he had killed two years ago and the*

bigger one McCaslin had killed before he was born, to the book-
case beneath the mounted head of his first buck, and returned with
the book and sat down again and opened it. 'Listen,' he said. He
read the five stanzas aloud and closed the book on his finger and
looked up. 'All right,' he said. 'Listen,' and read again, but only
one stanza this time and closed the book and laid it on the table.
'She cannot fade, though thou hast not thy bliss,' McCaslin said:
'Forever wilt thou love, and she be fair.'
    'He's talking about a girl,' he said.
    'He had to talk about something,' McCaslin said. Then he said,
'He was talking about truth. Truth is one. It doesn't change. It
covers all things which touch the heart—honor and pride and pity
and justice and courage and love. Do you see now?' He didn't
know. Somehow it had seemed simpler than that, simpler than
somebody talking in a book about a young man and a girl he
would never need to grieve over because he could never approach
any nearer and would never have to get any further away. He had
heard about an old bear and finally got big enough to hunt it and
he hunted it four years and at last met it with a gun in his hands
and he didn't shoot. Because a little dog—But he could have shot
long before the fyce covered the twenty yards to where the bear
waited, and Sam Fathers could have shot at any time during the
interminable minute while Old Ben stood on his hind legs over
them. . . . He ceased. McCaslin watched him, still speaking, the
voice, the words as quiet as the twilight itself was: 'Courage and
honor and pride, and pity and love of justice and of liberty. They
all touch the heart, and what the heart holds to becomes truth, as
far as we know truth. Do you see now?' and he could still hear
them, intact in this twilight as in that one seven years ago, no
louder still because they did not need to be because they would
endure: and he had only to look at McCaslin's eyes beyond the
thin and bitter smiling, the faint lip-lift which would have had to
be called smiling;—his kinsman, his father almost, who had been
born too late into the old time and too soon for the new, the two
of them juxtaposed and alien now to each other against their
ravaged patrimony, the dark and ravaged fatherland still prone
and panting from its etherless operation:

'Habet then.—So this land is, indubitably, of and by itself cursed:' and he

'Cursed:' and again McCaslin merely lifted one hand, not even speaking and not even toward the ledgers: so that, as the stereopticon condenses into one instantaneous field the myriad minutia of its scope, so did that slight and rapid gesture establish in the small cramped and cluttered twilit room not only the ledgers but the whole plantation in its mazed and intricate entirety—the land, the fields and what they represented in terms of cotton ginned and sold, the men and women whom they fed and clothed and even paid a little cash money at Christmas-time in return for the labor which planted and raised and picked and ginned the cotton, the machinery and mules and gear with which they raised it and their cost and upkeep and replacement—that whole edifice intricate and complex and founded upon injustice and erected by ruthless rapacity and carried on even yet with at times downright savagery not only to the human beings but the valuable animals too, yet solvent and efficient and, more than that: not only still intact but enlarged, increased; brought still intact by McCaslin, himself little more than a child then, through and out of the debacle and chaos of twenty years ago where hardly one in ten survived, and enlarged and increased and would continue so, solvent and efficient and intact and still increasing so long as McCaslin and his McCaslin successors lasted, even though their surnames might not even be Edmonds then: and he: 'Habet too. Because that's it: not the land, but us. Not only the blood, but the name too; not only its color but its designation: Edmonds, white, but, a female line, could have no other but the name his father bore; Beauchamp, the elder line and the male one, but, black, could have had any name he liked and no man would have cared, except the name his father bore who had no name—' and McCaslin

'And since I know too what you know I will say now, once more let me say it: And one other, and in the third generation too, and the male, the eldest, the direct and sole and white and still McCaslin even, father to son to son—' and he

'I am free:' and this time McCaslin did not even gesture, no inference of fading pages, no postulation of the stereoptic whole, but the frail and iron thread strong as truth and impervious as evil and longer than life itself and reaching beyond record and patrimony both to join him with the lusts and passions, the hopes and dreams and griefs, of bones whose names while still fleshed and capable even old Carothers' grandfather had never heard: and he: 'And of that too:' and McCaslin

'Chosen, I suppose (I will concede it) out of all your time by Him as you say Buck and Buddy were from theirs. And it took Him a bear and an old man and four years just for you. And it took you fourteen years to reach that point and about that many, maybe more, for Old Ben, and more than seventy for Sam Fathers. And you are just one. How long then? How long?' and he

'It will be long. I have never said otherwise. But it will be all right because they will endure—' and McCaslin

'And anyway, you will be free.—No, not now nor ever, we from them nor they from us. So I repudiate too. I would deny even if I knew it were true. I would have to. Even you can see that I could do no else. I am what I am; I will be always what I was born and have always been. And more than me. More than me, just as there were more than Buck and Buddy in what you called His first plan which failed:' and he

'And more than me:' and McCaslin

'No. Not even you. Because mark. You said how on that instant when Ikkemotubbe realised that he could sell the land to Grandfather, it ceased forever to have been his. All right; go on: Then it belonged to Sam Fathers, old Ikkemotubbe's son. And who inherited from Sam Fathers, if not you? co-heir perhaps with Boon, if not of his life maybe, at least of his quitting it?' and he

'Yes. Sam Fathers set me free.' And Isaac McCaslin, not yet Uncle Ike, a long time yet before he would be uncle to half a county and still father to none, living in one small cramped fireless rented room in a Jefferson boardinghouse where petit juries were domiciled during court terms and itinerant horse- and mule-traders stayed, with his kit of brand-new carpenter's tools and the shotgun McCaslin had given him with his name engraved in silver and old General Compson's compass (and, when the General died, his silver-mounted horn too) and the iron cot and mattress

and the blankets which he would take each fall into the woods
for more than sixty years and the bright tin coffee-pot

there had been a legacy, from his Uncle Hubert Beauchamp,
his godfather, that bluff burly roaring childlike man from whom
Uncle Buddy had won Tomey's Terrel's wife Tennie in the poker-
game in 1859—'posible strait against three Treys in sigt Not
called'—; no pale sentence or paragraph scrawled in cringing fear
of death by a weak and trembling hand as a last desperate sop
flung backward at retribution, but a Legacy, a Thing, possessing
weight to the hand and bulk to the eye and even audible: a silver
cup filled with gold pieces and wrapped in burlap and sealed with
his godfather's ring in the hot wax, which (intact still) even before his Uncle Hubert's death and long before his own majority,
when it would be his, had become not only a legend but one of
the family lares. After his father's and his Uncle Hubert's sister's
marriage they moved back into the big house, the tremendous
cavern which old Carothers had started and never finished, cleared
the remaining negroes out of it and with his mother's dowry completed it, at least the rest of the windows and doors and moved
into it, all of them save Uncle Buddy who declined to leave the
cabin he and his twin had built, the move being the bride's notion
and more than just a notion and none ever to know if she really
wanted to live in the big house or if she knew before hand that
Uncle Buddy would refuse to move: and two weeks after his
birth in 1867, the first time he and his mother came down stairs,
one night and the silver cup sitting on the cleared dining-room
table beneath the bright lamp and while his mother and his father
and McCaslin and Tennie (his nurse: carrying him)—all of them
again but Uncle Buddy—watched, his Uncle Hubert rang one by
one into the cup the bright and glinting mintage and wrapped it
into the burlap envelope and heated the wax and sealed it and
carried it back home with him where he lived alone now without
even his sister either to hold him down as McCaslin said or to
try to raise him up as Uncle Buddy said, and (dark times then
in Mississippi) Uncle Buddy said most of the niggers gone and
the ones that didn't go even Hub Beauchamp could not have
wanted: but the dogs remained and Uncle Buddy said Beauchamp
fiddled while Nero fox-hunted

they would go and see it there; at last his mother would prevail and they would depart in the surrey, once more all save Uncle
Buddy and McCaslin to keep Uncle Buddy company until one
winter Uncle Buddy began to fail and from then on it was himself, beginning to remember now, and his mother and Tennie and
Tomey's Terrel to drive: the twenty-two miles into the next
county, the twin gateposts on one of which McCaslin could remember the half-grown boy blowing a fox-horn at breakfast dinner and supper-time and jumping down to open to any passer who
happened to hear it but where there were no gates at all now, the
shabby and overgrown entrance to what his mother still insisted
that people call Warwick because her brother was if truth but
triumphed and justice but prevailed the rightful earl of it, the
paintless house which outwardly did not change but which on the
inside seemed each time larger because he was too little to realise
then that there was less and less in it of the fine furnishings, the
rosewood and mahogany and walnut which for him had never existed anywhere anyway save in his mother's tearful lamentations
and the occasional piece small enough to be roped somehow onto
the rear or the top of the carriage on their return (And he remembered this, he had seen it: an instant, a flash, his mother's
soprano 'Even my dress! Even my dress!' loud and outraged in
the barren unswept hall; a face young and female and even lighter
in color than Tomey's Terrel's for an instant in a closing door; a
swirl, a glimpse of the silk gown and the flick and glint of an
ear-ring: an apparition rapid and tawdry and illicit yet somehow
even to the child, the infant still almost, breathless and exciting
and evocative: as though, like two limpid and pellucid streams
meeting, the child which he still was had made serene and absolute and perfect rapport and contact through that glimpsed nameless illicit hybrid female flesh with the boy which had existed at
that stage of inviolable and immortal adolescence in his uncle for
almost sixty years; the dress, the face, the ear-rings gone in that
same aghast flash and his uncle's voice: 'She's my cook! She's my
new cook! I had to have a cook, didn't I?' then the uncle himself,
the face alarmed and aghast too yet still innocently and somehow
even indomitably of a boy, they retreating in their turn now, back
to the front gallery, and his uncle again, pained and still amazed,

in a sort of desperate resurgence if not of courage at least of self-assertion: 'They're free now! They're folks too just like we are!' and his mother: 'That's why! That's why! My mother's house! Defiled! Defiled!' and his uncle: 'Damn it, Sibbey, at least give her time to pack her grip:' then over, finished, the loud uproar and all, himself and Tennie and he remembered Tennie's inscrutable face at the broken shutterless window of the bare room which had once been the parlor while they watched, hurrying down the lane at a stumbling trot, the routed compounder of his uncle's uxory: the back, the nameless face which he had seen only for a moment, the once-hooped dress ballooning and flapping below a man's overcoat, the worn heavy carpet-bag jouncing and banging against her knee, routed and in retreat true enough and in the empty lane solitary young-looking and forlorn yet withal still exciting and evocative and wearing still the silken banner captured inside the very citadel of respectability, and unforgettable.)

the cup, the sealed inscrutable burlap, sitting on the shelf in the locked closet, Uncle Hubert unlocking the door and lifting it down and passing it from hand to hand: his mother, his father, McCaslin and even Tennie, insisting that each take it in turn and heft it for weight and shake it again to prove the sound, Uncle Hubert himself standing spraddled before the cold unswept hearth in which the very bricks themselves were crumbling into a litter of soot and dust and mortar and the droppings of chimney-sweeps, still roaring and still innocent and still indomitable: and for a long time he believed nobody but himself had noticed that his uncle now put the cup only into his hands, unlocked the door and lifted it down and put it into his hands and stood over him until he had shaken it obediently until it sounded then took it from him and locked it back into the closet before anyone else could have offered to touch it, and even later, when competent not only to remember but to rationalise, he could not say what it was or even if it had been anything because the parcel was still heavy and still rattled, not even when, Uncle Buddy dead and his father, at last and after almost seventy-five years in bed after the sun rose, said: 'Go get that damn cup. Bring that damn Hub Beauchamp too if you have to:' because it still rattled though his uncle no longer put it even into his hands now but carried it him-

self from one to the other, his mother, McCaslin, Tennie, shaking
it before each in turn, saying: 'Hear it? Hear it?' his face still
innocent, not quite baffled but only amazed and not very amazed
and still indomitable: and, his father and Uncle Buddy both gone
now, one day without reason or any warning the almost completely empty house in which his uncle and Tennie's ancient and
quarrelsome great-grandfather (who claimed to have seen Lafayette and McCaslin said in another ten years would be remembering God) lived, cooked and slept in one single room, burst into
peaceful conflagration, a tranquil instantaneous sourceless una-
nimity of combustion, walls floors and roof: at sunup it stood where
his uncle's father had built it sixty years ago, at sundown the four
blackened and smokeless chimneys rose from a light white powder
of ashes and a few charred ends of planks which did not even
appear to have been very hot: and out of the last of evening, the
last one of the twenty-two miles, on the old white mare which
was the last of that stable which McCaslin remembered, the two
old men riding double up to the sister's door, the one wearing his
fox-horn on its braided deerhide thong and the other carrying the
burlap parcel wrapped in a shirt, the tawny wax-daubed shapeless
lump sitting again and on an almost identical shelf and his uncle
holding the half-opened door now, his hand not only on the knob
but one foot against it and the key waiting in the other hand, the
face urgent and still not baffled but still and even indomitably not
very amazed and himself standing in the half-opened door looking
quietly up at the burlap shape become almost three times its original height and a good half less than its original thickness and
turning away and he would remember not his mother's look this
time nor yet Tennie's inscrutable expression but McCaslin's dark
and aquiline face grave insufferable and bemused: then one night
they waked him and fetched him still half-asleep into the lamp
light, the smell of medicine which was familiar by now in that
room and the smell of something else which he had not smelled
before and knew at once and would never forget, the pillow, the
worn and ravaged face from which looked out still the boy innocent and immortal and amazed and urgent, looking at him and
trying to tell him until McCaslin moved and leaned over the bed

and drew from the top of the night shirt the big iron key on the
greasy cord which suspended it, the eyes saying Yes Yes Yes now,
and cut the cord and unlocked the closet and brought the parcel
to the bed, the eyes still trying to tell him even when he took the
parcel so that was still not it, the hands still clinging to the parcel
even while relinquishing it, the eyes more urgent than ever trying
to tell him but they never did; and he was ten and his mother was
dead too and McCaslin said, 'You are almost halfway now. You
might as well open it:' and he: 'No. He said twenty-one:' and he
was twenty-one and McCaslin shifted the bright lamp to the center of the cleared dining-room table and set the parcel beside it
and laid his open knife beside the parcel and stood back with
that expression of old grave intolerant and repudiating and he
lifted it, the burlap lump which fifteen years ago had changed its
shape completely overnight, which shaken gave forth a thin
weightless not-quite-musical curiously muffled clatter, the bright
knife-blade hunting amid the mazed intricacy of string, the knobby
gouts of wax bearing his uncle's Beauchamp seal rattling onto the
table's polished top and, standing amid the collapse of burlap
folds, the unstained tin coffee-pot still brand new, the handful of
copper coins and now he knew what had given them the muffled
sound: a collection of minutely-folded scraps of paper sufficient
almost for a rat's nest, of good linen bond, of the crude ruled
paper such as negroes use, of raggedly-torn ledger-pages and the
margins of newspapers and once the paper label from a new pair
of overalls, all dated and all signed, beginning with the first one
not six months after they had watched him seal the silver cup
into the burlap on this same table in this same room by the light
even of this same lamp almost twenty-one years ago:

> *I owe my Nephew Isaac Beauchamp McCaslin five (5)*
> *pieces Gold which I,O.U constitues My note of hand with*
> *Interest at 5 percent.*
>
> *Hubert Fitz-Hubert Beauchamp*
> *at Warwick 27 Nov 1867*

and he: 'Anyway he called it Warwick:' once at least, even if no
more. But there was more:

Isaac 24 Dec 1867 I.O.U. 2 pieces Gold H.Fh.B. I.O.U.
Issac 1 piece Gold 1 Jan 1868 H.Fh.B.

then five again then three then one then one then a long time and
what dream, what dreamed splendid recoup, not of any injury or
betrayal of trust because it had been merely a loan: nay, a partnership:

I.O.U. Beauchamp McCaslin or his heirs twenty-five (25)
pieces Gold This & All preceeding constituting My notes of
hand at twenty (20) percentum compounded annually. This
date of 19th January 1873

                                                    Beauchamp

no location save that in time and signed by the single not name
but word as the old proud earl himself might have scrawled Ne-
vile: and that made forty-three and he could not remember himself of course but the legend had it at fifty, which balanced: one:
then one: then one: then one and then the last three and then the
last chit, dated after he came to live in the house with them and
written in the shaky hand not of a beaten old man because he had
never been beaten to know it but of a tired old man maybe and
even at that tired only on the outside and still indomitable, the
simplicity of the last one the simplicity not of resignation but
merely of amazement, like a simple comment or remark, and not
very much of that:

One silver cup. Hubert Beauchamp

and McCaslin: 'So you have plenty of coppers anyway. But they
are still not old enough yet to be either rarities or heirlooms. So
you will have to take the money:' except that he didn't hear Mc-
Caslin, standing quietly beside the table and looking peacefully at
the coffee-pot and the pot sitting one night later on the mantel
above what was not even a fireplace in the little cramped icelike
room in Jefferson as McCaslin tossed the folded banknotes onto
the bed and, still standing (there was nowhere to sit save on the
bed) did not even remove his hat and overcoat: and he
    'As a loan. From you. This one:' and McCaslin
    'You cant. I have no money that I can lend to you. And you

will have to go to the bank and get it next month because I wont
bring it to you:' and he could not hear McCaslin now either, looking peacefully at McCaslin, his kinsman, his father almost yet no
kin now as, at the last, even fathers and sons are no kin: and he
  'It's seventeen miles, horseback and in the cold. We could both
sleep here:' and McCaslin
  'Why should I sleep here in my house when you wont sleep
yonder in yours?' and gone, and he looking at the bright rustless
unstained tin and thinking and not for the first time how much it
takes to compound a man (Isaac McCaslin for instance) and of
the devious intricate choosing yet unerring path that man's (Isaac
McCaslin's for instance) spirit takes among all that mass to make
him at last what he is to be, not only to the astonishment of them
(the ones who sired the McCaslin who sired his father and Uncle
Buddy and their sister, and the ones who sired the Beauchamp
who sired his Uncle Hubert and his Uncle Hubert's sister) who
believed they had shaped him, but to Isaac McCaslin too
  as a loan and used it though he would not have had to: Major
de Spain offered him a room in his house as long as he wanted it
and asked nor would ever ask any question, and old General
Compson more than that, to take him into his own room, to sleep
in half of his own bed and more than Major de Spain because he
told him baldly why: 'You sleep with me and before this winter
is out, I'll know the reason. You'll tell me. Because I dont believe
you just quit. It looks like you just quit but I have watched you in
the woods too much and I dont believe you just quit even if it
does look damn like it:' using it as a loan, paid his board and
rent for a month and bought the tools, not simply because he was
good with his hands because he had intended to use his hands and
it could have been with horses, and not in mere static and hopeful
emulation of the Nazarene as the young gambler buys a spotted
shirt because the old gambler won in one yesterday, but (without
the arrogance of false humility and without the false humbleness
of pride, who intended to earn his bread, didn't especially want to
earn it but had to earn it and for more than just bread) because
if the Nazarene had found carpentering good for the life and
ends He had assumed and elected to serve, it would be all right
too for Isaac McCaslin even though Isaac McCaslin's ends, al-

though simple enough in their apparent motivation, were and
would be always incomprehensible to him, and his life, invincible
enough in its needs, if he could have helped himself, not being the
Nazarene, he would not have chosen it: and paid it back. He had
forgotten the thirty dollars which McCaslin would put into the
bank in his name each month, fetched it in to him and flung it
onto the bed that first one time but no more; he had a partner
now or rather he was the partner: a blasphemous profane clever
old dipsomaniac who had built blockade-runners in Charleston in
'62 and '3 and had been a ship's carpenter since and appeared in
Jefferson two years ago nobody knew from where nor why and
spent a good part of his time since recovering from delirium
tremens in the jail; they had put a new roof on the stable of the
bank's president and (the old man in jail again still celebrating
that job) he went to the bank to collect for it and the president
said, 'I should borrow from you instead of paying you:' and it had
been seven months now and he remembered for the first time, two-
hundred-and-ten dollars, and this was the first job of any size and
when he left the bank the account stood at two-twenty, two-forty
to balance, only twenty dollars more to go, then it did balance
though by then the total had increased to three hundred and
thirty and he said, 'I will transfer it now:' and the president said,
'I cant do that. McCaslin told me not to. Haven't you got another
initial you could use and open another account?' but that was all
right, the coins the silver and the bills as they accumulated knotted
into a handkerchief and the coffee-pot wrapped in an old shirt as
when Tennie's great-grandfather had fetched it from Warwick
eighteen years ago, in the bottom of the iron-bound trunk which
old Carothers had brought from Carolina and his landlady said,
'Not even a lock! And you dont even lock your door, not even
when you leave!' and himself looking at her as peacefully as he
had looked at McCaslin that first night in this same room, no kin
to him at all yet more than kin as those who serve you even for
pay are your kin and those who injure you are more than brother
or wife

   and had the wife now, got the old man out of jail and fetched
him to the rented room and sobered him by superior strength, did
not even remove his own shoes for twenty-four hours, got him up

and got food into him and they built the barn this time from the ground up and he married her: an only child, a small girl yet curiously bigger than she seemed at first, solider perhaps, with dark eyes and a passionate heart-shaped face, who had time even on that farm to watch most of the day while he sawed timbers to the old man's measurements: and she: 'Papa told me about you. That farm is really yours, isn't it?' and he

'And McCaslin's:' and she

'Was there a will leaving half of it to him?' and he

'There didn't need to be a will. His grandmother was my father's sister. We were the same as brothers:' and she

'You are the same as second cousins and that's all you ever will be. But I dont suppose it matters:' and they were married, they were married and it was the new country, his heritage too as it was the heritage of all, out of the earth, beyond the earth yet of the earth because his too was of the earth's long chronicle, his too because each must share with another in order to come into it and in the sharing they become one: for that while, one: for that little while at least, one: indivisible, that while at least irrevocable and unrecoverable, living in a rented room still but for just a little while and that room wall-less and topless and floorless in glory for him to leave each morning and return to at night; her father already owned the lot in town and furnished the material and he and his partner would build it, her dowry from one: her wedding-present from three, she not to know it until the bungalow was finished and ready to be moved into and he never know who told her, not her father and not his partner and not even in drink though for a while he believed that, himself coming home from work and just time to wash and rest a moment before going down to supper, entering no rented cubicle since it would still partake of glory even after they would have grown old and lost it: and he saw her face then, just before she spoke: 'Sit down:' the two of them sitting on the bed's edge, not even touching yet, her face strained and terrible, her voice a passionate and expiring whisper of immeasurable promise: 'I love you. You know I love you. When are we going to move?' and he

'I didn't—I didn't know—Who told you—' the hot fierce palm clapped over his mouth, crushing his lips into his teeth, the fierce curve of fingers digging into his cheek and only the palm slacked off enough for him to answer:

'The farm. Our farm. Your farm:' and he

'I—' then the hand again, finger and palm, the whole enveloping weight of her although she still was not touching him save the hand, the voice: 'No! No!' and the fingers themselves seeming to follow through the cheek the impulse to speech as it died in his mouth, then the whisper, the breath again, of love and of incredible promise, the palm slackening again to let him answer:

'When?' and he

'I—' then she was gone, the hand too, standing, her back to him and her head bent, the voice so calm now that for an instant it seemed no voice of hers that he ever remembered: 'Stand up and turn your back and shut your eyes:' and repeated before he understood and stood himself with his eyes shut and heard the bell ring for supper below stairs and the calm voice again: 'Lock the door:' and he did so and leaned his forehead against the cold wood, his eyes closed, hearing his heart and the sound he had begun to hear before he moved until it ceased and the bell rang again below stairs and he knew it was for them this time and he heard the bed and turned and he had never seen her naked before, he had asked her to once, and why: that he wanted to see her naked because he loved her and he wanted to see her looking at him naked because he loved her but after that he never mentioned it again, even turning his face when she put the nightgown on over her dress to undress at night and putting the dress on over the gown to remove it in the morning and she would not let him get into bed beside her until the lamp was out and even in the heat of summer she would draw the sheet up over them both before she would let him turn to her: and the landlady came up the stairs up the hall and rapped on the door and then called their names but she didn't move, lying still on the bed outside the covers, her face turned away on the pillow, listening to nothing, thinking of nothing, not of him anyway he thought then the landlady went away and she said, 'Take off your clothes:' her head still turned away, looking at nothing, thinking of nothing, waiting for nothing, not even him, her hand moving as though with volition and vision of its own, catching his wrist at the exact moment when he paused beside the bed so that he never paused but merely changed the direction of moving, downward now, the hand drawing him and she moved at last, shifted, a movement one single complete inherent not practiced and one time older than man, looking at him now, drawing him still downward with the one hand down and down and he neither saw nor felt it shift, palm flat against his chest now and holding him away with the same apparent lack of any effort or any need for strength, and not looking at him now, she didn't need to, the chaste woman, the wife, already looked upon all the men who ever rutted and now her whole body had changed, altered, he had never seen it but once and now it was not even the one he had seen but composite of all woman-flesh since man that ever of its own will reclined on its back and opened, and out of it somewhere, without any movement of lips even, the dying and invincible whisper: 'Promise:' and he

'Promise?'

'The farm.' He moved. He had moved, the hand shifting from his chest once more to his wrist, grasping it, the arm still lax and only the light increasing pressure of the fingers as though arm and hand were a piece of wire cable with one looped end, only the hand tightening as he pulled against it. 'No,' he said. 'No:' and she was not looking at him still but not like the other but still the hand: 'No, I tell you. I wont. I cant. Never:' and still the hand and he said, for the last time, he tried to speak clearly and he knew it was still gently and he thought, *She already knows more than I with all the man-listening in camps where there was nothing to read ever even heard of. They are born already bored with what a boy approaches only at fourteen and fifteen with blundering and aghast trembling:* 'I cant. Not ever. Remember:' and still the steady and invincible hand and he said Yes and he thought, *She is lost. She was born lost. We were all born lost* then he stopped thinking and even saying Yes, it was like nothing he had ever dreamed, let alone heard in mere man-talking until after a no-time he returned and lay spent on the insatiate immemorial beach and again with a movement one time more older than man she turned and freed herself and on their wedding night she had cried and he thought she was crying now at first, into the tossed and wadded pillow, the voice coming from somewhere between the

pillow and the cachinnation: 'And that's all. That's all from me.
If this dont get you that son you talk about, it wont be mine:' lying
on her side, her back to the empty rented room, laughing and
laughing

5.

He went back to the camp one more time before the lumber
company moved in and began to cut the timber. Major de Spain
himself never saw it again. But he made them welcome to use the
house and hunt the land whenever they liked, and in the winter
following the last hunt when Sam Fathers and Lion died, General
Compson and Walter Ewell invented a plan to corporate themselves, the old group, into a club and lease the camp and the
hunting privileges of the woods—an invention doubtless of the
somewhat childish old General but actually worthy of Boon
Hogganbeck himself. Even the boy, listening, recognised it for
the subterfuge it was: to change the leopard's spots when they
could not alter the leopard, a baseless and illusory hope to which
even McCaslin seemed to subscribe for a while, that once they had
persuaded Major de Spain to return to the camp he might revoke
himself, which even the boy knew he would not do. And he did
not. The boy never knew what occurred when Major de Spain
declined. He was not present when the subject was broached and
McCaslin never told him. But when June came and the time for
the double birthday celebration there was no mention of it and
when November came no one spoke of using Major de Spain's
house and he never knew whether or not Major de Spain knew
they were going on the hunt though without doubt old Ash probably told him: he and McCaslin and General Compson (and that
one was the General's last hunt too) and Walter and Boon and
Tennie's Jim and old Ash loaded two wagons and drove two days
and almost forty miles beyond any country the boy had ever seen
before and lived in tents for the two weeks. And the next spring
they heard (not from Major de Spain) that he had sold the timber-
rights to a Memphis lumber company and in June the boy came to
town with McCaslin one Saturday and went to Major de Spain's

office—the big, airy, book-lined second-storey room with windows
at one end opening upon the shabby hinder purlieus of stores and
at the other a door giving onto the railed balcony above the
Square, with its curtained alcove where sat a cedar water-bucket
and a sugar-bowl and spoon and tumbler and a wicker-covered
demijohn of whiskey, and the bamboo-and-paper punkah swinging
back and forth above the desk while old Ash in a tilted chair beside the entrance pulled the cord.

"Of course," Major de Spain said. "Ash will probably like to
get off in the woods himself for a while, where he wont have to
eat Daisy's cooking. Complain about it, anyway. Are you going
to take anybody with you?"

"No sir," he said. "I thought that maybe Boon—" For six
months now Boon had been town-marshall at Hoke's; Major de
Spain had compounded with the lumber company—or perhaps
compromised was closer, since it was the lumber company who
had decided that Boon might be better as a town-marshall than
head of a logging gang.

"Yes," Major de Spain said. "I'll wire him today. He can meet
you at Hoke's. I'll send Ash on by the train and they can take
some food in and all you will have to do will be to mount your
horse and ride over."

"Yes sir," he said. "Thank you." And he heard his voice again.
He didn't know he was going to say it yet he did know, he had
known it all the time: "Maybe if you . . ." His voice died. It
was stopped, he never knew how because Major de Spain did not
speak and it was not until his voice ceased that Major de Spain
moved, turned back to the desk and the papers spread on it and
even that without moving because he was sitting at the desk with
a paper in his hand when the boy entered, the boy standing there
looking down at the short plumpish grey-haired man in sober fine
broadcloth and an immaculate glazed shirt whom he was used to
seeing in boots and muddy corduroy, unshaven, sitting the shaggy
powerful long-hocked mare with the worn Winchester carbine
across the saddlebow and the great blue dog standing motionless
as bronze at the stirrup, the two of them in that last year and to
the boy anyway coming to resemble one another somehow as two

people competent for love or for business who have been in love
or in business together for a long time sometimes do. Major de
Spain did not look up again.

"No. I will be too busy. But good luck to you. If you have it,
you might bring me a young squirrel."

"Yes sir," he said. "I will."

He rode his mare, the three-year-old filly he had bred and raised
and broken himself. He left home a little after midnight and six
hours later, without even having sweated her, he rode into Hoke's,
the tiny log-line junction which he had always thought of as Major
de Spain's property too although Major de Spain had merely sold
the company (and that many years ago) the land on which the
sidetracks and loading-platforms and the commissary store stood,
and looked about in shocked and grieved amazement even though
he had had forewarning and had believed himself prepared: a new
planing-mill already half completed which would cover two or
three acres and what looked like miles and miles of stacked steel
rails red with the light bright rust of newness and of piled crossties
sharp with creosote, and wire corrals and feeding-troughs for two
hundred mules at least and the tents for the men who drove them;
so that he arranged for the care and stabling of his mare as rapidly
as he could and did not look any more, mounted into the log-train
caboose with his gun and climbed into the cupola and looked no
more save toward the wall of wilderness ahead within which he
would be able to hide himself from it once more anyway.

Then the little locomotive shrieked and began to move: a rapid
churning of exhaust, a lethargic deliberate clashing of slack
couplings traveling backward along the train, the exhaust changing
to the deep slow clapping bites of power as the caboose too began
to move and from the cupola he watched the train's head complete the first and only curve in the entire line's length and vanish
into the wilderness, dragging its length of train behind it so that
it resembled a small dingy harmless snake vanishing into weeds,
drawing him with it too until soon it ran once more at its maxi-
mum clattering speed between the twin walls of unaxed wilderness
as of old. It had been harmless once. Not five years ago Walter
Ewell had shot a six-point buck from this same moving caboose,
and there was the story of the half-grown bear: the train's first

trip in to the cutting thirty miles away, the bear between the rails, its rear end elevated like that of a playing puppy while it dug to see what sort of ants or bugs they might contain or perhaps just to examine the curious symmetrical squared barkless logs which had appeared apparently from nowhere in one endless mathematical line overnight, still digging until the driver on the braked engine not fifty feet away blew the whistle at it, whereupon it broke frantically and took the first tree it came to: an ash sapling not much bigger than a man's thigh and climbed as high as it could and clung there, its head ducked between its arms as a man (a woman perhaps) might have done while the brakeman threw chunks of ballast at it, and when the engine returned three hours later with the first load of outbound logs the bear was halfway down the tree and once more scrambled back up as high as it could and clung again while the train passed and was still there when the engine went in again in the afternoon and still there when it came back out at dusk; and Boon had been in Hoke's with the wagon after a barrel of flour that noon when the train-crew told about it and Boon and Ash, both twenty years younger then, sat under the tree all that night to keep anybody from shooting it and the next morning Major de Spain had the log-train held at Hoke's and just before sundown on the second day, with not only Boon and Ash but Major de Spain and General Compson and Walter and Mc-Caslin, twelve then, watching, it came down the tree after almost thirty-six hours without even water and McCaslin told him how for a minute they thought it was going to stop right there at the barrow-pit where they were standing and drink, how it looked at the water and paused and looked at them and at the water again, but did not, gone, running, as bears run, the two sets of feet, front and back, tracking two separate though parallel courses.

It had been harmless then. They would hear the passing log-train sometimes from the camp; sometimes, because nobody bothered to listen for it or not. They would hear it going in, running light and fast, the light clatter of the trucks, the exhaust of the diminutive locomotive and its shrill peanut-parcher whistle flung for one petty moment and absorbed by the brooding and inattentive wilderness without even an echo. They would hear it going out, loaded, not quite so fast now yet giving its frantic and

toylike illusion of crawling speed, not whistling now to conserve
steam, flinging its bitten laboring miniature puffing into the immemorial woodsface with frantic and bootless vainglory, empty
and noisy and puerile, carrying to no destination or purpose sticks
which left nowhere any scar or stump as the child's toy loads and
transports and unloads its dead sand and rushes back for more,
tireless and unceasing and rapid yet never quite so fast as the
Hand which plays with it moves the toy burden back to load the
toy again. But it was different now. It was the same train, engine
cars and caboose, even the same enginemen brakeman and conductor to whom Boon, drunk then sober then drunk again then
fairly sober once more all in the space of fourteen hours, had
bragged that day two years ago about what they were going to do
to Old Ben tomorrow, running with its same illusion of frantic
rapidity between the same twin walls of impenetrable and impervious woods, passing the old landmarks, the old game crossings
over which he had trailed bucks wounded and not wounded and
more than once seen them, anything but wounded, bot out of the
woods and up and across the embankment which bore the rails and
ties then down and into the woods again as the earth-bound supposedly move but crossing as arrows travel, groundless, elongated,
three times its actual length and even paler, different in color, as if
there were a point between immobility and absolute motion where
even mass chemically altered, changing without pain or agony not
only in bulk and shape but in color too, approaching the color of
wind, yet this time it was as though the train (and not only the
train but himself, not only his vision which had seen it and his
memory which remembered it but his clothes too, as garments
carry back into the clean edgeless blowing of air the lingering
effluvium of a sick-room or of death) had brought with it into the
doomed wilderness even before the actual axe the shadow and
portent of the new mill not even finished yet and the rails and
ties which were not even laid; and he knew now what he had
known as soon as he saw Hoke's this morning but had not yet
thought into words: why Major de Spain had not come back, and
that after this time he himself, who had had to see it one time
other, would return no more.

Now they were near. He knew it before the engine-driver

whistled to warn him. Then he saw Ash and the wagon, the reins without doubt wrapped once more about the brake-lever as within the boy's own memory Major de Spain had been forbidding him for eight years to do, the train slowing, the slackened couplings jolting and clashing again from car to car, the caboose slowing past the wagon as he swung down with his gun, the conductor leaning out above him to signal the engine, the caboose still slowing, creeping, although the engine's exhaust was already slatting in mounting tempo against the unechoing wilderness, the crashing of draw-bars once more travelling backward along the train, the caboose picking up speed at last. Then it was gone. It had not been. He could no longer hear it. The wilderness soared, musing, inattentive, myriad, eternal, green; older than any mill-shed, longer than any spur-line. "Mr Boon here yet?" he said.

"He beat me in," Ash said. "Had the wagon loaded and ready for me at Hoke's yistiddy when I got there and setting on the front steps at camp last night when I got in. He already been in the woods since fo daylight this morning. Said he gwine up to the Gum Tree and for you to hunt up that way and meet him." He knew where that was: a single big sweet-gum just outside the woods, in an old clearing; if you crept up to it very quietly this time of year and then ran suddenly into the clearing, sometimes you caught as many as a dozen squirrels in it, trapped, since there was no other tree near they could jump to. So he didn't get into the wagon at all.

"I will," he said.

"I figured you would," Ash said, "I fotch you a box of shells." He passed the shells down and began to unwrap the lines from the brake-pole.

"How many times up to now do you reckon Major has told you not to do that?" the boy said.

"Do which?" Ash said. Then he said: "And tell Boon Hoggan-beck dinner gonter be on the table in a hour and if yawl want any to come on and eat it."

"In an hour?" he said. "It aint nine oclock yet." He drew out his watch and extended it face-toward Ash. "Look." Ash didn't even look at the watch.

"That's town time. You aint in town now. You in the woods."

"Look at the sun then."

"Nemmine the sun too," Ash said. "If you and Boon Hoggan-beck want any dinner, you better come on in and get it when I tole you. I aim to get done in that kitchen because I got my wood to chop. And watch your feet. They're crawling."

"I will," he said.

Then he was in the woods, not alone but solitary; the solitude closed about him, green with summer. They did not change, and, timeless, would not, anymore than would the green of summer and the fire and rain of fall and the iron cold and sometimes even snow

the day, the morning when he killed the buck and Sam marked his face with its hot blood, they returned to camp and he remembered old Ash's blinking and disgruntled and even outraged disbelief until at last McCaslin had had to affirm the fact that he had really killed it: and that night Ash sat snarling and unapproachable behind the stove so that Tennie's Jim had to serve the supper and waked them with breakfast already on the table the next morning and it was only half-past one oclock and at last out of Major de Spain's angry cursing and Ash's snarling and sullen rejoinders the fact emerged that Ash not only wanted to go into the woods and shoot a deer also but he intended to and Major de Spain said, 'By God, if we dont let him we will probably have to do the cooking from now on.' and Walter Ewell said, 'Or get up at midnight to eat what Ash cooks:' and since he had already killed his buck for this hunt and was not to shoot again unless they needed meat, he offered his gun to Ash until Major de Spain took command and allotted that gun to Boon for the day and gave Boon's unpredictable pump gun to Ash, with two buckshot shells but Ash said, 'I got shells:' and showed them, four: one buck, one of number three shot for rabbits, two of bird-shot and told one by one their history and their origin and he remembered not Ash's face alone but Major de Spain's and Walter's and General Compson's too, and Ash's voice: 'Shoot? In course they'll shoot! Genl Cawmpson guv me this un'—the buckshot—'right outen the same gun he kilt that big buck with eight years ago. And this un'—it was the rabbit shell: triumphantly—'is oldern thisyer boy!' And that morning he loaded the gun himself, reversing the order: the bird-shot, the rabbit, then the buck so that the buckshot would feed first into the chamber, and himself without a gun, he and Ash walked beside Major de Spain's and Tennie's Jim's horses and the dogs (that was the snow) until they cast and struck, the sweet strong cries ringing away into the muffled falling air and gone almost immediately, as if the constant and unmurmuring flakes had already buried even the unformed echoes beneath their myriad and weightless falling, Major de Spain and Tennie's Jim gone too, whooping on into the woods; and then it was all right, he knew as plainly as if Ash had told him that Ash had now hunted his deer and that even his tender years had been forgiven for having killed one, and they turned back toward home through the falling snow—that is, Ash said, 'Now whut?' and he said, 'This way'—himself in front because, although they were less than a mile from camp, he knew that Ash, who had spent two weeks of his life in the camp each year for the last twenty, had no idea whatever where they were, until quite soon the manner in which Ash carried Boon's gun was making him a good deal more than just nervous and he made Ash walk in front, striding on, talking now, an old man's garrulous monologue beginning with where he was at the moment then of the woods and of camping in the woods and of eating in camps then of eating then of cooking it and of his wife's cooking then briefly of his old wife and almost at once and at length of a new light-colored woman who nursed next door to Major de Spain's and if she didn't watch out who she was switching her tail at he would show her how old was an old man or not if his wife just didn't watch him all the time, the two of them in a game trail through a dense brake of cane and brier which would bring them out within a quarter-mile of camp, approaching a big fallen tree-trunk lying athwart the path and just as Ash, still talking, was about to step over it the bear, the yearling, rose suddenly beyond the log, sitting up, its forearms against its chest and its wrists limply arrested as if it had been surprised in the act of covering its face to pray: and after a certain time Ash's gun yawed jerkily up and he said, 'You haven't got a shell in the barrel yet. Pump it:' but the gun already snicked and he said, 'Pump it. You haven't got a shell in the barrel yet:' and Ash pumped the action and in a certain time the gun steadied again and snicked and he said, 'Pump it:' and watched the buckshot shell jerk, spinning heavily, into the cane. This is the rabbit shot: he thought and the gun snicked and he thought: The next is bird-shot: and he didn't have to say Pump it; he cried, 'Dont shoot! Dont shoot!' but that was already too late too, the light dry vicious snick! before he could speak and the bear turned and dropped to all-fours and then was gone and there was only the log, the cane, the velvet and constant snow and Ash said, 'Now whut?' and he said, 'This way. Come on:' and began to back away down the path and Ash said, 'I got to find my shells:' and he said, 'Goddamn it, goddamn it, come on:' but Ash leaned the gun against the log and returned and stooped and fumbled among the cane roots until he came back and stooped and found the shells and they rose and at that moment the gun, untouched, leaning against the log six feet away and for that while even forgotten by both of them, roared, bellowed and flamed, and ceased: and he carried it now, pumped out the last mummified shell and gave that one also to Ash and, the action still open, himself carried the gun until he stood it in the corner behind Boon's bed at the camp

—; summer, and fall, and snow, and wet and saprife spring in their ordered immortal sequence, the deathless and immemorial phases of the mother who had shaped him if any had toward the man he almost was, mother and father both to the old man born of a Negro slave and a Chickasaw chief who had been his spirit's father if any had, whom he had revered and harkened to and loved and lost and grieved: and he would marry someday and they too would own for their brief while that brief unsubstanced glory which inherently of itself cannot last and hence why glory: and they would, might, carry even the remembrance of it into the time when flesh no longer talks to flesh because memory at least does last: but still the woods would be his mistress and his wife.

He was not going toward the Gum Tree. Actually he was getting farther from it. Time was and not so long ago either when he would not have been allowed here without someone with him, and a little later, when he had begun to learn how much he did not know, he would not have dared be here without someone with him, and later still, beginning to ascertain, even if only dimly, the limits of what he did not know, he could have attempted and car-

ried it through with a compass, not because of any increased belief in himself but because McCaslin and Major de Spain and
Walter and General Compson too had taught him at last to believe
the compass regardless of what it seemed to state. Now he did
not even use the compass but merely the sun and that only subconsciously, yet he could have taken a scaled map and plotted at
any time to within a hundred feet of where he actually was; and
sure enough, at almost the exact moment when he expected it,
the earth began to rise faintly, he passed one of the four concrete
markers set down by the lumber company's surveyor to establish
the four corners of the plot which Major de Spain had reserved
out of the sale, then he stood on the crest of the knoll itself, the
four corner-markers all visible now, blanched still even beneath
the winter's weathering, lifeless and shockingly alien in that place
where dissolution itself was a seething turmoil of ejaculation
tumescence conception and birth, and death did not even exist.
After two winters' blanketings of leaves and the flood-waters of
two springs, there was no trace of the two graves anymore at all.
But those who would have come this far to find them would not
need headstones but would have found them as Sam Fathers himself had taught him to find such: by bearings on trees: and did,
almost the first thrust of the hunting knife finding (but only to see
if it was still there) the round tin box manufactured for axel-
grease and containing now Old Ben's dried mutilated paw, resting
above Lion's bones.

He didn't disturb it. He didn't even look for the other grave
where he and McCaslin and Major de Spain and Boon had laid
Sam's body, along with his hunting horn and his knife and his
tobacco-pipe, that Sunday morning two years ago; he didn't have
to. He had stepped over it, perhaps on it. But that was all right.
*He probably knew I was in the woods this morning long before I
got here,* he thought, going on to the tree which had supported one
end of the platform where Sam lay when McCaslin and Major de
Spain found them—the tree, the other axel-grease tin nailed to the
trunk, but weathered, rusted, alien too yet healed already into the
wilderness' concordant generality, raising no tuneless note, and
empty, long since empty of the food and tobacco he had put into
it that day, as empty of that as it would presently be of this which

he drew from his pocket—the twist of tobacco, the new bandanna
handkerchief, the small paper sack of the peppermint candy which
Sam had used to love; that gone too, almost before he had turned
his back, not vanished but merely translated into the myriad life
which printed the dark mold of these secret and sunless places with
delicate fairy tracks, which, breathing and biding and immobile,
watched him from beyond every twig and leaf until he moved,
moving again, walking on; he had not stopped, he had only paused,
quitting the knoll which was no abode of the dead because there
was no death, not Lion and not Sam: not held fast in earth but
free in earth and not in earth but of earth, myriad yet undiffused of
every myriad part, leaf and twig and particle, air and sun and
rain and dew and night, acorn oak and leaf and acorn again, dark
and dawn and dark and dawn again in their immutable progression
and, being myriad, one: and Old Ben too, Old Ben too; they would
give him his paw back even, certainly they would give him his
paw back: then the long challenge and the long chase, no heart to
be driven and outraged, no flesh to be mauled and bled— Even as
he froze himself, he seemed to hear Ash's parting admonition. He
could even hear the voice as he froze, immobile, one foot just taking his weight, the toe of the other just lifted behind him, not
breathing, feeling again and as always the sharp shocking inrush
from when Isaac McCaslin long yet was not, and so it was fear all
right but not fright as he looked down at it. It had not coiled yet
and the buzzer had not sounded either, only one thick rapid con-
traction, one loop cast sideways as though merely for purchase
from which the raised head might start slightly backward, not in
fright either, not in threat quite yet, more than six feet of it, the
head raised higher than his knee and less than his knee's length
away, and old, the once-bright markings of its youth dulled now
to a monotone concordant too with the wilderness it crawled and
lurked: the old one, the ancient and accursed about the earth,
fatal and solitary and he could smell it now: the thin sick smell of
rotting cucumbers and something else which had no name, evocative of all knowledge and an old weariness and of pariah-hood and
of death. At last it moved. Not the head. The elevation of the head
did not change as it began to glide away from him, moving erect
yet off the perpendicular as if the head and that elevated third were

complete and all: an entity walking on two feet and free of all
laws of mass and balance and should have been because even now
he could not quite believe that all that shift and flow of shadow
behind that walking head could have been one snake: going and
then gone; he put the other foot down at last and didn't know it,
standing with one hand raised as Sam had stood that afternoon six
years ago when Sam led him into the wilderness and showed him
and he ceased to be a child, speaking the old tongue which Sam
had spoken that day without premeditation either: "Chief," he
said: "Grandfather."

He couldn't tell when he first began to hear the sound, because
when he became aware of it, it seemed to him that he had been
already hearing it for several seconds—a sound as though someone were hammering a gun-barrel against a piece of railroad iron,
a sound loud and heavy and not rapid yet with something frenzied
about it, as the hammerer were not only a strong man and an
earnest one but a little hysterical too. Yet it couldn't be on the
log-line because, although the track lay in that direction, it was
at least two miles from him and this sound was not three hundred
yards away. But even as he thought that, he realised where the
sound must be coming from: whoever the man was and whatever
he was doing, he was somewhere near the edge of the clearing
where the Gum Tree was and where he was to meet Boon. So far,
he had been hunting as he advanced, moving slowly and quietly
and watching the ground and the trees both. Now he went on, his
gun unloaded and the barrel slanted up and back to facilitate its
passage through brier and undergrowth, approaching as it grew
louder and louder that steady savage somehow queerly hysterical
beating of metal on metal, emerging from the woods, into the old
clearing, with the solitary gum tree directly before him. At first
glance the tree seemed to be alive with frantic squirrels. There appeared to be forty or fifty of them leaping and darting from
branch to branch until the whole tree had become one green
maelstrom of mad leaves, while from time to time, singly or in
twos and threes, squirrels would dart down the trunk then whirl
without stopping and rush back up again as though sucked violently back by the vacuum of their fellows' frenzied vortex. Then
he saw Boon, sitting, his back against the trunk, his head bent,

hammering furiously at something on his lap. What he hammered with was the barrel of his dismembered gun, what he hammered at was the breech of it. The rest of the gun lay scattered about him in a half-dozen pieces while he bent over the piece on his lap his scarlet and streaming walnut face, hammering the disjointed barrel against the gun-breech with the frantic abandon of a madman. He didn't even look up to see who it was. Still hammering, he merely shouted back at the boy in a hoarse strangled voice:

"Get out of here! Dont touch them! Dont touch a one of them! They're mine!"

Seven Approaches to

THE BEAR

Introduction

Part of a great writer's greatness is his penetrating and unique vision of man and his world, and its expression in language of power and beauty. His works are more than explicit statements; they are alive with implications. What he may mean, but does not say explicitly, can be as important as the thematic statements that seem to shout from his pages.

Because his expression is evocative, it is often difficult to evaluate objectively. Moreover, the idea of style is itself a subjective matter; even scholars and critics often do not agree on the value of certain styles. Standards of judgment, methods of analysis, and general conclusions about style are important—especially if, as some critics maintain, meaning lies as much in the way something is said as in what is said.

William Faulkner is a "difficult" writer for two reasons. First, his viewpoint of man, his attitude toward events, is one that attempts to embrace all human affairs; he touches upon history, economics, sociology, psychology, scientific advancement, and the arts. He peoples his works with babies, with young boys struggling to maturity, young lovers fearing marriage, women accepting nature or the Bible, aging men facing economic debilitation, old folk preparing for death. His works deal with Indians, Negroes, white men, and animals; and he gives to each character he creates some distinctive trait and, thereby, some place in the land he writes about. His imagination has such breadth and power that out of it he creates an entire county, builds its towns and plantations, and peoples its sidewalks and backlands. He gives the county a history —from its settlement by Indians to its present threat by a machine-ridden economy. He creates a social system, with classes that differ sharply in values, in what men believe and fight for. Like America in miniature, he makes some men farmers and some merchants and some jobless; he makes some men religious, some pantheistic, and others atheistic; he makes some brimful with love, and some afraid to love, and others capable only of hate.

He has the power of words to match this vision; his language surges forth. His sentences are often long and labyrinthine; the words match the sentences in complexity. He breaks the limiting convention of progressive, linear time and juxtaposes past and present in an attempt to find a new meaning, new truth about the characters he creates and observes. Deliberately rejecting the objective view, he digs into the minds of his characters, exploring their consciousness, the ideas they have that never see the daylight of action. He finds that his own ideas cannot be fit into one novel, and reworks lives and events again and again from book to book.

Thus the reasons that make Faulkner great also make him challenging to read. One cannot just thumb through his works; they need rereading and study. That is perhaps the single conviction commonly held by the various contributors to this volume. Focusing on *The Bear,* they apply their own experiences and studies, their own attitudes and viewpoints, to Faulkner's works, and find that he is saying many significant things in a single work.

Part two of this book attempts to present some of the most penetrating articles written by and about Faulkner which relate to *The Bear*. The text of *The Bear* itself has been chosen because parts one, two, three, and five represent Faulkner as fiction writer, writing at his best. Part four of *The Bear* states, in his most complex style but in his most concise statement, Faulkner's own theories of the South: how it came to be, what it was, and where its weaknesses lay. In part four are comments on man—his love, his pride, his humility, his courage, his greed, his lust. There, also, are comments on man's society—its historical growth, its economic basis, its structure of status and class, its population groupings in city, farm, and woods. *The Bear* is Faulkner's whole world in small: it is his place and his people.

The seven approaches suggested here handle the totality of *The Bear* without dividing it artificially into such categories as plot, characterization, and atmosphere or setting. But they clarify Faulkner's themes and techniques by examining *The Bear* from various single vantage points.

The biographical approach, for example, explores the role of personal experience in Faulkner's work. This approach assumes that, whatever else may be true, a work of art is, first and last, a human product. Presented here is a biographical essay on Faulkner's life which, from facts, from interviews with Faulkner and his friends, and from an examination of reports on Faulkner, attempts to arrange a mosaic of the man who was also artist. In using the biographical approach, one considers *The Bear* as an expression of an individual man with his own experiences, observations, and interests.

The background approach is concerned with what anecdotes and other stories about Old Ben reveal about *The Bear*. Sometimes the genesis of a story can be traced, but this is not the case with *The Bear*. Although Faulkner has written closely related stories, their precise dates of composition are not known. Still, Faulkner made remarks to Cynthia Grenier about his hunting, other anecdotes have been recorded by a hunting companion, and two other versions of Old Ben, one titled "Lion" and the other also titled "The Bear," appeared in magazines in 1935 and 1942, respectively. Even lacking dates, it is useful to examine in juxtaposition Faulkner's and John B. Cullen's recitals of real hunts and Faulkner's variations of his fictional bear hunt. One final story, "A Bear Hunt," in *The Saturday Evening Post* for February 10, 1934, is merely an unrelated tall tale and is not included here.

The canonical approach is particularly relevant since Faulkner, like Thomas Hardy, usually wrote of a single region—in this case, the county of Yoknapatawpha in Mississippi. Included here is an essay by Millar MacLure which introduces the Faulkner *canon* or body of works; Faulkner's own Nobel Prize Address, which is the closest he came to a formal credo; and selections from other Faulkner stories which provide additional information about Sam Fathers, Ike McCaslin, and Boon Hogganbeck.

The cultural approach is, despite some neglect, basic to understanding Faulkner's work. Anthropologists and students of American culture can show the beliefs and literary traditions in which

Faulkner's work took root. For instance, hunting bears has for centuries been a vital function of societies in America, whether or not Faulkner studied them in detail, and *The Bear* takes on whole new areas of meaning once such rituals are compared with the hunt of Old Ben. Incorporated in this collection is a report of a primitive bear hunt, A. Irving Hallowell's discussion of Eastern Woodlands bear ceremonialism, and three descriptions of initiations.

Another relevant part of the cultural approach is the modes and mores of living in the southern United States as expressed in both fact and fiction. W. J. Cash authoritatively analyzes the realities of Southern character and thought as well as the myths which obscure and interpret them. Whether or not the writings by Thomas Bangs Thorpe and Samuel Clemens are direct sources for *The Bear,* they surely reflect the literary context out of which this work could have grown: *The Big Bear of Arkansas,* which concentrates on the hunt and the tall-tale technique, and *Huckleberry Finn,* which shows how another Southern boy, like young Ike Mc-Caslin, is asked to examine his culture and transcend its flaws. In this section, Thorpe tells of the bear, Clemens and Cash of the man, and the anthropologists of the god. The final essay, "Pride and Humility," synthesizes these three views.

The interpretive approach consists of attempts to answer the most frequently asked question, "What does it mean?" Critics do this by giving their own "readings," employing in different ways their own special knowledge and experience. This collection attempts to give some of the best of the interpretations Faulkner's work allows and sometimes demands. Thomas J. Wertenbaker's relation of the elaborate chronology of events on *The Bear* is as objective as critics may get, but his commentary on time is nevertheless wholly interpretive. The possible variety of approaches to the single Faulkner text is also illustrated here by R. W. B. Lewis, who focuses on the Christian and ritualistic aspects of *The Bear;* John Lydenberg, who sees it as myth; and Walter Taylor, who concentrates on its historical and social implications. David H. Stewart points out Ike's failings. Still other critics offer other readings, so that all major points of view are represented.

The stylistic approach explores the relation of style and meaning in Faulkner's work. Is there a single style which best relates certain ideas, or must theme be reflected in stylistic rhythms, or is the meaning buried *in* style—are they one and the same? Or, can style obscure meaning, perhaps so much that readers fail to unwrap the cloak of rhetoric to find the body underneath? Much dispute has raged over Faulkner's style: some praise his writing as poetic or prophetic prose, while others condemn it for high-flown language or obscurity. The stylistic approach—investigating *how* something is said to determine *why*—does two important things. It considers such matters as a work's characteristic strengths and weaknesses, its own peculiar hallmarks; and it shows how the expression affects meaning. Included in this section of Part II are studies which approve of Faulkner's style, and those which disapprove of it, as well as a parody which by exaggeration highlights some of the signposts of style by which Faulkner is most commonly known.

The developmental approach compares the relationship between "Delta Autumn" and *The Bear*. Faulkner has been called inconsistent, but part of his alleged inconsistency stems from his ability to grow *with* his characters, to see them in newer lights, in greater depth. "Delta Autumn," which immediately follows *The Bear* in *Go Down, Moses,* shows Ike McCaslin, many years after his appearance in *The Bear,* thinking back on the hunt for Old Ben. In this story, much later in time, Faulkner provides new perspectives through Ike's new interpretation of former events—and through subsequent events as well.

These are seven ways to begin reading *The Bear*. Which is best? Partly, this depends on the reader. It may be one or a combination of several approaches. Or, perhaps, the ideal approach synthesizes the best of all seven.

The answer is, ultimately, the reader's answer to himself. Yet whatever that is, the results will still be the same: an exciting literary experience and the establishment of an individual methodology for reading. For Faulkner is great, too, because he is both varied enough for the first of these, and a worthy starting point for the latter.

The Role of
Personal Experience in
Faulkner's Work

William Faulkner: A Biographical Sketch

MICHAEL MILLGATE

❦

Faulkner himself [1] was born on 25 Sept. 1897, at New Albany (about thirty-five miles from Oxford), the eldest of the four sons of Murray C. Falkner and his wife, Maud Butler of Oxford. The family moved to Oxford while Faulkner was still a child, and it was there that he grew up and went to school. He made no particular impression upon either neighbours or teachers and left high school without graduating. He seems at first to have done

FROM *William Faulkner* (New York: Grove Press, 1961), pp. 6-13. Reprinted by permission of the publishers: Grove Press, Inc. and Oliver & Boyd Ltd., Edinburgh. Copyright © 1961 by Michael Millgate.
[1] There is no biography of Faulkner as yet. The outline of his life [here] is particularly indebted to [Robert] Cantwell, "The Faulkners [: Recollections of a Gifted Family," *New World Writing* 2 (1952), 306], Robert Coughlan, *The Private World of William Faulkner* (1954), and William Van O'Connor, *The Tangled Fire of William Faulkner* (1954).

little but wander about and read without much sense of purpose or direction, but in 1914 began his friendship with Phil Stone, who already had degrees from the University of Mississippi and from Yale. Stone, four years his senior, told him what to read, talked with him about literature and about the South, and encouraged and criticised his writing, which at that time and for some time afterwards was mostly verse.

When the United States entered the First World War, Faulkner, rejected by the American army as underweight, managed to join the Royal Air Force of Canada and became a pilot. Despite the legends that have grown up around him, he never went to Europe. Back in Oxford after the war he seems to have devoted himself for a time to the cultivation of mild eccentricities. For a short while he attended the University of Mississippi, doing quite well in Spanish and French but failing disastrously in English. Late in 1920, at the invitation of Stark Young, who was also from northern Mississippi, he made his first visit to New York. He worked in a book-shop for a time, but the only useful result of the trip seems to have been his friendship with Elizabeth Prall, whose marriage to Sherwood Anderson was to give Faulkner his first introduction to a really lively literary circle. For the moment, however, Faulkner returned to Oxford to become university postmaster. He is said to have discharged the functions of that office with notable inefficiency and, on the occasion of his dismissal or resignation (the evidence is conflicting), to have declared that at least he would no longer be at the beck and call of anyone who happened to have two cents for a stamp.

By this time he had published several poems in the University's year-book and in its newspaper, *The Mississippean,* and one each in the *New Republic* and the New Orleans "little magazine," the *Double Dealer*; and in 1924, the year the postmastership ended, Phil Stone financed the private publication of a small volume of Faulkner's verse entitled *The Marble Faun.* This was Faulkner's first experience of book-publication, and an unhappy one, for the book attracted few sales and little attention. Shortly afterwards he set off for New Orleans, where he intended to take a boat to Europe. But he met Sherwood Anderson (married by now to Elizabeth Prall), and stayed on in the city for six months, enjoying his first experience of literary society and publishing sketches in the *Times-Picayune* newspaper and in the *Double Dealer*. Anderson, at this time, was at the height of his reputation, and the recognition and encouragement he gave Faulkner was an extremely important factor in the younger man's career. It seems to have been largely Anderson's influence that turned Faulkner to fiction, and it was certainly Anderson who helped him publish his first novel, *Soldiers' Pay,* which he wrote during the New Orleans visit.

Anderson was by no means Faulkner's only friend in New Orleans, however, and with one of the others, the artist William Spratling, Faulkner collaborated in the production of *Sherwood Anderson & other Famous Creoles* published in New Orleans at the end of 1926. This little book of fifty-one pages was primarily a collection of Spratling's drawings, but Faulkner contributed a brief introduction, signed "W.F.," in a parody of Anderson's rather uneven literary style. The exercise was much milder and much less extended than Hemingway's parody of Anderson in *The Torrents of Spring,* published the same year, but Anderson was offended and broke off his friendship with Faulkner, though he continued to speak highly of him as a writer. In the meantime Faulkner had gone to Europe with Spratling in July 1925. He visited northern Italy, spent some time in Paris without becoming converted to the current fashion of expatriation, and returned to the United States in December.

Soldiers' Pay was published by Liveright early in 1926, and had a mild critical success. The book sold poorly, but Liveright signed a contract for a second novel, *Mosquitoes,* which was written at Pascagoula, on the Gulf coast of Mississippi, during 1926 and published early in 1927. The reviews were less favorable than those of *Soldiers' Pay,* even fewer copies of the book were sold, and the publisher's contract was not renewed. Despite this setback, Faulkner continued to write, living at home in Oxford and picking up a little money here and there by doing odd jobs. In Faulkner's introduction to the Modern Library edition of *Sanctuary,* published in 1932, he speaks of painting houses and carpentering, and of a job on the night-shift at the town power plant shovelling coal for the boilers. Faulkner says that on this job, using the slack hours between midnight and 4 a.m., and working on a table contrived from a wheel-barrow, he was able to write *As I Lay Dying* in six weeks during the summer of 1929 [*Sanctuary,* p. vii.]

It was in 1929 that Faulkner married Estelle Oldham, an Oxford girl whom he had known for many years and who had two children by a previous marriage; and the year was an important one in his life for other reasons as well. In January, Harcourt, Brace published *Sartoris,* after Liveright had turned it down. Sales were again low, but in writing the book Faulkner had made important discoveries about himself and his region. He later told Robert Cantwell that when he was half-way through the book, " 'suddenly I discovered that writing was a mighty fine thing—you could make people stand on their hind legs and cast a shadow.' " More recently still, he told an interviewer for the *Paris Review:*

> With *Soldiers' Pay* and *Mosquitoes* I wrote for the sake of writing because it was fun. Beginning with *Sartoris* I discovered that my own little postage stamp of native soil was worth writing about and that I would never live long enough to exhaust it, and that by sublimating the actual into the apocryphal I would have complete liberty to use whatever talent I might have to its absolute top. It opened up a gold mine of other people, so I created a cosmos of my own.

The astonishing outcome of this discovery—astonishing in its own right, still more astonishing when seen against the background of his earlier novels—was *The Sound and the Fury,* published in October 1929 by Jonathan Cape and Harrison Smith. Critical reception of *The Sound and the Fury* was mixed, but it was always respectful and sometimes warm. Faulkner, who for the first time had "written [his] guts" into a book without worrying about whether or not it would sell, had also received his first important encouragement from beyond the circle of his own acquaintance.

From this time onwards he seems to have devoted himself to writing—despite his favourite habit of telling interviewers he is essentially a farmer who writes for fun—and his adoption of professional status was made memorable by the publication of his sensational novel *Sanctuary*. The sensationalism, according to Faulkner's own account in the introduction to the Modern Library edition, was entirely deliberate. His previous novels had brought him a certain amount of critical praise but little financial reward: now he would write a book expressly designed to make money. Faulkner says that he "invented the most horrific tale I could imagine," wrote it out in three weeks or so, and sent it straight off to his publisher, though he extensively revised the book before it was finally published by Cape and Smith in February 1931 [*Sanctuary,* pp. vi-viii].

Sanctuary certainly shocked its readers—nowhere more obviously than in Oxford itself—but it was undoubtedly a popular success. It made Faulkner the money he had needed. It made him, too, a popular reputation of a kind he had never expected and did not particularly want. Paramount bought the story and made from it a film called *The Story of Temple Drake,* and from this time dates Faulkner's long, legendary and mutually profitable relationship with Hollywood.

In the 'thirties and 'forties Faulkner made several visits to Hollywood lasting weeks or months at a time and worked as scriptwriter on a variety of films including those of Hemingway's *To Have and to Have Not* and Raymond Chandler's *The Big Sleep*. Anecdotes of his Hollywood visits abound: there is a collection of them in the eighth chapter of Robert Coughlan's *The Private World of William Faulkner,* and Faulkner gave his own version of some of them in his *Paris Review* interview with Jean Stein. The world of Hollywood has had unfortunate effects upon a good many American writers who have been attracted there. That Faulkner has escaped these effects seems to be largely due to his refusal to become involved in Hollywood social life and to his acceptance of script-writing as neither an artistic challenge nor a way of life, but as a short-term job of craftsmanship to be done honestly and then left behind. Faulkner seems to have thoroughly disliked Hollywood itself, and one of the best-known stories about him tells of his asking the studio if he could work at home for a while, and of his employers' horror at receiving, some while later, a card bearing the postmark "Oxford, Mississippi."

Faulkner's sole reason for going to Hollywood was to make money. In the early 'thirties he purchased a handsome house built before the Civil War, and this involved him in heavy expenses. His fondness for flying was also costly, though he gave this up almost completely after the death of his youngest brother Dean in a flying accident in 1935. Another expense was his attachment to strong drink: Coughlan describes in some detail what he calls Faulkner's "alcoholic holidays from reality." Faulkner did not pursue the vein of *Sanctuary,* and his next books sold comparatively few copies. From 1930 onwards he was selling stories to the magazines at a fairly steady rate—in 1934, for example, he placed four stories with the *Saturday Evening Post,* one each with *Harper's, Scribner's* and *American Mercury,* and two elsewhere— but his occasional trips to Hollywood provided a useful supplementary income.

Apart from these visits, and business trips to New York to see his publisher, Faulkner seems rarely to have moved from Oxford during the 'thirties and 'forties. He and his wife lost their first child, but they have a second daughter, Jill, and Mrs. Faulkner's two children lived at home until they married and left Oxford. His family, the old house, the small farm, and his writing, seemed at one time to occupy the whole of Faulkner's life. For many years he lived in Oxford in something like seclusion, refusing to be interviewed, rarely engaging in correspondence, apparently not even writing a great deal. Between *The Hamlet,* published in 1940 and *Intruder in the Dust,* published in 1948, Faulkner's only book was *Go Down, Moses,* 1942, mostly made up of previously-published short stories—though some of them were extensively revised.

Intruder in the Dust, a novel with overt social and political intentions, heralded a new phase of Faulkner's career as a writer, and he has since published four[2] new novels as well as a number of other books. It also heralded a new development in his relationship with the world, which became even more marked following the award of the Nobel Prize. His famous address on the occasion of the Nobel Prize ceremonies in Stockholm in 1950 has

[2] The publication of *The Reivers* (New York: Randon House, Inc., 1962) brings the total to five.—*Eds.*

been the forerunner of a remarkable number of speeches, articles, letters to newspapers, and other public statements, in which he has forcibly expressed his views on the past, present, and future of the South, the United States, and the human race. He has made public appearances on several occasions and has travelled abroad a good deal, notably to Europe and Japan.

To make the break with his former life even more decisive, Faulkner has now moved away from Oxford and seems to have settled permanently in Charlottesville, Virginia, where the University of Virginia is situated. And, as writer-in-residence at the University, this formerly retiring man has not only submitted himself to a series of study-sessions, in which he discussed his work with students, but allowed these sessions to be recorded on tape and then published, in an edited version, under the title *Faulkner in the University*.

The contrasts between the Faulkner of this last stage and the Faulkner of legend add a final twist to the already difficult problem of describing him as a man. The evidence of those who know him is highly contradictory. We find him described in one place as pleasant in manner, in another as stiff; as warm, and coldly reserved; as modest, and fiercely proud; as courteous, and capable of insult; as a kind and thoughtful friend and father, and as a man with a streak of intolerance and even of cruelty. It need not greatly worry us, however, that Faulkner remains for the moment an enigmatic figure. His books offer enigmas enough, and the puzzling personality of their author may safely be left for his biographers to unravel. It seems quite possible that he is a far simpler man than his readers are at present ready to believe. The novels themselves are not simple, and are unlikely ever to seem so, but they are among the great books of the twentieth century. And that is what matters.[3]

---

[3] As his last published work, *The Reivers,* reached the best-seller list, William Faulkner died of a heart attack on July 6, 1962, in his home town of Oxford, Mississippi. He was sixty-four.—*Eds.*

Anecdotes and
Other Stories About
Old Ben

The Art of Fiction:
An Interview with William Faulkner—September, 1955

CYNTHIA GRENIER

❦

INT: Tell me, was there a real Big Ben and a Lion?

WF: Yes. There used to be a bear like Big Ben in our county when I was a boy. He'd gotten one paw caught in a trap, and 'cause of that, folks used to call him Reel Foot, 'cause of the way he walked. He got killed too, though not so spectacularly as I killed him in the story of course . . . (drawing on pipe reflectively.) I took Hogganbeck from a fella that worked for my father. He was about thirty, but had the mind of a fourteen-year-old. I was about eight or nine. 'Course, me being the boss's son, we always did what I wanted to do. It's a wonder we survived, some of the things we got into. It's a wonder. . . .

FROM *Accent*, XVI (Summer, 1956), 174. Reprinted by permission of *Accent*.

FROM *Old Times in the Faulkner Country*

JOHN B. CULLEN IN COLLABORATION
WITH FLOYD C. WATKINS

❧

Many hunters have killed much more game than the men in our camp, but few have had more fun or enjoyed being together more than we have. Of all the men with whom I first hunted in the Delta, Uncle Bud Miller is the only one still alive. All the rest are gone. On my first hunt, old Dr. A. C. Bramlett sent Uncle Bud Miller and Joe Butler, two of our best woodsmen and hunters, to what was known as Brown's Deadening to see if old Reel Foot was still there. Faulkner says [in the interview with Miss Grenier reprinted above] that he had in mind this famous old bear when he wrote the story about Old Ben in "The Bear." Old Reel Foot had lost two of the toes off his left front paw; Joe measured his tracks, and they were eight inches wide. For twenty years, Old Doc said, he had lived in this jungle, which had sprung up after fire swept through the area and killed all the timber. Thickets of vines and cane grew there, and when the dead trees fell into the tangle it became impossible for man to penetrate it with any speed. Old Reel Foot had either whipped or killed every pack of dogs that followed him into his jungle lair. On my first hunting trip there, a pack of twenty-seven dogs followed Old Reel Foot into the thicket, and only two of them came out alive. How he killed so many dogs so quickly I will never know. . . .

I left the state and spent one year out West and three in the army during World War I. When I returned, the great hunting grounds I had remembered were gone. Towns and cotton fields had taken their place. Today, about all that is left is a little

FROM *Old Times in the Faulkner Country* (Chapel Hill: The University of North Carolina Press, 1961), pp. 27-44 (excerpts). Reprinted by permission of the University of North Carolina Press. Mr. Cullen, a native and lifelong resident of Mississippi, has been on several of the same hunting parties as Faulkner.

scrubby timber on overflow lands. We have often wondered what became of Old Reel Foot after his home was destroyed. I hope that this resourceful old rascal did migrate, find a good home, and die of old age. . . .

In Old Reel Foot's days a man could travel for miles under the open timber and never see a road. . . . The Carrier Lumber Company or Lamb Fish, a big-time lumberman, cut the timber and sold the land to people who started farming. In 1915 and 1916 near Charleston, Mississippi, there were miles of lumber in stacks high as a man could make them. Now levees and farms have replaced the timber, and where the game was there are fields of cotton, corn, and soybeans and pastures. Even though this is progress and even though it is wise to graze thousands of cattle on land that once produced only a few wild deer, I am sad because this period has come to an end. The day of the bear hunter is over, and the day of the deer hunter soon will be ended. Now I think each season is going to be the last one for me.

William Faulkner loves to hunt with men who love the woods and wild life. He likes to camp with a few good fellows in a tent. We are confident that it was around our campfire that he got the background for his story of Ike McCaslin and the bear. And this story expresses better than anyone else ever could the great sadness of change and the terrible sorrow of the loss of the wilderness. . . .

Once William Faulkner got a shot at a deer but did not say whether it was an easy shot or a hard one. All he had to say when I asked him if he saw a deer was, "Yes, I got a shot." Since he did not bring the deer to camp, I took it for granted that he must have missed it. Had this been any of the other hunters, they would have explained in detail why they failed to kill the deer. But William Faulkner never explains very much. . . .

Faulkner's "The Bear," his best fiction about hunting in the Delta, is based on men and animals and natural settings that he has seen and heard about in stories told in our camp. He never saw Old Reel Foot, I believe, or even his tracks, but he has heard many hunters tell tales about him. Probably he never went hunting with Uncle Ad Bush, but old Ash in "The Bear" is like Uncle Ad, and Simon in "Race at Morning" wakes the hunters with

Uncle Ad's call—"Raise up raise up and get fo o'clock coffee"—which Faulkner has heard us repeat. Uncle Ad went on one camp with us when he was eighty-five years old.

The story about Boon Hogganbeck's going with Isaac McCaslin to Memphis for whisky is, I believe, a true story from the Stone camp. Faulkner says in an interview in *The Paris Review* that he took Boon from the character of a man who worked for his father. But I never knew a hunter exactly like that, even though I have known Faulkner's father and men who worked for him. An old fellow a little like Boon lived in the bottom, a great big bear-looking type of man, but he was not tall. He had eyes like a wild animal, and he let hair grow all over his face. He went bare-footed, walking around among the rattlesnakes in the bottoms. We never killed anything but he was there to claim part of it. He was just a buzzard after the kill. He had little shoe-button eyes like Boon's and a great red beard. The bottom was a hide-out, a wild hide-out.

Lion: A Story

WILLIAM FAULKNER

❧

A good part of the lives of dogs—I mean hunting dogs, bear and deer dogs—is whiskey. That is, the men who love them, who hunt hard the hard-hunting and tireless and courageous dogs, drink hard too. I know certainly that the best, the finest talk about dogs which I have heard took place over a bottle or two or three bottles maybe, in the libraries of town houses and the offices of plantation houses or, better still, in the camps themselves; before the burning logs on hearths when there were houses, or before the high blazing of nigger-fed wood before stretched and earth-pegged tarpaulins when there were not. So this story might just as well begin with whiskey too.

FROM *Harper's Monthly Magazine*, CLXXII (December, 1925), 67-77. Copyright 1935 and renewed 1963 by Estelle Faulkner and Jill Faulkner Summers. Reprinted by permission of Random House, Inc.

It was December; it was the coldest December I ever saw. We —I was just sixteen that year—had been in camp a week now and the men had run out of whiskey, and so Boon Hogganbeck and I went in to Memphis with a suitcase and a note from Major de Spain to get some more. That is, Major de Spain sent Boon in to get the whiskey, and he sent me along to get Boon back to camp with the whiskey in the suitcase and not in Boon. Boon was part Indian. They said half, but I don't think so. I think it was his grandmother who was the Chickasaw woman, niece of the chief who once owned the land which Major de Spain now owned and over which we hunted.

Boon was four inches over six feet, and he had the mind of a child and the heart of a horse and the ugliest face I ever saw. It looked as if somebody had found a walnut a little smaller than a basket ball and with a machinist's hammer had shaped the features of the face and then painted it, mostly red. Not Indian red: a fine bright ruddy color that whiskey might have had something to do with but probably mostly just happy and violent out-of-door life. The wrinkles in it—he must have been forty years old —must have come just from squinting into the sun or into the gloom of cane brakes where game had run, or have been baked into his face by camp fires while he tried to sleep on the cold November or December ground while waiting for daylight so he could get up and hunt again—as though time were just something he walked through as he did in air, to age him no more than air did. The eyes were like shoebuttons, without depth, without meanness or generosity or viciousness or gentleness or anything at all: just something to see with. He didn't have any profession or trade or even job: he just did whatever Major de Spain told him to do. Later, after Lion died, Major de Spain had him appointed marshal of Hoke's, the little town on the edge of Major de Spain's preserve. But that had not happened yet; Lion was not dead yet.

We got up at three o'clock this morning. Ad had breakfast ready and we ate, hearing the dogs under the kitchen, wakened too by the smell of the frying ham or maybe by Ad's feet on the floor overhead; we could hear Lion then, just once, short and peremptory, as the best hunter in any crowd has only to speak once to all the others except the ones that are fools, and there were no fools among Major de Spain's dogs. As he said, sometimes he had fools in the house because now and then he could not help himself. But that did not matter so much because he did not intend to hunt with them or depend on them to hunt.

Ad had the mules in the wagon, waiting too, and it was cold, the ground frozen and the stars hard and bright. I was not shivering, I was just shaking slow and steady and hard, the breakfast I had just eaten warm and comfortable inside me and my stomach still warm from it and the outside of me shaking slow and hard as if my stomach were floating loose inside me like the globe of a floating compass.

"They won't run this morning, anyway," I said. "No dog will have any nose to-day."

"Cep' Lion," Ad said. "He run a bear thu a thousand-acre ice house. Ketch him too. Other dogs don't matter because they don't keep up wid Lion nohow."

"Well, they ain't going to run this morning," Boon said, harsh and positive. "Major promised they wouldn't run till me and Quentin get back."

He was sitting on the jolting seat, his feet wrapped in towsacks and a quilt from his pallet in the kitchen wrapped around him and over his head so that he didn't look like anything at all. Ad laughed. "I like to know why Major need to wait on you. Hit's Lion he gonter use; I ain't never heard tell of you bringing no bear nor any yuther kind of meat into this camp."

"By God, he ain't going to put Lion or no other dog on nothing until I get back," Boon said. "Because he promised me. Whup up them mules; you want me to freeze to death?"

He and Ad were funny. It was Lion that made the difference, because Boon had a bad name among negroes. Yet Ad talked to him, when Lion was a factor (even though he was not mentioned), just as if Ad were another white man; and Boon let him do it. They were funny about Lion. Neither one of them owned him or had any hope of ever owning him and I don't believe it ever occurred to either of them to think, *I wish I owned that dog.* Because you didn't think of Lion as belonging to anyone, any more than you thought about a man belonging to anybody, not even to Major de Spain. You thought of the house and the woods as belonging to him and even the deer and the bear in them; even the deer and bear killed by other people were shot by them on Major de Spain's courtesy, given to them through his kindness and will. But not Lion. Lion was like the chiefs of Aztec and Polynesian tribes who were looked upon as being not men but both more and less than men. Because we were not men either while we were in camp: we were hunters, and Lion the best hunter of us all, and Major de Spain and Uncle Ike McCaslin next; and Lion did not talk as we talked, not because he could not but because he was the chief, the Sunbegotten, who knew the language which we spoke but was superior to using it himself; just as he lived under the house, under the kitchen, not because he was a dog, an animal, but for the same reason as the Aztec or the Polynesian whose godhead required that he live apart. Lion did not belong to Major de Spain at all but just happened to like him better than he did any of the rest of us, as a man might have.

Ad and Boon were funny about him. You would have almost thought that Lion was a woman, a beautiful woman. I used to listen to them; they would wait until Major de Spain had settled down to the poker game or maybe was in bed, if we were going out early, and then Boon and Ad would each try to get Lion in to sleep on his pallet with him, Ad in the kitchen and Boon in the shed room. It would be funny. They would be so deadly serious about it, not arguing with each other but each one trying to work on Lion, persuade or tempt him; and he not caring which one he slept with, and not staying long with either one even when they persuaded him, because always Major de Spain would carry the lamp into Boon's shed or into the kitchen, as the case might be, and make them put Lion outdoors. "Damn it," he would say, "if he slept with either one of you for half the night he wouldn't even be able to trace a polecat to-morrow."

So we went on, under the iron stars, the wagon jolting in the iron ruts, the woods impenetrable and black on either hand. Once we heard two wildcats squalling and fighting off to the right and not far away. We came to the dummy line and Boon flagged the early log train and we rode into Hoke's in the warm caboose, while I slept behind the red stove and Boon and the conductor and brakeman talked about Lion and Old Ben as people talked about Sullivan and Kilrain or Dempsey and Tunney. Old Ben was a bear and we were going to run him to-morrow as we did once every year, every time in camp. He was known through the country as well as Lion was. I don't know why they called him Old Ben nor who named him except that it was a long time ago. He was known well for the shoats he had stolen and the corn cribs he had broken into and the dogs he had killed and the number of times he had been bayed and the lead which he carried (it was said that he had been shot at least two dozen times, with buckshot and even with rifles). Old Ben had lost three toes from his nigh hind foot in a steel trap, and every man in the country knew his track, even discounting the size, and so he should have been called Two-Toe. That is, that's what they had been calling two-toed bears in this country for a hundred years. Maybe it was because Old Ben was an extra bear—the head bear, Uncle Ike Mc-Caslin called him—and everyone knew that he deserved a better name.

We were in Hoke's by sun-up, Boon and me, getting out of the warm caboose in our hunting clothes, our muddy boots, and stained khaki. Boon hadn't shaved since we came into camp, but that was all right because Hoke's was just a sawmill and a few stores, and most of the men in it wore muddy boots and khaki too. Then the accommodation came; Boon bought three packages of molasses-covered popcorn and a bottle of soda pop from the news butch and I went to sleep to the sound of his chewing. But in Memphis we did not look all right. The tall buildings and the hard pavements and the street cars made our boots and khaki look a little rougher and muddier and made Boon's whiskers look worse and his face more and more as if he should never have brought it out of the woods at all or at least out of reach of Major de Spain or somebody who knew it and could say, "Don't be afraid. He's all right; he won't hurt you"—Boon walking through the station, on the tile floor, his face moving where he was still working the popcorn out of his teeth with his tongue, his legs spraddled a little and a little stiff in the hips as if he were walking on buttered glass, and that blue stubble on his face and chin like used steel wool or like ravelings from screen wire.

We went straight and had the suitcase filled and Boon bought a bottle for himself, to take home after we broke camp, he said. But by the time we reached Hoke's again at sundown, it was all gone. He drank the first time in the washroom at the station. A man in uniform came in to tell Boon he couldn't drink there and took one look at Boon's face and didn't say anything. The next time he drank from his water glass, filling it under the edge of the counter where we were eating dinner and the waitress did tell him he could not. In the meantime he had been telling the waitress and all the other customers about Lion and Old Ben. Then he got on to the subject of the zoo some way, and his plan was to hurry back to camp, get Lion and return to the zoo where, he said, the bears were fed lady fingers and ice cream and where we would match Lion against them all, tigers and elephants included. But I got him and the suitcase aboard the train, so we were all right then, with Boon drinking right in the aisle and telling the other passengers about Lion and Old Ben; the men he button-holed no more dared to act as if they did not want to listen than the man in the washroom had dared to tell Boon he couldn't drink there. We were back in Hoke's at sundown and I waked him and got him and the suitcase off and persuaded him to eat supper.

When we got on the caboose of the evening log train which went back into the woods, the sun was going down red and it already seemed warmer. I was the one who went to sleep again now, sitting behind the stove again while Boon and the brakeman and the conductor talked about Lion and Old Ben and the drive to-morrow; they knew what Boon was talking about. Once I waked; it was dark now and the brakeman was leaning out the window. "It's overcast," he said. "It will thaw to-night and to-morrow scent will lie to a dog's nose. Maybe Lion will get him to-morrow."

It would have to be Lion or somebody. It would not be Boon. He never could shoot. He never had killed anything bigger than a squirrel that anybody knew of, except that nigger that time. That was several years ago. They said he was a bad nigger, but I don't know. All I know is, there was some trouble and the nigger told Boon he'd better have a pistol next time he came to town and Boon borrowed a pistol from Major de Spain and sure enough that afternoon he met the nigger and the nigger outs with a dollar-

and-a-half mail order pistol and he would have burned Boon up with it only it never went off. It just snapped five times and the nigger kept coming, and Boon shot four times and broke a plate-glass window and shot in the leg a nigger woman who happened to be passing before he managed to hit the nigger in the face at six feet with the last shot. He never could shoot. The first day in camp, the first drive we made, the buck ran right over him; we measured later and the buck's tracks and the five exploded shells were not fifty feet apart. We heard Boon's old pump gun go *whow whow whow whow whow* and then we heard him; they could have heard him clean up to Hoke's: "God damn, here he comes! Head him! Head him!"

The next morning we had company, people from Hoke's and from Jefferson too, who came every year for the day when Major de Spain drove Old Ben. It was gray and warmer; we ate break-fast by lamplight, with Boon frying the eggs and still talking, looking wilder and more unpredictable and more uncurried in the face than ever, and Ad sitting on his box beside the stove, push-ing the heavy solid greasy cartridges into Major de Spain's car-bine. And we could hear the dogs too now, in the yard where Ad had already coupled them in pairs and tied them to the fence —the snarling bursts of almost hysterical uproar; we could hear them all except Lion.

There was no sound from him, there never was; I remember how after breakfast we went out and into the damp, gray, faint light and there he stood, apart from the other dogs and not tied, just standing there and looking huge as a calf looks, or an ele-phant or buffalo calf, huge despite its actual size. He was part Walker, but most of him was mastiff; he was the color of a blue sorrel horse, though perhaps it was his topaz-colored eyes that made him look so dark. I remember how he stood there—big-footed, with his strong grave head and a chest almost as big as mine. Beneath the skin you could feel the long, easy, quiet, strong muscles that did not flinch with either pleasure or distaste from any touch, Major de Spain's or Boon's or Ad's or any stranger's. He stood like a horse, only different from a horse because a horse promises only speed while Lion promised—with that serene and comforting quality of a promise from a man whom you trust absolutely—an immeasurable capacity not only for courage and skill and will to pursue and kill, but for endurance, the will to endure beyond any imaginable limit to which his flesh and heart might be called. I remember him in the summer when we would go in for squirrels, how when the other dogs would be all over the bottom, chasing coon and wildcat and anything that ran and left scent, Lion would not go. He would stay in camp with us, not especially following Major de Spain or Boon or Ad in particular; just lying nearby somewhere in the attitude in which they carve lions in stone, with his big head raised and his big feet quiet before him; you would go to him and speak to him or pat him and he would turn his head slowly and look at you with those topaz eyes that were as impenetrable as Boon's, as free of meanness or generosity or gentleness or viciousness but a good deal more intelligent. Then he would blink and then you would realize that he was not looking at you at all, not seeing you at all. You didn't know what he was seeing, what he was thinking. It was like when you are sitting with your feet propped against a column on the gallery and after a while you are not even aware that you are not seeing the very column your feet are propped against.

The two mules were ready too, one for Major de Spain, who was going with Boon and Ad and the dogs; and the other for Uncle Ike McCaslin, who was going to put us on the stands. Because he and Major de Spain knew Old Ben as well as they knew each other. They knew where he denned and where he used and which direction he took when dogs jumped him. That was why we had been in camp a week and hadn't run him yet; that was the way Major de Spain did. Each year he ran Old Ben just one time, unless Old Ben happened to let himself be caught out of bounds on a visit or something and the dogs started him by accident, which did happen the second day in camp. We heard them strike something and carry it down toward the river; Lion was not with them. They went out of hearing and after a while Boon came up, cussing. But hunting was over for that day and so we went back to camp. We had not heard them again, but when we reached camp the dogs were already there, crouched back under the kitchen, huddled together as far back as they could go and Boon squatting down and peering under the kitchen at them and cussing, and Uncle Ike said it was Old Ben they had struck. Because they knew Old Ben too and the ones that didn't know him probably found out pretty quick. They were not cowards. It was just that Lion hadn't been with them to lead them in on him and bay him and hold him. Lion was with Major de Spain; they came in about an hour later with Lion on the leash and Major de Spain said it was Old Ben, that he had seen the track, still having to hold Lion on the leash because he was saving Old Ben for to-day. I remember him sitting on the mule in the gray light with his rifle across the saddle, and Boon with his old gun slung over his shoulder by a piece of cotton rope and still cussing while he and Ad struggled to hold the dogs while they untied them, and only Lion and Major de Spain calm and Major de Spain looking around at us and saying, "No deer this morning, boys. This is Old Ben's race."

He meant there must be no shooting, no noise that might turn Old Ben because he wanted everybody to have a fair chance. Uncle Ike explained that to me when he put me on my stand, after we watched Major de Spain ride away, with Lion heeled and pacing along beside the mule and Ad and Boon in front, stooped over and half running in a surging uproar of dogs as if they were running in surf.

"Stay here until you kill a bear or hear a horn, or until you haven't heard a dog in an hour," Uncle Ike said. "If Lion bays him, me or Major or Boon will blow everybody in. If you don't hear anything after a while, go back to camp. If you get lost, stand right still and holler and listen. Some of the boys will hear you."

"I've got my compass," I said.

"All right. Stay right still now. He may cross the bayou right here; I have known him to do it. Don't move around. If he comes over you, give him time to get close. Then hold right on his neck." Then he rode away, into the gray gloom.

It was full daylight now; that is, it was full daylight up above the trees, because it would never be very light down here that day. I had never been in this part of the bottom before, because Major de Spain had not let us hunt here lest we disturb Old Ben before the right day. I stood there under a gum tree beside the bayou, where the black, still water ran out of the cane and across a little clearing and into the cane again. I had been on stand before where you might see a bear and I had seen bear signs. But this was different; I was just sixteen then; I kept on thinking about those dogs huddled back there under the kitchen that day and I could smell the solitude, the loneliness, something breathing out of this place which human beings had merely passed through without altering it, where no axe or plow had left a scar, which looked exactly as it had when the first Indian crept into it and looked around, arrow poised and ready. I thought about how just twenty miles away was Jefferson, the houses where people were getting ready to wake up in comfort and security, the stores and offices where during the day they would meet to buy and sell and talk, and I could hardly believe it; I thought *It's just twenty miles away. What's the matter with you?* but then the other side of me, the other thing in me would say, *Yes, and you are just a puny assortment of bones and meat that cannot get one mile from where you stand without that compass to help you and could not spend one night where you are and live without fire to keep you warm and perhaps that gun to protect yourself.*

I had forgotten that I had a gun. I had completely forgotten it. I was telling myself that black bears are not dangerous, they won't hurt a man unless they are cornered, when all of a sudden I thought, with a kind of amazed surprise, *Besides, I have a gun. Why, I have a gun!* I had clean forgotten it. I hadn't even loaded it; I broke it quickly, fumbling in my coat for shells. I was not scared any more now; I was just suffering one of those mindless and superstitious illusions which people get—I do anyway. I believed that by getting scared and failing to load my gun, I was going to fail the others and let Old Ben through. I had conferred supernatural powers on him now. I had a picture of him lurking back in the cane, watching his chance and waiting for one of us who barred his way to make a mistake, and I had made it; I believed, knew, that he would charge out of the cane and pass me before I could get loaded. I thought I should never pick up the two shells, and then I had a terrible impulse to read the size of the shot printed on the wadding to be sure, even though I knew

I had only buckshot. But I didn't; I got the gun loaded and
snapped it shut, already swinging toward the spot of cane where
I had hypnotized myself to believe he would emerge. I think that
if a bird had moved in it I should have fired.

But I never saw him. I just heard the dogs. Suddenly I knew
that I had been hearing them for a second or two before I realized
what it was. That must have been when they jumped him because
I heard Lion, just once. His voice was not deep especially, it was
just strong and full; he bayed just once somewhere in the gray
light maybe a mile away, and that was all, as if he had said, "All
right, Old Man. Let's go." It was the other dogs making the
racket. But I never saw any of them. At the closest time they were
a half mile away and they didn't pass near any stand because I
heard no shots. I just stood there, crouched, holding my breath,
with the safety off even though father had taught me never to
take it off until I saw what I was going to shoot at; and I heard
the dogs pass me and go on. Then the sound died away. I didn't
move; I waited. I was thinking, maybe he will turn and come
back. But I knew that he would not. He must have known where
all of us were standing; he probably picked the one gap where he
could have got through unseen. Because he had lived too long
now, been run too many times. I stood there, still holding my gun
forward, though I did slip the safety back on. I don't know how
long it was; then I whirled. But it was only father. "You didn't
see him?" father said.

"No, sir. But it was Old Ben, wasn't it?"

"Yes. So Uncle Ike says. He's gone across the river. He won't
come back to-day. So we might as well go back to camp."

We went back to camp. Major de Spain was already there,
sitting on the mule with Boon's gun in the rope sling over his
shoulder now (he told how Boon had stopped just long enough
to throw the gun at him and say, "Here, take the damn thing. I
can't hit him with it nohow"). They had the other team in the
wagon, and some of them were just loading the boat into the
wagon when we came up, and Major de Spain told us how Old
Ben and the dogs had crossed the river, and that Ad and Boon
had swum it too, and that Uncle Ike was waiting at the river
while he came back for the boat.

"He killed Kate this side of the river without even stopping," Major de Spain said. "Come on, boys. Lion wasn't five hundred yards behind him. He will bay him soon and then we will get him."

So we all went back to the river. But the boat was just a duck boat, so it wouldn't hold any more than Major de Spain and Uncle Ike. Theophilus McCaslin, Uncle Ike's grandson, said he knew about a log drift across the river about three miles down, so he and some of the others went to look for it. I wanted to go too, but father said I'd better come on back to camp so the rest of us came back to camp, with the mules and the wagon and the dead dog.

It began to rain before we got back; it rained slowly and steadily all afternoon, and we ate dinner and then Theophilus and the others came in and said they had got across the river but they couldn't hear anything and so they came back. The men played cards some but not much because every now and then somebody would go to the window and look out across the field to where the woods began, the black trees standing in the rain like a picture in ink beginning to dissolve. "He must have carried them clean out of the country," somebody said.

It was still raining at dark. But we didn't eat supper yet; we waited, and now there was somebody watching the woods all the time, and just before dark Theophilus McCaslin began to blow a horn every five minutes to guide them in. Yet when they did come, nobody saw them at all; we were all inside at the fire; we just heard the noise at the back door and then in the hall; we were still sitting down when Boon walked into the room. He was carrying something big wrapped in his hunting coat, but we didn't even look to see what it was because we were looking at Boon. He was wet and muddy and there was blood all over him, streaked by the rain. But that wasn't it. It was his face, his head. There was a bloody furrow (you could see the five claw-marks) wide as my hand starting up in his hair and running down the side of his head and right on down his arm to the wrist; there was a bloody blob hanging on the side of his head that I didn't know until the next day was his left ear, and his right breeches' leg had been ripped off and the leg under it looking like raw beef and the blood from it staining his boot darker than the rain. But that wasn't it either. Because then we saw that what he was carrying in the coat was Lion. He stood there in the door, looking at us, and he began to cry. I never had seen a man cry before. He stood there in the lamplight, looking big as all outdoors and bloody as a hog, with that tough unshaven face of his crinkled up and more like a dried walnut than ever, and the tears streaming down it fast as rain.

"Good God, Boon!" father said. We got up then; we all kind of surged toward him and somebody tried to touch the coat; I hadn't even seen Major de Spain standing behind him until then.

"Get to hell away!" Boon hollered to the one who touched the coat. "His guts are all out of him." Then he hollered, "Saddle me a mule! Hurry!" and turned, with all of us following now, and crossed the hall into the shed where he slept and laid Lion on his pallet. "Damn it to hell, get me a mule!" he hollered.

"A mule?" somebody said.

"Yes!" Boon hollered. "I'm going to Hoke's and get a doctor!"

"No, you're not," Major de Spain said. "You need a doctor yourself. One of the other boys will go."

"The hell I ain't!" Boon hollered. He looked wild, bloody and wild as he glared round at us, then he ran out, the torn bloody clothes flapping behind him, still hollering, "Help me catch a mule!"

"Go and help them," father said, pushing me toward the door. There were three of us. We were almost too late to help any; we had to run to keep up with him. Maybe he was still crying, or maybe he was in too much of a hurry to cry now. We kept on trying to find out what happened but Boon couldn't even seem to hear the questions; he was talking to himself, saddling the mule fast, cussing and panting.

"I tried to get him back, make him stay out," he said. "I tried to. And them others wouldn't help him, wouldn't go in." And he did try. Ad said (Ad was there; he saw it all) that when Boon ran in, Lion was already on the ground and that Boon caught him by the hind leg and flung him twenty feet away, but that Lion hit the ground already running and that he beat Boon back to Old Ben.

Then Boon got into the saddle without even touching the stir-

rups and was gone; we could hear the mule already loping. Then
we went back to the house, where Major de Spain was sitting on
the pallet with Lion's head in his lap, soaking a rag in a pan of
water and squeezing it into Lion's mouth. Lion was still wrapped
in the coat and under a blanket, to keep the air away from his
entrails. But I don't think he was suffering now. He just lay there
with his head on Major de Spain's knee and his eyes open a little
and looking yellower than ever in the lamplight; once I saw his
tongue come out and touch Major de Spain's hand. Then about
midnight (Major de Spain had sent the wagon back to the river
before he followed Boon into the house) Uncle Ike and Ad came
in with Old Ben; and Ad stood in the door too, as Boon had
done, with the tears running down his face too, and Uncle Ike
told about it, what Ad had told him: about how Lion had bayed
Old Ben against a down tree top and the other dogs would not
go in, and how Old Ben caught Lion and had him on the ground,
and Boon ran in with the hunting knife and jerked Lion back,
but he would not stay out; and how this time Boon jumped strad-
dle of Old Ben's back and got the knife into him, under the
shoulder; Ad said that Boon picked Old Ben clean up from behind, his arm round Old Ben's neck and Old Ben striking backward at Boon's head and arm while Boon worked the knife blade
round until he touched the life.

Boon got back just before daylight with the doctor, and the
doctor told about that too: how Boon busted past the doctor's
wife when she opened the door and how the first thing the doctor
knew was when Boon waked him up dragging him out of the bed
like a sack of meal. He thought Boon was crazy, especially when
he saw him, the blood and all. Boon wouldn't even wait long
enough to have himself attended to; he didn't even want to wait
long enough for the doctor to put on his clothes. He wouldn't let
the doctor do anything for him now until he had fixed Lion; he
just stood there in his blood and his torn clothes and with his
wild face, saying, "Save him, Doc. By God, you had better save
him!"

They couldn't give Lion chloroform; they didn't dare. They
had to put his entrails back and sew him up without it. But I still
don't think he felt it, suffered. He just lay there on Boon's pallet,

with his eyes half open and Major de Spain holding his head, until the doctor was through. And not even Boon said, "Will he live?" We just sat there and talked quietly until the light came and we went out to look at Old Ben with his eyes open too and his lips snarled back and the neat slit just in front of the shoulder where Boon had finally found his life, and the mutilated hind foot and the little hard lumps under his skin which were the old bullets, the old victories. Then Ad said breakfast was ready. We ate, and I remember how that was the first time we could not hear any dogs under the kitchen, though I asked Ad and he said that they were there. It was as though Old Ben, even dead and harmless out there in the yard, was a more potent force than they were alive without Lion to lead them in, and they knew it.

The rain had stopped before midnight and about noon a thin sun came out and we moved Lion out onto the porch, in the sun. It was Boon's idea. "Damn it," he said, "he never did like to stay in the house. You know that. At least let's take him out where he can see the woods." So Boon loosened the floor boards under the pallet so that we could pick up the pallet without changing Lion's position, and we carried him out to the porch and we sat there now. The people at Hoke's had heard that we had got Old Ben and about Lion; there must have been a hundred men came in during the afternoon to look at Old Ben and then come and look at Lion, to sit and talk quietly about Lion, the races he had made and the bears he had brought to bay, and now and then Lion would open his eyes (Boon had laid him so he could look at the woods without moving) not as if he was listening to what they were saying but as if he was looking at the woods for a moment before closing his eyes again, remembering the woods again or seeing that they were still there. Maybe he was, because he waited until dark before he died. We broke camp that night; we went out in the wagon, in the dark. Boon was quite drunk by then. He was singing, loud.

This is how Lion's death affected the two people who loved him most—if you could have called Boon's feeling for him, for anything, love. And I suppose you could, since they say you al-

ways love that which causes you suffering. Or maybe Boon did
not consider being clawed by a bear suffering.

Major de Spain never went back again. But we did; he made
us welcome to go; it seemed to please him when we went. Father
and the others who had been there that time would talk about it,
about how maybe if they could just persuade him to go back
once . . . But he would not; he was almost sharp when he refused. I remember the day in the next summer when I went to his
office to ask permission to go in and hunt squirrels. "Help yourself," he said. "Ad will be glad to have some company. Do you
want to take anybody with you?"

"No, sir," I said. "I thought if maybe Boon . . ."

"Yes," he said. "I'll wire him to meet you there." Boon was
the marshal at Hoke's now; Major de Spain called his secretary
and sent Boon the wire right away. We didn't need to wait for
an answer; Boon would be there; he had been doing what Major
de Spain told him to for twenty years now at least. So I thanked
him and then I stood there and after a minute I got up my nerve
and said it:

"Maybe if you would come . . ."

But he stopped me. I don't know how he did it because he
didn't say anything at once. He just seemed to turn to his desk
and the papers on it without moving; and I stood there looking
down at a little plumpish gray-headed man in expensive, unobtru-
sive clothes and an old-fashioned immaculate boiled shirt, whom
I was used to seeing in muddy khaki, unshaven, sitting the mule
with the carbine across the saddle, and Lion standing beside him
as a thoroughbred horse stands and motionless as a statue, with
his strong grave head and his fine chest; the two of them somehow queerly alike, as two people get who have been closely associated for many years in doing something which both of them
love and respect. He didn't look at me again.

"No. I will be too busy. But if you have luck, you might bring
me a few squirrels when you come back."

"Yes, sir," I said. "I will." So I reached Hoke's early and
caught the morning log train into the woods and they put me off
at our crossing. It was the same, yet different, because they were

summer woods now, in full leaf, not like that iron dawn when Boon and I had flagged the train to go in to Memphis. And it was hot too. Ad was there with the wagon to meet me; we shook hands. "Mr. Boon here yet?" I said.

"Yes, suh. He got in last night. He in de woods fo daylight. Gone up to de Gum Tree."

I knew where that was. It was a single big gum just outside the woods, in an old clearing. If you crept up to it quietly just after daylight this time of year, sometimes you would catch a dozen squirrels in it, trapped there because they could not jump to another tree and dared not descend. So I told Ad to take my duffel on to the house; I would hunt up through the woods and meet Boon. I didn't say I was going by the holly knoll, but he must have known that I was, because the point where he put me down was on a direct line with the knoll and the Gum Tree. "Watch out for snakes," he said. "Dey's crawling now."

"I will," I said. He went on and I entered the woods. They were changed, different. Of course it was just the summer; next fall they would be again as I remembered them. Then I knew that that was wrong; that they would never again be as I remembered them, as any of us remembered them, and I, a boy, who had owned no Lion, knew now why Major de Spain knew that he would never return and was too wise to try to. I went on. Soon the earth began to lift under my feet and then I saw the hollies, the four pale trunks marking the four corners and inside them the wooden cross with Old Ben's dried mutilated paw nailed to it. There was no trace of grave any more; the spring flood water had seen to that. But that was all right because it was not Lion who was there; not Lion. Maybe it was nice for him now, nice for him and Old Ben both now—the long challenge and the long chase, the one with no heart to be driven and outraged, the other with no flesh to be mauled and bled. It was hot and the mosquitoes were too bad to stand still in, besides it was too late to hunt any more this morning; I would go on and pick up Boon and go back to camp. I knew these woods and presently I knew that I could not be very far from the Gum Tree.

Then I began to hear a curious sound. It sounded like a blacksmith shop—someone hammering fast on metal. It grew louder as

I approached. Then I saw the clearing, the sun; the hammering, the furious hammering on metal, was quite loud now, and the trees broke and I saw the Gum Tree and then I saw Boon. It was the same Boon; he had not changed; the same Boon who had almost missed that nigger and had missed that buck; who could not shoot even when his old worn-out gun held together. He was sitting under the tree, hammering at something in his lap, and then I saw that the tree was apparently alive with frightened squirrels. I watched them rush from limb to limb, trying to escape, and rush, dart, down the trunk and then turn and dart back up again. Then I saw what Boon was hammering at. It was a section of his gun; drawing nearer, I saw the rest of it scattered in a dozen pieces about him on the ground where he sat, hunched over, hammering furiously at the part on his lap, his walnut face wild and urgent and streaming with sweat. He was living, as always, in the moment; nothing on earth—not Lion, not anything in the past—mattered to him except his helpless fury with his broken gun. He didn't stop; he didn't even look up to see who I was; he just shouted at me in a hoarse desperate voice.

"Get out of here!" he said. "Don't touch them! They're mine!"

The Bear (*Saturday Evening Post* version)

WILLIAM FAULKNER

❦

He was ten. But it had already begun, long before that day when at last he wrote his age in two figures and he saw for the first time the camp where his father and Major de Spain and old General Compson and the others spent two weeks each November and two weeks again each June. He had already inherited then, without ever having seen it, the tremendous bear with one trap-ruined foot which, in an area almost a hundred miles deep, had

FROM *Saturday Evening Post*, CCXIV (May 9, 1942), 30-31, 74, 76-77. Copyright 1942 by The Curtis Publishing Co. Reprinted by permission of Random House, Inc.

earned for itself a name, a definite designation like a living man.

He had listened to it for years: the long legend of corncribs rifled, of shotes and grown pigs and even calves carried bodily into the woods and devoured, of traps and deadfalls overthrown and dogs mangled and slain, and shotgun and even rifle charges delivered at point-blank range and with no more effect than so many peas blown through a tube by a boy—a corridor of wreckage and destruction beginning back before he was born, through which sped, not fast but rather with the ruthless and irresistible deliberation of a locomotive, the shaggy tremendous shape.

It ran in his knowledge before he ever saw it. It looked and towered in his dreams before he even saw the unaxed woods where it left its crooked print, shaggy, huge, red-eyed, not malevolent but just big—too big for the dogs which tried to bay it, for the horses which tried to ride it down, for the men and the bullets they fired into it, too big for the very country which was its constricting scope. He seemed to see it entire with a child's complete divination before he ever laid eyes on either—the doomed wilderness whose edges were being constantly and punily gnawed at by men with axes and plows who feared it because it was wilderness, men myriad and nameless even to one another in the land where the old bear had earned a name, through which ran not even a mortal animal but an anachronism, indomitable and invincible, out of an old dead time, a phantom, epitome and apotheosis of the old wild life at which the puny humans swarmed and hacked in a fury of abhorrence and fear, like pygmies about the ankles of a drowsing elephant; the old bear solitary, indomitable and alone, widowered, childless and absolved of mortality—old Priam reft of his old wife and having outlived all his sons.

Until he was ten, each November he would watch the wagon containing the dogs and the bedding and food and guns and his father and Tennie's Jim, the Negro, and Sam Fathers, the Indian, son of a slave woman and a Chickasaw chief, depart on the road to town, to Jefferson, where Major de Spain and the others would join them. To the boy, at seven and eight and nine, they were not going into the Big Bottom to hunt bear and deer, but to keep yearly rendezvous with the bear which they did not even intend to kill. Two weeks later they would return, with no trophy, no head and skin. He had not expected it. He had not even been afraid it would be in the wagon. He believed that even after he was ten and his father would let him go too, for those two November weeks, he would merely make another one, along with his father and Major de Spain and General Compson and the others, the dogs which feared to bay it and the rifles and shotguns which failed even to bleed it, in the yearly pageant of the old bear's furious immortality.

Then he heard the dogs. It was in the second week of his first time in the camp. He stood with Sam Fathers against a big oak beside the faint crossing where they had stood each dawn for nine days now, hearing the dogs. He had heard them once before, one morning last week—a murmur, sourceless, echoing through the wet woods, swelling presently into separate voices which he could recognize and call by name. He had raised and cocked the gun as Sam told him and stood motionless again while the uproar, the invisible course, swept up and past and faded; it seemed to him that he could actually see the deer, the buck, blond, smoke-colored, elongated with speed, fleeing, vanishing, the woods, the gray solitude, still ringing even when the cries of the dogs had died away.

"Now let the hammers down," Sam said.

"You knew they were not coming here too," he said.

"Yes," Sam said. "I want you to learn how to do when you didn't shoot. It's after the chance for the bear or the deer has done already come and gone that men and dogs get killed."

"Anyway," he said, "it was just a deer."

Then on the tenth morning he heard the dogs again. And he readied the too-long, too-heavy gun as Sam had taught him, before Sam even spoke. But this time it was no deer, no ringing chorus of dogs running strong on a free scent, but a moiling yapping an octave too high, with something more than indecision and even abjectness in it, not even moving very fast, taking a long time to pass completely out of hearing, leaving even then somewhere in the air that echo, thin, slightly hysterical, abject, almost grieving, with no sense of a fleeing, unseen, smoke-colored, grass-eating shape ahead of it, and Sam, who had taught him first of all to cock the gun and take position where he could see everywhere and then never move again, had himself moved up beside him; he could hear Sam breathing at his shoulder and he could see the arched curve of the old man's inhaling nostrils.

"Hah," Sam said. "Not even running. Walking."

"Old Ben!" the boy said. "But up here!" he cried. "Way up here!"

"He do it every year," Sam said. "Once. Maybe to see who in camp this time, if he can shoot or not. Whether we got the dog yet that can bay and hold him. He'll take them to the river, then he'll send them back home. We may as well go back, too; see how they look when they come back to camp."

When they reached the camp the hounds were already there, ten of them crouching back under the kitchen, the boy and Sam squatting to peer back into the obscurity where they huddled, quiet, the eyes luminous, glowing at them and vanishing, and no sound, only that effluvium of something more than dog, stronger than dog and not just animal, just beast, because still there had been nothing in front of that abject and almost painful yapping save the solitude, the wilderness, so that when the eleventh hound came in at noon and with all the others watching—even old Uncle Ash, who called himself first a cook—Sam daubed the tattered ear and the raked shoulder with turpentine and axle grease, to the boy it was still no living creature, but the wilderness which, leaning for the moment down, had patted lightly once the hound's temerity.

"Just like a man," Sam said. "Just like folks. Put off as long as she could having to be brave, knowing all the time that sooner or later she would have to be brave once to keep on living with herself, and knowing all the time beforehand what was going to happen to her when she done it."

That afternoon, himself on the one-eyed wagon mule which did not mind the smell of blood nor, as they told him, of bear, and with Sam on the other one, they rode for more than three hours through the rapid, shortening winter day. They followed no path, no trail even that he could see; almost at once they were in a country which he had never seen before. Then he knew why Sam had made him ride the mule which would not spook. The sound one stopped short and tried to whirl and bolt even as Sam got down, blowing its breath, jerking and wrenching at the rein while Sam held it, coaxing it forward with his voice, since he could not risk tying it, drawing it forward while the boy got down from the marred one.

Then, standing beside Sam in the gloom of the dying afternoon, he looked down at the rotted overturned log, gutted and scored with claw marks and, in the wet earth beside it, the print of the enormous warped two-toed foot. He knew now what he had smelled when he peered under the kitchen where the dogs huddled. He realized for the first time that the bear which had run in his listening and loomed in his dreams since before he could remember to the contrary, and which, therefore, must have existed in the listening and dreams of his father and Major de Spain and even old General Compson, too, before they began to remember in their turn, was a mortal animal, and that if they had departed for the camp each November without any actual hope of bringing its trophy back, it was not because it could not be slain, but because so far they had had no actual hope to.

"Tomorrow," he said.

"We'll try tomorrow," Sam said. "We ain't got the dog yet."

"We've got eleven. They ran him this morning."

"It won't need but one," Sam said. "He ain't here. Maybe he ain't nowhere. The only other way will be for him to run by accident over somebody that has a gun."

"That wouldn't be me," the boy said. "It will be Walter or Major or ——"

"It might," Sam said. "You watch close in the morning. Because he's smart. That's how come he has lived this long. If he gets hemmed up and has to pick out somebody to run over, he will pick out you."

"How?" the boy said. "How will he know ——" He ceased. "You mean he already knows me, that I ain't never been here before, ain't had time to find out yet whether I ——" He ceased again, looking at Sam, the old man whose face revealed nothing until it smiled. He said humbly, not even amazed, "It was me he was watching. I don't reckon he did need to come but once."

The next morning they left the camp three hours before daylight. They rode this time because it was too far to walk, even the dogs in the wagon; again the first gray light found him in a place which he had never seen before, where Sam had placed him and told him to stay and then departed. With the gun which was too big for him, which did not even belong to him, but to Major de Spain, and which he had fired only once—at a stump on the first day, to learn the recoil and how to reload it—he stood against a gum tree beside a little bayou whose black still water crept without movement out of a canebrake and crossed a small clearing and into cane again, where, invisible, a bird—the big woodpecker called Lord-to-God by Negroes—clattered at a dead limb.

It was a stand like any other, dissimilar only in incidentals to the one where he had stood each morning for ten days; a territory new to him, yet no less familiar than that other one which, after almost two weeks, he had come to believe he knew a little—the same solitude, the same loneliness through which human beings had merely passed without altering it, leaving no mark, no scar, which looked exactly as it must have looked when the first ancestor of Sam Fathers' Chickasaw predecessors crept into it and looked about, club or stone ax or bone arrow drawn and poised; different only because, squatting at the edge of the kitchen, he smelled the hounds huddled and cringing beneath it and saw the raked ear and shoulder of the one who, Sam said, had had to be brave once in order to live with herself, and saw yesterday in the earth beside the gutted log the print of the living foot.

He heard no dogs at all. He never did hear them. He only heard the drumming of the woodpecker stop short off and knew that the bear was looking at him. He never saw it. He did not know whether it was in front of him or behind him. He did not move, holding the useless gun, which he had not even had warning to cock and which even now he did not cock, tasting in his saliva that taint as of brass which he knew now because he had smelled it when he peered under the kitchen at the huddled dogs.

Then it was gone. As abruptly as it had ceased, the woodpecker's dry, monotonous clatter set up again, and after a while he even believed he could hear the dogs—a murmur, scarce a sound even, which he had probably been hearing for some time before he even remarked it, drifting into hearing and then out again, dying away. They came nowhere near him. If it was a bear they ran, it was another bear. It was Sam himself who came out of the cane and crossed the bayou, followed by the injured bitch of yesterday. She was almost at heel, like a bird dog, making no sound. She came and crouched against his leg, trembling, staring off into the cane.

"I didn't see him," he said. "I didn't, Sam!"

"I know it," Sam said. "He done the looking. You didn't hear him neither, did you?"

"No," the boy said. "I ——"

"He's smart," Sam said. "Too smart." He looked down at the hound, trembling faintly and steadily against the boy's knee. From the raked shoulder a few drops of fresh blood oozed and clung. "Too big. We ain't got the dog yet. But maybe someday. Maybe not next time. But someday."

So I must see him, he thought. *I must look at him.* Otherwise, it seemed to him that it would go on like this forever, as it had gone on with his father and Major de Spain, who was older than his father, and even with old General Compson, who had been old enough to be a brigade commander in 1865. Otherwise, it would go on so forever, next time and next time, after and after and after. It seemed to him that he could see the two of them, himself and the bear, shadowy in the limbo from which time emerged, becoming time; the old bear absolved of mortality and himself partaking, sharing a little of it, enough of it. And he knew now what he had smelled in the huddled dogs and tasted in his saliva. He recognized fear. *So I will have to see him,* he thought, without dread or even hope. *I will have to look at him.*

It was in June of the next year. He was eleven. They were in camp again, celebrating Major de Spain's and General Compson's birthdays. Although the one had been born in September and the other in the depth of winter and in another decade, they had met for two weeks to fish and shoot squirrels and turkey and run coons and wildcats with the dogs at night. That is, he and Boon Hoggenbeck and the Negroes fished and shot squirrels and ran the coons and cats, because the proved hunters, not only Major de Spain and old General Compson, who spent those two weeks sitting in a rocking chair before a tremendous iron pot of Bruns-

wick stew, stirring and tasting, with old Ash to quarrel with about
how he was making it and Tennie's Jim to pour whisky from the
demijohn into the tin dipper from which he drank it, but even the
boy's father and Walter Ewell, who were still young enough,
scorned such, other than shooting the wild gobblers with pistols
for wagers on their marksmanship.

Or, that is, his father and the others believed he was hunting
squirrels. Until the third day he thought that Sam Fathers believed
that too. Each morning he would leave the camp right after breakfast. He had his own gun now, a Christmas present. He went back
to the tree beside the little bayou where he had stood that morning. Using the compass which old General Compson had given
him, he ranged from that point; he was teaching himself to be
a better-than-fair woodsman without knowing he was doing it. On
the second day he even found the gutted log where he had first
seen the crooked print. It was almost completely crumbled now,
healing with unbelievable speed, a passionate and almost visible
relinquishment, back into the earth from which the tree had
grown.

He ranged the summer woods now, green with gloom; if anything, actually dimmer than in November's gray dissolution,
where, even at noon, the sun fell only in intermittent dappling
upon the earth, which never completely dried out and which
crawled with snakes—moccasins and water snakes and rattlers,
themselves the color of the dappled gloom, so that he would not
always see them until they moved, returning later and later, first
day, second day, passing in the twilight of the third evening the
little log pen enclosing the log stable where Sam was putting up
the horses for the night.

"You ain't looked right yet," Sam said.

He stopped. For a moment he didn't answer. Then he said
peacefully, in a peaceful rushing burst as when a boy's miniature
dam in a little brook gives way, "All right. But how? I went to
the bayou. I even found that log again. I ——"

"I reckon that was all right. Likely he's been watching you.
You never saw his foot?"

"I," the boy said—"I didn't—I never thought ——"

"It's the gun," Sam said. He stood beside the fence, motionless

—the old man, the Indian, in the battered faded overalls and the frayed five-cent straw hat which in the Negro's race had been the badge of his enslavement and was now the regalia of his freedom. The camp—the clearing, the house, the barn and its tiny lot with which Major de Spain in his turn had scratched punily and evanescently at the wilderness—faded in the dusk, back into the immemorial darkness of the woods. *The gun,* the boy thought. *The gun.*

"Be scared," Sam said. "You can't help that. But don't be afraid. Ain't nothing in the woods going to hurt you unless you corner it, or it smells that you are afraid. A bear or a deer, too, has got to be scared of a coward the same as a brave man has got to be."

The gun, the boy thought.

"You will have to choose," Sam said.

He left the camp before daylight, long before Uncle Ash would wake in his quilts on the kitchen floor and start the fire for breakfast. He had only the compass and a stick for snakes. He could go almost a mile before he would begin to need the compass. He sat on a log, the invisible compass in his invisible hand, while the secret night sounds, fallen still at his movements, scurried again and then ceased for good, and the owls ceased and gave over to the waking of day birds, and he could see the compass. Then he went fast yet still quietly; he was becoming better and better as a woodsman, still without having yet realized it.

He jumped a doe and a fawn at sunrise, walked them out of the bed, close enough to see them—the crash of undergrowth, the white scut, the fawn scudding behind her faster than he had believed it could run. He was hunting right, upwind, as Sam had taught him; not that it mattered now. He had left the gun; of his own will and relinquishment he had accepted not a gambit, not a choice, but a condition in which not only the bear's heretofore inviolable anonymity but all the old rules and balances of hunter and hunted had been abrogated. He would not even be afraid, not even in the moment when the fear would take him completely—blood, skin, bowels, bones, memory from the long time before it became his memory—all save that thin, clear, quenchless, immortal lucidity which alone differed him from this bear and from all the other bear and deer he would ever kill in the humility and pride of his skill and endurance, to which Sam had spoken when he leaned in the twilight on the lot fence yesterday.

By noon he was far beyond the little bayou, farther into the new and alien country than he had ever been. He was traveling now not only by the compass but by the old, heavy, biscuit-thick silver watch which had belonged to his grandfather. When he stopped at last, it was for the first time since he had risen from the log at dawn when he could see the compass. It was far enough. He had left the camp nine hours ago; nine hours from now, dark would have already been an hour old. But he didn't think that. He thought, *All right. Yes. But what?* and stood for a moment, alien and small in the green and topless solitude, answering his own question before it had formed and ceased. It was the watch, the compass, the stick—the three lifeless mechanicals with which for nine hours he had fended the wilderness off; he hung the watch and compass carefully on a bush and leaned the stick beside them and relinquished completely to it.

He had not been going very fast for the last two or three hours. He went no faster now, since distance would not matter even if he could have gone fast. And he was trying to keep a bearing on the tree where he had left the compass, trying to complete a circle which would bring him back to it or at least intersect itself, since direction would not matter now either. But the tree was not there, and he did as Sam had schooled him—made the next circle in the opposite direction, so that the two patterns would bisect somewhere, but crossing no print of his own feet, finding the tree at last, but in the wrong place—no bush, no compass, no watch— and the tree not even the tree, because there was a down log beside it and he did what Sam Fathers had told him was the next thing and the last.

As he sat down on the log he saw the crooked print—the warped, tremendous, two-toed indentation which, even as he watched it, filled with water. As he looked up, the wilderness coalesced, solidified—the glade, the tree he sought, the bush, the watch and the compass glinting where a ray of sunlight touched them. Then he saw the bear. It did not emerge, appear; it was just there, immobile, solid, fixed in the hot dappling of the green and windless noon, not as big as he had dreamed it, but as big as he had expected it, bigger, dimensionless against the dappled obscurity, looking at him where he sat quietly on the log and looked back at it.

Then it moved. It made no sound. It did not hurry. It crossed the glade, walking for an instant into the full glare of the sun; when it reached the other side it stopped again and looked back at him across one shoulder while his quiet breathing inhaled and exhaled three times.

Then it was gone. It didn't walk into the woods, the under-growth. It faded, sank back into the wilderness as he had watched a fish, a huge old bass, sink and vanish back into the dark depths of its pool without even any movement of its fins.

He thought, *It will be next fall.* But it was not next fall, nor the next nor the next. He was fourteen then. He had killed his buck, and Sam Fathers had marked his face with the hot blood, and in the next year he killed a bear. But even before that accolade he had become as competent in the woods as many grown men with the same experience; by his fourteenth year he was a better woods-man than most grown men with more. There was no territory within thirty miles of the camp that he did not know—bayou, ridge, brake, landmark tree and path. He could have led anyone to any point in it without deviation, and brought them out again. He knew game trails that even Sam Fathers did not know; in his thirteenth year he found a buck's bedding place, and unbeknown to his father he borrowed Walter Ewell's rifle and lay in wait at dawn and killed the buck when it walked back to the bed, as Sam had told him how the old Chickasaw fathers did.

But not the old bear, although by now he knew its footprint better than he did his own, and not only the crooked one. He could see any one of the three sound ones and distinguish it from any other, and not only by its size. There were other bears within those thirty miles which left tracks almost as large, but this was more than that. If Sam Fathers had been his mentor and the back-yard rabbits and squirrels at home his kindergarten, then the wilderness the old bear ran was his college, the old male bear itself, so long unwifed and childless as to have become its own ungendered progenitor, was his alma mater. But he never saw it.

He could find the crooked print now almost whenever he liked, fifteen or ten or five miles, or sometimes nearer the camp than that. Twice while on stand during the three years he heard the dogs strike its trail by accident; on the second time they jumped it seemingly, the voices high, abject, almost human in hysteria, as on that first morning two years ago. But not the bear itself. He would remember that noon three years ago, the glade, himself and the bear fixed during that moment in the windless and dappled blaze, and it would seem to him that it had never happened, that he had dreamed that too. But it had happened. They had looked at each other, they had emerged from the wilderness old as earth, synchronized to that instant by something more than the blood that moved the flesh and bones which bore them, and touched, pledged something, affirmed something more lasting than the frail web of bones and flesh which any accident could obliterate.

Then he saw it again. Because of the very fact that he thought of nothing else, he had forgotten to look for it. He was still-hunting with Walter Ewell's rifle. He saw it cross the end of a long blow-down, a corridor where a tornado had swept, rushing through rather than over the tangle of trunks and branches as a locomotive would have, faster than he had ever believed it could move, almost as fast as a deer even, because a deer would have spent most of that time in the air, faster than he could bring the rifle sights up to it, so that he believed the reason he never let off the shot was that he was still behind it, had never caught up with it. And now he knew what had been wrong during all the three years. He sat on a log, shaking and trembling as if he had never seen the woods before nor anything that ran them, wondering with incredulous amazement how he could have forgotten the very thing which Sam Fathers had told him and which the bear itself had proved the next day and had now returned after three years to reaffirm.

And he now knew what Sam Fathers had meant about the right dog, a dog in which size would mean less than nothing. So when he returned alone in April—school was out then, so that the sons of farmers could help with the land's planting, and at last his father had granted him permission, on his promise to be back in four days—he had the dog. It was his own, a mongrel of the sort called by Negroes a fyce, a ratter, itself not much bigger than a rat and possessing that bravery which had long since stopped being courage and had become foolhardiness.

It did not take four days. Alone again, he found the trail on the first morning. It was not a stalk; it was an ambush. He timed the meeting almost as if it were an appointment with a human being. Himself holding the fyce muffled in a feed sack and Sam Fathers with two of the hounds on a piece of plowline rope, they lay down wind of the trail at dawn of the second morning. They were so close that the bear turned without even running, as if in surprised amazement at the shrill and frantic uproar of the released fyce, turning at bay against the trunk of a tree, on its hind feet; it seemed to the boy that it would never stop rising, taller and taller, and even the two hounds seemed to take a sort of desperate and despairing courage from the fyce, following it as it went in.

Then he realized that the fyce was actually not going to stop. He flung, threw the gun away, and ran; when he overtook and grasped the frantically pinwheeling little dog, it seemed to him that he was directly under the bear.

He could smell it, strong and hot and rank. Sprawling, he looked up to where it loomed and towered over him like a cloudburst and colored like a thunderclap, quite familiar, peacefully and even lucidly familiar, until he remembered: This was the way he had used to dream about it. Then it was gone. He didn't see it go. He knelt, holding the frantic fyce with both hands, hearing the abased wailing of the hounds drawing farther and farther away, until Sam came up. He carried the gun. He laid it down quietly beside the boy and stood looking down at him.

"You've done seed him twice now with a gun in your hands," he said. "This time you couldn't have missed him."

The boy rose. He still held the fyce. Even in his arms and clear of the ground, it yapped frantically, straining and surging after the fading uproar of the two hounds like a tangle of wire springs. He was panting a little, but he was neither shaking nor trembling now.

"Neither could you!" he said. "You had the gun! Neither did you!"

"And you didn't shoot," his father said. "How close were you?"

"I don't know, sir," he said. "There was a big wood tick inside his right hind leg. I saw that. But I didn't have the gun then."

"But you didn't shoot when you had the gun," his father said. "Why?"

But he didn't answer, and his father didn't wait for him to, rising and crossing the room, across the pelt of the bear which the boy had killed two years ago and the larger one which his father had killed before he was born, to the bookcase beneath the mounted head of the boy's first buck. It was the room which his father called the office, from which all the plantation business was transacted; in it for the fourteen years of his life he had heard the best of all talking. Major de Spain would be there and sometimes old General Compson, and Walter Ewell and Boon Hoggenbeck and Sam Fathers and Tennie's Jim, too, because they, too, were hunters, knew the woods and what ran them.

He would hear it, not talking himself but listening—the wilderness, the big woods, bigger and older than any recorded document of white man fatuous enough to believe he had bought any fragment of it or Indian ruthless enough to pretend that any fragment of it had been his to convey. It was of the men, not white nor black nor red, but men, hunters with the will and hardihood to endure and the humility and skill to survive, and the dogs and the bear and deer juxtaposed and reliefed against it, ordered and compelled by and within the wilderness in the ancient and unremitting contest by the ancient and immitigable rules which voided all regrets and brooked no quarter, the voices quiet and weighty and deliberate for retrospection and recollection and exact remembering, while he squatted in the blazing firelight as Tennie's Jim squatted, who stirred only to put more wood on the fire and to pass the bottle from one glass to another. Because the bottle was always present, so that after a while it seemed to him that those fierce instants of heart and brain and courage and wiliness and speed were concentrated and distilled into that brown liquor which not women, not boys and children, but only hunters drank, drinking not of the blood they had spilled but some condensation of the wild immortal spirit, drinking it moderately, humbly even, not with the pagan's base hope of acquiring thereby the virtues of cunning and strength and speed, but in salute to them.

His father returned with the book and sat down again and opened it. "Listen," he said. He read the five stanzas aloud, his voice quiet and deliberate in the room where there was no fire now because it was already spring. Then he looked up. The boy watched him. "All right," his father said. "Listen." He read again, but only the second stanza this time, to the end of it, the last two lines, and closed the book and put it on the table beside him. " 'She cannot fade, though thou hast not thy bliss, for ever wilt thou love, and she be fair,' " he said.

"He's talking about a girl," the boy said.

"He had to talk about something," his father said. Then he said, "He was talking about truth. Truth doesn't change. Truth is one thing. It covers all things which touch the heart—honor and pride and pity and justice and courage and love. Do you see now?"

He didn't know. Somehow it was simpler than that. There was an old bear, fierce and ruthless, not merely just to stay alive, but with the fierce pride of liberty and freedom, proud enough of that liberty and freedom to see it threatened without fear or even alarm; nay, who at times even seemed deliberately to put that freedom and liberty in jeopardy in order to savor them, to remind his old strong bones and flesh to keep supple and quick to defend and preserve them. There was an old man, son of a Negro slave and an Indian king, inheritor on the one side of the long chronicle of a people who had learned humility through suffering, and pride through the endurance which survived the suffering and injustice, and on the other side, the chronicle of a people even longer in the land than the first, yet who no longer existed in the land at all save in the solitary brotherhood of an old Negro's alien blood and the wild and invincible spirit of an old bear. There was a boy who wished to learn humility and pride in order to become skillful and worthy in the woods, who suddenly found himself becoming so skillful so rapidly that he feared he would never become worthy because he had not learned humility and pride, although he had tried to, until one day and as suddenly he discovered that an old man who could not have defined either had led him, as though by the hand, to that point where an old bear and a little mongrel dog showed him that, by possessing one thing other, he would possess them both.

And a little dog, nameless and mongrel and many-fathered, grown, yet weighing less than six pounds, saying as if to itself, "I can't be dangerous, because there's nothing much smaller than I am; I can't be fierce, because they would call it just noise; I can't be humble, because I'm already too close to the ground to genuflect; I can't be proud, because I wouldn't be near enough to it for anyone to know who was casting that shadow, and I don't even know that I'm not going to heaven, because they have already decided that I don't possess an immortal soul. So all I can be is brave. But it's all right. I can be that, even if they still call it just noise."

That was all. It was simple, much simpler than somebody talking in a book about a youth and a girl he would never need to grieve over, because he could never approach any nearer her and would never have to get any farther away. He had heard about a bear, and finally got big enough to trail it, and he trailed it four years and at last met it with a gun in his hands and he didn't shoot. Because a little dog —— But he could have shot long before the little dog covered the twenty yards to where the bear waited, and Sam Fathers could have shot at any time during that interminable minute while Old Ben stood on his hind feet over them. He stopped. His father was watching him gravely across the springrife twilight of the room; when he spoke, his words were as quiet as the twilight, too, not loud, because they did not need to be because they would last, "Courage, and honor, and pride," his father said, "and pity, and love of justice and of liberty. They all touch the heart, and what the heart holds to becomes truth, as far as we know truth. Do you see now?"

Sam, and Old Ben, and Nip, he thought. And himself too. He had been all right too. His father had said so. "Yes, sir," he said.

The Bear
in Relation to
Faulkner's Other Works

The Historic Ages of Yoknapatawpha County

MILLAR MACLURE

❦

Like the history of Europe, the story of Yoknapatawpha County
is divided into three periods: ancient, medieval and modern. The
antique world is peopled by the Chickasaws, who are in many
ways Faulkner's most successful creations. Remote, immensely
dignified, partners of the wilderness, they accepted the penalties
of ownership, of property in slaves, with comic resignation. Dispossessed, they departed uncorrupted; their symbol, the bear,
remained to be hunted by their successors. The age of chivalry
began with the irruption into the wilderness of the Anglo-Saxon
barbarians, the reckless bandits and daring settlers who founded
the old Southern houses. They and their children established a
feudal order which was destroyed in the Civil War; their symbol,

FROM "William Faulkner," *Queen's Quarterly*, LXIII:3 (Autumn, 1956),
336-7. Reprinted by permission of the author.

the centaur, the man on a horse, persists into modern times, appears for example in the night-ride of Chick Mallison in *Intruder in the Dust*. The modern age began with the Reconstruction; it is dominated by the Snopeses, the parasitic poor-whites whose descendants and allies are the politicians, the cotton-brokers, the twentieth-century despoilers of men and land. The modern symbol is the automobile, which kills old Bayard Sartoris, which carries Temple Drake to her degradation. Ground-bass to these melodies is the constant triad: nigger-mule-land. These endure through the generations, when all that is left of the wilderness is an image in the memory of the old hunter Isaac McCaslin, and the great houses have surrendered to fire and to dust.

Tradition, Moral Confusion, the Negro: Themes in Faulkner's Work

ROBERT PENN WARREN

❦

It is important, I think, that Faulkner's work be regarded not in terms of the South against the North, but in terms of issues which are common to our modern world. The legend is not merely a legend of the South, but is also a legend of our general plight and problem. The modern world is in moral confusion. It does suffer from a lack of discipline, of sanctions, of community of values, of a sense of a mission. It is a world in which self-interest, workableness, success, provide the standards. It is a world which is the victim of abstraction and of mechanism, or at least, at moments, feels itself to be. It can look back nostalgically upon the old world of traditional values and feel loss and perhaps despair—upon the world in which, as one of Faulkner's characters puts it, men "had the gift of living once or dying once instead of being diffused and scattered creatures drawn blindly from a grab bag and assembled"

FROM "William Faulkner," *Selected Essays of Robert Penn Warren* (New York: Random House, 1958), pp. 59-79. Copyright 1946, 1958 by Robert Penn Warren. Reprinted by permission of Random House, Inc.

—a world in which men were, "integer for integer," more simple and complete.

If it be objected that Faulkner's view is unrealistic, that had the old order satisfied human needs it would have survived, and that it is sentimental to hold that it was killed from the outside, the answer is clear in the work: the old order did not satisfy human needs—the Southern old order or any other—for it, not being founded on justice, was "accursed" and held the seeds of its own ruin in itself. But even in terms of the curse the old order, as opposed to the new order (in so far as the new is to be equated with Snopesism), allowed the traditional man to define himself as human by setting up codes, concepts of virtues, obligations, and by accepting the risks of his humanity. Within the traditional order was a notion of truth, even if man in the flow of things did not succeed in realizing that truth. Take, for instance, the pas-sage from "The Bear":

> "All right," he said. "Listen," and read again, but only one stanza this time and closed the book and laid it on the table. "She cannot fade, though thou hast not thy bliss," Mc-Caslin said: "Forever wilt thou love, and she be fair."
>
> "He's talking about a girl," he said.
>
> "He had to talk about something," McCaslin said. Then he said, "He was talking about truth. Truth is one. It doesn't change. It covers all things which touch the heart—honor and pride and pity and justice and courage and love. Do you see now?"

The human effort is what is important, the capacity to make the effort to rise above the mechanical process of life, the pride to endure, for in endurance there is a kind of self-conquest.

When it is said, as it is often said, that Faulkner's work is "backward-looking," the answer is that the constant ethical center is to be found in the glorification of the human effort and of human endurance, which are not in time, even though in modernity they seem to persist most surely among the despised and rejected. It is true that Faulkner's work contains a savage attack on modernity, but it is to be remembered that Elizabethan tragedy, for instance, contained just such an attack on its own special "modernity." (Ambition is the most constant tragic crime, and ambition is the attitude special to an opening society; all villains are rationalists and appeal to "nature" beyond traditional morality for justification, and rationalism is, in the sense implied here, the attitude special to the rise of a secular and scientific order before a new morality can be formulated.)

It is not ultimately important whether the traditional order (Southern or other) as depicted by Faulkner fits exactly the picture which critical historical method provides. Let it be granted, for the sake of discussion, that Faulkner does oversimplify the matter. What is ultimately important, both ethically and artistically, is the symbolic function of that order in relation to the world which is set in opposition to it. The opposition between the old order and the new does not, however, exhaust the picture. What of the order to come? "We will have to wait," old Ike McCaslin says to the mulatto girl who is in love with a white man. A curse may work itself out in time; and in such glimpses, which occur now and then, we get the notion of a grudging meliorism, a practical supplement to the idealism, like Ike McCaslin's, which finds compensation in the human effort and the contemplation of "truth."

The discussion, even at a larger scope and with more satisfactory analysis, of the central theme of Faulkner would not exhaust the interest of his work. In fact, the discussion of this question always runs the risk of making his work appear too schematic, too dry and too complacent when in actual fact it is full of rich detail, of shadings and complexities of attitude, of ironies and ambivalences.

. . . It is slavery, not the Negro, which is defined, quite flatly, as the curse [of the South in Faulkner's novels] over and over again, and the Negro is the black cross in so far as he is the embodiment of the curse, the reminder of the guilt, the incarnation of the problem. That is the basic point. But now and then, as a kind of tangential irony, we have the notion, not of the burden of the white on the black, but of the burden of the black on the white, the weight of obligation, inefficiency, and so on, as well as the weight of guilt (the notion we find in the old story of the plantation mistress who, after the Civil War, said: "Mr. Lincoln thought he was emancipating those slaves, but he was really emancipating me."). For instance, we get hints of this notion in "Red Leaves": one of the Indians, sweating in the chase of the runaway Negro who is to be killed for the Man's funeral, says, "Damn that Negro," and the other Indian replies, "Yao. When have they been anything but a trial and a care to us?" But the black cross is, fundamentally, the weight of the white man's guilt, the white man who now sells salves and potions to "bleach the pigment and straighten the hair of Negroes that they might resemble the very race which for two hundred years had held them in bondage and from which for another hundred years not even a bloody civil war would have set them completely free." The curse is still operative, as the crime is still compounded.

The actual role of the Negro in Faulkner's fiction is consistently one of pathos or heroism. It is not merely, as has been suggested more than once, that Faulkner condescends to the good and faithful servant, the "white folks' nigger." There are figures like Dilsey, but they are not as impressive as the Negro in "Red Leaves" or Sam Fathers who, with the bear, is the hero of "The Bear." The fugitive, who gains in the course of the former story a shadowy symbolic significance, is told in the end by one of the Indians who overtake him, "You ran well. Do not be ashamed," and when he walks among the Indians, he is "the tallest there, his high, close, mud-caked head looming above them all." And Sam Fathers is the fountainhead of the wisdom which Ike McCaslin finally gains, and the repository of the virtues which are central for Faulkner—"an old man, son of a Negro slave and an Indian king, inheritor on the one hand of the long chronicle of a people who had learned humility through suffering and learned pride through the endurance which survived suffering, and on the other side the chronicle of a people even longer in the land than the first, yet who now existed there only in the solitary brotherhood of an old and childless Negro's alien blood and the wild and invincible spirit of an old bear."

Speech of Acceptance upon the Award of the Nobel Prize for Literature

WILLIAM FAULKNER

❧

I feel that this award was not made to me as a man, but to my work—a life's work in all the agony and sweat of the human spirit, not for glory and least of all for profit, but to create out of the materials of the human spirit something which did not exist before. So this award is only mine in trust. It will not be difficult to find a dedication for the money part of it commensurate with the purpose and significance of its origin. But I would like to do the same with the acclaim too, by using this moment as a pinnacle from which I might be listened to by the young men and women already dedicated to the same anguish and travail, among whom is already that one who will some day stand here where I am standing.

Our tragedy today is a general and universal physical fear so long sustained by now that we can even bear it. There are no longer problems of the spirit. There is only the question: When will I be blown up? Because of this, the young man or woman writing today has forgotten the problems of the human heart in conflict with itself which alone can make good writing because only that is worth writing about, worth the agony and the sweat.

He must learn them again. He must teach himself that the basest of all things is to be afraid; and, teaching himself that, forget it forever, leaving no room in his workshop for anything but the old verities and truths of the heart, the old universal truths lacking which any story is ephemeral and doomed—love and honor and pity and pride and compassion and sacrifice. Until he does so, he labors under a curse. He writes not of love but of lust, of defeats in which nobody loses anything of value, of victories without hope and, worst of all, without pity or compassion.

Delivered in Stockholm, December 10, 1950.

His griefs grieve on no universal bones, leaving no scars. He writes not of the heart but of the glands.

Until he relearns these things, he will write as though he stood among and watched the end of man. I decline to accept the end of man. It is easy enough to say that man is immortal simply because he will endure; that when the last ding-dong of doom has clanged and faded from the last worthless rock hanging tideless in the last red and dying evening, that even then there will still be one more sound: that of his puny inexhaustible voice, still talking. I refuse to accept this. I believe that man will not merely endure: he will prevail. He is immortal, not because he alone among creatures has an inexhaustible voice, but because he has a soul, a spirit capable of compassion and sacrifice and endurance. The poet's, the writer's, duty is to write about these things. It is his privilege to help man endure by lifting his heart, by reminding him of the courage and honor and hope and pride and compassion and pity and sacrifice which have been the glory of his past. The poet's voice need not merely be the record of man, it can be one of the props, the pillars to help him endure and prevail.

On Method and Theme in Faulkner

MALCOLM COWLEY

Faulkner's novels have the quality of being lived, absorbed, remembered rather than merely observed. And they have what is rare in the novels of our time, a warmth of family affection, brother for brother and sister, the father for his children—a love so warm and proud that it tries to shut out the rest of the world. Compared with that affection, married love is presented as something calculating, and illicit love as a consuming fire. And because the blood relationship is central in his novels, Faulkner finds it

FROM the Introduction to *The Portable Faulkner* (New York: The Viking Press, 1946), p. 21. Copyright 1946 by Malcolm Cowley. Reprinted by permission of The Viking Press.

hard to create sympathetic characters between the ages of twenty and forty. He is better with children, Negro and white, and incomparably good with older people who preserve the standards that have come down to them "out of the old time, the old days."

FROM *The Hamlet**

WILLIAM FAULKNER

❦

A mile back he had left the rich, broad, flat river-bottom country and entered the hills—a region which topographically was the final blue and dying echo of the Appalachian mountains. Chickasaw Indians had owned it, but after the Indians it had been cleared where possible for cultivation, and after the Civil War, forgotten save by the small peripatetic sawmills which had vanished too now, their sites marked only by the mounds of rotting sawdust which were not only their gravestones but the monuments of a people's heedless greed.

Sam Fathers†

WILLIAM FAULKNER

❦

Quentin Compson describes Sam Fathers, here a carpenter on the Compson farm. Mr. Stokes is the overseer for the Compsons.

He talked like a nigger—that is, he said his words like niggers do, but he didn't say the same words—and his hair was nigger hair.

---

* FROM *The Hamlet* (New York: Random House, 1940), p. 196. Reprinted by permission of Random House, Inc. Copyright 1940 by William Faulkner.
† FROM "A Justice," *Collected Stories of William Faulkner* (New York: Random House, 1950), p. 344. Reprinted by permission of Random House, Inc. Copyright 1931, and renewed 1959, by William Faulkner.

But his skin wasn't quite the color of a light nigger and his nose
and his mouth and chin were not nigger nose and mouth and
chin. And his shape was not like the shape of a nigger when he
gets old. He was straight in the back, not tall, a little broad, and
his face was still all the time, like he might be somewhere else all
the while he was working or when people, even white people,
talked to him, or while he talked to me. It was just the same all
the time, like he might be away up on a roof by himself, driving
nails. Sometimes he would quit work with something half-finished
on the bench, and sit down and smoke. And he wouldn't jump up
and go back to work when Mr. Stokes or even Grandfather came
along.

FROM *Was*

WILLIAM FAULKNER

❧

Isaac McCaslin, 'Uncle Ike', past seventy and nearer eighty than
he ever corroborated any more, a widower now and uncle to half
a county and father to no one

this was not something participated in or even seen by himself,
but by his elder cousin, McCaslin Edmonds, grandson of Isaac's
father's sister and so descended by the distaff, yet notwithstanding
the inheritor, and in his time the bequestor, of that which some
had thought then and some still thought should have been Isaac's,
since his was the name in which the title to the land had first been
granted from the Indian patent and which some of the descendants
of his father's slaves still bore in the land. But Isaac was not one of
these:—a widower these twenty years, who in all his life had
owned but one object more than he could wear and carry in his
pockets and his hands at one time, and this was the narrow iron
cot and the stained lean mattress which he used camping in the

FROM "Was," *Go Down, Moses* (New York: Random House, 1942), p. 34.
Reprinted by permission of Random House, Inc. Copyright 1942 by William
Faulkner.

woods for deer and bear or for fishing or simply because he loved
the woods; who owned no property and never desired to since
the earth was no man's but all men's, as light and air and weather
were; who lived still in the cheap frame bungalow in Jefferson
which his wife's father gave them on their marriage and which his
wife had willed to him at her death and which he had pretended to
accept, acquiesce to, to humor her, ease her going but which was
not his, will or not, chancery dying wishes mortmain possession
or whatever, himself merely holding it for his wife's sister and her
children who had lived in it with him since his wife's death, holding himself welcome to live in one room of it as he had during his
wife's time or she during her time or the sister-in-law and her
children during the rest of his and after

not something he had participated in or even remembered except from the hearing, the listening, come to him through and from
his cousin McCaslin born in 1850 and sixteen years his senior and
hence, his own father being near seventy when Isaac, an only child,
was born, rather his brother than cousin and rather his father than
either, out of the old time, the old days

The Blood Ritual of Isaac McCaslin

WILLIAM FAULKNER

At first there was nothing. There was the faint, cold, steady rain,
the gray and constant light of the late November dawn, with the
voices of the hounds converging somewhere in it and toward them.
Then Sam Fathers, standing just behind the boy as he had been
standing when the boy shot his first running rabbit with his first
gun and almost with the first load it ever carried, touched his
shoulder and he began to shake, not with any cold. Then the buck

FROM "The Old People," *Go Down, Moses* (New York: Random House,
1942), pp. 163-184. Reprinted by permission of Random House, Inc. Copyright 1940 by William Faulkner.

was there. He did not come into sight; he was just there, looking not like a ghost but as if all of light were condensed in him and he were the source of it, not only moving in it but disseminating it, already running, seen first as you always see the deer, in that split second after he has already seen you, already slanting away in that first soaring bound, the antlers even in that dim light looking like a small rocking-chair balanced on his head.

"Now," Sam Fathers said, "shoot quick, and slow."

The boy did not remember that shot at all. He would live to be eighty, as his father and his father's twin brother and their father in his turn had lived to be, but he would never hear that shot nor remember even the shock of the gun-butt. He didn't even remember what he did with the gun afterward. He was running. Then he was standing over the buck where it lay on the wet earth still in the attitude of speed and not looking at all dead, standing over it shaking and jerking, with Sam Fathers beside him again, extending the knife. "Dont walk up to him in front," Sam said. "If he aint dead, he will cut you all to pieces with his feet. Walk up to him from behind and take him by the horn first, so you can hold his head down until you can jump away. Then slip your other hand down and hook your fingers in his nostrils."

The boy did that—drew the head back and the throat taut and drew Sam Fathers' knife across the throat and Sam stooped and dipped his hands in the hot smoking blood and wiped them back and forth across the boy's face. Then Sam's horn rang in the wet gray woods and again and again; there was a boiling wave of dogs about them, with Tennie's Jim and Boon Hogganbeck whipping them back after each had had a taste of the blood, then the men, the true hunters—Walter Ewell whose rifle never missed, and Major de Spain and old General Compson and the boy's cousin, McCaslin Edmonds, grandson of his father's sister, sixteen years his senior and, since both he and McCaslin were only children and the boy's father had been nearing seventy when he was born, more his brother than his cousin and more his father than either—sitting their horses and looking down at them: at the old man of seventy who had been a negro for two generations now but whose face and bearing were still those of the Chickasaw chief who had been his father; and the white boy of twelve with the prints of the bloody hands on his face, who had nothing to do now but stand straight and not let the trembling show.

"Did he do all right, Sam?" his cousin McCaslin said.

"He done all right," Sam Fathers said.

They were the white boy, marked forever, and the old dark man sired on both sides by savage kings, who had marked him, whose bloody hands had merely formally consecrated him to that which, under the man's tutelage, he had already accepted, humbly and joyfully, with abnegation and with pride too; the hands, the touch, the first worthy blood which he had been found at last worthy to draw, joining him and the man forever, so that the man would continue to live past the boy's seventy years and then eighty years, long after the man himself had entered the earth as chiefs and kings entered it;—the child, not yet a man, whose grandfather had lived in the same country and in almost the same manner as the boy himself would grow up to live, leaving his descendants in the land in his turn as his grandfather had done, and the old man past seventy whose grandfathers had owned the land long before the white men ever saw it and who had vanished from it now with all their kind, what of blood they left behind them running now in another race and for a while even in bondage and now drawing toward the end of its alien and irrevocable course, barren, since Sam Fathers had no children. . . .

That was seventy years ago. The Sam Fathers whom the boy knew was already sixty—a man not tall, squat rather, almost sedentary, flabby-looking though he actually was not, with hair like a horse's mane which even at seventy showed no trace of white and a face which showed no age until he smiled, whose only visible trace of negro blood was a slight dullness of the hair and the fingernails, and something else which you did notice about the eyes, which you noticed because it was not always there, only in repose and not always then—something not in their shape nor pigment but in their expression, and the boy's cousin McCaslin told him what that was: not the heritage of Ham, not the mark of servitude but of bondage; the knowledge that for a while that part of his blood had been the blood of slaves. "Like an old lion or a bear in a cage," McCaslin said. "He was born in the cage and has been in it all his life; he knows nothing else. Then he smells something. It might be anything, any breeze blowing past anything and then into his nostrils. But there for a second was the hot sand or the cane-brake that he never even saw himself, might not even know if he did see it and probably does know he couldn't hold his own with it if he got back to it. But that's not what he smells then. It was the cage he smelled. He hadn't smelled the cage until that minute. Then the hot sand or the brake blew into his nostrils and blew away, and all he could smell was the cage. That's what makes his eyes look like that."

"Then let him go!" the boy cried. "Let him go!"

His cousin laughed shortly. Then he stopped laughing, making the sound that is. It had never been laughing. "His cage aint McCaslins," he said. "He was a wild man. When he was born, all his blood on both sides, except the little white part, knew things that had been tamed out of our blood so long ago that we have not only forgotten them, we have to live together in herds to protect ourselves from our own sources. He was the direct son not only of a warrior but of a chief. Then he grew up and began to learn things, and all of a sudden one day he found out that he had been betrayed, the blood of the warriors and chiefs had been betrayed. Not by his father," he added quickly. "He probably never held it against old Doom for selling him and his mother into slavery, because he probably believed the damage was already done before then and it was the same warriors' and chiefs' blood in him and Doom both that was betrayed through the black blood which his mother gave him. Not betrayed by the black blood and not wilfully betrayed by his mother, but betrayed by her all the same, who had bequeathed him not only the blood of slaves but even a little of the very blood which had enslaved it; himself his own battle-ground, the scene of his own vanquishment and the mausoleum of his defeat. His cage aint us," McCaslin said. "Did you ever know anybody yet, even your father and Uncle Buddy, that ever told him to do or not do anything that he ever paid any attention to?" . . .

White man's work, when Sam did work. Because he did nothing else: farmed no allotted acres of his own, as the other ex-slaves of old Carothers McCaslin did, performed no field-work for daily wages as the younger and newer negroes did—and the boy never knew just how that had been settled between Sam and old Carothers, or perhaps with old Carothers' twin sons after him. For, although Sam lived among the negroes, in a cabin among the other cabins in the quarters, and consorted with negroes (what of consorting with anyone Sam did after the boy got big enough to walk alone from the house to the blacksmith-shop and then to carry a gun) and dressed like them and talked like them and even went with them to the negro church now and then, he was still the son of that Chickasaw chief and the negroes knew it. And, it seemed to the boy, not only negroes. Boon Hogganbeck's grandmother had been a Chickasaw woman too, and although the blood had run white since and Boon was a white man, it was not chief's blood. To the boy at least, the difference was apparent immediately you saw Boon and Sam together, and even Boon seemed to know it was there—even Boon, to whom in his tradition it had never occurred that anyone might be better born than himself. A man might be smarter, he admitted that, or richer (luckier, he called it) but not better born. Boon was a mastiff, absolutely faithful, dividing his fidelity equally between Major de Spain and the boy's cousin McCaslin, absolutely dependent for his very bread and dividing that impartially too between Major de Spain and McCaslin, hardy, generous, courageous enough, a slave to all the appetites and almost unratiocinative. In the boy's eyes at least it was Sam Fathers, the negro, who bore himself not only toward his cousin McCaslin and Major de Spain but toward all white men, with gravity and dignity and without servility or recourse to that impenetrable wall of ready and easy mirth which negroes sustain between themselves and white men, bearing himself toward his cousin McCaslin not only as one man to another but as an older man to a younger.

. . . But the solitude did not breathe again. It should have suspired again then but it did not. It was still facing, watching, what it had been watching and it was not here, not where he and Sam stood; rigid, not breathing himself, he thought, cried *No! No!*, knowing already that it was too late, thinking with the old despair

of two and three years ago: *I'll never get a shot.* Then he heard it
—the flat single clap of Walter Ewell's rifle which never missed.
Then the mellow sound of the horn came down the ridge and something went out of him and he knew then he had never expected
to get the shot at all.

"I reckon that's it," he said. "Walter got him." He had raised
the gun slightly without knowing it. He lowered it again and had
lowered one of the hammers and was already moving out of the
thicket when Sam spoke.

"Wait."

"Wait?" the boy cried. And he would remember that—how he
turned upon Sam in the truculence of a boy's grief over the missed
opportunity, the missed luck. "What for? Dont you hear that
horn?"

And he would remember how Sam was standing. Sam had not
moved. He was not tall, squat rather and broad, and the boy had
been growing fast for the past year or so and there was not much
difference between them in height, yet Sam was looking over the
boy's head and up the ridge toward the sound of the horn and the
boy knew that Sam did not even see him; that Sam knew he was
still there beside him but he did not see the boy. Then the boy saw
the buck. It was coming down the ridge, as if it were walking out
of the very sound of the horn which related its death. It was not
running, it was walking, tremendous, unhurried, slanting and tilting its head to pass the antlers through the undergrowth, and the
boy standing with Sam beside him now instead of behind him as
Sam always stood, and the gun still partly aimed and one of the
hammers still cocked.

Then it saw them. And still it did not begin to run. It just
stopped for an instant, taller than any man, looking at them; then
its muscles suppled, gathered. It did not even alter its course, not
fleeing, not even running, just moving with that winged and effort-
less ease with which deer move, passing within twenty feet of
them, its head high and the eye not proud and not haughty but
just full and wild and unafraid, and Sam standing beside the boy
now, his right arm raised at full length, palm-outward, speaking
in that tongue which the boy had learned from listening to him and

Joe Baker in the blacksmith shop, while up the ridge Walter Ewell's horn was still blowing them in to a dead buck.[1]

"Oleh, Chief," Sam said. "Grandfather."

Race at Morning*

WILLIAM FAULKNER

❧

With two others, the narrator, a twelve-year-old boy, has come to hunt in the Big Woods in the same section Uncle Ike McCaslin, Will Legate, Roth Edmonds, and Walter Ewell have come to the day before.

. . . all three of us now turned like one agreement to walk back home, not together in a bunch because we didn't want to worry or tempt one another, because what we had all three spent this morning doing was no play-acting jest for fun, but was serious, and all three of us was still what we was—that old buck that had to run, not because he was skeered, but because running was what he done the best and was proudest at; and Eagle and the dogs that chased him, not because they hated or feared him, but because that was the thing they done the best and was proudest at; and me and Mister Ernest and Dan, that run him not because we wanted his meat, which would be tough to eat anyhow, or his head to hang on a wall, but because now we could go back and work hard for eleven months making a crop, so we would have the right to come back here next November—all three of us going back home now, peaceful and separate, but still side by side, until next year, next time.

. . . all of a sudden I thought about how maybe planting and

---

[1] But, we learn, really a spike buck, nearly a fawn, that Ewell thinks is the big buck, because he killed it in the older deer's tracks. Although Sam and young Ike realize the truth, they do not tell Ewell; later, Ike tells his cousin back in Jefferson.—*Eds.*

* FROM *Big Woods* (New York: Random House, 1935), pp. 188, 195. Reprinted by permission of Random House, Inc. Copyright 1955 by the Curtis Publishing Company.

working and then harvesting oats and cotton and beans and hay wasn't jest something me and Mister Ernest done three hundred and fifty-one days, to fill in the time until we could come back hunting again, but it was something we had to do, and do honest and good during the three hundred and fifty-one days, to have the right to come back into the big woods and hunt for the other fourteen; and the fourteen days that old buck run in front of dogs wasn't jest something to fill his time until the three hundred and fifty-one when he didn't have to, but the running and the risking in front of guns and dogs was something he had to do for fourteen days to have the right not to be bothered for the other three hundred and fifty-one. And so the hunting and the farming wasn't two different things at all—they was jest the other side of each other.

Boon Hogganbeck

WILLIAM FAULKNER

❧

This account is given by Lucius Priest, a descendant of the Mc-Caslins, who refers to Ike as "Cousin Ike." The actual relationship between Lucius and Ike is unclear.

[Boon's] grandmother had been the daughter of one of old Issetibbeha's Chickasaws who married a white whiskey trader; at times, depending on the depth of his cups, Boon would declare himself to be at least ninety-nine one-hundredths Chickasaw and in fact a lineal royal descendant of old Issetibbeha himself; the next time he would offer to fight any man who dared even intimate that he had one drop of Indian blood in his veins.

He was tough, faithful, brave and completely unreliable; he was six feet four inches tall and weighed two hundred and forty pounds and had the mentality of a child. . . .

FROM *The Reivers* (New York: Random House, 1962), pp. 19-23. © Copyright 1962 by William Faulkner. Reprinted by permission of Random House, Inc.

In fact, although he was obviously a perfectly normal flesh-and-blood biological result (vide the moments in his cups when he was not merely ready and willing but even eager to fight any man or men either pro or con, depending on how the drink had taken him, for the right to ancestry) and hence he had to have been somewhere during those first nine or ten or eleven years, it was as if Boon had been created whole and already nine or ten or eleven years old, by the three of us, McCaslin-De Spain-Compson, as a solution to a dilemma one day at Major de Spain's hunting camp. . . .

But then, when Boon materialized at the camp one day, full panoplied and already ten or eleven or twelve years old, there were only twenty miles for Major de Spain and General Compson and McCaslin Edmonds and Walter Ewell and old Bob Legate and the half-dozen others who would come and go, to travel. But General Compson, although he had commanded troops not too unsuccessfully as a colonel at Shiloh, and again not too unsuccessfully as a brigadier during Johnston's retreat on Atlanta, was a little short in terrain, topography, and would promptly get lost ten minutes after he left camp (the mule he preferred to ride would have brought him back at any time but, not only a paroled Confederate general but a Compson too, he declined to accept counsel or advice from a mule), so as soon as the last hunter was in from the morning's drive, everyone would take turns blowing a horn until General Compson at last got in. Which was satisfactory, anyway served, until General Compson's hearing began to fail too. Until finally one afternoon Walter Ewell and Sam Fathers, who was half Negro and half Chickasaw Indian, had to track him down and camp in the woods with him all night, facing Major de Spain with the alternative of either forbidding him to leave the tent or expelling him from the club, when lo, there was Boon Hogganbeck, already a giant, even at ten or eleven already bigger than General Compson, whose nurse he became—a waif, who seemed to have nothing and know nothing but his name; even Cousin Ike is not sure whether it was McCaslin Edmonds or Major de Spain who found Boon first where whoever bore him had abandoned him. All Ike knows—remembers—is that Boon was already there, about twelve years old, out at old Carothers Mc-

Caslin's place, where McCaslin Edmonds was already raising Ike as if he was his father and now and without breaking stride took over Boon too as though he had been Boon's father also, though at that time McCaslin Edmonds himself was only thirty.

Anyway, as soon as Major de Spain realized that he must either expel General Compson from the club, which would be difficult, or forbid him to leave the camp, which would be impossible, and hence he must equip General Compson with something resembling a Boon Hogganbeck, there was the Boon Hogganbeck, produced either by McCaslin Edmonds or perhaps by both of them— Edmonds and De Spain himself—in simultaneous crisis. Ike could remember that: the loading of the bedding and guns and food into the wagon on the fourteenth of November, with Tennie's Jim (grandfather of this Bobo Beauchamp of whom you will hear presently) and Sam Fathers and Boon (he, Ike, was only five or six then; another four or five years before he would be ten and could make one also) and McCaslin himself riding ahead on the horse, to the camp where each morning Boon would follow General Compson on a second mule until by simple force probably, since at twelve Boon was already bigger than his charge, Boon would compel him to the right direction in time to reach camp before dark.

Thus General Compson made a woodsman of Boon despite himself, you might say, in simple self-defense. But even eating at the same table and ranging the same woods and sleeping in the same rain even with Walter Ewell never made a marksman of him; one of the camp's favorite stories was about Boon's shooting, told by Walter Ewell: of being on a stand where he had left Boon (old General Compson had gone to his fathers at last—or to whatever bivouac old soldiers of that war, blue or gray either, probably insisted on going to since probably no place would suit them for anything resembling a permanent stay—and now Boon was a regular hunter like anybody else) and of hearing the hounds and realising that the deer was going to cross at Boon's stand, then of hearing the five shots from Boon's ramshackle pump gun (General Compson had bequeathed it to him; it had never been in the best condition while Compson owned it and Walter said his real surprise was that the gun had fired even twice without jam-

ming, let alone five times) and then Boon's voice across the woods
between them: "God damn! Yonder he goes! Head him! Head
him!" And how he—Walter—hurried across to Boon's stand and
found the five exploded shells on the ground and not ten paces
away the prints of the running buck which Boon had not even
touched.

The Cultural Roots of
The Bear

How to Catch Bears (*Twenyucis's Dream*)

FRANK G. SPECK AND JESSE MOSES

❧

This "dream" is from a text composed by Nekatcit or Nicodemus Peters, "an Indian sage of the Delaware Nation," and represents his memory of the Bear Sacrifice Ceremony of the Munsee-Mahican branches of the Eastern Woodlands people. It was collected along with other traditions in the Hudson Valley in 1932-1938.

Twenyucis had a dream. Then she told the chief, about the time of the new moon when we celebrate the feast, "I know where the bear is living. So you call these young men to go and bring the bear." The chief went and brought Maxkok. The chief told Maxkok, "Twelve men will go with you. All twelve men of the Big House." Then Twenyucis told Maxkok, "Very near daybreak you will reach there. Then you will see a little creek which runs by. And the tree standing there is an oak. A little hole will be visible. Then the bear's nose will appear as though it comes out of the

FROM *The Celestial Bear Comes Down to Earth* (Reading, Pa., 1945), pp. 61-62. Reprinted by permission of the Reading Public Museum and Art Gallery.

hole pushed through, his nose icy about the edge. Do not bring him. That is not a good one, it is a smooth bear. You will go on, down past him. Then you will see an elm tree leaning toward the east. Then you will look up. You will see a hole. That is the bear's home. Thence you cannot come back. There, accordingly, you stay all night. And then standing by that tree there, you are all standing around. Then you hit that tree standing up with your bow on that tree. Three times you will hit that tree. You tell the bear, 'I find you.' Then nothing will be heard. Then also you hit that tree three times. Tell the bear, 'I find you.' "

Then they heard him moving about. Once more the tree was hit. He told him. "You we have found." All these men look upward. All saw the bear's head sticking out. Then Maxkok told the bear, "Come down! The chief wants your body." Then that bear climbed down. Then that bear came down on the ground. Then that bear let his head hang down on the ground. "Surely like a dog he was ashamed of something." Maxkok told the bear, "The chief wants your body." Then he told the bear to turn around. Then that bear turned around. Maxkok told this bear, "That's enough." He told him, "Now you go and take the lead." The bear went on ahead. Then these men all came behind him. Then they reached the little creek here. Then that bear lay down. Maxkok told him, "What is wrong? Get up!" Truly that bear did not move. Then Maxkok told these men, "The bear will come to the Big House." Then Maxkok appointed one man. He told him, "So, you will tell the chief that the bear refuses to come. You will go there yourself." Then the chief came there. Then Maxkok told him, "The bear will not come to the Big House. So no more will there be a feast dance. Therefore you will have to kill the bear right here." Then the chief told the bear, "Right here we will have to kill you. We want your body for the Big House." Then that bear got up. His head was still hanging down on the ground, his eyes were closed. The chief hit him. Then he died. He never kicked. Then these men skinned him. Then that Maxkok picked up the bear skin. He gave it to the chief. Then the chief told these men, "Now will we go to the Big House. You men carry the bear. We, with the dead bear, will take the lead. You will come behind."

Then they reached the Big House. Then they went into the Big

House, to the middle of the building. Then they lowered that bear on the ground.

Then that chief untied the old bear hide and put the old bear hide down on the ground. Then he wrapped the new hide around the center post, a little below where these False Faces were hanging. Then that chief told the woman and one appointed man, "You cut up that bear. Help these women in the cooking."

Then that chief stood in the center of the house. "Therefore indeed we are thankful, all of us, that God should help us. All of us people, we should help one another, that we do not steal, not to steal your brother's wife."

Then all of us people came into the Big House. A new moon elevated as high as the tree tops sets and goes down. Then the chief stands right in the middle of the floor of the Big House and talks to these people. He tells them, "All be good to one another, do not cheat one's living companions." Then the moon goes down. Then the chief tells them, "Go home, don't be trifling, be good to one another."

FROM *Bear Ceremonialism in the Northern Hemisphere*

A. IRVING HALLOWELL

❧

Eastern Woodlands Area.—When a bear is discovered in its winter retreat, or attacked in the woods, it is customary among the Algonkian tribes to dispatch the animal by means of a spear or an axe. Although one might expect that upon the introduction of firearms and steel traps, such methods would have fallen into almost immediate decadence, such was not actually the case. Contemporary practice, as well as traditional testimony indicates the use of the more primitive weapons in many instances, even when guns are

FROM *Bear Ceremonialism in the Northern Hemisphere* (Philadelphia: University of Pennsylvania Press, 1926), pp. 33-35, 75-76. Reprinted by permission of the author.

available. This appears to be due to an inhibition which, although difficult to define except in rather vague terms, seems, nevertheless, to be connected with the whole ideology of which the bear is the focus. It is simply the feeling, conserved from a remote past, perhaps, that in killing a bear the most appropriate weapon for the task must be one of an aboriginal type. The Montagnais-Naskapi as well as the Penobscot, for example, consider it proper to strike the animal with an axe as it emerges from its den. In the old days the latter people say that sometimes the bear would be attacked in the open by three or four hunters, armed only with their knives lashed on canoe poles or staves. After the animal was brought to bay and surrounded, one of them would throw a freshly cut balsam branch into the beast's clutches. This served to confuse the bear who would start to maul it, giving the hunters time to run him through. If the animal turned in one direction a man from the opposite side would attack, and so on until the bear was overcome.

Among the northern Saulteaux there is a specific prohibition upon shooting bears in their winter lairs. Custom prescribes that the animal be killed by a blow on the head with a club as it emerges from its refuge. Among the Cree, "in the old days, the hunters engaged the bear in hand to hand conflicts and clubbed it to death, for the bow and arrows were not considered strong enough weapons." "Even at present," Skinner says, "bears caught in steel traps are sometimes killed by striking them over the head with an axe, although they are usually shot." For the central Algonkian generally, there is traditional information, so Mr. Skinner tells me, to the effect that good sportsmanship dictated that the bear should be attacked only with weapons such as the spear or axe. There was no taboo upon other instruments of the chase, but, because the bear was considered such an unusual sort of animal, it was thought that the use of these weapons was the manly way of attacking the beast. One met it on more common ground, as it were, by this manner of combat. . . .

The account which Curtis gives of the Kwakiutl is also worth quoting. The procedure closely parallels that given by Jewitt, although several details of interest are added. It is to be noted that he states that the ceremony follows the killing of the *first* bear of the season. "The hunter," he says, "would bring it to the village, and while yet a short distance away he would call, 'I have a visitor!' Then all of the people very solemnly and quietly would assemble in his house. The bear was placed in a sitting posture in the place of honor at the middle of the back part of the room, with a ring of cedar bark about its neck and eagle down on its head. Food was then given to each person and a portion was placed before the bear. Great solemnity prevailed. The bear was treated as an honored guest, and was so addressed in the speeches. The people, one by one, would advance and take its paws in their hands as if uttering a supplication. After the ceremonial meal was over, the bear was skinned and prepared for food." Another Kwakiutl procedure is described as follows: "When a black bear is killed, the hunter steps up to it and says: 'Thank you, friend, for meeting me. I did not do any harm to you. You came to meet me sent by our creator that I should shoot you that I may eat together with my wife and friend.' Thus he says and after he has said this he turns the bear over and places the blade of the knife at the chin of the bear and pretends to cut it. This is repeated three times. The fourth time he really cuts. He takes off the skin. Then he takes the skin with the right hand at the head and with the left hand at the small of the back, holds up the skin, and if it is a female bear he will say, 'Now, friend, call your husband to come to me also.' Then he throws down the skin on the body of the bear. He takes it up again and says, 'Now call your father to come here also.' Again he throws down the skin and says, holding it up, 'Oh friend, call your mother to come here also.' Then he throws down the skin on the body. He holds up the skin and says, 'Now call your children to come here also,' and throws down the skin on the body. Then the hunter himself answers his prayer saying, 'I am going to do so.' "

The Pattern of Initiation

Mircea Eliade

❦

Everywhere one meets with mysteries of initiation, and everywhere, even in the most archaic societies, they include the symbolism of a death and a new birth. We cannot here undertake a historical analysis of initiation—such as might enable us to elucidate the relations between this and that cultural structure and the types of initiation—but let us retain at least certain characteristic features that are common to the majority of these secret ceremonies.

(1) Everywhere the mystery begins with the separation of the neophyte from his family, and a "retreat" into the forest. In this there is already a symbolisation of death; the forest, the jungle and the darkness symbolise "the beyond," the Shades. In certain places it is believed that a tiger comes and carries the candidates into the jungle on its back; the wild animal incarnates the mythical Ancestor, the Master of the initiation who conducts the adolescents to the Shades. In other places the neophyte is supposed to be swallowed by a monster—an initiatory motif that will claim our attention later on: for the moment we are concerned with the symbolism of darkness. In the belly of the monster it is cosmic Night; this is the embryonic mode of existence, both upon the plane of the cosmos and on the plane of human life.

(2) In many regions, there is a hut for initiations in the bush. It is there that young candidates undergo a part of their ordeals and are instructed in the secret traditions of the tribe. And the initiation-cabin symbolises the maternal womb.[1] The death of the neophyte signifies a regression to the embryonic state, but this

---

FROM *Myths, Dreams, and Mysteries* (New York: Harper & Bros., 1960), pp. 197-200. Reprinted by permission of Harper & Row, Publishers, Incorporated, New York.

[1] R. Thurnwald, "Primitive Initiations- und Wiedergeburtsriten," p. 393. See also Frazer, *Spirits of the Corn*, I, pp. 225ff.

must not be understood only in terms of human physiology but also, and chiefly, in cosmological terms; the fœtal condition is equivalent to a temporary regression into the *virtual,* or precosmic mode of being before "the dawn of the first day" as the Karadjeri say. We shall have an opportunity to return to this multivalent symbol of a new birth expressed in terms of gestation. For the present, let us add this: the candidate's regression to the pre-natal stage is meant to render him contemporary with the creation of the world. He now lives no longer in the maternal womb as he did before his biological birth, but in the cosmic Night and in expectation of the "dawn"—that is, of the Creation. To become a new man, he has to re-live the cosmology.

(3) Other rituals throw light upon the symbolism of the initiatory death. Among certain peoples, the candidates are buried or laid out in newly dug graves. They are either covered with branches, and remain motionless like the dead; or they are rubbed with a white powder to make them look like ghosts. The neophytes also imitate the behaviour of ghosts: they do not use their fingers in eating, but pick up the food directly with the teeth as the souls of the dead are believed to do. Finally, the tortures that they undergo, and which of course have a multitude of meanings, have this one among others: the tortured and mutilated neophyte is supposed to be tortured, dismembered, boiled or grilled by the demon-masters of initiation—that is by the mythic Ancestors. His physical sufferings correspond to the situation of the man who is "eaten" by the demonic wild animal, is cut to pieces between the jaws of that initiatory monster and is digested in his belly. The initiates' mutilations, too, are charged with a symbolism of death. The majority of those mutilations come under the lunar deities. Now, the Moon disappears—that is, dies—periodically, to be born again three nights later; and this lunar symbolism stresses the idea that death is the first condition of all mystical regeneration.

(4) Besides specific operations—such as circumcision and subincision—and apart from initiatory mutilations (extractions of teeth, amputations of fingers, etc.), there are other external marks of death and resurrection, such as tattooings and scarifications. As for the symbolism of the mystical rebirth, it presents itself in

many forms. The candidates are given new names which for the future are to be their real names. In certain tribes, the young initiates are deemed to have forgotten all their previous lives; immediately after initiation they are fed like little children, led by the hand and taught how to behave in every way, as though they were babies. In the bush, they generally learn a new language, or at least a secret vocabulary known only to the initiates. Thus, we see, at an initiation everything begins anew. *Incipit vita nova.* Sometimes the symbolism of the "second birth" is expressed in concrete gestures. Among some Bantu peoples the boy who is to be circumcised is the object of a ceremony known explicitly as "being born anew." [2] The father sacrifices a ram; and three days later he envelops the child in the animal's stomach-membrane and in its skin. Before being thus attired, the child has to climb into the bed beside his mother and cry like a new-born infant. He remains in the ram's skin for three days and, on the fourth, the father cohabits with his wife. Among these same people, the dead are buried in rams' skins and in the embryonic position. We will say no more here about the symbolism of the mystical rebirth for which one is ritually dressed in the skin of an animal—a symbolism that is attested both in ancient Egypt and in India. [3]

(5) Finally, we must say a few words about another motif which appears in a great many initiations, and not always in the most primitive societies. It concerns the injunction to kill a man. Here, for instance, is what happens among the Papuan Koko. [4] The candidate has first to undergo ordeals analogous to those of any other initiation—prolonged fasting, solitude, tortures, the revelation of the bull-roarer and traditional instruction. But in the end they say to him: "Now you have seen the Spirit, and you are a real man. In order to prove that in your own eyes, you must

---

[2] M. Canney, "The Skin of Rebirth," in *Man*, July, 1939, No. 91, pp. 104-105; *cf.* C. W. Hobley, *Bantu Beliefs and Magic*, London, 1922, pp. 78ff. and 98ff.

[3] *Cf.* E. A. Wallis Budge, *From Fetish to God in Ancient Egypt*, Oxford, 1934, p. 494; S. Stevenson, *The Rites of the Twice-born*, London, 1920, pp. 33, 40, etc.

[4] E. W. P. Chinnery and W. N. Beaver, "Notes on the Initiation Ceremony of the Koko; Papua" in *Journal of the Royal Anthropological Institute*, No. 45, 1915 (pp. 69-78), especially pp. 76ff.

slay a man." Head-hunting, and certain forms of cannibalism, are parts of the same initiatory schema. Before pronouncing a moral judgment upon these customs, one should remember this—that to kill a man, and eat him or preserve his head as a trophy, is to imitate the behaviour of the Spirits, or of the gods. Thus, replaced in its own context, the act is a religious one, a ritual. The neophyte must kill a man because the god did so before him; furthermore he, the neophyte, has just been killed by the god during initiation; he has known death. He has to repeat what has been revealed to him: the mystery instituted by the gods in mythic times.

We have alluded to this type of ritual because it has played a very great part in military initiations, above all in proto-historical Europe. The warrior hero is not only a killer of dragons and other monsters; he is also a killer of men. The heroic duel is a sacrifice: war is a decadent ritual in which a holocaust of innumerable victims is offered up to the gods of victory.

An Indian Boy's Initiation into Manhood in the Omaha Tribe

A. C. FLETCHER AND F. LAFLESCHE

In the ceremony of cutting the hair the priest in charge gathered a tuft from the crown of the boy's head, tied it, then cut it off and laid it away in a parfleche case, which was kept as a sacred repository, singing as he cut the lock a ritual song explanatory of the action. The severing of the lock was an act that implied the consecration of the life of the boy to Thunder, the symbol of the power that controlled the life and death of the warrior—for every man had to be a warrior in order to defend the home and the tribe. The ritual song which followed the cutting of the lock indi-

FROM *The Omaha Tribe* (Bureau of American Ethnology, 27th Annual Report, Washington, 1911), pp. 122-132 (excerpts). Reprinted by permission of the Bureau of American Ethnology, Smithsonian Institution.

cated the acceptance of the offering made; that is, the life of the warrior henceforth was under the control of the Thunder to prolong or to cut short at will. . . .

From this ritual song we learn that the lock laid away in the sacred case in care of the Thunder priest symbolically was sent to the Thunder god dwelling "far above on high," who was ceremonially addressed as "Grandfather"—the term of highest respect in the language. The hair of a person was popularly believed to have a vital connection with the life of the body, so that anyone becoming possessed of a lock of hair might work his will on the individual from whom it came. In ceremonial expressions of grief the throwing of locks of hair upon the dead was indicative of the vital loss sustained. In the light of customs that obtained among the people, the hair, under certain conditions, might be said to typify life. Because of the belief in the continuity of life a part could stand for the whole, so in this rite by the cutting off of a lock of the boy's hair and giving it to the Thunder the life of the child was given into the keeping of the god. It is to be noted that later, when the hair was suffered to grow on the boy's head, a lock on the crown of the head was parted in a circle from the rest of the hair and kept constantly distinct and neatly braided. Upon this lock the war honors of the warrior were worn, and it was this lock that was cut from the head of a slain enemy and formed the central object in the triumph ceremonies, for the reason that it preeminently represented the life of the man who had been slain in battle. . . .

The next stage in the life of the Omaha youth was marked by the rite known by the name of $No^{n'}zhi^{n}zho^{n}$. The literal meaning of the word is "to stand sleeping"; it here implies that during the rite the person stands as if oblivious of the outward world and conscious only of what transpires within himself, his own mind. This rite took place at puberty, when the mind of the child had "become white." This characterization was drawn from the passing of night into day. It should be remembered that in native symbolism night is the mother of day; so the mind of the new-born child is dark, like the night of its birth; gradually it begins to discern and remember things as objects seen in the early dawn; finally it is able to remember and observe discriminatingly; then its mind is said to be "white," as with the clear light of day. At the period when the youth is at the verge of his conscious individual life, is "old enough to know sorrow," it was considered time that through the rite No$^{n'}$zhi^{n}zho^n he should enter into personal relations with the mysterious power that permeates and controls all nature as well as his own existence. . . .

Four days and nights the youth was to fast and pray provided he was physically able to bear so long a strain. No matter how hungry he became, he was forbidden to use the bow and arrows put into his hands by his father when he left his home for this solitary test of endurance. When he fell into a sleep or a trance, if he saw or heard anything, that thing was to become a special medium through which the youth could receive supernatural aid. . . .

When going forth to fast, the youth went silently and unobserved. No one accosted him or gave him counsel or direction. He passed through his experience alone, and alone he returned to his father's lodge. No one asked him of his absence, or even mentioned the fact that he had been away. For four days he must rest, eat little, and speak little. After that period he might go to an old and worthy man who was known to have had a similar vision. After eating and smoking with the old man, when they were quite alone it was permitted the youth to mention that he had had a vision like that of his host, of beast, or bird, or whatever it might have been. Should he speak of his vision before the expiration of the four days, it would be the same as lost to him. After the youth had spoken to the old man it became his duty to travel until he should meet the animal or bird seen in his vision, when he had to slay it, and preserve either the whole or a part of its body. This trophy became the visible sign of his vision and the most sacred of his possessions. He might wear it on his scalp lock or elsewhere on his person during sacred festivals, when going to war, or on some other important occasions. This article has been spoken of by some writers as the man's "personal totem." When the vision came in the form of a cloud or the sound of the thunder, these were symbolized by certain objects or were typified in designs painted on the man or on his belongings.

Some visions were regarded as "lucky," as giving special and

helpful advantages to the man. Hawks were "lucky"—they helped
to success and prowess in war. Bears, being slow and clumsy, were
"not so good," although possessing great recuperative power. The
elk was fleet. Snakes were "not good," etc.

A Girls' Initiation Ceremony Among the Bemba
of Northern Rhodesia

AUDREY I. RICHARDS

❀

CALENDAR OF EVENTS AT CHISUNGU
PERFORMED AT CHINSALI, NORTH-EASTERN
RHODESIA, IN 1931

1st Day   *Entry into the hut* (*Ukuingishya*).
> The blessing of the girls.
> The hiding of the girls (*ukusakila*).
> The first jump.
> The first triumphant return to the village.
> The teasing of the girls.

7th Day   *The first woodland ceremony.*
> The gardening mimes.
> Honouring the *musuku* tree.
> Preparation of the emblem bundles.
> First appearance of the mock bridegrooms.
> Bringing the firewood back to the village.
> *The hut ceremonies.*
> The first test of maturity (*njelele*).
> The girls made free to offer food.
> The ritual lighting of the girls' fire.
> The setting on of the girls' pot.
> The ritual cooking of the seeds (*namushimwa*).

8th Day   *The painting of the wall designs.*

FROM *Chisingu* (New York: Grove Press, 1956), pp. 110-111. Reprinted
by permission of Faber and Faber, Ltd., Publishers, London.

9th Day	*The modelling of the sun rays.*
	The modelling of the brother and sister and the bed.
10th Day	*The modelling of the guinea-fowl.*
11th Day	*The festive porridge eating.*
	The girls made free to eat food.
	The washing of the husband's hands.
13th Day	*The modelling of the snake.*
	The modelling of the fool.
14th Day	*The whitening magic.*
	Blessing of the ancestral spirits.
15th Day	*Modelling of the shelter.*
	Modelling of the screen.
17th Day	*The second woodland ceremony.*
	The honouring of the *mwenge* tree.
	The beer rite.
	The preparation of the jumping hoop.
	The triumphant return of the lion-killers.
	The final jump (ukushimpa umupeto).
	The modelling of the lion.
	Arrival of the blind bridegroom.
	The presentation of the pottery emblems.
	The bridegroom with the bow and arrow.
	The second test of maturity—killing of the chicken.
18th Day	*The communal eating of the chickens.*
	The bathing of the girls.
19th Day	*Obeisance of the bride to the village.*
23rd Day	*The congratulation ceremony (ukushikula).*

FROM *The Mind of the South*

W. J. CASH

❧

The Southerner, however, was primarily a direct product of the soil, as the peasant of Europe is the direct product of the soil. His way of life was his, not—John Crowe Ransom to the contrary notwithstanding—as one "considered and authorized," not because he himself or his ancestors or his class had deliberately chosen it as against something else, not even because it had been tested through centuries and found to be good, but because, given his origins, it was the most natural outcome of the conditions in which he found himself.

The whole difference can be summed up in this: that, though he galloped to hounds in pursuit of the fox precisely as the squire did, it was for quite other reasons. It was not that hoary and so-phisticated class tradition dictated it as the proper sport for gen-tlemen. It was not even, in the first place, that he knew that Eng-lish squires so behaved, and hungered to identify himself with them by imitation, though this of course was to play a great part in confirming and fixing the pattern. It was simply and primarily for the same reason that, in his youth and often into late man-hood, he ran spontaneous and unpremeditated foot-races, wres-tled, drank Gargantuan quantities of raw whisky, let off wild yells, and hunted the possum:—because the thing was already in his mores when he emerged from the backwoods, because on the frontier it was the obvious thing to do, because he was a hot, stout fellow, full of blood and reared to outdoor activity, because of a primitive and naïve zest for the pursuit in hand.

I do not forget the Virginians and their artificializing influence. I shall have, indeed, presently to report our Southerner as devel-oping a striking self-consciousness and as growing somewhat more

FROM *The Mind of the South* (New York: Alfred A. Knopf, 1941), pp. 43-44, 46, 55-58, 63-64, 73-74, 94-95, 137, 425-426. Reprinted by permis-sion of Alfred A. Knopf, Inc. Copyright 1941 by Alfred A. Knopf, Inc.

complex. But this is what he almost invariably was in the begin- ning, and what he remained at bottom right down to the end. This simple, rustic figure is the true center from which the Old South proceeded—the frame about which the conditions of the planta- tion threw up the whole structure of the Southern mind.

Inevitably, then, the dominant trait of this mind was an intense individualism—in its way, perhaps the most intense individualism the world has seen since the Italian Renaissance and its men of "terrible fury." The simple man in general invariably tends to be an individualist. Everywhere and invariably his fundamental atti- tude is purely personal—and purely self-asserting. . . .

And what is true of the planter is true also, *mutatis mutandis,* for the poorer whites under this plantation order. The farmers and the crackers were in their own way self-sufficient too—as fiercely careful of their prerogatives of ownership, as jealous of their sway over their puny domains, as the grandest lord. No man felt or acknowledged any primary dependence on his fellows, save perhaps in the matter of human sympathy and entertainment— always a pressing one in a wide and lonely land. . . .

And when to that was added the natural effect on the planters of virtually unlimited sway over their bondsmen, and the natural effect on the common whites of the example of these planters, it eventuated in this: that the individualism of the plantation world would be one which, like that of the backcountry before it, would be far too much concerned with bald, immediate, unsupported assertion of the ego, which placed too great stress on the inviola- bility of personal whim, and which was full of the chip-on-shoul- der swagger and brag of a boy—one, in brief, of which the es- sence was the boast, voiced or not, on the part of every South- erner, that he would knock hell out of whoever dared to cross him.

This character is of the utmost significance. For its corollary was the perpetuation and acceleration of the tendency to violence which had grown up in the Southern backwoods as it naturally grows up on all frontiers. Other factors, some of which we shall glance at later on, played their part in perpetuating and elaborat- ing this pattern, too. But none was more decisive than this one. However careful they might be to walk softly, such men as these of the South were bound to come often into conflict. And being what they were—simple, direct, and immensely personal—and their world being what it was—conflict with them could only mean immediate physical clashing, could only mean fisticuffs, the gouging ring, and knife and gun play.

Nor was it only private violence that was thus perpetuated. The Southerner's fundamental approach carried over into the realm of public offenses as well. What the direct willfulness of his individualism demanded, when confronted by a crime that aroused his anger, was immediate satisfaction for itself—catharsis for personal passion in the spectacle of a body dancing at the end of a rope or writhing in the fire—now, within the hour—and not some ponderous abstract justice in a problematic tomorrow. And so, in this world of ineffective social control, the tradition of vigilante action, which normally lives and dies with the frontier, not only survived but grew so steadily that already long before the Civil War and long before hatred for the black man had begun to play any direct part in the pattern (of more than three hundred persons said to have been hanged or burned by mobs between 1840 and 1860, less than ten per cent were Negroes) the South had become peculiarly the home of lynching.

But if I show you Southern individualism as eventuating in violence, if I imply that the pride which was its root was in some sense puerile, I am very far from suggesting that it ought to be held in contempt. For it reached its ultimate incarnation in the Confederate soldier.

To the end of his service this soldier could not be disciplined. He slouched. He would never learn to salute in the brisk fashion so dear to the hearts of the professors of mass murder. His "Cap'n" and his "Gin'ral" were likely to pass his lips with a grin —were charged always with easy, unstudied familiarity. He could and did find it in himself to jeer openly and unabashed in the face of Stonewall Jackson when that austere Presbyterian captain rode along his lines. And down to the final day at Appomattox his officers knew that the way to get him to execute an order without malingering was to flatter and to jest, never to command too brusquely and forthrightly. And yet—and yet—and by virtue of precisely these unsoldierly qualities, he was, as no one will care to deny, one of the world's very finest fighting men.

Allow what you will for *esprit de corps,* for this or for that, the thing that sent him swinging up the slope at Gettysburg on that celebrated, gallant afternoon was before all else nothing more or less than the thing which elsewhere accounted for his violence —was nothing more or less than his conviction, the conviction of every farmer among what was essentially only a band of farmers, that nothing living could cross him and get away with it.

But already, by implication, I have been taking you deep into the territory of a second great Southern characteristic which deserves to be examined thoroughly in its own right. I mean the tendency toward unreality, toward romanticism, and, in intimate relation with that, toward hedonism. And rightly to understand this tendency, we cannot begin better than by returning upon the simple figure which I have posed as the center about which the Southern pattern would be built.

A common impression to the contrary notwithstanding, the simple man in general rarely has any considerable capacity for the real. What is ordinarily taken for realism in him is in fact only a sort of biological pragmatism—an intuitive faculty of the practical, like that exhibited by those astounding wasps and bees celebrated by Jean-Henri Fabre—born of the circumstance that he has nearly everywhere and always been the driven slave of the belly, and confined to the narrow sphere of interests and activities marked out by the struggle for mere animal existence.

Relax that drive a little, let him escape a little from this struggle, and the true tenor of his nature promptly appears: he stands before us, has always stood before us in such circumstances, as a romantic and a hedonist. And this, indeed, inheres in the very terms of the equation. To say that he is simple is to say in effect that he necessarily lacks the complexity of mind, the knowledge, and, above all, the habit of skepticism essential to any generally realistic attitude. It is to say that he is inevitably driven back upon imagination, that his world-construction is bound to be mainly a product of fantasy, and that his credulity is limited only by his capacity for conjuring up the unbelievable. And it is to say also that he is the child-man, that the primitive stuff of humanity lies very close to the surface in him, that he likes naïvely to play, to expand his ego, his senses, his emotions, that he will accept what pleases him and reject what does not, and that in general he will prefer the extravagant, the flashing, and the brightly colored—in a word, that he displays the whole catalogue of qualities we mean by romanticism and hedonism. . . .

Such is the primary picture. But I must not leave the theme without calling your attention specifically to the stimulation of the tendency to violence which these things obviously involved. Nor must I leave it without pointing to two significant patterns which grew up in the closest association with this romanticism and hedonism and served it as channels of discharge.

The first of these is the Southern fondness for rhetoric. A gorgeous, primitive art, addressed to the autonomic system and not to the encephalon, rhetoric is of course dear to the heart of the simple man everywhere. In its purest and most natural form, oratory, it flourishes wherever he forgathers—and particularly in every new land where bonds are loosed and imagination is vaulting. It flourished over the whole American country in these days of continental expansion, as it has rarely flourished elsewhere at any time.

But in the South, to recapitulate, there was the rising flood of romanticism and hedonism clamoring for expression, and in the South there was the daily impact upon the white man of the example of the Negro, concerning whom nothing is so certain as his remarkable tendency to seize on lovely words, to roll them in his throat, to heap them in redundant profusion one upon another until meaning vanishes and there is nothing left but the sweet, canorous drunkenness of sound, nothing but the play of primitive rhythm upon the secret springs of emotion. Thus rhetoric flourished here far beyond even its American average; it early became a passion—and not only a passion but a primary standard of judgment, the *sine qua non* of leadership. The greatest man would be the man who could best wield it.

But to speak of the love of rhetoric, of oratory, is at once to suggest the love of politics. The two, in fact, were inseparable. Hand in hand they emerged from the frontier tradition, flourished over the swelling territory of the young Republic of the West, and grew into romantic Southern passions. . . .

. . . running counter, as we have seen, to the stream of its time, and, above all, running counter to the moral notions of that time in embracing slavery at the hour when the rest of the West was decisively giving it up, [the South] had to stand against the whole weight of the world's question and even of the world's frown.

And, worst of all, there was the fact that the South itself definitely shared in these moral notions—in its secret heart always carried a powerful and uneasy sense of the essential rightness of the nineteenth century's position on slavery. The evangelical religious sects had all begun by denouncing it, and were still muttering over it as late as the early 1830's. Of the 130 abolition societies established before 1827 by Lundy, the forerunner of Garrison, more than a hundred, with four-fifths of the total membership, were in the South. And in the days of their sway the old colonial gentry had been so disturbed by the institution that numbers of them had followed the lead of Christopher Gadsden of South Carolina and Thomas Jefferson in pronouncing it an insufferable crime. In the State of Virginia itself, as is well known, they had twice come close to abolishing it.

This Old South, in short, was a society beset by the specters of defeat, of shame, of guilt—a society driven by the need to bolster its morale, to nerve its arm against waxing odds, to justify itself in its own eyes and in those of the world. Hence a large part—in a way, the very largest part—of its history from the day that Garrison began to thunder in Boston is the history of its efforts to achieve that end, and characteristically by means of romantic fictions.

And of all these fictions, the most inevitable and obviously indicated was just that one which we know today as the legend of the Old South—the legend of which the backbone is, of course, precisely the assumption that every planter was in the most rigid sense of the word a gentleman.

Enabling the South to wrap itself in contemptuous superiority, to sneer down the Yankee as low-bred, crass, and money-grubbing, and even to beget in his bourgeois soul a kind of secret and envious awe, it was a nearly perfect defense-mechanism. And the stage was magnificently set for its acceptance. For the Yankee, accustomed by long habit and the myopia usual in such cases to thinking of the South purely in terms of its nearest and for so many years most important part, Virginia, had the association of plantation and aristocrat fixed in his mind with axiomatic force; he invariably assumed the second term of the equation when he thought of the first. And what was true of the Yankee was equally true of the world in general, which received the body of its impressions of the South directly from him.

Nor was this all. It was for the principal Western nations, as is commonly known, an age of nostalgia. An age in which, underneath all the optimistic trumpeting for the Future, all the solemn self-congratulation on Progress, there was an intense revulsion against the ugliness of the new industrialism and the drab monotony of the new rule of money-bags miscalled democracy, and a yearning back toward the colorfulness and the more or less imaginary glory of the aristocratic and purely agricultural past. An age which, producing such various phenomena of dissatisfaction as the reaction which began with Chateaubriand and flowered in Joseph de Maistre, the romanticism of Byron and the Blue Flower, the bitter tirades of John Ruskin, and the transcendental outpourings of Coleridge, Carlyle, and Emerson, found perhaps the most perfect expression for this part of its spirit in the cardboard medievalism of the Scotch novels. It was an age, in other words, of which it may be truthfully said, I think (and however paradoxical it may seem, I include Yankeedom in the allegation), that it was not only ready but eager to believe in the Southern legend—that it fell with a certain distinct gladness on this last purely agricultural land of the West as a sort of projection ground for its own dreams of a vanished golden time. . . .

Just as plain was the fact that the institution [of slavery] was brutalizing—to white men. Virtually unlimited power acted inevitably to call up, in the coarser sort of master, that sadism which lies concealed in the depths of universal human nature— bred angry impatience and a taste for cruelty for its own sake, with a strength that neither the kindliness I have so often referred to (it continued frequently to exist unimpaired side by side, and in the same man, with this other) nor notions of honor could effectually restrain. And in the common whites it bred a savage and ignoble hate for the Negro, which required only opportunity to break forth in relentless ferocity; for all their rage against the "white-trash" epithet concentrated itself on him rather than on the planters.

There it stood, then—terrible, revolting, serving as the very school of violence, and lending mordant point to the most hysterical outcries of the Yankee.

But the South could not and must not admit it, of course. It must prettify the institution and its own reactions, must begin to boast of its own Great Heart. To have heard them talk, indeed, you would have thought that the sole reason some of these planters held to slavery was love and duty to the black man, the earnest, devoted will not only to get him into heaven but also to make him happy in this world. He was a child whom somebody had to look after. More, he was in general, and despite an occasional spoiled Nat Turner, a grateful child—a contented, glad, loving child. Between the owner and the owned there was everywhere the most tender and beautiful relationship.

Mrs. Stowe did not invent the figure of Uncle Tom, nor did Christy invent that of Jim Crow—the banjo-picking, heel-flinging, hi-yi-ing happy jack of the levees and the cotton fields. All they did was to modify them a little for their purposes. In essentials, both were creations of the South—defense-mechanisms, answers to the Yankee and its own doubts, projections from its own mawkish tears and its own mawkish laughter over the black man, incarnations of its sentimentalized version of slavery. And what is worth observing also is that the Negro, with his quick, intuitive understanding of what is required of him, and his remarkable talents as a mime, caught them up and bodied them forth so convincingly that his masters were insulated against all question as to their reality—were enabled to believe in them as honestly as they believed in so many other doubtful things.

But there was another factor which was perhaps even more important for the growth of sentimentality than this: the influence of the presence of the Negro in increasing the value attaching to Southern woman. For, as perpetuator of white superiority in legitimate line, and as a creature absolutely inaccessible to the males of the inferior group, she inevitably became the focal center of the fundamental pattern of Proto-Dorian pride.

Nor, in this connection, must we overlook the specific role played by the Negro woman. Torn from her tribal restraints and taught an easy complaisance for commercial reasons, she was to be had for the taking. Boys on and about the plantation inevitably learned to use her, and having acquired the habit, often continued it into manhood and even after marriage. For she was natural, and could give herself up to passion in a way impossible to wives inhibited by Puritanical training. And efforts to build up a taboo against miscegenation made little real progress. I do not mean to imply, certainly, that it was universal. There were many men in the South who rigidly abstained from such liaisons, and scorned those who indulged. . . .

The South's perpetual need for justifying its career, and the will to shut away more effectually the vision of its mounting hate and brutality toward the black man, entered into the equation also and bore these people yet further into the cult of the Great Southern Heart. The Old South must be made not only the happy country but the happy country especially for the Negro. The lash? A lie, sir; it had never existed. The only bonds were those of tender understanding, trust, and loyalty. And to prove it, here about us in this very hour of new freedom and bitter strife are hundreds of worn-out Uncle Toms and black mammies still clinging stubbornly to the old masters who can no longer feed them, ten thousand Jim Crows still kicking their heels and whooping for the smile of a white man. Such is the Negro, sir, when he is not corrupted by meddling fools. Hate him? My good friend, we love him dearly—and we alone, for we alone know him.

Do I again seem to satirize them for sniveling hypocrites? Then I must assure you once more that they were not. They believed in their professions here more fully than they had ever done. And they did love the thing, compounded of one part fact and three parts fiction and the black man's miming, which subsisted in their minds under the denomination of the Good Negro.

Lastly, the increased centrality of woman, added up with the fact that miscegenation, though more terrifying than it had been even in the Old South, showed little tendency to fall off despite efforts to build up standards against it, served to intensify the old interest in gyneolatry, and to produce yet more florid notions about Southern Womanhood and Southern Virtue, and so to foster yet more precious notions of modesty and decorous behavior for the Southern female to live up to. . . .

This analysis might be carried much farther. But the book is already too long, and so I think I shall leave it at this. The basic picture of the South is here, I believe. And it was that I started out to set down.

Proud, brave, honorable by its lights, courteous, personally generous, loyal, swift to act, often too swift, but signally effective, sometimes terrible, in its action—such was the South at its best. And such at its best it remains today, despite the great falling away in some of its virtues. Violence, intolerance, aversion and suspicion toward new ideas, an incapacity for analysis, an inclination to act from feeling rather than from thought, an exaggerated individualism and a too narrow concept of social responsibility, attachment to fictions and false values, above all too great attachment to racial values and a tendency to justify cruelty and injustice in the name of those values, sentimentality and a lack of realism—these have been its characteristic vices in the past. And, despite changes for the better, they remain its characteristic vices today.

In the coming days, and probably soon, it is likely to have to prove its capacity for adjustment far beyond what has been true in the past. And in that time I shall hope, as its loyal son, that its virtues will tower over and conquer its faults and have the making of the Southern world to come. But of the future I shall venture no definite prophecies. It would be a brave man who would venture them in any case. It would be a madman who would venture them in face of the forces sweeping over the world in the fateful year of 1940.

The Big Bear of Arkansas

THOMAS BANGS THORPE

❧

This story, one of the finest of the Southwest tall tales, first appeared in the periodical The Spirit of the Times *(March 27, 1841). William T. Porter, editor of* The Spirit, *reprinted it often in a volume* The Big Bear of Arkansas and Other Sketches *(1845, 1846, 1850, 1851, 1855, and possibly 1858). The author, however, was Thomas Bangs Thorpe, and he included it in his* The Hive of "The Bee-Hunter," A Repository of Sketches *(New York: D. Appleton & Co., 1854). Blair's edition appears to be based on one of the later editions of Porter, since it varies from the first edition slightly, but lacks the auctorial revisions of* The Hive, *most of which are improvements. One, perhaps, is not: the self-conscious substitution of "bear" for "bar" in the first edition. Professor Utley has collated the last auctorial edition of Thorpe with the periodical version, using a copy of* The Hive *in the Ohio State University Library, and a photograph of* The Spirit *provided through the courtesy of Lawrence Roberts of the University of Kentucky Library. A few variants in the original edition deserve mention: it is headed "(Written for the 'Spirit of the Times.')" and "*BY THE AUTHOR OF TOM OWEN, THE BEE HUNTER.*" and at the end appear the initials "T.B.T." and the postscript "Louisiana, Feb., 1841." There are fewer commas in Thorpe's version, and many more paragraph separations. The game "checkers and roulette" of our text was "chickens and roulette" in the original print; the editor changed some dialect words into their standard forms: "tuck" became "took," "diggins" became "diggings," and so forth. Thorpe's later version contains "pre-emption" for "land," and this may well have been an auctorial revision, for the* Dictionary of Americanisms *cites the word for the first time in 1844 as applied to "A piece of land obtained or to be obtained by pre-emption"; what readers of Westerns would call a* homestead *or a* claim.

These and several other major changes indicate that the best text is Thorpe's own supervised text, which is reproduced here.

The quotation from Carvel Collins in Prof. Utley's essay "Pride and Humility," the final selection in this section, indicates the striking major agreements between Thorpe and Faulkner. Many others might be cited: Jim Doggett's "greenness" in New Orleans resembles that of Boon in Memphis; there is a remarkable dog, Bowieknife, who participates in the climactic hunt; and a brave but foolhardy little pup whom the Big Bar destroys; the Bar is hunted for several years before the climax; the hunter is the hunted for the Big Bar like a devil "hunted me"; Jim's gun fails and he helps his dog with a knife, as Boon does; the Big Bar tends to exchange his identity with the hunter. Perhaps the most striking agreement is Jim's boast about predicting an earlier bear's length by marks on the trees. Comically he says, "I swelled up considerably—I've been a prouder man ever since. So I went on, larning something every day, until I was reckoned a buster, and allowed to be decidedly the best bear hunter in my district. . . ." Here, one might argue, is the germ of the initiation theme, of the "pride and humility" paradox of Faulkner's story.

A steamboat on the Mississippi, frequently, in making her regular trips, carries between places varying from one to two thousand miles apart; and, as these boats advertise to land passengers and freight at "all intermediate landings," the heterogeneous character of the passengers of one of these up-country boats can scarcely be imagined by one who has never seen it with his own eyes.

Starting from New Orleans in one of these boats, you will find yourself associated with men from every State in the Union, and from every portion of the globe; and a man of observation need not lack for amusement or instruction in such a crowd, if he will take the trouble to read the great book of character so favorably opened before him.

Here may be seen, jostling together, the wealthy Southern planter and the pedler of tin-ware from New England—the Northern merchant and the Southern jockey—a venerable bishop, and a desperate gambler—the land speculator, and the honest farmer —professional men of all creeds and characters—Wolvereens,

Suckers, Hoosiers, Buckeyes, and Corncrackers, beside a "plenti-ful sprinkling" of the half-horse and half-alligator species of men, who are peculiar to "old Mississippi," and who appear to gain a livelihood by simply going up and down the river. In the pursuit of pleasure or business, I have frequently found myself in such a crowd.

On one occasion, when in New Orleans, I had occasion to take a trip of a few miles up the Mississippi, and I hurried on board the well-known "high-pressure-and-beat-every-thing" steamboat "Invincible," just as the last note of the last bell was sounding; and when the confusion and bustle that is natural to a boat's getting under way had subsided, I discovered that I was associated in as heterogeneous a crowd as was ever got together. As my trip was to be of a few hours' duration only, I made no endeavors to become acquainted with my fellow-passengers, most of whom would be together many days. Instead of this, I took out of my pocket the "latest paper," and more critically than usual examined its contents; my fellow-passengers, at the same time, disposed of themselves in little groups.

While I was thus busily employed in reading, and my compan-ions were more busily still employed, in discussing such subjects as suited their humors best, we were most unexpectedly startled by a loud Indian whoop, uttered in the "social hall," that part of the cabin fitted off for a bar; then was to be heard a loud crow-ing, which would not have continued to interest us—such sounds being quite common in that *place of spirits*—had not the hero of these windy accomplishments stuck his head into the cabin, and hallooed out, "Hurra for the Big Bear of Arkansaw!"

Then might be heard a confused hum of voices, unintelligible, save in such broken sentences as "horse," "screamer," "lightning is slow," &c.

As might have been expected, this continued interruption, at-tracted the attention of every one in the cabin; all conversation ceased, and in the midst of this surprise, the "Big Bear" walked into the cabin, took a chair, put his feet on the stove, and looking back over his shoulder, passed the general and familiar salute— "Strangers, how are you?"

He then expressed himself as much at home as if he had been at "the Forks of Cypress," and "prehaps a little more so."

Some of the company at this familiarity looked a little angry, and some astonished; but in a moment every face was wreathed in a smile. There was something about the intruder that won the heart on sight. He appeared to be a man enjoying perfect health and contentment; his eyes were as sparkling as diamonds, and good-natured to simplicity. Then his perfect confidence in himself was irresistibly droll.

"Prehaps," said he, "gentlemen," running on without a person interrupting, "prehaps you have been to New Orleans often; I never made *the first visit before,* and I don't intend to make another in a crow's life. I am thrown away in that ar place, and useless, that ar a fact. Some of the gentlemen thar called me *green*—well, prehaps I am, said I, *but I arn't so at home;* and if I aint off my trail much, the heads of them perlite chaps themselves wern't much the hardest; for according to my notion, they were *real know-nothings,* green as a pumpkin-vine—couldn't, in farming, I'll bet, raise a crop of turnips; and as for shooting, they'd miss a barn if the door was swinging, and that, too, with the best rifle in the country. And then they talked to me 'bout hunting, and laughed at my calling the principal game in Arkansaw poker, and high-low-jack.

" 'Prehaps,' said I, 'you prefer checkers and roulette;' at this they laughed harder than ever, and asked me if I lived in the woods, and didn't know what *game* was?

"At this, I rather think *I* laughed.

" 'Yes,' I roared, and says, I, 'Strangers, if you'd asked me *how we got our meat* in Arkansaw, I'd a told you at once, and given you a list of varmints that would make a caravan, beginning with the bar, and ending off with the cat; that's *meat* though, not game.

"Game, indeed,—that's what city folks call it; and with them it means chippen-birds and shite-pokes; may be such trash live in my diggins, but I arn't noticed them yet: a bird anyway is too trifling. I never did shoot at but one, and I'd never forgiven myself for that, had it weighed less than forty pounds. I wouldn't draw a rifle on any thing less heavy than that; and when I meet with another wild turkey of the same size, I will drap him."

"A wild turkey weighing forty pounds!" exclaimed twenty voices in the cabin at once.

"Yes, strangers, and wasn't it a whopper? You see, the thing was so fat that it couldn't fly far; and when he fell out of the tree, after I shot him, on striking the ground he bust open behind, and the way the pound gobs of tallow rolled out of the opening was perfectly beautiful."

"Where did all that happen?" asked a cynical-looking Hoosier.

"Happen! happened in Arkansaw: where else could it have happened, but in the creation State, the finishing-up country—a State where the *sile* runs down to the centre of the 'arth, and government gives you a title to every inch of it? Then its airs—just breathe them, and they will make you snort like a horse. It's a State without a fault, it is."

"Excepting mosquitoes," cried the Hoosier.

"Well, stranger, except them; for it ar a fact that they are rather *enormous,* and do push themselves in somewhat troublesome. But, stranger, they never stick twice in the same place; and give them a fair chance for a few months, and you will get as much above noticing them as an alligator. They can't hurt my feelings, for they lay under the skin; and I never knew but one case of injury resulting from them, and that was to a Yankee: and they take worse to foreigners, any how, than they do to natives. But the way they used that fellow up! first they punched him until he swelled up and busted; then he sup-per-a-ted, as the doctor called it, until he was as raw as beef; then, owing to the warm weather, he tuck the ager, and finally he tuck a steamboat and left the country. He was the only man that ever tuck mosquitoes at heart that I knowd of.

"But mosquitoes is natur, and I never find fault with her. If they ar large, Arkansaw is large, her varmints ar large, her trees ar large, her rivers ar large, and a small mosquito would be of no more use in Arkansaw than preaching in a cane-brake."

This knock-down argument in favor of big mosquitoes used the Hoosier up, and the logician started on a new track, to explain how numerous bear were in his "diggins," where he represented them to be "about as plenty as blackberries, and a little plenti-fuller."

Upon the utterance of this assertion, a timid little man near me inquired, if the bear in Arkansaw ever attacked the settlers in numbers?

"No," said our hero, warming with the subject, "no, stranger, for you see it ain't the natur of bear to go in droves; but the way they squander about in pairs and single ones is edifying.

"And then the way I hunt them—the old black rascals know the crack of my gun as well as they know a pig's squealing. They grow thin in our parts, it frightens them so, and they do take the noise dreadfully, poor things. That gun of mine is a perfect *epidemic among bear:* if not watched closely, it will go off as quick on a warm scent as my dog Bowieknife will: and then that dog—whew! why the fellow thinks that the world is full of bear, he finds them so easy. It's lucky he don't talk as well as think; for with his natural modesty, if he should suddenly learn how much he is acknowledged to be ahead of all other dogs in the universe, he would be astonished to death in two minutes.

"Strangers, that dog knows a bear's way as well as a horse-jockey knows a woman's: he always barks at the right time, bites at the exact place, and whips without getting a scratch.

"I never could tell whether he was made expressly to hunt bear, or whether bear was made expressly for him to hunt; any way, I believe they were ordained to go together as naturally as Squire Jones says a man and woman is, when he moralizes in marrying a couple. In fact, Jones once said, said he, 'Marriage according to law is a civil contract of divine origin; it's common to all countries as well as Arkansaw, and people take to it as naturally as Jim Doggett's Bowieknife takes to bear.'"

"What season of the year do your hunts take place?" inquired a gentlemanly foreigner, who, from some peculiarities of his baggage, I suspected to be an Englishman, on some hunting expedition, probably at the foot of the Rocky Mountains.

"The season for bear hunting, stranger," said the man of Arkansaw, "is generally all the year round, and the hunts take place about as regular. I read in history that varmints have their fat season, and their lean season. That is not the case in Arkansaw, feeding as they do upon the *spontenacious* productions of the sile, they have one continued fat season the year round; though in winter things in this way is rather more greasy than in summer, I must admit. For that reason bear with us run in warm weather, but in winter they only waddle.

"Fat, fat! its an enemy to speed; it tames every thing that has plenty of it. I have seen wild turkeys, from its influence, as gentle as chickens. Run a bear in this fat condition, and the way it improves the critter for eating is amazing; it sort of mixes the ile up with the meat, until you can't tell t'other from which. I've done this often.

"I recollect one perty morning in particular, of putting an old he fellow on the stretch, and considering the weight he carried, he run well. But the dogs soon tired him down, and when I came up with him wasn't he in a beautiful sweat—I might say fever; and then to see his tongue sticking out of his mouth a feet, and his sides sinking and opening like a bellows, and his cheeks so fat that he couldn't look cross. In this fix I blazed at him, and pitch me naked into a briar patch, if the steam didn't come out of the bullet-hole ten foot in a straight line. The fellow, I reckon, was made on the high-pressure system, and the lead sort of bust his biler."

"That column of steam was rather curious, or else the bear must have been very *warm*," observed the foreigner, with a laugh.

"Stranger, as you observe, that bear was WARM, and the blowing off of the steam show'd it, and also how hard the varmint had been run. I have no doubt if he had kept on two miles farther his insides would have been stewed; and I expect to meet with a varmint yet of extra bottom, that will run himself into a skinfull of bear's grease: it is possible; much onlikelier things have happened."

"Whereabouts are these bears so abundant?" inquired the foreigner, with increasing interest.

"Why, stranger, they inhabit the neighborhood of my settlement, one of the prettiest places on old Mississipp—a perfect location, and no mistake; a place that had some defects until the river made the 'cut-off' at 'Shirt-tail bend,' and that remedied the evil, as it brought my cabin on the edge of the river—a great advantage in wet weather, I assure you, as you can now roll a barrel of whiskey into my yard in high water from a boat, as easy as falling off a log. It's a great improvement, as toting it by land in a jug, as I used to do, *evaporated* it too fast, and it became expensive.

"Just stop with me, stranger, a month or two, or a year, if you like, and you will appreciate my place. I can give you plenty to eat; for beside hog and hominy, you can have bear-ham, and bear-sausages, and a mattrass of bear-skins to sleep on, and a wildcat-skin, pulled off hull, stuffed with corn-shucks, for a pillow. That bed would put you to sleep if you had the rheumatics in every joint in your body. I call that ar bed, a *quietus*.

"Then look at my 'pre-emption'—the government aint got another like it to dispose of. Such timber, and such bottom land,— why you can't preserve any thing natural you plant in it unless you pick it young, things thar will grow out of shape so quick.

"I once planted in those diggins a few potatoes and beets; they took a fine start, and after that, an ox team couldn't have kept them from growing. About that time I went off to old Kaintuck on business, and did not hear from them things in three months, when I accidentally stumbled on a fellow who had drapped in at my place, with an idea of buying me out.

" 'How did you like things?' said I.

" 'Pretty well,' said he; 'the cabin is convenient, and the timber land is good; but that bottom land aint worth the first red cent.' "

" 'Why?' said I.

" ' 'Cause,' said he.

" ' 'Cause what?' said I.

" ' ' 'Cause it's full of cedar stumps and Indian mounds, and *can't be cleared.*'

" 'Lord,' said I, 'them ar "cedar stumps" is beets, and them ar "Indian mounds" tater hills.'

"As I had expected, the crop was overgrown and useless: the sile is too rich, *and planting in Arkansaw is dangerous.*

"I had a good-sized sow killed in that same bottom land. The old thief stole an ear of corn, and took it down to eat where she slept at night. Well, she left a grain or two on the ground, and lay down on them: before morning the corn shot up, and the percussion killed her dead. I don't plant any more: natur intended Arkansaw for a hunting ground, and I go according to natur."

The questioner, who had thus elicited the description of our hero's settlement, seemed to be perfectly satisfied, and said no more; but the "Big Bear of Arkansaw" rambled on from one thing to another with a volubility perfectly astonishing, occasionally disputing with those around him, particularly with a "live Sucker" from Illinois, who had the daring to say that our Arkansaw friend's stories "smelt rather tall."

The evening was nearly spent by the incidents we have detailed; and conscious that my own association with so singular a personage would probably end before morning, I asked him if he would not give me a description of some particular bear hunt; adding, that I took great interest in such things, though I was no sportsman. The desire seemed to please him, and he squared himself round towards me, saying, that he could give me an idea of a bear hunt that was never beat in this world, or in any other. His manner was so singular, that half of his story consisted in his excellent way of telling it, the great peculiarity of which was, the happy manner he had of emphasizing the prominent parts of his conversation. As near as I can recollect, I have italicized the words, and given the story in his own way.

"Stranger," said he, "in bear hunts *I am numerous,* and which particular one, as you say, I shall tell, puzzles me.

"There was the old she devil I shot at the Hurricane last fall—then there was the old hog thief I popped over at the Bloody Crossing, and then—Yes, I have it! I will give you an idea of a hunt, in which the greatest bear was killed that ever lived, *none excepted;* about an old fellow that I hunted, more or less, for two or three years; and if that aint a *particular bear hunt,* I ain't got one to tell.

"But in the first place, stranger, let me say, I am pleased with you, because you aint ashamed to gain information by asking and listening; and that's what I say to Countess's pups every day when I'm home; and I have got great hopes of them ar pups, because they are continually *nosing* about; and though they stick it sometimes in the wrong place, they gain experience any how, and may learn something useful to boot.

"Well, as I was saying about this big bear, you see when I and some more first settled in our region, we were drivin to hunting naturally; we soon liked it, and after that we found it an easy matter to make the thing our business. One old chap who had pioneered 'afore us, gave us to understand that we had settled in the right place. He dwelt upon its merits until it was affecting, and showed us, to prove his assertions, more scratches on the bark of the sassafras trees, than I ever saw chalk marks on a tavern door 'lection time.

" 'Who keeps that ar reckoning?' said I.

" 'The bear,' said he.

" 'What for?' said I.

" 'Can't tell,' said he; 'but so it is: the bear bite the bark and wood too, at the highest point from the ground they can reach, and you can tell, by the marks,' said he, 'the length of the bear to an inch.'

" 'Enough,' said I; 'I've learned something here a'ready, and I'll put it in practice.'

"Well, stranger, just one month from that time I killed a bar, and told its exact length before I measured it, by those very marks; and when I did that, I swelled up considerably—I've been a prouder man ever since.

"So I went on, larning something every day, until I was reckoned a buster, and allowed to be decidedly the best bear hunter in my district; and that is a reputation as much harder to earn than to be reckoned first man in Congress, as an iron ramrod is harder than a toadstool.

"Do the varmints grow over-cunning by being fooled with by greenhorn hunters, and by this means get troublesome, they send for me, as a matter of course; and thus I do my own hunting, and most of my neighbors'. I walk into the varmints though, and it has become about as much the same to me as drinking. It is told in two sentences—

"A bear is started, and he is killed.

"The thing is somewhat monotonous now—I know just how much they will run, where they will tire, how much they will growl, and what a thundering time I will have in getting their meat home. I could give you the history of the chase with all the

particulars at the commencement, I know the signs so well—
Stranger, I'm certain. Once I met with a match, though, and I will
tell you about it; for a common hunt would not be worth relating.

"On a fine fall day, long time ago, I was trailing about for bear,
and what should I see but fresh marks on the sassafras trees, about
eight inches above any in the forests that I knew of. Says I, 'Them
marks is a hoax, or it indicates the d——t bear that was ever
grown.' In fact, stranger, I couldn't believe it was real, and I
went on. Again I saw the same marks, at the same height, and *I
knew the thing lived.* That conviction came home to my soul like
an earthquake.

"Says I, 'Here is something a-purpose for me: that bear is
mine, or I give up the hunting business.' The very next morning,
what should I see but a number of buzzards hovering over my
corn-field. 'The rascal has been there,' said I, 'for that sign is
certain:' and, sure enough, on examining, I found the bones of
what had been as beautiful a hog the day before, as was ever
raised by a Buckeye. Then I tracked the critter out of the field to
the woods, and all the marks he left behind, showed me that he
was *the bear.*

"Well, stranger, the first fair chase I ever had with that big
critter, I saw him no less than three distinct times at a distance:
the dogs run him over eighteen miles and broke down, my horse
gave out, and I was as nearly used up as a man can be, made on
my principle, *which is patent.*

"Before this adventure, such things were unknown to me as
possible; but, strange as it was, that bear got me used to it before
I was done with him; for he got so at last, that he would leave me
on a long chase *quite easy.* How he did it, I never could understand.

"That a bear runs at all, is puzzling; but how this one could
tire down and bust up a pack of hounds and a horse, that were
used to overhauling every thing they started after in no time, was
past my understanding. Well, stranger, that bear finally got so
sassy, that he used to help himself to a hog off my premises whenever he wanted one; the buzzards followed after what he left, and
so, between *bear and buzzard,* I rather think I got *out of pork.*

"Well, missing that bear so often took hold of my vitals, and I wasted away. The thing had been carried too far, and it reduced me in flesh faster than an ager. I would see that bear in every thing I did: *he hunted me,* and that, too, like a devil, which I began to think he was.

"While in this shaky fix, I made preparations to give him a last brush, and be done with it. Having completed every thing to my satisfaction, I started at sunrise, and to my great joy, I discovered from the way the dogs run, that they were near him. Finding his trail was nothing, for that had become as plain to the pack as a turnpike road.

"On we went, and coming to an open country, what should I see but the bear very leisurely ascending a hill, and the dogs close at his heels, either a match for him this time in speed, or else he did not care to get out of their way—I don't know which. But wasn't he a beauty, though! I loved him like a brother.

"On he went, until he came to a tree, the limbs of which formed a crotch about six feet from the ground. Into this crotch he got and seated himself, the dogs yelling all around it; and there he sat eyeing them as quiet as a pond in low water.

"A greenhorn friend of mine, in company, reached shooting distance before me, and blazed away, hitting the critter in the centre of his forehead. The bear shook his head as the ball struck it, and then walked down from that tree, as gently as a lady would from a carriage.

" 'Twas a beautiful sight to see him do that—he was in such a rage, that he seemed to be as little afraid of the dogs as if they had been sucking pigs; and the dogs warn't slow in making a ring around him at a respectful distance, I tell you; even Bowieknife himself, stood off. Then the way his eyes flashed!—why the fire of them would have singed a cat's hair; in fact, that bear was in a *wrath all over.* Only one pup came near him, and he was brushed out so totally with the bear's left paw, that he entirely disappeared; and that made the old dogs more cautious still. In the mean time, I came up, and taking deliberate aim, as a man should do, at his side, just back of his foreleg, *if my gun did not snap,* call me a coward, and I won't take it personal.

"Yes, stranger, *it snapped,* and I could not find a cap about my person. While in this predicament, I turned round to my fool

friend—'Bill,' says I, 'you're an ass—you're a fool—you might as
well have tried to kill that bear by barking the tree under his
belly, as to have done it by hitting him in the head. Your shot has
made a tiger of him; and blast me, if a dog gets killed or wounded
when they come to blows, I will stick my knife into your liver, I
will ——.' My wrath was up. I had lost my caps, my gun had
snapped, the fellow with me had fired at the bear's head, and I
expected every moment to see him close in with the dogs and
kill a dozen of them at least. In this thing I was mistaken; for the
bear leaped over the ring formed by the dogs, and giving a fierce
growl, was off—the pack, of course, in full cry after him. The run
this time was short, for coming to the edge of a lake, the varmint
jumped in, and swam to a little island in the lake, which it reached,
just a moment before the dogs.

" 'I'll have him now,' said I, for I had found my caps in the
lining of my coat—so, rolling a log into the lake, I paddled myself
across to the island, just as the dogs had cornered the bear in a
thicket. I rushed up and fired—at the same time the critter leaped
over the dogs and came within three feet of me, running like mad;
he jumped into the lake, and tried to mount the log I had just
deserted, but every time he got half his body on it, it would roll
over and send him under; the dogs, too, got around him, and
pulled him about, and finally Bowieknife clenched with him, and
they sunk into the lake together.

"Stranger, about this time I was excited, and I stripped off my
coat, drew my knife, and intended to have taken a part with
Bowieknife myself, when the bear rose to the surface. But the
varmint staid under—Bowieknife came up alone, more dead than
alive, and with the pack came ashore.

" 'Thank God!' said I, 'the old villain has got his deserts at last.'

"Determined to have the body, I cut a grape-vine for a rope,
and dove down where I could see the bear in the water, fastened
my rope to his leg, and fished him, with great difficulty, ashore.
Stranger, may I be chawed to death by young alligators, if the
thing I looked at wasn't a *she bear, and not the old critter after all*.

"The way matters got mixed on that island was onaccountably
curious, and thinking of it made me more than ever convinced that
I was hunting the devil himself. I went home that night and took

to my bed—the thing was killing me. The entire team of Arkansaw in bear-hunting acknowledged himself used up, and the fact sunk into my feelings as a snagged boat will in the Mississippi. I grew as cross as a bear with two cubs and a sore tail. The thing got out 'mong my neighbors, and I was asked how come on that individ-u-al that never lost a bear when once started? and if that same individ-u-al didn't wear telescopes when he turned a she-bear, of ordinary size, into an old he one, a little larger than a horse?

" 'Prehaps,' said I, 'friends'—getting wrathy—'prehaps you want to call somebody a liar?'

" 'Oh, no,' said they, 'we only heard of such things being *rather common* of late, but we don't believe one word of it; oh, no,'—and then they would ride off, and laugh like so many hyenas over a dead nigger.

"It was too much, and I determined to catch that bear, go to Texas, or die,—and I made my preparations accordin'.

"I had the pack shut up and rested. I took my rifle to pieces, and iled it.

"I put caps in every pocket about my person, *for fear of the lining.*

"I then told my neighbors, that on Monday morning—naming the day—I would start THAT B(E)AR, and bring him home with me, or they might divide my settlement among them, the owner having disappeared.

"Well, stranger, on the morning previous to the great day of my hunting expedition, I went into the woods near my house, taking my gun and Bowieknife along, just *from habit,* and there sitting down, also from habit, what should I see, getting over my fence, but *the bear!* Yes, the old varmint was within a hundred yards of me, and the way he walked *over that fence*—stranger; he loomed up like a *black mist,* he seemed so large, and he walked right towards me.

"I raised myself, took deliberate aim, and fired. Instantly the varmint wheeled, gave a yell, and *walked through the fence,* as easy as a falling tree would through a cobweb.

"I started after, but was tripped up by my inexpressibles, which, either from habit or the excitement of the moment, were about my heels, and before I had really gathered myself up, I heard the old varmint groaning, like a thousand sinners, in a thicket near by, and, by the time I reached him, he was a corpse.

"Stranger, it took five niggers and myself to put that carcass on a mule's back, and old long-ears waddled under his load, as if he was foundered in every leg of his body; and with a common whopper of a bear, he would have trotted off, and enjoyed himself.

" 'Twould astonish you to know how big he was: I made a *bed-spread of his skin,* and the way it used to cover my bear mattress, and leave several feet on each side to tuck up, would have delighted you. It was, in fact, a creation bear, and if it had lived in Samson's time, and had met him in a fair fight, he would have licked him in the twinkling of a dice-box.

"But, stranger, I never liked the way I hunted him, *and missed him.* There is something curious about it, that I never could understand,—and I never was satisfied at his giving in so *easy at last.* Prehaps he had heard of my preparations to hunt him the next day, so he jist guv up, like Captain Scott's coon, to save his wind to grunt with in dying; but that ain't likely. My private opinion is, that that bear was an *unhuntable bear, and died when his time come.*"

When this story was ended, our hero sat some minutes with his auditors, in a grave silence; I saw there was a mystery to him connected with the bear whose death he had just related, that had evidently made a strong impression on his mind. It was also evident that there was some superstitious awe connected with the affair,—a feeling common with all "children of the wood," when they meet with any thing out of their every-day experience.

He was the first one, however, to break the silence, and, jumping up, he asked all present to "liquor" before going to bed,—a thing which he did, with a number of companions, evidently to his heart's content.

Long before day, I was put ashore at my place of destination, and I can only follow with the reader, in imagination, our Arkansas friend, in his adventures at the "Forks of Cypress," on the Mississippi.

You Can't Pray a Lie

SAMUEL L. CLEMENS

❧

Huck's white companions on the raft, the Duke and the King, have been trying all sorts of swindling and thieving games, mostly without remarkable success. They get into a fight at a saloon and Huck runs back to the raft determined to run off from them. He calls for his Negro friend Jim and cannot find him. A boy tells Huck that Jim is captive at Silas Phelps's place, and that they will return Jim to his owner for the reward of two hundred dollars. It is clear that the Duke and the King have betrayed Jim, for "forty dirty dollars."

I went to the raft, and set down in the wigwam to think. But I couldn't come to nothing. I thought till I wore my head sore, but I couldn't see no way out of the trouble. After all this long journey, and after all we'd done for them scoundrels, here was it all come to nothing, everything all busted up and ruined, because they could have the heart to serve Jim such a trick as that, and make him a slave again all his life, and amongst strangers, too, for forty dirty dollars.

Once I said to myself it would be a thousand times better for Jim to be a slave at home where his family was, as long as he'd *got* to be a slave, and so I'd better write a letter to Tom Sawyer and tell him to tell Miss Watson where he was. But I soon give up

---

Chapter XXXI, *Adventures of Huckleberry Finn* (*Tom Sawyer's Comrade*) (New York: Charles L. Webster and Co., 1885). An early state of the first American edition, from the Ohio State University Library Rare Book Room, has been used, with points such as "with the was" on p. 57 and the erroneous "p. 88" in the Table of Contents. For the complex bibliographical problem of this famous American "first edition" (anticipated by an English edition in 1884), see Merle Johnson, *A Bibliography of the Works of Mark Twain* (New York: Harper and Brothers, 1935), pp. 43-50; Walter Blair, *Mark Twain and Huck Finn* (Berkeley: University of California Press, 1960), pp. 385-387, 422; Lucille Adams, *Huckleberry Finn: A Descriptive Bibliography of the Huckleberry Finn Collection at the Buffalo Public Library* (Buffalo, 1950), pp. 11-13.

that notion, for two things: she'd be mad and disgusted at his rascality and ungratefulness for leaving her, and so she'd sell him straight down the river again; and if she didn't, everybody naturally despises an ungrateful nigger, and they'd make Jim feel it all the time, and so he'd feel ornery and disgraced. And then think of *me!* It would get all around, that Huck Finn helped a nigger to get his freedom; and if I was to ever see anybody from that town again, I'd be ready to get down and lick his boots for shame. That's just the way: a person does a low-down thing, and then he don't want to take no consequences of it. Thinks as long as he can hide it, it ain't no disgrace. That was my fix exactly. The more I studied about this, the more my conscience went to grinding me, and the more wicked and low-down and ornery I got to feeling. And at last, when it hit me all of a sudden that here was the plain hand of Providence slapping me in the face and letting me know my wickedness was being watched all the time from up there in heaven, whilst I was stealing a poor old woman's nigger that hadn't ever done me no harm, and now was showing me there's One that's always on the lookout, and ain't agoing to allow no such miserable doings to go only just so fur and no further, I most dropped in my tracks I was so scared. Well, I tried the best I could to kinder soften it up somehow for myself, by saying I was brung up wicked, and so I warn't so much to blame; but something inside of me kept saying, "There was the Sunday school, you could a gone to it; and if you'd a done it they'd a learnt you, there, that people that acts as I'd been acting about that nigger goes to everlasting fire."

It made me shiver. And I about made up my mind to pray; and see if I couldn't try to quit being the kind of a boy I was, and be better. So I kneeled down. But the words wouldn't come. Why wouldn't they? It warn't no use to try and hide it from Him. Nor from *me,* neither. I knowed very well why they wouldn't come. It was because my heart warn't right; it was because I warn't square; it[1] was because I was playing double. I was letting *on* to give up sin, but away inside of me I was holding on to the biggest one of all. I was trying to make my mouth *say* I would do the right thing and the clean thing, and go and write to that nigger's owner and

---

[1] This state of the first edition has "is."—*Eds.*

tell where he was; but deep down in me I knowed it was a lie—and He knowed it. You can't pray a lie—I found that out.

So I was full of trouble, full as I could be; and didn't know what to do. At last I had an idea; and I says, I'll go and write the letter —and *then* see if I can pray. Why, it was astonishing, the way I felt as light as a feather, right straight off, and my troubles all gone. So I got a piece of paper and a pencil, all glad and excited, and set down and wrote:

> Miss Watson your runaway nigger Jim is down here two mile below Pikesville and Mr. Phelps has got him and he will give him up for the reward if you send.   HUCK FINN.

I felt good and all washed clean of sin for the first time I had ever felt so in my life, and I knowed I could pray now. But I didn't do it straight off, but laid the paper down and set there thinking—thinking how good it was all this happened so, and how near I come to being lost and going to hell. And went on thinking. And got to thinking over our trip down the river; and I see Jim before me, all the time, in the day, and in the night-time, sometimes moonlight, sometimes storms, and we a floating along, talking, and singing, and laughing. But somehow I couldn't seem to strike no places to harden me against him, but only the other kind. I'd see him standing my watch on top of his'n, stead of calling me, so I could go on sleeping; and see him how glad he was when I come back out of the fog; and when I come to him again in the swamp, up there where the feud was; and such-like times; and would always call me honey, and pet me, and do everything he could think of for me, and how good he always was; and at last I struck the time I saved him by telling the men we had small-pox aboard, and he was so grateful, and said I was the best friend old Jim ever had in the world, and the *only* one he's got now; and then I happened to look around, and see that paper.

It was a close place. I took it up, and held it in my hand. I was a trembling, because I'd got to decide, forever, betwixt two things, and I knowed it. I studied a minute, sort of holding my breath, and then says to myself:

"All right, then, I'll *go* to hell"—and tore it up.

It was awful thoughts, and awful words, but they was said. And

I let them stay said; and never thought no more about reforming.
I shoved the whole thing out of my head; and said I would take up
wickedness again, which was in my line, being brung up to it, and
the other warn't. And for a starter, I would go to work and steal
Jim out of slavery again; and if I could think up anything worse,
I would do that, too; because as long as I was in, and in for good,
I might as well go the whole hog.

Cultural Primitivism in William Faulkner's The Bear

KENNETH LABUDDE

❦

Students and critics have commented on the opposition between
civilization and nature in the work of William Faulkner. Robert
Penn Warren has noted that Faulkner associates "the right attitude
toward nature" with "the right attitude toward man." [1] A special
and significant aspect of Faulkner's conception of man's relationship to nature is found in his long story called "The Bear."

This story is presented as if Isaac McCaslin, now near eighty,
were reliving the years of his boyhood and youth.[2] The bear hunt
furnishes the prologue to Isaac's attainment of spiritual maturity.
The importance of the hunt in the spiritual development of the
boy Ike is revealed first of all by the significance of the bear it-

FROM *American Quarterly,* II:4 (1950), 322-328. Reprinted by permission
of the author and *American Quarterly.* Copyright, *American Quarterly.*

[1] "William Faulkner," *Forms of Modern Fiction,* William Van O'Connor,
ed. (Minneapolis: University of Minnesota Press, 1948) 133.

[2] The narrative does not have a conventional chronology because Isaac
does not relive the story in that manner. In a later article I will use "The
Bear" for a study of Faulkner's writing technique. At that time I will take
up the question of the earlier stories which furnished material for this long
story published first in *Go Down, Moses.* These stories are "A Bear Hunt,"
Saturday Evening Post, vol. 206, pp. 8-9, 74, 76 (February 10, 1934);
"Lion," *Harper's,* vol. 172, pp. 66-67 (December 1935); and "The Bear,"
Saturday Evening Post, vol. 214, pp. 30-31, 74, 76-77 (May 9, 1942). For
the location of these stories I am indebted to Robert W. Daniel's *A Catalogue of the Writings of William Faulkner* (New Haven: Yale University
Library, 1942).

self. Before considering Faulkner's use of the bear, we might well observe the statement by the anthropologist A. Irving Hallowell that of all the game hunted "no other animal was found to attain such universal prominence as the bear, nor to have associated with it, over such a wide geographical area, such a large series of customs." [3]

Old Ben, the name given to the bear by the hunters, takes on a semihuman aspect. Sam, the old Negro, in telling the young Ike about Old Ben testifies to the way he feels about the bear: "He don't care no more for bear than he does for dogs or men neither. He came to see who's here, who's new in camp this year, whether he can shoot or not, can stay or not. Whether we got the dog yet that can bay and hold him until a man gets there with a gun. Because he's the head bear. He's the man." Ike attributed to Old Ben the feeling of courting death, that "he don't want it to last any longer." In later years the man Isaac muses: "If Sam Fathers had been his mentor and the backyard rabbits and squirrels his kindergarten, then the wilderness the old bear ran was his college and the old male bear itself, so long unwifed and childless as to have become its own ungendered progenitor, was his alma mater." One is reminded here that Sam too was "unwifed and childless," which is a significant parallelism.

When Ike comes close to him, Old Ben takes on the stance of a human being. When Ike rescued the ratter, Old Ben "loomed and towered over him like a thunderclap." In the account of the closing in on the bear we are told that "it caught the dog in both arms, almost loverlike, and they both went down." A moment later after Boon jumped astride Old Ben "the bear surged erect, raising with the man and dog too, and turned and still carrying the man and the dog it took two or three steps toward the woods on its hind feet as a man would have walked . . ."

Primitive people observed the sagacious qualities, the omnivorous habits, and the wide range of facial and bodily expression of emotional behavior in the bear. They were struck by seeing the bear rise on his hind legs and sit up against a tree just as if he

---

[3] *Bear Ceremonialism in the Northern Hemisphere* (Philadelphia, 1926), 184. Unless otherwise noted this is the authority for my interpretation of the bear in Faulkner's story.

were a man. The fact that a bear, unlike other animals, walks on the sole of his foot with the heel touching the ground and leaves a footprint of heel, toe, and arch like that of a human being had a great impact on the mind of primitive man. Perhaps these unique qualities help explain the importance Old Ben had for Faulkner's characters who live in the primitive world of the hunter. The hunters revere the powers of Old Ben and they see themselves playing a heroic game with the bear. Frazer testifies to the reverence of hunters for the bear that they kill.[4] Boon's killing of Old Ben by stabbing the bear with his knife is therefore appropriate.

Other details in the story are allied to primitive customs. The bear is usually referred to as Old Ben or "he." Hallowell points out that "one of the most constant and distinctive practices associated with bears is the custom of referring or speaking to the animal by some other term than the generic name for it." Primitive people would address a bear as if he were a relative. They would make conciliatory speeches to the bear asking him to come out to be killed and begging his pardon for having to kill it. Major de Spain, it will be remembered, told the other hunters why Old Ben must be killed as if an excuse had to be given. "I'm disappointed in him. He has broken the rules. I didn't think he would have done that. He has killed mine and McCaslin's dogs, but that was all right. We gambled the dogs against him; we gave each other warning. But now he has come into my house and destroyed my property, out of season too. He broke the rules."

When one reads in Hallowell that it was a custom for the killer to cut off a paw of the bear, one recalls that Boon had done just that. Ike senses that hunting Old Ben is something more than a matter of marksmanship:

> for the first time he realized that the bear which had run in his listening and loomed in his dreams since before he could remember and which therefore must have existed in the listening and the dreams of his cousin and Major de Spain and even old General Compson before they began to remember in their turn, was a mortal animal and that they had departed

[4] J. G. Frazer, *Golden Bough* (London: Macmillan, 1907), Part V, vol. 2, p. 224.

for the camp each November with no actual intention of slaying it, not because it could not be slain but because so far
they had no actual hope of being able to.

Among more primitive peoples the important stages of life are
expressed in ritualistic customs which have certain marked characteristics.[5] In "The Bear" one finds much which resembles the prevailing characteristics of the rituals of puberty.

Isolation of the boy is requisite in these rituals. Ike was taken
into the big woods for the first time at the age of ten to be in the
company of a few men, his elders. There he was cut off from the
comforts of civilization as if he had to be purified from them.
Faulkner speaks of the "coarse, rapid food—which men ate,
cooked by men who were hunters first and cooks afterward." He
tells us that Ike "slept in harsh blankets as hunters slept." No
woman enters into the account of the hunt. Sam took Ike to his
stand the first few times, but the morning came when Ike had to
go alone. Ike must undergo isolation before he can be reborn into
the social group.

Essential in the rituals of puberty is the ordeal of physical suffering which tests the right for the boy to be considered able to
bear pain as a man would. Ike recognized his fear as he "tasted
his own saliva." Sam told him, "Be scared. You can't help that.
But don't be afraid. Ain't nothing in the woods going to hurt you
if you don't corner it or it don't smell that you are afraid." It was
Sam who convinced him that in order to see the bear he would
have to leave his gun behind, his gun which represents man's bar-
rier against the wilderness. But Ike knew he must purify himself
still further by leaving behind his compass and watch as well. One
symbolizes the time and the other the direction in space as civilization defines them for the boy. Ike soon became lost, but he did as
"Sam coached and drilled him." This was the time Ike saw the
footprint of the bear. Ike had met his ordeal.

Instruction in tribal usages relating to obedience, courage, and
perseverance is a part of the rituals of puberty. Ike had to prove
himself fit at each point before he could be initiated into the suc-

---

[5] W. D. Hambly, *Origins of Education Among Primitive Peoples* (London: Macmillan, 1926), 128-32.

cessive stages of the hunt. Before the youth could know the wilderness and be accepted by it, he must realize its greatness. He had the necessary humility, but he had to acquire patience because the process of initiation extended over six years. Not until the third morning on the hunt was the boy able to hear the dogs running. At the end of two weeks he still could not expect the hunt to come his way, but he had learned how to take his stand alone and how to return to camp without guidance.

As youth is instructed by its elders in primitive cultures, Ike was taught the use of the compass by his cousin McCaslin, Major de Spain, Walter Ewell, and General Compson. These men represented the social caste into which Isaac was born, the planter aristocracy, now down at heel. But none of these was the great teacher of Ike. His "spirit's father was Sam," the "old man born of a Negro slave and a Chickasaw chief." It was Sam who taught him how to find his way into the wilderness without his watch and compass and how to handle a gun, when to shoot and when not to. When Ike was thirteen, Sam had led him straight to the great cypress—"he had known the buck would pass exactly there because there was something running in Sam Fathers' veins which ran in the veins of the buck too." After Ike killed his buck, it was Sam who performed the primitive ritual of marking the boy's face with blood. Sam represents the ancient wisdom of the wilderness.

The tests which Ike was submitted to and the instruction which he received from his elders are actually those given to a youth destined for an exalted position among his people. The symbolism of the name *Isaac* is obvious. He had the instinct of his people to a superior degree so that when he went into the woods for the first time he moved instinctively. The scene was something he had always known, for it had been in his very blood.

The boy felt the same intuitional compulsion when he heard the dogs the first time: "a murmur, sourceless, almost indistinguishable, yet he knew what it was although he had never before heard that many dogs running at once." There was something in Ike meant to receive the wisdom of the wilderness, for "he was teaching himself to be better than a fair woodsman without knowing he was doing it." He could feel the bear looking at him, and the bear itself was known to Ike from the beginning. During Ike's third hunting trip his little ratter overcame the bear—this little ratter which symbolizes the foolhardy bravado which Ike must learn was useless to him. "When he overtook and grasped the shrill, frantically pinwheeling little dog, it seemed to him that he was directly under the bear. He could smell it, strong and hot and rank. Sprawling, he looked up where it loomed and towered over him like a thunderclap. It was quite familiar, until he remembered: this was the way he had used to dream about it."

General Compson, the man of highest rank among the hunters but now too old for the chase, recognized Ike's inherent superiority. When the General announced that he wanted Ike to ride his horse there was a transfer of power from an elder to a novice. After Old Ben was killed, Ike pleaded to be allowed to remain in the woods instead of having to return to school right away. He was the only one who knew that Sam was going to die. The General opposed McCaslin when he told his young cousin Ike that he must go back to town: " 'And you shut up, Cass,' he said, though McCaslin had not spoken. 'You've got one foot straddled into a farm and the other foot straddled into a bank; you ain't even got a good hand-hold where this boy was already an old man long before you damned Sartorises and Edmondses invented farms and banks to keep yourselves from having to find out what this boy was born knowing, and fearing too maybe, but without being afraid.' "

Ike's almost legendary knowledge of the wilderness not only makes him a superior hunter, but also serves as a symbol of the youth's coming of age spiritually. With his own instincts encouraged, nurtured, and given shape by Sam, Ike comes to possess what he must have before he can see the capture and killing of Old Ben: pride and humility. Ike must realize his own smallness in the vastness of the wilderness. He must be scared, but he must not be afraid. In other words, Ike must attain the sense of being and of the unity of his being with the wilderness. The bear had not been killed earlier because it was to show Ike what the wilderness meant just as Sam had taught Ike what it meant. Sam and the bear are so much a part of each other that Sam dies soon after the killing of the bear.

Ike's spiritual wisdom becomes evident in the long *parenthèse,*

Part IV, of the story. While it is true that the hunting story is left intact without that part, the reader who omits it has only a story of adolescence. Part IV is the story of the man Isaac McCaslin. Ike expresses that knowledge through an act which defines his individuality as a man. The hunting story is the prelude to, the preparation for that act.

Ike, in learning of the wilderness, had learned of God. Knowing God meant he had learned that he must do what he could to fulfill the plan of God. Ike's father had attempted retribution for evil by means of the legacy left to the children who carried in their veins the intermingled blood of the McCaslins and their slaves. But the legacy was not enough. Ike told McCaslin that the only way to eradicate evil was "to hold the earth mutual and intact in the communal anonymity of brotherhood, and all the fee He asked was pity and humility and sufferance and endurance and sweat of his face for bread."

The wisdom which he acquired in the wilderness became a code that enabled Ike to decipher the ledgers in the commissary. Ike saw those ledgers on the shelf when he was a young boy watching the men go off for the bear hunts. Then he had no desire to examine them. However, when he was sixteen and had learned the lesson of the wilderness, he took down the ledgers as if moved by intuition. "He knew what he was going to find before he found it." What he found was the record of evil and the attempts to obliterate it. Ike saw for himself the worthlessness of those attempts when he went on his "abortive trip into Tennessee with the still-intact third of old Carothers' legacy to his Negro son and his descendants."

Therefore, when Ike was twenty-one, he told McCaslin, who, as the General said, could never know the meaning of the wilderness, that he must renounce the land left to him. Ike proclaimed, "Sam Fathers set me free." That was Sam's legacy to Ike. Then we have the ironical juxtaposing of the account of Ike's other legacy, the one from his godfather, his Uncle Hubert Beauchamp. In Beauchamp's silver cup filled with gold pieces we have the symbol of the civilization of the white aristocratic caste to which Ike belonged by birth. On Ike's twenty-first birthday he opened the parcel which was supposed to contain the silver cup only to

find a tin coffee-can filled with a handful of copper coins and
I.O.U.s.

In Part IV we realize "The Bear" is an affirmation of primitivism. Civilization is evil. ("This whole land, the whole South is
cursed, and all of us who derive from it.") The only means of
salvation is to sweep all this man-made structure away so that
man will hold "the earth mutual and intact in the communal
anonymity of brotherhood." The prince among men is the seventy-
year-old son of an Indian chief and a Negro slave. Sam is a noble
savage, and it is from him that Ike learned wisdom. Ike learned
about God in the wilderness: "There are some things He said in
the Book, and some things reported of Him that He did not say.
And I know what you will say now: That if truth is one thing to
me and another to you, how will we choose which is truth? You
don't need to choose. The heart already knows." Wisdom is
achieved by intuition schooled by nature rather than by reason
fashioned according to the ways of men.

Pride and Humility:
The Cultural Roots of Ike McCaslin

FRANCIS LEE UTLEY

❦

I

Out of the "driving complexity" of Faulkner's *The Bear* many
strands may be unwoven; like *Don Quixote* or *Hamlet,* the story
allows an infinity of readings. Here we shall seek one which
recognizes the culture from which Ike derives and which he represents and transcends. It is the tall tale of an epic hunt for an
immortal Hunted Bear who like God is also mortal, the realistic
tale of how one boy is initiated into pride and humility, and the
romantic tale of how that boy is prepared by his culture for one
massive and courageous act of repudiation of a land tainted by
slavery and miscegenation. Ike's rejection of his inheritance makes

him momentarily like the Carpenter who repudiated (and perpetuated) the Law; since he was but mortal, it left him drained, a
no-'count poor white hunter despite his high-born ancestry, a
sterile sacrifice to truth and humanity. The temptation to narrow
such a tale to the religious, the social, the local is great; we shall
try to view it in its breadth without reduction.

A good hunting story has a wide appeal; New England has its
great cosmic yarn of a hunt—Ahab's pursuit of Moby Dick. But
the hunting culture of America is found at its most intense in the
Old South, with its wildernesses old and new. What W. J. Cash has
called the "romantic and hedonistic" character of his native region[1] finds some of its most natural expression in the hunt, exclusively male, or as Faulkner puts it "the best game of all, the
best of all breathing and forever the best of all listening." Many
Northern boys know a hobby called hunting; most Southern boys
know hunting as a way of life. Hunting is a masculine democracy:
the gentry like Major de Spain and General Compson drink, play
poker and hunt with or beside Sam Fathers and Tennie's Jim,
both of whom have Negro blood; the poor whites, swampers and
farmers and loggers, collect to witness the climactic battle between
their own Boon Hogganbeck, the dog Lion, and the bear Old Ben.

Faulkner, it is rumored, had to be assured of good hunting in
Virginia before he could settle down as a writer in residence at
Jefferson's University. He has often insisted that *The Bear,* if
printed out of the historical context of the "novel" *Go Down,
Moses,* should drop its lengthy and surrealistic fourth part, which
demonstrates how Ike renounced his plantation heritage.[2] Some
of this conviction, which is rarely shared by critics[3] (who would as
soon lose the last chapter of Joyce's *Ulysses* because it likewise
violates the norms of English punctuation), comes from Faulk-

---

[1] W. J. Cash, *The Mind of the South* (New York: Vintage Books, 1954),
pp. 46-49.
[2] Frederick L. Gwynn and Joseph L. Blotner, ed., *Faulkner in the University* (Charlottesville: University of Virginia Press, 1959), pp. 3-4, 273.
[3] One exception is Richard J. Stonsifer, "Faulkner's 'The Bear': A Note on
Structure," *College English,* XXIII (1961), pp. 219-223. Stonsifer's search
for sevens to equate with Ishtar's descent into the underworld is an example
of mythical legerdemain of the kind I hope this essay does not sponsor,
despite its use of ritual metaphors.

ner's knowledge that he had several times written an earlier form of the story, of which "Lion," a pure hunting yarn, is perhaps the most successful example. Faulkner knows that the story of the Last Great Hunt in the dying Wilderness will appeal directly to his people, who may be distracted by the revolutionary repudiation of Part IV. The distraction is less in the full setting of *Go Down, Moses,* which puts Ike himself in perspective, strengthens the element of initiation in the story, shows us the heroism of the Old South, white and black, and the pride and humility of the New South, white and black. But above all one assumes that Faulkner's fellow-Southerners love the hunt so intensely that they will take a good deal from a tale which celebrates it. If we, following the lead of other critics, remove the tale from its literary context, we must grant the tale its cultural context as reparation.

Now that we have a hunt, what of the quarry? Clearly there is a closeness between hunter and hunted, of the kind missed by the American in England who was rebuked by the Master of the Hunt for a breach of etiquette. When he saw the fox he did not shout "Tally-ho!" as he should, but "There goes the little son of a bitch!" Hunting, one of the most ancient of sports, breeds ceremony, and the center of the ceremony must be respected. Old Ben is a monster like Beowulf's Grendel, ageless, "a phantom, epitome and apotheosis of the old, wild life which the little puny humans swarmed and hacked at in a fury of abhorrence and fear, like pygmies about the ankles of a drowsing elephant;—the old bear, solitary, indomitable, and alone; widowered, childless, and absolved of mortality—old Priam reft of his old wife and outlived all his sons." He appears to Ike in a series of ritual epiphanies—eight of them in all. At ten Ike only hears him, in the company of his priest and tutor, Sam Fathers. Here the Bear is not the hunted but the hunter. " 'He come to see who's here, who's new in camp this year, whether he can shoot or not, can stay or not. . . . Because he's the head bear. He's the man.' " The Man, like Sam's own ancestor Doom or "du Homme," an Indian adventurer whose acquisition of these lands by questionable means but with no lack of force and leadership sets the whole sequence of *Go Down, Moses* in motion. Two weeks later Ike merely senses that Ben looks at him; the bear is still the Hunter. The third time Ike, courageously alone and ritually naked of gun, watch and compass, confronts Old Ben directly; a mystic link between them is riveted. The fourth and fifth meetings occur in Part II when Ike is thirteen; a new source of *mana* or spirit power, the dog Lion, has joined the destined hunters. Once, "still hunting with Walter Ewell's rifle," Ike sees the Bear from a distance. Later, in the company of his "frantic fyce," a little dog who is the essence of courage because he cannot aspire to Lion's strength, Ike sees Old Ben once more; he fails to shoot him because he would kill the absurd fyce, who is surrounding Ben on all sides. But he comes close enough to smell the Bear, "strong and hot and rank." The sixth time Lion, the destined antagonist of Ben, is present, but Ben escapes the dog and the hunters by covering his trail with the river. Next November Lion jumps Ben and General Compson draws blood; Boon shoots five times but misses him, and nearly dies of shame. A year later (Part III), when Ike is sixteen, the yearly ritual of pursuit continues, but this time Old Ben comes to his fated end, bringing down with him Lion and Sam Fathers, the ancient Chief and Hunter.

This climactic ladder of pursuits and escapes is obviously, among other things, a repeated ritual dealing with the destinies of gods and men. Master of the rite is Sam Fathers, who knows the destinies and teaches craft and wisdom to Ike, his fosterling. He foresees that if Ben "gets hemmed up and has got to pick out somebody to run over, he will pick out you," a prophecy of the fifth epiphany, when Ben looms above Ike and the fyce. Sam knows that one particular dog (not yet chosen) will be Old Ben's Nemesis, and Ike, who is learning second sight from Sam, echoes him with "So it won't be until the last day. When even he don't want it to last any longer." Sam's foreknowledge, against the rationalizations of his social "betters," leads him to lure Lion out of the wilderness and to tame him for the fated task, which coincides with the death of Ben, Lion, and Sam himself. On the "last day," only Ike knows that Sam is going to die: "Sam's eyes were probably open again on that profound look which saw further than them or the hut, further than the death of a bear and the dying of a dog." As in all rituals, in which man follows the ways of the gods in order to control them, the borderline between man's choice and man's fate becomes blurred. Sam directs Boon, his acolyte, to the last rites, including those of his own funeral.

Similarly, in a Munsee-Mahican Bear Sacrifice ceremony related by Nicodemus Peters, an Indian sage of the Delaware Nation,[4] the twelve male participants seek the very real bear they want to sacrifice. They come upon a bear in an oak tree, his nose showing through a little hole, and they reject him. Then they find an elm tree containing the right bear, and knock four times on the tree, crying out "You we have found." The Bear comes out, acts ashamed, like a dog. The hero Maxkok orders the bear to come and to take the lead towards the Big House where the sacrifice is to take place. The bear lies down and makes further difficulties. Maxkok says "The bear will not come to the Big House. So no more will there be a feast dance. Therefore you will have to kill the bear right here." Courteously they order the bear to get up, he does, and they kill him, skin him, and complete the ceremony.

Here also, then, we have a fated bear, a "right" one, whose cooperation in his own death is demanded, since as the god he will want to share in all parts of the sacrifice which honors him with death. The bridge from the mythical to the real bear is crossed pragmatically by anticipation of some apparent lack of cooperation: if he runs away he is leading them; if he lies down he is ritually refusing to come; if, threatened by death, he rises to run again he is making it possible for the hunters to kill him. Folk wisdom has caught up the humor of this kind of situation in the proverbial dialogue: "I have caught a bear. —Bring it here. —It won't come. —Then come yourself. —It won't let me go." Catching a bear is like catching a Tartar.[5] The Hunted and the Hunter, as in Francis Thompson's *Hound of Heaven,* are one and the same.

Like Sam and the Munsee bear, Old Ben knows his fatal day. Here we find Faulkner reflecting[6] one of the greatest tall tales of

---

[4] Frank G. Speck and Jesse Moses, *The Celestial Bear Comes Down to Earth* (Reading, Pa., 1945), pp. 61-62. (See pp. 185-187 above.)

[5] Archer Taylor, *The Proverb* (Cambridge: Harvard University Press, 1931), p. 156.

[6] Faulkner's warnings about research find special appropriateness when we seek for examples of ritual parallels among the Choctaw and Chickasaw aborigines of Yoknapatawpha County. A. I. Hallowell, *Bear Ceremonialism*

the American Southwest, Thomas B. Thorpe's *The Big Bear of Arkansas,* of which Carvel Collins says:

> In Thorpe as in Faulkner the hunted animal is extraordinarily large, competent, and mysterious. Its hunters, with varying intensity, see it as supernatural and an embodiment of large principles. Even in minor matters the two works are parallel with each other and with the basic folktale: these details include a plunge through water at a climax of the hunt, the temporary substitution of an inferior for the real quarry, and the inability of the hunters to confront the bear when they are conventionally prepared for the hunt.[7]

Conventional preparation is of the real world; ritual demands special conditions, and any small omission may destroy the efficacy of the ceremony. So Ike must abandon watch, compass, gun and stick even to have a view of the god; and Boon must finish him off with a woodsman's knife, since guns will not work,[8] being tainted with novelty.

Thorpe's hero, Jim Doggett, hunted his quarry many times without success until one day, in an embarrassing posture while answering a call of nature, he saw the bear who, in his words:

> "loomed up like a *black mist,* he seemed so large, and he walked right towards me. I raised myself, took deliberate aim,

---

in the Northern Hemisphere (Philadelphia, 1926), p. 72, notes that "no rites accompanying the killing or eating of a bear have been reported for the peoples of" the Southeastern region or the related Iroquois. John R. Swanton's definitive *The Indians of the Southeastern United States* (Bureau of American Ethnology Bulletin 137, Washington, D.C., 1946) offers little or nothing on the "universal" custom of initiation (see the *huskanaw* on p. 712); only a little on the bear hunt with less on ceremonial (pp. 321-324); and something on burial customs as reflected in Sam Fathers' platform (p. 728).

[7] Carvel Collins, "Faulkner and Certain Earlier Southern Fiction," *College English,* XVI (1954), 96.

[8] Faulkner did not make it a *flint* knife, which it must be in many hypothetical rites which antedate the age of iron. See James G. Frazer, *The Golden Bough* (New York: Macmillan, 1935), III, 225-236; Hallowell, pp. 33-35. The pioneer iron knife of Daniel "Boon" is enough to show the conservative nature of ritual. LaBudde, *American Quarterly,* II (1950), 324, interprets the stabbing with the knife as "reverence" for the quarry; ritual conservatism is a better explanation to serve both his purposes and those of this essay.

and fired. Instantly the varmint wheeled, gave a yell, and *walked through the fence,* as easy as a falling tree would through a cobweb. I started after, but was tripped up by my inexpressibles, which, either from habit or the excitement of the moment, were about my heels, and before I had really gathered myself up, I heard the old varmint groaning, like a thousand sinners, in a thicket near by, and, by the time I reached him, he was a corpse. . . . It was, in fact, a creation bear, and if it had lived in Samson's time, and had met him in a fair fight, he would have licked him in the twinkling of a dice-box.

But, stranger, I never liked the way I hunted him, *and missed him.* There is something curious about it, that I never could understand,—and I never was satisfied at his giving in so *easy at last.* Perhaps he had heard of my preparations to hunt him the next day, so he jist guv up, like Captain Scott's coon, to save his wind to grunt with in dying; but that ain't likely. My private opinion is, that that bear was *an unhuntable bear, and died when his time come."* [9]

The dying god, in short, knows his destiny. One need not regard these parallels from Thorpe and the Munsee-Mahicans as "sources," but rather as cultural roots, as evidence of the closeness of Faulkner's story to the land from which it is taken. Faulkner at Virginia elaborately disclaimed direct sources:

As far as I know I have never done one page of research. Also, I doubt if I've ever forgotten anything I ever read too. . . . That what research I read, I read exactly as I do fiction because it's people, man, in motion, and the writer, as I say, never forgets that, he stores it away.[10]

At the same time he admits indirect or unconscious sources, and it is unlikely that the author of *The Bear* and *Spotted Horses,* the latter with its tell-tale teller Ratliff, did not know Davy Crockett,

---

[9] In Wright Morris's *Ceremony in Lone Tree* (New York: Atheneum, 1960), p. 66, the grandfather of a Nebraska family, aged ninety, remarks: "One thing nobody in the world knows is when his time is come. That is God's secret."

[10] Gwynn and Blotner, p. 251.

Thorpe, James Baldwin, Sut Lovingood and other Münchhausens of flush times in Mississippi, Georgia, Tennessee, and Arkansas Travellers. The Munsee-Mahican Bear Ceremony was published by Speck after *The Bear* was written; yet if Old Ben could foresee his own end and die "when his time come," he could surely anticipate a collector of traditions like Speck.[11]

Old Ben, like Thorpe's Big Bear, has cosmic dimensions; he is the God of the Wilderness. At his death the Wilderness dies, or at least shrinks to a tiny plot of hunting land surrounding the graves of the ritual dead: Lion, Old Ben, Sam Fathers. Ike, fleeing a Snopesian civilization and the raucous planing-mill which is its symbol, revisits the "dead." Like gods they never die. "It was as if the old bear, even dead there in the yard, was a more potent terror still than they could face without Lion between them." Death and life are earth's cycles. The graves are gone:

> He passed one of the four concrete markers set down by the lumber company's surveyor to establish the four corners of the plot which Major de Spain had reserved out of the sale, then he stood on the crest of the knoll itself, the four corner-markers all visible now, blanched still even beneath the winter's weathering, lifeless and shockingly alien in that place where dissolution itself was a seething turmoil of ejaculation tumescence conception and birth, and death did not even exist. . . . he had not stopped, he had only paused, quitting the knoll which was no abode of the dead because there was no death, not Lion and not Sam held fast in earth but free in earth and not in earth but of earth, myriad yet undiffused of every myriad part . . . dark and dawn and dark and dawn again in their immutable progression, and, being myriad, one: and Old Ben too. Old Ben too! they would give his paw back even.

Ike's recollections of the seasonal myths and the resurrection of the god are interrupted by the sight of a rattlesnake, the snake of

---

[11] Speck (p. xii) collected the ritual from Nekatcit in 1938; his informant died in 1939. The first version of *The Bear* (*Lion*) appeared in *Harper's Magazine* in 1935; the final magazine version in *The Saturday Evening Post* in 1942. *Go Down, Moses* was also published in 1942. See LaBudde, *American Quarterly*, II (1950), 322 [pp. 226-233 above].

this diminished Eden—the immortal snake who stole life from man and who is the prototype of the logging train which devours the wilderness.

II

Gods do not exist without their cults or without their priests. The hunt, as in many cultures, is blended in the story with initiation or puberty ritual. For if this is the story of a Bear, it is also the story of a Boy who achieves pride and humility through a lengthy testing in the woods. The unprecedented appeal of this story to young and old alike is partly the result of Faulkner's meticulous account of Ike's precocious growth as a "man's hunter." Mircea Eliade's classic definition of initiation as Birth and Rebirth might have been written with Ike specifically in mind:

> In philosophical terms, initiation is equivalent to a basic change in existential condition; the novice emerges from his ordeal endowed with a totally different being from that which he possessed before his initiation; he has become *another*.
> . . . Initiation introduces the candidate into the human community and into the world of spiritual and cultural values.
> . . . he learns the mystical relations between the tribe and the Supernatural Beings as those relations were established at the beginning of Time. . . . Initiatory death is indispensable for the beginning of spiritual life. Its function must be understood in relation to what it prepares: birth to a higher mode of being. As we shall see farther on, initiatory death is often symbolized, for example, by darkness, by cosmic night, by the telluric womb, the hut, the belly of a monster.[12]

So Ike "entered his novitiate to the true wilderness with Sam beside him as he had begun his apprenticeship in miniature to manhood after the rabbits and such with Sam beside him, the two of them wrapped in the damp, warm, Negro-rank quilt, while the wilderness closed behind his entrance as it had opened momentarily to accept him, opening before his advancement as it closed behind

---

[12] Mircea Eliade, *Birth and Rebirth* (New York: Harper and Brothers, 1958), pp. x-xiv. See pp. 190-193 above.

his progress. . . . It seemed to him that at the age of ten he was witnessing his own birth." [13]

The subtle steps by which Ike approaches the god, never close enough to be hurt by him as Lion was in body and Boon in mind, are the vicarious paths a good society (the hunter's society, not the world of the present) provides for its adolescents to make them men. The rites coincide with "the yearly pageant-rite of the old bear's furious immortality," but they are not identical with it; except for one close call as he saves the frantic fyce, Ike never comes really in contact with the Godhead. But he grows in hunting wisdom and also in spiritual perception; he abandons the tainted weapons of civilization; he progresses until General Compson can decry the conventional schoolhouse from which Ike wants to play hookey so that he may tend the dying Sam:

> "And you shut up, Cass. . . . You've got one foot straddled into a farm and the other foot straddled into a bank; you ain't even got a good hand-hold where this boy was already an old man . . . that could go ten miles on a compass because he wanted to look at a bear none of us had ever got near enough to put a bullet in and looked at the bear and came the ten miles back on the compass in the dark."

Ike then is the responsive initiate, like young Marlow in Conrad's *Youth,* Nick Adams in Hemingway's *Big Two-Hearted River,* or the boy soldier in Stephen Crane's *Red Badge of Courage.* Sam is the priest and Boon the acolyte, and Boon, who completes the killing of the Bear, goes mad, while Sam loses his

---

[13] Mordecai Marcus, who is skeptical of the too extensive use of the word "initiation" to characterize a host of modern stories, gives *The Bear* a clean bill. The marking of Ike's forehead with the blood of his first slain deer and the abandonment of watch, gun and compass "combine psychological compulsion and the sense of a half-intuited myth, the feeling that nature demands a certain rite. More distinctly psychological are the ritualistic intensity with which Ike pores over his grandfather's ledgers . . . and Ike's decision to renounce the land. . . . Faulkner's primitive and psychological rituals are always convincing." See "What Is an Initiation Story?" *Journal of Aesthetics and Art Criticism,* XIX (1960), 226-227. I would think the decision to renounce the land is ritually strengthened historical action, rather than ritual itself.

life as part of the sacrifice. "Sam was the chief, the prince; Boon, the plebeian, was his huntsman." In keeping with the return to nature, to Eliade's "telluric womb," the various animals of the story closely parallel the three human ritual actors. They share in the rite like the totemic ancestors, ancestral beasts, or culture heroes; they are shadows of the men and the boy, or rather the doubles, for it is uncertain here just who is shadow and who is substance. Spiritually speaking Sam is Ike's "Chief, Grandfather"; his father, Uncle Buck, has died long ago, and his grandfather Carothers is the compulsive villain of the story, archetypal slave-owner and seducer of his Negro women, one of them his own daughter. Sam, like the priest of Nemi, is identical with the god he must kill and be killed by. By juxtaposition Faulkner makes the equation clear: "an old bear, fierce and ruthless with the fierce pride of liberty and freedom . . . an old man, son of a Negro slave and an Indian king, inheritor on the one hand of the long chronicle of a people who had learned humility through suffering and learned pride through the endurance which survived the suffering, and on the other side the chronicle of a people even longer in the land than the first, yet who now existed there only in the solitary brotherhood of an old and childless Negro's alien blood and the wild and invincible spirit of an old bear." To them comes "a boy who wished to learn humility and pride in order to become skillful and worthy in the woods but found himself becoming so skillful so fast that he feared he would never become worthy, because he had not learned humility and pride though he had tried, until one day an old man, who could not have defined either, led him as though by the hand to where an old bear and a little mongrel dog showed him that, by possessing one thing other, he would possess them both." The one thing other is bravery; the fyce, who is as clearly Ike as Old Ben is Sam, is neither humble nor proud but only brave, although the world would "probably call that too just noise."

And if these equations hold, there is no trouble with the last one, Boon's identity with Lion. One of the magnificent things of this story is the love affair between the giant poor white Boon and "the great grave blue dog" who helps him kill Old Ben. Their relationship comes directly out of Southern culture.[14] Faulkner knows his Southern songs: the "Go Down, Moses" of the novel; "That Evening Sun," from "St. Louis Blues," with its tragic implications for Dilsey's daughter Nancy; Dilsey's own endurance, which owes much to various spirituals; and the widely-known song "Old Blue," which mingles rite with humor. A Mississippi version of the last, which Faulkner may have known, begins:

> I had an old dog, his name was Blue;
> I tell you boys, he was a rounder too.

Blue catches a possum, but dies of the exertion.

> Old Blue died; I laid him in the shade,
> I dug his grave with a silver spade.
> CHORUS: Come on, Blue, Come on Blue,
>   You old rascal you.

> I let him down with a golden chain;
> Link by link slipped through my hand.

> There is only one thing that bothers my mind;
> Blue went to heaven and left me behind.

> When I get there, the first thing I'll do,
> Grab me a horn and blow for Old Blue.[15]

Like the singer of this song, Boon is a whiskey-drinking rounder; Lion is a savage mongrel, not from the pack but out of the wilderness. Lion's use is confined to his obsessive desire to kill Old Ben, but he has the power which the brave little fyce lacked; he dies with Old Ben, his mortal enemy, and Boon cares for him

---

[14] The clearest mark of poor-white or hillfolk status is the hound-dog, according to James West (pseud. for George Withers), *Plainsville U.S.A.* (New York: Columbia University Press, 1961), pp. 20, 132, 138. See also William H. Nicholls, *Southern Tradition and Regional Progress* (Chapel Hill: University of North Carolina Press, 1960), pp. 37, 39, 125.

[15] Arthur P. Hudson, *Folksongs of Mississippi and Their Background* (Chapel Hill: University of North Carolina Press, 1936), pp. 201-202; see also Henry M. Belden and Arthur P. Hudson, *Folk Songs from North Carolina* (Durham: Duke University Press, 1952), pp. 252-253; Vance Randolph, *Ozark Folksongs* (State Historical Society of Missouri, 1946-50), II, 383, and my forthcoming book on *Folksongs of the Flood.*

like a human being. Boon defies Major de Spain and demands a
doctor, not for himself or for Sam Fathers, as one might think,
but for the great blue dog. He digs his grave, and no doubt expects to meet him in heaven. As Ike had refrained from shooting
Ben for the fyce's sake, Boon refrains for Lion's sake. Boon fed
Lion, slept with him, and lived for him; they were as one. At the
beginning of the climactic hunt, the final epiphany, Lion "moved
its head and looked at" Ike "across the trivial uproar of the
hounds, out of the yellow eyes as depthless as Boon's, as free as
Boon's of meanness or generosity or gentleness or viciousness.
They were just cold and sleepy."

Thus the initiate Ike viewed a ritual drama which made a man
of him, which taught him finally the "pride and humility" he
needed. These paradoxical words move like a *leitmotif* throughout the story; I count at least twenty occurrences of them separate
or combined. Though they are as hard for us to define as they
were for Sam Fathers, they are in a sense the key to the story.
Hunters need "humility and skill" to survive; Ike learns humility
on his first hunting trip—how to prepare his gun when he doesn't
shoot; his mentor Sam is "passionate and proud"; Ike at ten has
dedicated his life "to the wilderness with patience and humility";
his eagerness for hunting is tempered with "an abjectness, a sense
of his own fragility and impotence against the timeless woods";
he is too humble to know that he will be the first to come near to
the bear, be "run over" by him; he relinquishes his gun "in humility and peace and without regret"; he approaches Old Ben with
beating heart but with steadiness.

In Part II the keywords strangely vanish until one significant
paragraph at the end. It is because this section is in a measure an
exemplum of pride and independence, and of the fixing of the
fates which consists in the finding of the proper instruments for
the climactic ceremony. The words are not needed, for the action
is enough. In Part I Ike had learned humility as well as skill, but
the skill, too personal, had not yet become pride to balance the
humility. In Part II we have the episode of the fyce which ambushed the Bear, which bayed on the hounds and ran to Old Ben
with insane courage, forcing Ike to do the same until "it seemed
to him that he was directly under the bear. He could smell it,

strong and hot and rank. Sprawling, he looked up where it loomed and towered over him like a thunderclap."

Neither Ike nor the fyce, though brave even to foolhardiness, are the proper instruments. Those instruments are Boon and Lion, and the section is devoted to showing how Lion's independence is tamed by Sam and Boon, but tamed only insofar as to make him obsessed with a need to kill Old Ben. Here humility is not made into pride, but pride is tempered. Boon becomes so much Lion's double that he defies his employer Major de Spain, who had ordered Lion outside so that his scent would not be ruined by "the smell of Boon's unwashed body and his wet hunting-clothes." The next night he is back with Boon. With humor the Major admits that he is outsmarted. And Boon is right—the powerful odor of Old Ben, which had come so close to Ike, was not likely to be obscured by Boon and Lion's common bed. On Old Ben's seventh appearance, just before the climactic kill, Boon fails, to his utter shame, to shoot him. He laments, concerned only with Lion's reaction: "I ain't fit to sleep with him." The section closes with Ike's meditation: "So he should have hated and feared Lion. Yet he did not. It seemed to him that there was a fatality in it. It seemed to him that something, he didn't know what, was beginning; had already begun. It was like the last act on a set stage. It was the beginning of the end of something, he didn't know what except that he would not grieve. He would be humble and proud that he had been found worthy to be a part of it too or even just to see it too." Ike has learned that the pride comes from sharing the rite, from collective rather than individual action. He must not hate Lion, who replaces his double the fyce as major actor just as Boon replaces Ike. Boon's apparent independence and pride is a part of the sense of collective destiny; he must not be separated from Lion, for their *mana* or spirit power is reciprocal. Boon's "humility" when he fails Lion is the other side of the coin; to us it is almost absurd sensitivity, but Boon knows that he has not yet performed his task rightly, and that Lion knows it.

By Part III, Ike possesses the pair of virtues. In Memphis with Boon, the Major has put him in charge of the money, with orders to give Boon nothing for whiskey. But Ike is loyal to Boon, who had once saved him from a wild, unbroken horse, and he disobeys the Major and gives Boon a dollar. Waiting outside the saloon, Ike "felt the old lift of the heart, as pristine as ever, as on the first day; he would never lose it, no matter how old in hunting and pursuit: the best, the best of all breathing, the humility and the pride." The episode is not mere comedy; Boon's drinking, while it demonstrates his warfare with the town, has no ill effects. It is a necessary communion with the wine which will strengthen him for his final role. Ike remains true to his basic ties with Boon, as the keywords illustrate. Once more Boon exemplifies pride and valor; working in partnership with Lion he kills Old Ben and now, more openly, defies the Major:

> "Boon!" Major de Spain said. They looked at one another. Boon was a good head taller than Major de Spain; even the boy was taller now than Major de Spain.
> "I've got to get the doctor," Boon said. "His goddam guts ———"
> "All right," Major de Spain said.

The whiskey-soaked, no-'count half-breed, who can do nothing but drink in town because he is so alien there, and who must through his feeling of inferiority brag through liquor of Lion and the chase of Old Ben, rises finally to the greatest height of physical valor and pride of any character in the story, as he confronts the great Bear and kills him. After the kill, disregarding his own injuries and those of Sam Fathers, he tends the disembowelled Lion like the lover that he is. It is pride overcoming humility; through great, rash heedless acts, compelled by destiny and by love, Boon will pay for his excess of virtue; by the last act Boon, mad with contact with the God and the loss of his beloved Wilderness and his beloved Lion, is a mass of shivering hysteria. Part V is merely a coda to Part III; Ike pays humble tribute to the graves of Sam and Lion and Old Ben; Boon smashes his gun while the squirrels leap about—ostensibly because it had jammed, actually becaused it is a tainted weapon, unlike the primitive woodsman's knife[16] with which he had killed Old Ben. His final cry is ironic:

---

[16] See note 8.

"Get out of here! Don't touch them! Don't touch a one of them! They're mine!" On the surface he means the squirrels, the last vestige of the wild beings to whom his life had been devoted. But the mad cry is of greed, directed to his best human friend Ike; the craving is for the pride of possession, the vice which has destroyed the wilderness. Ike has learned the humility of pride; Boon has never learned the humility; he is in imbalance, out of *mesure,* mad.

III

So far we have said nothing of Part IV and its treatment of pride and humility; we have reserved it for an assault on our final problem—how the apparently incoherent flashback fits the story as a whole. Pride and humility, learned from initiation and cli-mactic Hunt, lead Ike to transcend his culture and to do it by strength gained from the culture itself. In no section, except the first, are the keywords more significantly used.

The narrative now moves out of its hunting context, from the protecting womb of the wilderness, to the stages of history and of the cosmos, to a real and not a vicarious testing of Isaac McCaslin. Ike declares that his repudiation of the land is no repudiation be-cause the earlier owners had never owned it. God had given it to men; He had allowed them "to hold the earth mutual and intact in the communal anonymity of brotherhood, and all the fee He asked was pity and humility and sufferance and endurance and the sweat of his face for bread." God, though blind and dis-possessed of Eden, suffered through the corruptions of Roman bagnios and Germanic hordes "until He used a simple egg to dis-cover to them a new world where a nation of people could be founded in humility and pity and sufferance and pride of one to another." It becomes clear that the true pride and endurance lies in the humblest of status—in the Northern Negro who defies Cass and marries Fonsiba, Ike's first cousin by Carothers's miscegena-tion, who proudly dotes on the white man's weapon, the book, at the risk of losing his livelihood on the farm which he cannot run; even more so in the Southern Negro Lucas, Fonsiba's young-est brother, biggety and defiant and proud, who on his twenty-first birthday demands his heritage from Cass.

The destinies are working themselves out; even God must await them. Having created man, "He could have known no more of hope than He could of pride and grief, but He didn't hope He just waited because He had made them." Humility is of the Godhead itself. But "He had seen how in individual cases" men "were capable of anything." There were Buck and Buddy, Lucas, Sam and Ike, all of whom learned both pride and humility, not through reason but, like the frantic fyce, through an irrational bravery. Keats's eternal truth and beauty "covers all things which touch the heart—honor and pride and pity and justice and courage and love. . . . what the heart holds to becomes truth, as far as we know truth." With this discovery that one must rest one's mortal case not on reason or conformity or the social pressures, or even on the marked-out destinies, Ike learns that he is free to repudiate his heritage. Cass, a lesser soul though a worthy one, who half understands Ike as he tries to dissuade him, denies the freedom of choice. Negro and White shall never be free, "we from them nor they from us . . . I am what I am; I will be always what I was born and have always been." Not so, says Ike, "Sam Fathers set me free." And he adopts the mystic role of the Carpenter[17] who had also repudiated the World, the Flesh, and the Devil. Ike gives up his land, and tries to live a life free from the obsessions of property and the taint of slavery. But he makes his great gesture "not in mere static and hopeful emulation of the Nazarene . . . (without the arrogance of false humility and without the false humbleness of pride, who intended to earn his bread, didn't especially want to earn it but had to earn his bread . . .) because if the Nazarene had found carpentering good for the life and ends He had assumed and elected to serve, it would be all right too for Isaac McCaslin."

Ike's exact ends are unclear; like Sam Fathers he could have defined completely neither pride nor humility. Though it is plain that the paradoxical words mean much to Faulkner, critics have said little about them. Perhaps there has been some fear that the author is a mere slave to the verbal fashions of a time when Eliot

---

[17] My colleague, John Muste, has prepared a study underlining the irony which lies in Ike's choice of a profession—timber, the product of the logger and the sawmill, is the raw material of the carpenter's craft. Hence the destruction of the wilderness is essential for Ike's act of repudiation.

and Empson have encouraged literary ambivalences. Yet it is easy to show that the linking of pride and humility is much older than the Freudian present. Macarius, a saint of the Egyptian desert in the early days of Christian asceticism, forces the devil, ancient symbol of pride, to complain:

> "In only one thing dost thou overmaster me." And when the saint asked what that might be, he answered "In thy humility." And the saint fell on his knees—it may be to repel this last and subtlest temptation—and the devil vanished into the air.[18]

We will recall the fourth and final temptation which assailed Eliot's Becket in *Murder in the Cathedral*. The deadliest sin of all may be pride in one's own humility. So Christianity: it was the essence of the Renaissance to penetrate to a juncture between the two. Erwin Panofsky tells us:

> It is from this ambivalent conception of *humanitas* that humanism was born. It is not so much a movement as an attitude which can be defined as the conviction of the dignity of man, based on both the insistence on human values (rationality and freedom) and the acceptance of human limitations (fallibility and frailty); from this two postulates result —responsibility and tolerance.[19]

Is there a better statement of the forces which strengthened Ike to his great repudiation—the responsibility of pride and the tolerance of humility?

The validity of the ambivalence is shown in two great antagonistic eighteenth-century figures, the hedonistic mystic William Blake and the stern moralist Immanuel Kant. Blake reverses, in his fragmentary *The Everlasting Gospel,* the usual meaning of the words:

> I was standing by when Jesus died;
> What I call'd humility, they call'd pride.

---

[18] Helen Waddell, *The Desert Fathers* (Ann Arbor Paperbacks, 1960), pp. 12-13.

[19] Erwin Panofsky, *Meaning in the Visual Arts* (New York: Anchor Books, 1955), p. 2.

> He who loves his enemies betrays his friends.
> This is surely not what Jesus intends;
> But the sneaking pride of heroic schools,
> And the Scribes' and Pharisees' virtuous rules,
> For He acts with honest, triumphant pride,
> And this is the cause that Jesus died.
> He did not die with Christian ease,
> Asking pardon of His enemies:
> If He had, Caiaphas would forgive;
> Sneaking submission can always live. . . .
> God wants not man to humble himself:
> That is the trick of the Ancient Elf.
> This is the race that Jesus ran:
> Humble to God, haughty to man. . . .
> "Thou art a Man: God is no more:
> Thy own Humanity learn to adore,
> For that is My spirit of life." . . .
> But when Jesus was crucified,
> Then was perfected His galling pride.[20]

Blake does not expect his transvaluation of values to gain immediate acceptance:

> I am sure this Jesus will not do,
> Either for Englishman or Jew.

But Blake, though perhaps much akin to the mature and transcending Ike McCaslin, is scarcely a respectable authority for the
joining of pride and humility. Hence we may turn to Immanuel
Kant, the moral giant of Königsberg, and ancestor of modern
philosophy:

> The moral law is holy (unyielding) and demands holiness of
> morals, although all moral perfection to which man can attain
> is only virtue . . . consequently, man can achieve only a
> self-esteem combined with humility. . . . Fontanelle says,

---

[20] John Sampson, ed., *The Poetical Works of William Blake* (New York:
Oxford University Press, 1958), pp. 150-151, 157. See Milton O. Percival,
William Blake's Circle of Destiny (New York: Columbia University Press,
1938), pp. 188, 195.

"I bow to a great man, but my mind does not bow." I can add; to a humble plain man, in whom I perceive righteousness in a higher degree than I am conscious of in myself, *my mind bows* whether I choose or not, and however high I carry my head that he may not forget my superior position. Why? His example holds a law before me which strikes down my self-conceit when I compare my own conduct with it. . . . Nevertheless . . . when once we renounce our self-conceit and respect has established its practical influence, we cannot ever satisfy ourselves in contemplating the majesty of this law, and the soul believes itself to be elevated in proportion as it sees the holy law as elevated over it and its frail nature.[21]

Humility and the pride of perfection, in other words, are closely allied: in Saint Macarius, Renaissance humanism, Kant's man, and Blake's and Faulkner's Nazarene.

IV

Being a modern man Ike does not seek celibacy, as Christ and His followers had done, but marries a woman who soon betrays that her eye is on the land which he had repudiated but could, she believes, have back again if he wished. Basically frigid by nature, she tries to seduce him with her body and the promise of a son and heir, but Ike refuses the temptation and the marriage breaks up with a hysterical laughter on her possessive part which is repeated in the hysteria of Boon, also dispossessed, at the end of the story. Ike himself is repudiated by the nameless woman who for a brief time shares his bed.

This passage means many things, and it is not certain just which of them Faulkner wishes to keep uppermost. In his public comments he has interpreted the episode wholly in a particular vein, without universal significance: a good woman might have helped Ike in his battle with the results of Negro slavery and

---

[21] Lewis W. Beck, ed., *The Critique of Practical Reason* (Chicago: The University of Chicago Press, 1949), copyright 1949 by The University of Chicago, pp. 184-185, 231; see also pp. 39, 41, 181; see also *Critique of Pure Reason* (London: J. M. Dent, 1942), p. 468 (pride or humility depends on a subjective or objective view of belief in God).

miscegenation.[22] But we might predict that Ike's initiation and skill in the hunt, won in exclusively masculine company, could not be transferred to a world which included woman. As many a man has found, woman is a hostage to fortune: the commitment to dynastic aims rather than to the "pure" aims of the individual; the commitment to property because the freedom to choose repudiation becomes complex when one has a wife and child to support. Woman, moreover, meant miscegenation; the crimes of Carothers which forced Ike to his gesture are bound up in the lusts of the flesh and the pride of life.

Woman thus has no place in Ike's world of values; he refuses the rationalization which exalts the white woman at the expense of her black sister, and to the peril of her black brother. As W. J. Cash puts it:

> We strike back to the fact that this Southern woman's place
> in the Southern mind proceeded primarily from the natural
> tendency of the great basic pattern of pride in superiority of
> race to center upon her as the perpetuity of that superiority
> in legitimate line, and attached itself precisely, and before
> anything else, to her enormous remoteness from the males
> of the inferior group, to the absolute taboo on any sexual
> approach to her by the Negro. . . . What Southerners felt,
> therefore, was that any assertion of any kind on the part of
> the Negro constituted in a perfectly real manner an attack
> on the Southern woman . . . a condition for which the term
> "rape" stood as truly as for the *de facto* deed.[23]

Ike's renunciation of the world of woman goes back at least one generation to Uncle Buck, who was forced into marriage with Miss Sophonsiba by a card game and an intriguing brother. The gesture of Uncle Buck and Uncle Buddy, which had consisted of manumitting the Negroes and of building a house with their own hands (they are carpenters before Isaac) and the herding of the Negroes into the Big House of their father Carothers McCaslin, had to take place before the marriage. After Miss Sophonsiba, mother of Ike, has died, Uncle Buddy takes on the shaman's role

---

[22] Gwynn and Blotner, pp. 275-276.
[23] Cash, pp. 118-119.

of cook. Miss Sophonsiba does not share men's guilt; she drives her brother Hubert's black concubine away; if women had been masters there would have been no taint, and thus women cannot understand man's obsession with guilt and repentance.

But the guilt leads to powerful action in Ike's case, and he is sure that from time to time some, like the Nazarene, Uncle Buck and Uncle Buddy, and himself, will be able to transcend the cultural environment into which they are born, and make the gesture which casts off the tainted heritage, the original sin. In this he is like Huck Finn, torn between his cultural and his private values: "it hit me all of a sudden that here was the plain hand of Providence slapping me in the face and letting me know my wickedness was being watched all the time from up there in heaven, whilst I was stealing a poor old woman's nigger that hadn't ever done me no harm. . . ." The training of his society tells Huck clearly that he must give back his friend Nigger Jim, and he writes a letter to Jim's owner, Miss Watson. But observe the ambiguity in the illiterate boy's misplaced modifier. It was not only Miss Watson, but Jim as well, that "hadn't ever done me no harm." So Huck, like Ike, repudiates—here the letter and the heavenly climate: " 'All right, then, I'll *go* to hell'—and tore it up." He had tried to pray to God for what seemed to be help, but "the words wouldn't come," for, as he realized, "You can't pray a lie—I found that out." He was holding on to what seemed to be the greatest sin of all, before God Himself—the refusal to follow his culture's fiat and to give Jim up. But again the ambivalence— what, after all, is the lie?

These "transcendences" of two Southern boys in the face of the great problem of the Negro appear like heroism to one born in the North. And so they are; any man who learns to probe to the center of the unsolved problems of his community and to try, even as lonely individual, to once make the right gesture, is a hero, like Thoreau with his Civil Disobedience, or Antigone with her obeisance to the gods in the burial of her brothers and her defiance of Creon. But we must come up short before we end in regional condescension—a major obstacle to helping the South to solve its problem or the North to solve its kindred ones. The heroism is nothing without the ambivalence, without the genuine struggle

between old cultural and newly emerging values. Can anyone but
the Southern boy be involved in this particular kind of heroic
defiance? Can he achieve it without the aid of the values his culture has provided for him? It was the pride and humility gained
in the wilderness, surrounded by a simple world of masculine
values, and demonstrating the worth of every creature—the half-
breed Negro and Indian Sam Fathers; the drunken no-'count
Boon; Major de Spain and Cass, gentle in breeding and will but
as yet unwilling to forego the more obvious values of their culture;
the furious fyce and the calculating ominous Lion and the savage,
cunning and god-like Old Ben; the poor white swampers who are
in the main spectators but yet passionate followers of the Hunt—
all of these lie behind this Southern boy who makes a quixotic
gesture to erase, he hopes, the miscegenation of his fathers, and
condemns his own line to sterility and his own life to a compulsive
repetition of the patterns of his childhood initiation, the endless,
seasonal hunt. Such a chivalric gesture was only made possible by
the nature of the South itself, with its individualism learned in
the Edenic wilderness and its romanticism learned from Sir Walter
Scott.[24] The South provided the hunting culture, with Ike's long
training and testing in the hands of Sam Fathers, true heir, if there
was one, to the land—descendant of Doom and double of the
Bear that walked like a Man. While an initiation is a rebirth into
the culture which surrounds one, it paradoxically may give one
the strength to rise above the culture's own ostensible values. To
transcend one's culture one must learn from it, one must lean
upon it for the upward leap; if there is no agony in the cutting of
the ties it may be presumed that there are no ties of importance
to cut.

Kenneth LaBudde, in his study of "Cultural Primitivism in
William Faulkner's 'The Bear' "[25] shares with this essay of mine
an interest in the anthropological parallels to Ike's story. I cannot
agree with him, however, in reducing Faulkner's "driving complexity" to a Rousseauistic myth. His conclusion that "Wisdom
is achieved by intuition schooled by nature rather than by reason
fashioned according to the ways of men" is only part of the truth.

---

[24] Cash, pp. 198-200 above.
[25] LaBudde, pp. 322-328. See pp. 226-233 above.

The Bear is as ambiguous as Moby Dick; if he is the doomed integral Wilderness he is also the creator of "a corridor of wreckage and destruction beginning back before the boy was born . . . a phantom, epitome and apotheosis of the old, wild life which the little puny humans swarmed and hacked at in a fury of abhorrence and fear." There is similar irony in the Major's charge that Old Ben must now be hunted because he has threatened sacred "property" by killing the colt. Our radical instincts are aroused by this; it would seem that puny man puts property above heroism and excellence. Yet, radical or conservative, we are human beings, and we find it hard to divorce ourselves from the championing of mankind, collective or individual, against the destructive forces of nature, whether they are in the wilderness, the sea, or in outer space. Faulkner essentially justifies our position in his comments external to the text.[26] Discussing the destruction of Old Ben and the wilderness he says:

> change can destroy what is irreplaceable. . . . But if in the end that makes more education for more people, and more food for more people, more of the good things of life. . . . it was worth destroying the wilderness. But if all the destruction of the wilderness does is to give more people more automobiles just to ride around in, then the wilderness was better.

It is interesting to note that another Southern novelist also saw the lumber companies as a destructive force. Planning a novel about the decay of an aristocratic family just after the Civil War, Thomas Wolfe projected the following element in the plot: "Against Eugene's and his mother's protest that to sell their land at next to nothing is criminal, the Colonel hard-pressed for money, and unwilling to work or have his boys work, sells his 500,000 acres for 25 cents an acre to a New Eng. lumber firm." [27] The coincidence shows that there is a real as well as a symbolic basis for the wilderness theme; it is no mere noble savagery.

A simple primitivism is not borne out by other figures in the

---

[26] Gwynn and Blotner, p. 277.

[27] *Thomas Wolfe's Letters to His Mother,* ed., John K. Terry (New York: Charles Scribner's Sons, 1946), pp. 16, 26.

story besides Old Ben. Boon is the rugged hero of the hunt, who fights Old Ben face to face with knife rather than with gun and risks his own life to save Lion, yet in town he is a self-conscious yokel, forced to drink whiskey to hide his embarrassments and to build his ego, and at the end of the story he goes mad, incapable of coping with civilization. His drunkenness and his fidelity to the Major are both virtues (the Major) or both vices (Cass). General Compson exalts the Hunt above school as a means to education; yet it is clear that Ike has learned the tale of human history both broad and narrow, both from Eden on to the major present and in the pages of the family ledgers. One must *read* to do this, and reading is not an accomplishment of noble savages. The Negro's freedom and honor is the subject of *The Bear* and even more of "Delta Autumn"; yet the one Negro in the hunting story (eliminating the symbolic half-breed Sam Fathers) is Ash, the cook, who has never learned to hunt, and who through his jealousy of Ike's baptism of blood becomes the subject of a comic hunting story about a gun which went off by itself.

The poetic justices of primitivism are cancelled out by the tragic spirit. God looks "upon this land this South for which he had done so much with woods for game and streams for fish and deep rich soil for seed and lush springs to sprout it and long summers to mature it and serene falls to harvest it and short mild winters for men and animals, and saw no hope anywhere and looked beyond it where hope should have been, where to East North and West lay illimitable that whole hopeful continent dedicated as a refuge and sanctuary of liberty and freedom from what you called the old world's worthless evening, and saw the rich descendants of slavers, females of both sexes . . . passing resolutions about horror and outrage in warm and air-proof halls." Only John Brown transcended this universal depravity. The Negro, despite his role as Noble Savage, his potential for endurance and his primitive strength, is human enough to share original sin: "those upon whom freedom and equality had been dumped overnight and without warning or preparation or any training in how to employ it or even just endure it and who misused it, not as children would nor yet because they had been so long in bondage and then so suddenly freed, but misused it as human beings always misuse freedom." Faulkner, in short, pays the Negro his tribute as a man, but with it must come man's human weaknesses.

Ike's freedom, patterned upon the initiation or not, is an achieved success, a progress rather than a nostalgic regression, a dynamism of the future rather than a return to the past, however much it has its roots in the culture and hence in the history of the race. As Cass, envious of Ike's release but aware of his own lack of it, says, the great hunt of the story proper is linked to the gesture of repudiation. "Chosen, I suppose (I will concede it) out of all your time by Him, as you say Buck and Buddy were from theirs. And it took Him a bear and an old man and four years just for you. And it took you fourteen years to reach that point and about that many, maybe more, for Old Ben, and more than seventy for Sam Fathers. And you just one. How long then? How long?" This is tragedy, a tragic conflict aided by God between man and his own society, the slow inching upward of evolution, and not the regression of primitivism. Redemptive tragedy, for the individual falls by the wayside as he saves us all. The primitive provides strength for those who would make civilization civilized, not a haven for those merely weary of civilization. Ike's gesture, as we can see, was dynamic and redemptive, a step in the salvation of the oppressed, the primitive; his later life was a regression, as we shall see in "Delta Autumn," for he was himself caught in the static back-eddies of "repudiation." There is, after all, a snake in Eden, and it has been there from the beginning.

Fortified, then, by the long developed ceremonial of the hunt and by the individualism and romanticism of his Southern culture, Ike has the courage to make the initial repudiation, and to sustain it in spite of the demonic temptation offered by his greedy and hysterical wife. He has emulated the Nazarene, and he is one therefore of those many characters of Faulkner, like Joe Christmas in *Light in August* and the Corporal in *The Fable,* who seem to repeat among proud and humble men, the meek who shall inherit the earth, the story of the Passion. Faulkner's attitude towards such symbolic readings has always been cavalier and oblique:

And that Christ story is one of the best stories that man has invented, assuming that he did invent that story, and of

course it will recur. Everyone that has had the story of
Christ and the Passion as a part of his Christian background
will in time draw from that. There was no deliberate attempt
to repeat it. That the people to me come first. The symbolism comes second. . . . Well, one symbol was the bear
represented the vanishing wilderness. The little dog that
wasn't scared of the bear represented the indomitable spirit
of man. I'll have to dig back and get up some more of these
symbols, because I have learned around an even dozen that
I put into that story without knowing it.[28]

Some of this is chaff, of course, the protective coloration of an
author besieged by brash young students and persistent old women
to tell the inmost secrets of his craft, which are either in his eyes
inferrable from his text or else not worth pursuing. But it allows
us the identification of Ike with the Nazarene; Ike is at least a
diminished Christ.

Elsewhere Faulkner has said that Ike is really a "no-'count,"
a man who is anything but the hero of history. Here he would
seem to accept the doubts of Major de Spain, who fears that Ike,
in renouncing his heritage, has "just quit." The Major modifies his
remark by saying "I have watched you in the woods too much
and I don't believe you just quit even if it does look damn like it."
Perhaps this is mere persuasion, calculated to cause Ike to change
his course once again, though a comparison to the Nazarene
follows. But Ike does, to all respectable people, become a no-
'count, who gives up his farm and becomes a poor menial and
spends his life passing on the lore of Sam Fathers, second-hand,
to youngsters.

Faulkner has been careful not to endow him with omniscience.
His renunciation of the world of woman's love, which surely
means the natural world of society, may not be as wise as it
seems. Perhaps there is some deficiency in this hunter, initiated
into a man's world.

He triumphs, surely, in *The Bear*. But *The Bear* must be read
along with "Delta Autumn," in which a young Negro girl, seduced
by his kinsman Roth Edmonds, turns out to be a daughter of his

---

[28] Gwynn and Blotner, pp. 117, 280.

black cousin Tennie's Jim. Ike, who has the sensitivity and judgment to give her the horn which is a symbol of their mutual heritage, nevertheless urges her to go back North and to marry a man of her own race (as Fonsiba, without notable success, had done). The girl's proud words force a large salient of doubt into the assumption that Ike has really cut loose from his culture:

"Old man," she said, "have you lived so long and forgotten so much that you don't remember anything you ever knew or felt or even heard about love?"

If Ike is a Christ-figure, he is a much diminished one; he may in his youth have cast off Agape as well as Eros. Yet in his age he can still learn something: though the wall between the races is still thick and high, and its vanishing may be far in the future, it may, given some centuries, vanish completely. From a woman he learns of his deficiency, and with that knowledge he transcends not only the values of his people, his culture, but also those of the Hunt itself. The values of the Hunt had aided him to surmount the flaws of his immediate society, the South and the wider world of men's greed; the values of Love, learned from a Negro girl, may help him at last to surmount the limits of the cloistered Hunt.

"It was a doe," he said.

Critical Interpretations of
The Bear

Faulkner's Point of View and The Chronicle of Ike McCaslin

THOMAS J. WERTENBAKER, JR.

❧

One problem in reading Faulkner is to determine where for the moment to stop—within what boundaries to pause and look for a philosophical or even an artistic whole. Faulkner's work is an imaginative chronicle that lays down, layer on layer, transparent mosaics in widening, overlapping, ever larger and deeper patterns without end. From the particulars of almost any Faulkner story the narrative eye retreats in space and time until its perspective is that of memory in nearly infinite depth and vista. It is the eye of human insight, limited and fallible, extended by the fallible mirrors of report and legend. The chronicle of Yoknapatawpha crystallizes in haze as the reader apprehends it through the re-solving lens of a receding central intelligence, a lens which com-poses in mosaics of memory a succession of presents now past.

FROM *College English*, XXIV:3 (December, 1962), 169-178. Reprinted with the permission of the National Council of Teachers of English and the author.

(Sometimes the narrator seems to look forward from the point of his retrospection, as if to comprehend at once a past, a present, and a future.) This misty eye of memory ultimately justifies unreconciled details in Faulkner, just as it ultimately reveals the consistency of Faulkner's point of view. It is the point of view of man himself as he stands on the flat land through which the water runs slow. . . .

Again, man's memory is fallible, and to be true to it Faulkner probably wrote, as at Virginia he has suggested he did, not from a plan but from his own imagination and imagined memory. In his mind he no doubt pieced out as he wrote the mosaic panorama of the Yoknapatawpha chronicle. "The genealogy," he said, "developed itself." There are discrepancies in time as there are in other details, inconsistencies that trouble the tidying critic more than they do the sensitive reader. The distortions are terrifyingly expressive of a young man's grappling with a disjointed past as he seeks to synthesize it and set by it a path for the future; and they are faithful to the added perspective of the years. (Probably they reflect as well a casual, a careless, an almost disdainful regard for mere facts by an author who puts a higher faith in feelings.) Thus, for example, in "The Fire and the Hearth" Ike's pension from the McCaslin estate is fifty dollars a month and Fonsiba's is three dollars a week, whereas in "The Bear," Ike's is thirty and Fonsiba's three dollars a month. The very ledgers themselves record an inconsistency as if to demonstrate the fallible mind: the slave Phoebe ("Fibby"), freed in 1837, says she is fifty; yet she is the mother of Thucydides ("Thucydus"), who is simultaneously recorded as born in 1779. More typical are the discrepancies of a year or two, for example of whether the bear hunts on Major de Spain's property began before or after the Civil War in the light of the ages and aging of the various characters. Two further illustrations are these: the year of McCaslin Edmonds' birth is given as 1850 and that of Isaac McCaslin as late in 1867; yet McCaslin is said to be sixteen years Ike's senior; again, Ike is said to have gone on his first hunt at ten and to have killed his first buck at twelve; yet it is implied that he killed this deer the second fall, for his calendar is crowded thereafter with spaced events up to the killing of Old Ben in his sixteenth December.

Within appropriate limits, then, one may record somewhat painfully with aid from the rest of *Go Down, Moses* a chronology of the events rendered or alluded to in "The Bear," a chronology undoubtedly at slight variance with, perhaps somewhat more explicit than, the one in Faulkner's imagination which grew as the stories were written. There is precedent as well as justification for such an outline: a Compson chronology and genealogy is appended to the Modern Library edition of *Absalom, Absalom!* and a more eloquent Compson genealogy was composed by the author for Malcolm Cowley's *Portable Faulkner*. (It must be noted that the McCaslin family history does not in itself in any way reveal the meaning of the story: that rests upon a reading which the history only helps to clarify. With such a reading, however, a chronology of the events gives us more nearly the grasp, the command of the author and so permits us to search his meaning with clearer vision.) The McCaslin chronicle is here hazarded with minor inconsistencies (of a year or less) for the most part ignored or compromised and with reasonable inferences interpolated, often somewhat arbitrarily. [Two] charts are offered: (1) the McCaslin chronology from 1772; (2) the narrative sequence of Part 4. [The page references for entries referring to *The Bear* and *Delta Autumn* have been changed by the present editors to agree with pagination of the text in Part I of this volume; events not alluded to in *The Bear* and *Delta Autumn* are italicized and refer to the Modern Library edition of *Go Down, Moses*.]

CHRONOLOGY

1772	Lucius Quintus CAROTHERS McCASLIN is born in Carolina (62; cf. 163)
1779	Thucydides ("Thucydus") is born to the McCaslin slaves Roscius ("Roskus") and Phoebe ("Fibby") (62)
1787 ?	Carothers McCaslin brings his wife and slaves to Mississippi, buys land for a farm from Chickasaw Chief Ikkemotubbe (56; 60; cf. 36-37)

?	A girl is born to Carothers McCaslin and his wife. She is to become the grandmother of McCaslin Edmonds (3; 7)
1799 ?	Twin boys, Theophilus and Amodeus ("BUCK" and "BUDDY") McCaslin, are born to Carothers McCaslin and his wife (4; 7; 164)
1807	Eunice, a slave girl, is bought by Carothers McCaslin in New Orleans for $650 (63)
1809 ?	Sam Fathers, son of Ikkemotubbe and a negro woman, is born and traded with his mother by the chief to Carothers McCaslin for a gelding (23; 60; 87; 373; 164)
1809	Eunice is married to the McCaslin slave Thucydides (63)
1810	Tomasina ("Tomey" or "Tomy") is born to Eunice. The father is Carothers McCaslin (64-66)
?	The wife of Carothers McCaslin dies (65)
Dec. 25, 1832	Eunice, learning that her daughter is pregnant by Carothers McCaslin, drowns herself in a creek (63)
June 1833	Terrel ("Tomy's Turl") is born to Tomasina. The father is Carothers McCaslin. Tomasina dies in childbirth (65-66)
June 27, 1837	Carothers McCaslin dies. His will frees the old slaves Roscius and Phoebe and their son Thucydides, but none leaves. Thucydides refuses 10 acres of land, refuses $200 cash, stays on to earn his legacy (62)
	The will leaves $1000 to Tomey's Terrel upon his coming of age (65)
	Buck and Buddy McCaslin, now running the farm, build a log cabin to live in, move the slaves into the big house (59; 6)

1838	Tennie (Beauchamp) is born, a slave of Hubert Beauchamp and his sister Sophonsiba, distant neighbors of the McCaslins (66)
Nov. 3, 1841	Thucydides, having earned his $200 from the McCaslins, sets up a blacksmith shop in Jefferson (63)
1843 ?	Boon Hogganbeck, quarter-Indian, is born (33)
1851 ?	Carothers McCASLIN EDMONDS ("Cass") is born, a grandson of the sister of Buck and Buddy. Before he is 14 he is orphaned and comes under care of the McCaslins (67; *3; 4; 7; 10; 163*)
1852 ?	Buck and Buddy McCaslin establish a $1000 legacy for Tomey's Terrel in accordance with Carothers McCaslin's will (*105-106*)
Feb. 17, 1854	Thucydides dies (63)
June 1854	Tomey's Terrel comes of age, ignores his $1000 legacy, stays on (*105-106*)
March 3, 1856	Buck McCaslin buys the slave Percival Brownlee from slave dealer (later General) Nathan Bedford Forrest at Cold Water for $265 (61)
Oct. 3, 1856	Brownlee, having done $100 damage, is freed, refuses to leave, later disappears (62; 83)
1859	Buddy McCaslin wins the slave girl Tennie (Beauchamp) from neighbor Hubert Beauchamp in a poker game, to be married to Tomey's Terrel (See "Was" 66; 89; *105*)
1861	The Civil War begins. Buck McCaslin joins Col. Sartoris' horse, under command of General (formerly slave dealer) Nathan Bedford Forrest (38; 67; cf. 373)
1862	Percival Brownlee reappears, conducting revival meetings on the McCaslin farm (82)

	1863	Buck McCaslin, a Confederate cavalryman, is said to have ridden into Jefferson and out while it was held by Federal troops (38)

Dec. 29, 1864   After 3 children have died in infancy, James Thucydides ("Tennie's Jim") is born to Terrel and Tennie (67)

1865   The Civil War ends. Buck McCaslin returns to the farm (68)

Sophonsiba Beauchamp ("Sibbey"), Hubert's sister, is married to Buck McCaslin. They move into the big house on the McCaslin farm (59; 89)

1865 ?   Hunting parties begin on land in the Big Bottom of the Tallahatchie River bought by Major Cassius de Spain from Thomas Sutpen (106)

Participants with the major are:
General Compson, the major's friend
Walter Ewell, a crack shot
Uncle Ash, the major's camp cook
McCaslin Edmonds
Sam Fathers
Boon Hogganbeck
Tennie's Jim

1865   The logging train makes its first trips into the Big Bottom on Major de Spain's land. It is halted to let a frightened bear escape from a tree (103)

1866   Brownlee reappears in Jefferson, is seen by Buck McCaslin (82-83)

Ike's
age

0   Oct./Nov.   1867   ISAAC Beauchamp McCASLIN ("Ike") is born to Buck and Sibbey McCaslin (68; 89)

Hubert Beauchamp, Ike's uncle and godfather, seals 50 gold pieces in a silver cup as a legacy for Ike at 21 (89; 93)

1½		1869		Sophonsiba ("Fonsiba") is born to Terrel and Tennie (68)
		1870	?	Buck and Buddy McCaslin decide to let the legacy under Carothers Mc-Caslin's will accrue to provide $1000 each to the surviving children of Terrel and Tennie as they come of age (68)
3	Winter	1871	?	Uncle Buddy's health begins to fail; Ike accompanies his mother on visits to Uncle Hubert at "Warwick" (90)
4		1872	?	Sibbey McCaslin makes Hubert dismiss his new "cook" (90-91)
5		1873	?	First Buddy, then Buck McCaslin die within the year. Management of the farm passes to McCaslin Edmonds (74; 69; cf. 106; 114; 163)
5		1873	?	"Warwick" burns to the ground. Hubert and one Negro (Tennie's great-grandfather) come to live on the McCaslin farm (91-92; 96)
6		1874	?	The silver cup, wrapped in burlap and kept in a closet, changes shape overnight (92-93; 96)
6	March 17,	1874		Lucius ("Lucas" Beauchamp) is born to Terrel and Tennie (68)
7		1875	?	Hubert Beauchamp dies (92-93)
7		1875	?	Sam Fathers' Indian companion Joe Baker ("Jobaker") dies (172)
7		1875	?	Young Ike McCaslin shoots rabbits near the McCaslin farm (176)
8		1876	?	*Zachary Edmonds ("Zack") is born to McCaslin and his wife Alice (47; 104; 114)*
9	March	1877		Sam Fathers goes to live on Major de Spain's land in the Big Bottom (173)
9		1877	?	Sibbey McCaslin, Ike's mother, dies (93)
10	November	1877		Ike McCaslin is taken to the Big Bottom on his first deer-bear hunt (6; 7; 8; 9; 10; 15; 175)

10		1878 ?	Tomey's Terrel dies (66; cf. 106)
10		1878 ?	Ike, with Boon, buys a wild pony at an auction. The pony breaks away (37)
10½	June	1878	Ike goes alone into the woods, discards his gun, watch, and compass, sees Old Ben (17-19; 30)
11	November	1878	With Sam Fathers Ike kills his first buck ("The Old People"; 19; 111; 373)
			Ash, jealous, goes hunting with Ike, surprises a bear. His gun misfires (106-108)
11		1878	Boon Hogganbeck shoots at a Negro in Jefferson 5 times with a pistol, wounds a bystander (35)
12	November	1879	Ike kills his first bear (19; 85-86)
			Ike kills a buck after waiting at its bedding place (20)
			Ike sees Old Ben crossing a corridor of down timber (20-21; 41)
12½	June	1880 ?	With Sam, Ike and his little dog (a "fyce") corner Old Ben but let him escape (21; 85; 86; 88)
13	November	1880	Walter Ewell shoots a buck from the caboose of the logging train (102)
13	March	1881	A doe and fawn are found killed; later one of Major de Spain's colts is found killed. At first Old Ben is suspected (22)
13½	June	1881	Sam captures the killer, a wild mongrel Airedale, whom he trains and names "Lion" (24-28)
14	November	1881	Lion participates in the hunt for Old Ben as 7 strangers watch; the bear escapes (29-30)
15	November	1882	Lion is found to be sleeping on Boon's bed (28-29)

			With Lion the hunters twice corner Old Ben. Boon shoots 5 times and misses. General Compson "draws blood" (31)
16	December	1883	Ike accompanies Boon on an errand to Memphis for whiskey (6; 32-39)
			The hunters close in on Old Ben. With Lion, Boon kills the bear. Lion dies. Sam Fathers "quits" and dies, probably with Boon's help (5-6; 32; 47-48)
16	December	1883 ?	Ike reads the ledgers in the commissary on the McCaslin farm (59; 64; 68)
			The hunters (without Major de Spain) plan to incorporate and lease hunting rights on the land (100)
17	November	1884	The hunters (without Major de Spain) go farther into the woods to hunt (100)
17	December	1884	Major de Spain leases the timber rights on his land to a Memphis lumber company (100)
			Boon Hogganbeck becomes town marshal at Hoke's (101)
17½	June	1885	Ike revisits Major de Spain's land, meets Ash, visits the graves of Sam and Lion, finds Boon under a gum tree (101; 109; 111-112)
18	Dec.	29, 1885	Tennie's Jim disappears on his 21st birthday. Ike traces him to Tennessee to give him his $1000 but loses him (70; cf. 105)
18½	Summer	1886	A Negro man takes Fonsiba to Arkansas to be his wife (69)
		1886	McCaslin Edmonds hears that Percival Brownlee is now proprietor of a brothel in New Orleans (83)

19	December	1886	Ike carries Fonsiba's $1000 to Arkansas, deposits it in a bank at Midnight, orders her paid $3 a month (70; 74; cf. 107)
21	Oct./Nov.	1888	In the commissary on his 21st birthday, in conversation with his cousin McCaslin Edmonds, Ike relinquishes his title to the McCaslin farm (53-54; 74; 87; 373)
			Ike also opens his Uncle Hubert's "legacy," finds a tin coffee pot stuffed with coppers and I.O.U.'s (93)
			The next day Ike goes to Jefferson, accepts as a loan a "pension" of $30 a month from McCaslin Edmonds (94)
21½	June	1889	Ike, now a carpenter, repays to the bank his "loan" (96)
22		1890 ?	Ike marries a girl who has been living on a farm where he and his partner have rebuilt the barn (97)
27	March	17, 1895	Lucas, on his 21st birthday, appears at Jefferson and asks Ike for the rest of Carothers McCaslin's legacy (74; 107)
28		1896 ?	*Lucas marries Mollie (or "Molly" Worsham). McCaslin Edmonds builds them a house and allots them a field (35; 101; 110)*
30	Winter	1898	*Henry (Beauchamp) is born to Lucas and Mollie (45)*
30	Spring	1898	*Carothers Edmonds ("Roth") is born to Zachary and his wife; the wife dies in childbirth; Mollie nurses Roth (36; 45-46; 110; 118; 121)*
31	Autumn	1898	*Lucas fights Zachary over Mollie; Mollie returns (44)*
	Ca.	1900	Tennie dies (66)

47		1915	*Samuel (Worsham Beauchamp) is born to a daughter of Lucas and Mollie; the mother dies in childbirth (369-372; 376)*
48		1916 ?	*George Wilkins, a Negro on the Mc-Caslin farm, is born (40; 123)*
50		1918	Roth Edmonds fights in the World War (364)
53		1921	*Zachary Edmonds dies (116); Lucas sets up a still (35; 65)*
54		1922 ?	Ike's wife dies; her sister moves into the house (3; 4; cf. 374)
55		1923	*Nathalie ("Nat") Beauchamp is born to Lucas and Mollie (73; 117)*
66		1934 ?	*Samuel (Worsham Beauchamp) ("Butch"), having been run off the McCaslin farm by Roth Edmonds, breaks into a store in Jefferson and is jailed (372; 373)*
72	October	1940	*Nat (Beauchamp) is secretly married to George Wilkins (72)*
73	Summer	1941	*Samuel (Worsham Beauchamp) is electrocuted at Joliet (370)*
73		1941	Ike hunts the delta with descendants of his former companions, meets a granddaughter of Tennie's Jim and her child by Roth (364; 365; 368)
73		1941	Perspective of *Go Down, Moses* (81; 364; 365; 368; 3; 33; 61; 79; 103; 118; 121; 369-370)
80		1947 ?	Projected year of Ike McCaslin's death (16-18; 88-89; 163)

THE NARRATIVE SEQUENCE OF PART 4

Pages

53-59   In the commissary under the shelf of ledgers on his 21st birthday, Ike McCaslin ("he") begins his explanation to his cousin McCaslin Edmonds ("McCaslin") of why he is relinquishing his heritage of the McCaslin farm.

59-74   In a break in the dialogue Ike recalls the contents of the ledgers as he had read them five years before, and the narration projects the history of the Negroes recorded therein through 1895.

74-80   The dialogue between Ike and Cass resumes. They are exploring the history of the South as evidence of a divine plan for the salvation of man.

80-82   In a second break in the dialogue Ike recalls what he knew (largely from Cass) of the reconstruction era following the Civil War.

82   The scene in the commissary resumes without dialogue for a few lines.

82-84   Ike's thoughts turn to the fate of the McCaslin Negroes after the reconstruction era. Again the narration projects them to 1895.

84-85   Ike and Cass discuss the character of the Negro race and speculate on its destiny.

85-86   In a fourth break in the dialogue Ike recalls his discussion with Cass following a hunt in which with Sam and a fyce Ike had cornered Old Ben but let him escape. Cass had quoted Keats's "Ode on a Grecian Urn."

86-88   The dialogue in the commissary is concluded. Ike asserts his relinquishment.

88   The narrative takes the reader next day to Jefferson, where Ike will live.

89-94   In a break in the narrative Ike recalls the history of the tin coffee pot which he had unwrapped the day before and now has in Jefferson.

95-100   With narration and dialogue the story resumes and concludes:
    Cass offers Ike $30 a month as a "pension";
    Ike becomes a carpenter and marries;
    Ike's wife proffers her love to him only if he will return to the farm.

William Faulkner and the Land

DALE G. BREADEN

❦

William Faulkner, apparently with deliberate intent, is vitally aware of the land question, and in this awareness one detects a relation of his ideas to those philosophers of the past whose concepts were dependent upon a belief in natural law and natural rights, a belief especially popular in the late eighteenth and early nineteenth centuries.

Faulkner is, of course, a Southerner, and he possesses a deep feeling for the soil, a recognition of the land's importance and the effects it can have upon the men who put their lives into it, who fertilize it with their blood and water it with their sweat. It would be impossible, generally, for a Southerner to ignore the land, as impossible as it would be for him to ignore Negroes or the Civil War, for land is the basis of Southern life and economy, and upon it the legend of the South has been painfully and gloriously constructed.

Faulkner is an agrarian realist, but with profundity and depth, rising above Erskine Caldwell. His realism shows what is true in an agricultural society, his depth and profundity speak in glowing rhetoric of the land and the part it plays in almost every aspect of Southern life; and from his realism and his rhetoric, from his depth and his profundity, there evolves in his work a philosophy or a concept of land, its ownership and its fundamental character that is brilliant and humanitarian in its vastness of scope and its depth of understanding.

Bertrand Russell has pointed out that various philosophic ideas often evolve from the environments in which they are found, that they are both "an effect and a cause of the character of the various

FROM *American Quarterly,* X:3 (Fall, 1958), 344-357. Reprinted by permission of the author and *American Quarterly.*

communities in which"[1] they flourish. So it must be with Faulkner's concepts. From his agrarian world, from his realm of black soil and white cotton, where land is the heart and soul of existence, he has taken cognizance of the land question; and his realization of the importance of that question has led him to conclusions similar to those of another day and of another time; for such a world as his, such a realm as his, has existed before, and from it others sprang to develop similar concepts of land and the men who work it.

Such philosophers as John Locke, the Physiocrats and Henry George contend that the evils which plague mankind derive from the private ownership of land, that when men claim to possess the earth they claim to possess those who live upon it as well. Basically such a concept is founded upon a belief in natural rights, upon the idea that man holds certain rights from birth, and that to deny such rights is to violate those natural laws which govern man as definitely as the physical laws govern falling apples.

Natural law as it applies to the land question can be abstracted from the work of Locke, the Physiocrats and Henry George. . . .

From what George says, one must assume that in the natural state man holds only as much land as he can use. No man pays rent or plays the part of the tenant, for no man controls land for which he has no immediate use. All of man's labor, in the natural state, returns to him as food, clothing and shelter; none is taken from him. In this natural condition, therefore, no one actually owns land, he merely occupies and employs it, has tenure upon it. No one, generally, is without the means of life, for all have equal access to the land, the foundation of life. When one person, however, devises a method of controlling more land than the share he uses for his family's support, then destiny becomes perverted, evil stalks the earth, for natural law has been violated and the natural order disturbed.

Similar ideas of natural law can be found in the work of William Faulkner, especially as they pertain to the land question, that question upon whose answer depends the liberty and freedom of man. Faulkner seems to see the South as cursed by the origins of its land

---

[1] Bertrand Russell, *A History of Western Philosophy* (New York: Simon & Schuster, 1945), p. ix.

titles and by the fact that the land is owned at all. According to Robert Coughlan, Faulkner has been attempting to explain this curse all his life. . . . Coughlan says Faulkner, in his groping, found a philosophy centered around the land. " 'People don't own the land,' one of his characters says,[2] 'It's the land that owns the people.' If Faulkner has a philosophy, this may be its distillation; although it is less a philosophy than a mystique, a religious revelation." [3] In a way, this last idea, that Faulkner's philosophy is religious in nature, may be true, for, while he seems to adopt a natural rights concept of land, he includes in the concept an idea of the land turning and aiding in the destruction of those it has helped, unwillingly, to power, for "the earth would permit them to live on and out of it and use it only so long as they behaved and that if they did not behave right, it would shake them off just like a dog getting rid of fleas." [4] Also, such a religious attitude is perfectly typical of those who profess belief in the natural rights of man and in natural law. In this particular case, the land may stand as a symbol of the ancient sword of God striking back at iniquity and evil as personified by those who claim private ownership of the land.

In Faulkner's work the curse of land ownership falls upon the people of the South when the Indian Ikkemotubbe discovers that he can sell the land of his people. By means of this discovery, Ikkemotubbe curses his own people, for as time passes they vanish from Yoknapatawpha County, leaving only old Sam Fathers to remember the past which had been their glory. Faulkner recognizes, however, that the land was generally stolen from the Indians. . . .

Land titles, which give to a man what Faulkner calls the "legal fiction" [5] of ownership, are pictured as drenched in blood, not, necessarily, the blood of war, but the blood of those whose rights they deprive, whose labor they confiscate for the benefit of a few

---

[2] Coughlan fails to identify this character fully, yet the reference is probably to the beliefs of Buck and Buddy McCaslin. William Faulkner, *The Unvanquished* (New York: New American Library, 1952), p. 33.

[3] Coughlan, *Private World of William Faulkner* (New York: Harper and Brothers, 1954, p. 91.

[4] Faulkner, *The Unvanquished*, p. 33.

[5] Coughlan, *Private World*, p. 90.

who "own." And, doubtless, actual blood was shed in gaining particular titles. Even Ikkemotubbe killed to become the Man of his tribe.[6] All titles to land, in their origin, are false, for what claim can a man make to that which he has not made, to that which others have had and which others will deserve a share of, for, after all, this is the land,

> The big woods, bigger and older than any recorded document:—of white man fatuous enough to believe he had bought any fragment of it, of Indian ruthless enough to pretend that any fragment of it had been his to convey; bigger than Major de Spain and the scrap he pretended to, knowing better; older than old Thomas Sutpen of whom Major de Spain had had it and who knew better; older even than old Ikkemotubbe, the Chickasaw chief, of whom old Sutpen had had it and who knew better in his turn.[7]

An interesting point here is the striking similarity of tone and attitude between the above passage from Faulkner's *Go Down, Moses* and the following paragraph from Henry George's *Social Problems:*

> What more preposterous than that one tenant for a day of this rolling sphere should collect rent for it from his co-tenants, or sell to them for a price what was here ages before him and will be here ages after him? [8]. . . .

The land Faulkner speaks of was to be Isaac McCaslin's heritage, land which had come from the Indians, part of it from old Ikkemotubbe, who "knew . . . that not even a fragment of it had been his to relinquish or sell. . . ." But Isaac was to deny his heritage, feeling inside himself that the land could not be owned, that it was cursed and should not be owned, that it was cursed by slavery, too, but another kind of false ownership. . . .

Isaac felt as he did because he believed God's plan for earth, as seen in the Bible, was designed to raise man, not to degrade him or

---

[6] William Faulkner, "A Justice," *Collected Stories of William Faulkner* (New York: Random House, Inc., 1948), p. 349.

[7] William Faulkner, *Go Down, Moses* (New York: Modern Library, 1942), p. 191.

[8] Henry George, *Social Problems* (New York: Schalkenbach, 1953), pp. 204-5.

to make him the slave of other men. For God "made the earth first and peopled it with dumb creatures, and then He created man to be His overseer on the earth and to hold suzerainty over the earth and the animals on it in His name. . . ." [9] This man, Isaac McCaslin, whose story Faulkner tells in *Go Down, Moses,* is a symbol of the concept of natural rights as Faulkner seems to see it. He speaks the theory of man's right to the land time and time again, realizing as he does that his hold upon the land is "as trivial and without reality as the now faded and archaic script in the chancery book in Jefferson which allocated it" [10] to him. Isaac appears as the fictionalized conscience of man, revolting against the evils of land ownership, harking back to the natural state and the natural law which governed it. The Biblical claim he makes in support of his ideas is not an unusual one. Henry George called for such support upon three well-known Biblical quotations:

"The land shall not be sold forever." Leviticus 25:23
"The earth is Jehovah's." Exodus 9:29—Ps. 24:1—I Cor. 10:26
"The earth hath he given to the children of men." Ps. 115:16

These three quotations give, in essence, the basis of what Isaac implies. And if natural law is derived from reason, and if reason is bestowed on man by God, then surely nothing is more proper than the quoting of what is supposedly God's word in support of the natural order. . . .

Faulkner has written several stories concerning bear hunts, the most famous being "The Bear." One seldom heard of, called "A Bear Hunt," concerns a comic situation between one Lucius Provine and the sewing machine salesman V. K. Ratliff. While on a bear hunt with Major de Spain, Lucius develops a violent and seemingly incurable case of hiccoughs. Ratliff advises him to visit the Indians who will perhaps have some sort of cure. When Lucius expresses some doubt as to the value of such a venture, Ratliff assures him that the Indians would be more than happy to accommodate him. He says:

. . . the white folks have been so good to them—not only letting them keep that ere hump of dirt that don't nobody

[9] Faulkner, *Moses,* p. 257.
[10] *Moses,* p. 171.

want noways, but letting them use names like ourn and selling
them flour and sugar and farm tools at not more than a fair
profit above what they would cost a white man. I hyear tell
how pretty soon they are even going to start letting them
come to town once a week.[11]

This whole passage is superficially a comic one, yet below its surface lies an accusation against those whites who have taken the
land from the Indians and reduced that race to but a shade of its
once proud self. The Indians, probably more than any other single
group, suffered from man's greed for possession of the land, suffered so that they faced extinction in Mississippi. They were the
first to suffer the evils of private property in land in Yoknapatawpha County, yet they were, in many ways, responsible for their
own plight, for it was they who partially let loose the curse of the
land when they discovered they could sell the earth. They were
the first, but not the last, to pay for their decision to make private
property of land. . . .

[Faulkner] loves the South, and because he loves it he abhors
its injustices and its cruelties. The fact that men must live subject
to others, that they can never know the pleasure, the psychological
satisfaction, of exerting their labor upon their land (not his land
or her land) is a tragedy to him, for even in the twentieth century,
while much of the old order of aristocracy is gone, the land is still
owned. The Civil War did not end the concept of private ownership of land, it merely changed the agents of that ownership.

To Faulkner, when natural law is violated, when man's natural
rights to the land are denied, evil follows, for this is a jealous
God's, an outraged nature's reply to such violation. Those who
claim they can sell the land, those who claim they can own the
land, are cursed; for to own the land upon which a man must labor
is to own the man himself, and man cannot own man, for this,
too, is a violation of the natural law. Today man recognizes the
fact that slavery is an evil, yet he still fails to comprehend the
evils of land ownership. Faulkner seems to say, with the Brahmins
of long ago— " 'To whomsoever the soil at any time belongs, to

---

[11] Faulkner, "A Bear Hunt," *Stories,* pp. 71-72.

him belong the fruits of it. White parasols and elephants mad with pride are the flowers of a grant of land.' " [12] . . .

Faulkner's work, then, searches for and finds that for which he had groped as a young man, the answer to his family's fall, an answer based upon concepts of natural law similar to those of Locke, the Physiocrats and George, a reason for the great socio-historic change of the South, the idea that man can own the land privately.

In demonstrating the evils of private property in land and of its violation of natural rights, Faulkner is not only struggling for the disinherited yeoman, that man who must pay for the privilege of working, he is also urging the abstract "man" to save himself from the curse of the "legal fiction" of the private ownership of land. . . .

Primitivism and The Bear[*]

HARRY MODEAN CAMPBELL AND RUEL E. FOSTER

🌷

Primitivism—or what might be called "conceptual primitivism"—has to do with the impingement of the "nature as norm" concept on the fields of philosophy, religion, literature, sociology, ethics, politics, and economics. This phase of primitivism, whch has received a detailed and scholarly treatment in recent studies by George Boas and Arthur O. Lovejoy,[1] goes back at least to Greco-Roman antiquity. Its primary technique in art has been that of

[12] Henry George, *Progress and Poverty* (New York: Robert Schalkenbach Foundation, 1953), p. 296.

[*] FROM *William Faulkner: A Critical Appraisal* (Norman: University of Oklahoma Press, 1951), pp. 143, 147. Reprinted by permission of the publisher.

[1] The reference is to *Primitivism and Related Ideas in Antiquity* (Vol. I of *A Documentary History of Primitivism and Related Ideas*) (Baltimore: Johns Hopkins Press, 1935). No other volume in the series was completed. See also George Boas, *Essays in Primitivism and Related Ideas in the Middle Ages* (Baltimore: Johns Hopkins Press, 1948) and Arthur O. Lovejoy, *Essays in the History of Ideas* (Baltimore: Johns Hopkins, 1948).—*Eds.*

regression: the artist regresses in time to a far-off primal golden age (chronological primitivism); or regresses in culture to a simple, primitive savage stage (cultural primitivism); or regresses to childhood or to the domain of the subconscious (psychic primitivism). . . .

In terms of allegory, this story might be interpreted thus. It would seem there are two worlds: the primitive world of the old free fathers—the first world—the wilderness and the animals of the wilderness and the men who live by and in and through the wilderness; and the civilized world of contemporary man who has insulated himself against the primitive world by interposing houses, societies, and material values between himself and the land, the earth, nature. Ike is born into this latter world but soon learns the existence of the primitive world. Through the ritual of the hunt, he is initiated into the primitive world, prefers it, and decides that, although he cannot completely escape the civilized world, he will repudiate its values and live in terms of primitive values. His problem is how to live by the rules of the wilderness when the wilderness no longer exists—how to be a primitive while living in a small Southern town. What happens to Ike is what would happen to any true primitive caught in our present society. The curse of Ike is that familiar one of other moderns who are caught between two worlds and spread-eagled. . . .

Nature Myth in Faulkner's The Bear

JOHN LYDENBERG

❧

. . . But of course [Faulkner's] stories are not merely about the South; they are about men, or Man. Here appears the other type of myth [which is different from the myth of a Southern society]: the primitive nature myth. Perhaps one should not say "appears," for the myth lies imbedded in Faulkner's feeling about

FROM *American Literature,* XXIV (March, 1952), 62-72. Reprinted by permission of the author and the Duke University Press.

human actions and seldom appears as a readily visible outcropping, as does his conception of the mythical kingdom. Faulkner feels man acting in an eternity, in a timeless confusion of past and future, acting not as a rational Deweyan creature but as a natural, unthinking (but always moral) animal. These men do not "understand" themselves, and neither Faulkner nor the reader fully understands them in any naturalistic sense. Sometimes these creatures driven by instinct become simply grotesques; sometimes the inflated rhetoric gives the characters the specious portentousness of a gigantic gray balloon. But often the aura of something-moreness casts a spell upon the reader, makes him sense where he does not exactly comprehend the eternal human significance of the ritual activities carried out by these suprahuman beings. They are acting out magical tales that portray man's plight in a world he cannot understand or control. They are Man, the primordial and immortal, the creator and protagonist of myth.

This dual myth-making can best be demonstrated in the short story "The Bear." "The Bear" is by general agreement one of Faulkner's most exciting and rewarding stories. . . . beneath its other layers of meaning, the story is essentially a nature myth.

. . . On one level the story is a symbolic representation of man's relation to the land, and particularly the Southerner's conquest of his native land. In attempting to kill Old Ben, the men are contending with the wilderness itself. In one sense, as men, they have a perfect right to do this, as long as they act with dignity and propriety, maintaining their humility while they demonstrate the ability of human beings to master the brute forces of nature. The hunters from Jefferson are gentlemen and sportsmen, representing the ideals of the old order at its best, the honor, dignity, and courage of the South. In their rapport with nature and their contest with Old Ben, they regain the purity they have lost in their workaday world, and abjure the petty conventions with which they ordinarily mar their lives. But as Southerners they are part of "that whole edifice intricate and complex and founded upon injustice"; they are part of that South that has bought and sold land and has held men as slaves. Their original sins have alienated them irrevocably from nature. Thus their conquest of Old Ben becomes a rape. What might in other circumstances have been right, is now a violation of the wilderness and the Southern land.

Part IV makes explicit the social comment implied in the drama of Old Ben. It consists of a long and complicated account of the McCaslin family, white and mulatto, and a series of pronunciamentos by Ike upon the South, the land, truth, man's frailties and God's will. It is in effect Ike's spiritual autobiography given as explanation of his reasons for relinquishing and repudiating, for refusing to own land or participate actively in the life of the South. Ike discovers that he can do nothing to lift or lighten the curse the Southerners have brought on themselves, the monstrous offspring of their God-given free will. The price of purity, Ike finds, is non-involvement, and he chooses purity.

Thus Part IV carries us far beyond the confines of the story of the hunt. It creates a McCaslin myth that fits into the broad saga of Faulkner's mythical kingdom, and it includes in nondramatic form a good deal of direct social comment. The rest of "The Bear" cannot be regarded as *simply* a dramatic symbolization of Ike's conscientious repudiation. Its symbolism cannot fully be interpreted in terms of this social myth. One responds emotionally to the bear hunt as to a separate unit, an indivisible and self-sufficient whole. Part IV and Old Ben's story resemble the components of a binary star. They revolve about each other and even cast light upon each other. But each contains the source of its own light.[1]

II

It is the mythical quality of the bear hunt proper that gives the story its haunting power. Beneath its other meanings and symbolisms lies the magical tale enacted by superhuman characters. Here religion and magic are combined in a ritual demonstration of the eternal struggle between Man and Nature. A statement of the legend recounting their partial reconciliation would run somewhat as follows:

Every fall members of the tribe make a pilgrimage to the domain of the Great Beast, the bear that is more than a bear, the preternatural animal that symbolizes for them their relation to

---

[1] Two early versions of "The Bear" appeared in magazines; little of Part IV is to be found in either version.

Nature and thus to life. They maintain, of course, the forms of routine hunts. But beneath the conventional ritual lies the religious rite: the hunting of the tribal god, whom they dare not, and cannot, touch, but whom they are impelled to challenge. In this rite the established social relations dissolve; the artificial ranks of Jefferson give way to more natural relations as Sam Fathers is automatically given the lead. The bear and Sam are both taboo. Like a totem animal, Old Ben is at the same time sacred, and dangerous or forbidden (though in no sense unclean). Also he is truly animistic, possessing a soul of his own, initiating action, not inert like other creatures of nature. And Sam, the high priest, although alone admitted to the arcana and trusted with the tutelage of the young neophyte, is yet outside the pale, living by himself, irrevocably differentiated from the others by his Negro blood, and yet kept pure and attuned to nature by his royal Indian blood.

This particular legend of man and the Nature God relates the induction of Ike, the natural and pure boy, into the mysteries of manhood. Guided by Sam Fathers, Ike learns how to retain his purity and bring himself into harmony with the forces of Nature. He learns human woodlore and the human codes and techniques of the hunt. And he learns their limitations. Old Ben, always concerned with the doings of his mortals, comes to gaze upon Ike as he stands alone and unprepared in a clearing. Ike "knew that the bear was looking at him. He never saw it. He did not know whether it was facing him from the cane or behind him." His apprehension does not depend on human senses. Awareness of his coming relation to the bear grows not from rational processes, but from intuition: "he knew now that he would never fire at it."

Yet he must see, must meet, Old Ben. He will be vouchsafed the vision, but only when he divests himself of man-made signs of fear and vanity. "*The gun,* the boy thought. *The gun.* 'You will have to choose,' Sam said." So one day, before light, he starts out unarmed on his pilgrimage, alone and helpless, with courage and humility, guided by his newly acquired woodlore, and by compass and watch, traveling till past noon, past the time at which he should have turned back to regain camp in safety. He has not yet found the bear. Then he realizes that divesting himself of the gun, necessary as that is, will not suffice if he wishes to come into the presence. "He stood for a moment—a child, alien and lost in the green and soaring gloom of the markless wilderness. Then he relinquished completely to it. It was the watch and the compass. He was still tainted."

He takes off the two artifacts, hangs them from a bush, and continues farther into the woods. Now he is at last pure—and lost. Then the footprints, huge, misshapen, and unmistakable, appear, one by one, leading him back to the spot he could no longer have found unaided, to the watch and the compass in the sunlight of the glade.

Then he saw the bear. It did not emerge, appear; it was just there, immobile . . .

Ike has seen the vision. That is his goal, but it is not the goal for the tribe, nor for Sam Fathers who as priest must prepare the kill for them. They are under a compulsion to carry out their annual ritual at the time of "the year's death," to strive to conquer the Nature God whose very presence challenges them and raises doubts as to their power.

The priest has first to make the proper medicine; he has to find the right dog. Out of the wilds it comes, as if sent by higher powers, untamable, silent, like no other dog. Then Sam, magician as well as priest, shapes him into the force, the instrument, that alone can master Old Ben. Lion is almost literally bewitched— broken maybe, but not tamed or civilized or "humanized." He is removed from the order of nature, but not allowed to partake of the order of civilization or humanity.

Sam Fathers fashions the instrument; that is his duty as it has been his duty to train the neophyte, to induct him into the mysteries, and thus to prepare, in effect, his own successor. But it is not for the priest to perform the impious and necessary deed. Because he belongs to the order of nature as well as of man—as Ike does now—neither of them can do more than assist at the rites. Nor can Major de Spain or General Compson or other human hunters pair with Lion. That is for Boon, who has never hit any animal bigger than a squirrel with his shotgun, who is like Lion in his imperturbable nonhumanity. Boon is part Indian; "he had neither profession job nor trade"; he has "the mind of a child, the heart of a horse, and little hard shoe-button eyes without depth or meanness or generosity or viciousness or gentleness or anything else." So he takes Lion into his bed, makes Lion a part of him. Divorced from nature and from man—"the big, grave, sleepy-seeming dog which, as Sam Fathers said, cared about no man and no thing; and the violent, insensitive, hard-faced man with his touch of remote Indian blood and the mind almost of a child"— the two mavericks live their own lives, dedicated and fated.

The "yearly pageant-rite" continues for six years. Then out of the swamps come the rest of the tribe, knowing the climax is approaching, accepted by the Jefferson aristocrats as proper participants in the final rites. Ike, the young priest, is given the post of honor on the one-eyed mule which alone among the mules and horses will not shy at the smell of blood. Beside him stands the dog who "loved no man and no thing." . . .

The final hunt is short, for Old Ben can be downed only when his time has come, not by the contrived machinations of men, but by the destined ordering of events and his own free will. The hounds run the bear; a swamper fires; Walter Ewell fires;[2] Boon cannot fire.[3] Then the bear turns and Lion drives in, is caught in the bear's two arms and falls with him. Ike draws back the hammers of his gun. And Boon, like Lion, drives in, jumps on Ben's back and thrusts his knife into the bear's throat. Again they fall. Then "the bear surged erect, raising with it the man and the dog too, and turned and still carrying the man and the dog it took two or three steps towards the woods on its hind feet as a man would have walked and crashed down. It didn't collapse, crumple. It fell all of a piece, as a tree falls, so that all three of them, man dog and bear, seemed to bounce once."

The tribe comes up, with wagon and mules, to carry back to camp the dead bear, Lion with his guts raked out, Boon bleeding, and Sam Fathers who dropped, unscathed but paralyzed, at the

---

[2] In "The Old People," the story preceding "The Bear" in *Go Down, Moses,* Faulkner says that Walter Ewell never misses. Thus mention of his shooting and missing at this particular time takes on added significance.

[3] Boon explained that he could not fire because Lion was too close. That was, of course, not the "real" reason; Boon could not kill Ben with a civilized gun (to say nothing of the fact that he couldn't hit anything with his gun anyway).

moment that Ben received his death wound. The doctor from the near-by sawmill pushes back Lion's entrails and sews him up. Sam lies quiet in his hut after talking in his old unknown tongue, and then pleading, "Let me out, master. Let me go home."

Next day the swampers and trappers gather again, sitting around Lion in the front yard, "talking quietly of hunting, of the game and the dogs which ran it, of hounds and bear and deer and men of yesterday vanished from the earth, while from time to time the great blue dog would open his eyes, not as if he were listening to them but as though to look at the woods for a moment before closing his eyes again, to remember the woods or to see that they were still there. He died at sundown." And in his hut Sam quietly goes after the bear whose death he was destined to prepare and upon whose life his own depended, leaving behind the de Spains and Compsons who will no longer hunt in this wilderness and the new priest who will keep himself pure to observe, always from the outside, the impious destruction of the remaining Nature by men who can no longer be taught the saving virtues of pride and humility. They have succeeded in doing what they felt they had to do, what they thought they wanted to do. But their act was essentially sacrilegious, however necessary and glorious it may have seemed. They have not gained the power and strength of their feared and reverenced god by conquering him. Indeed, as human beings will, they have mistaken their true relation to him. They tried to possess what they could not possess, and now they can no longer even share in it.

Boon remains, but he has violated the fundamental taboo. Permitted to do this by virtue of his nonhumanity, he is yet in part human. He has broken the law, killed with his own hand the bear, taken upon himself the mastery of that which was no man's to master. So when the chiefs withdraw, and the sawmills grind their way into the forests, Boon polices the new desecrations. When Ike returns to gaze once more upon the remnants of the wilderness, he finds Boon alone in the clearing where the squirrels can be trapped in the isolated tree. Boon, with the gun he could never aim successfully, frenziedly hammers the barrel against the breech of the dismembered weapon, shouting at the intruder, any intruder, "Get out of here! Don't touch them! Don't touch a one of them! They're mine!" Having killed the bear, he now possesses all the creatures of nature, and will snarl jealously at the innocent who walks peacefully through the woods. The result of his impiety is, literally, madness.

III

That, of course, is not exactly Faulkner's "Bear." But it is part of it, an essential part. If a reading of the story as myth results in suppressions and distortions, as it does, any other reading leaves us unsatisfied. Only thus can we answer certain crucial questions that otherwise baffle us. The most important ones relate to the four central characters: Why can Ike or Sam not kill the bear? Why can Boon? Why are Boon and Lion drawn precisely so? And why does Sam Fathers die along with Old Ben?

Ike has developed and retained the requisite purity. He has learned to face nature with pride and humility. He is not tainted like de Spain and Compson by having owned slaves. According to Faulkner's version of the huntsman's code, Ike should be the one who has the right to kill Old Ben, as General Compson feels when he assigns him the one mule that can approach the bear. Or it might be argued that Sam Fathers, with his unsurpassed knowledge, instinct, and dignity, rightly deserves the honor. If Old Ben is merely the greatest of bears, it would seem fitting for either Ike or Sam to demonstrate his impeccable relationship to nature by accomplishing the task. But Faulkner rules differently.

Lion and Boon do it. At first glance that may seem explicable if we consider Old Ben's death as symbolizing man's destruction of the wilderness. Then the deed cannot be performed by Ike or Sam, for it would be essentially vicious, done in violation of the rules by men ignorant or disrespectful of the rules. Thus one may think it could be assigned to Boon, "the plebeian," and that strange, wild dog. But actually neither of them is "bad," neither belongs to a mean order of hunters. Boon and Lion are creatures set apart, dehumanized, possessing neither virtues nor vices. In their actions and in his words describing them, Faulkner takes great pains to link them together and to remove from them all human traits.[4]

---

[4] In "The Old People," Boon is referred to as "a mastiff."

Thus the killing of the bear cannot be explained by a natural-istic interpretation of the symbolism. Old Ben is not merely an extraordinary bear representing the wilderness and impervious to all but the most skillful or improper attacks. He is the totem ani-mal, the god who can never be bested by men with their hounds and guns, but only by a nonhuman Boon with Lion, the instru-ment fashioned by the priest.

Sam Fathers' death can likewise be explained only by the nature myth. If the conquest of Old Ben is the triumphant culmination of the boy's induction into the hunting clan, Sam, his mentor, would presumably be allowed a share in the triumph. If the bear's death symbolizes the destruction of the wild, Sam's demise can be seen as paralleling that of the nature of which he is so com-pletely a part. But then the whole affair would be immoral, and Sam could not manage and lead the chase so willingly, nor would he die placid and satisfied. Only as part of a nature rite does his death become fully understandable. It is as if the priest and the god are possessed of the same soul. The priest fulfils his function; his magic makes the god vulnerable to the men. He has to do it; and according to human standards he wins a victory for his tribe. But it is a victory for which the only fit reward is the death he is content to accept. The actors act out their ordained roles. And in the end the deed brings neither jubilation nor mourning—only retribution, tragic in the high sense, right as the things which are inevitable are right.

A further paradox, a seeming contradiction, appears in the con-junction of the two words which are repeated so often that they clearly constitute a major theme. Pride and humility. Here con-joined are two apparently polar concepts: the quintessence of Christianity in the virtue of humility; and the greatest of sins, the sin of Satan. Though at first the words puzzle one, or else slip by as merely a pleasant conceit, they soon gather up into themselves the entire "meaning" of the story. This meaning can be read in purely naturalistic terms: Faulkner gives these two qualities as the huntsman's necessary virtues. But they take on additional connota-tions. Humility becomes the proper attitude to the nature gods, with whom man can merely bring himself into harmony as Sam teaches Ike to do. The pride arises out of the individual's realization of his manhood: his acquisition of the self-control which permits him to perform the rituals as he should. Actually it is humanly impossible to possess these two qualities fully at the same time. Sam alone truly has them, and as the priest he has partly escaped from his humanity. Ike apparently believes he has developed them, finally; and Faulkner seems to agree with him. But Ike cannot quite become Sam's successor, for in acquiring the necessary humility—and insight—he loses the ability to act with the full pride of a man, and can only be an onlooker, indeed in his later life, as told in Part IV and "Delta Autumn," a sort of Ishmael.

In conclusion, then, "The Bear" is first of all a magnificent story. The inclusion of Part IV gives us specific insights into Faulkner's attitudes toward his Southern society and adds another legend to the saga of his mythical kingdom. The tale of Old Ben by itself has a different sort of effect. Our response is not intellectual but emotional. The relatively simple story of the hunting of a wise old bear suggests the mysteries of life, which we feel subconsciously and cannot consider in the rationalistic terms we use to analyze the "how" of ordinary life. Thus it appears as a nature myth, embodying the ambivalences that lie at the heart of primitive taboos, rituals, and religions, and the awe we feel toward that which we are unable to comprehend or master. From strata buried deep under our rationalistic understanding, it dredges up our feeling that the simple and the primitive—the stolid dignity and the superstitions of Sam Fathers—are the true. It evokes our terrible and fatal attraction toward the imperturbable, the powerful, the great—as symbolized in the immortal Old Ben. And it expresses our knowledge that as men we have to conquer and overcome, and our knowledge that it is beyond our human power to do so— that it is necessary and sacrilegious.

Let My People Go: The White Man's Heritage *in* Go Down, Moses

WALTER F. TAYLOR, JR.

❦

[In *Go Down, Moses*] Faulkner has more than anywhere else in his work set forth an extensive, historically conceived, literary vision which revolves around the problem of race relations in the South. Malcolm Cowley has made the most comprehensive statement of the central purposes of the book:

> Although it was published as a group of stories . . . [*Go Down, Moses*] is really a panoramic novel dealing with the white and black descendants of Carothers McCaslin through five generations. Its major theme is injustice to the Negroes, its minor theme is the destruction of the wilderness, and the two themes are closely interwoven.

This is an accurate statement of the underlying plan of the book; but Cowley, regrettably, has never had occasion to enlarge upon the statement. It needs to be enlarged. The theme of injustice to the Negroes is indeed central in *Go Down, Moses,* as is that of the destruction of the wilderness. But it would be more accurate to say, first of all, that the theme of injustice to the Negroes is included in the larger one of the tortured heritage of the white Southerner as seen in microcosm in the five generations of the McCaslin family, a heritage in which the Negro plays a central part. And by the same token, the theme of the destruction of the wilderness is better understood as a part of Faulkner's careful study of primitive American life. When one considers that Carothers McCaslin's grandson Isaac (Ike) McCaslin, the white character in the book who most nearly succeeds in transcending this tortured heritage, achieves his freedom through the adoption

FROM the *South Atlantic Quarterly,* LVIII:1 (Winter, 1959), 20-32. Reprinted with the permission of the Duke University Press.

of the virtues of these primitive peoples into his own life, the two themes assume much more than a "closely interwoven" relationship. *Go Down, Moses* is best seen as a historical vision which includes an extensive comparison of primitive society with modern society, the latter comprehended in the McCaslin dynasty. The virtues of primitive society are envisioned as cures for modern ills, specifically for those of the South.

Central to the Southern white's heritage as comprehended in *Go Down, Moses* is the fact that Faulkner sees all Southerners as living under a kind of Biblical curse brought on by the sins of the whites. As Ike McCaslin puts it in "The Bear," "This whole land, the whole South, is cursed, and all of us who derive from it . . . white and black both, lie under the curse." Each successive generation inherits this curse from the preceding one, and the story of each generation is the story of its struggle to free itself from it.

A central cause of the curse, as the book's title implies, is the problem of the mistreatment of Southern Negroes; but Faulkner, whose usual method is the presentation not simply of concrete examples based on historical problems but of historical visions, would not restrict himself to so explicit a statement. His many-sided vision of the white South, seen here in the story of Carothers McCaslin and his descendants, is that of a people cursed by their failure to live up to a trust given them by God.

Carothers McCaslin, like Thomas Sutpen in *Absalom, Absalom!* (1936), is portrayed as a ruthless ante-bellum Southerner who sought to build what amounted to his own small empire in the form of a huge plantation. Carothers had twin sons, Theophilus (Uncle Buck) and Amodeus (Uncle Buddy), and a daughter, unmentioned by name, who married a man named Edmonds. He also had one illegitimate daughter, Tomey, by a slave woman, and later a son, Turl, by this daughter, Tomey.

After Carothers' death, Buck and Buddy took over the plantation and saw it through the evil times of the Civil War and early Reconstruction. When they, in turn, died, their heir was young Ike McCaslin, the child of Buck's old age. Ike, however, was too young to run the plantation, and so it was taken over as a trusteeship by McCaslin (Cass) Edmonds, son of Carothers' white daughter. Cass, who runs it during much of the action of the book, is largely responsible for the fact that long before Ike McCaslin becomes twenty-one in 1888 the Negroes of the plantation are once more in bondage, this time as sharecroppers.

Ike McCaslin, meanwhile, has been brought up in a world in which two conflicting environmental forces shaped his mind. He has been reared into his McCaslin heritage by Cass Edmonds, who was more of a father to him than Buck, whom he scarcely remembers. He has also received another type of education during the annual hunting trips in the wilderness with old Sam Fathers, the aging half-Negro son of a Chickasaw chief. From him, Ike learned in his youth the simple virtues of the primitive Indian and Negro: courage, humility, pride, and endurance. These qualities have become so deeply ingrained in Ike that when he reaches his majority he believes it is wrong for him to take over the plantation, his birthright. His reasons for refusing it reveal Faulkner's vision of the curse of the white Southern heritage.

The source of this curse is self-aggrandizement at the expense of one's neighbors. It is an evil implicit in the history of Western European civilization. At the creation of the world, Ike says in "The Bear," God "created man to be His overseer on the earth and to hold suzerainty over the earth . . . in His name, not to hold for himself and his descendants inviolable title forever . . . but to hold the earth mutual and intact in the communal anonymity of brotherhood." From the first, however, individual men broke this trust in order to aggrandize themselves. This continual failure to obey God's will caused a moral degeneration, until, after thousands of years of Europe, mankind had degenerated to a point where, in "the old world's worthless twilight," they "snarled" like animals over "the old world's gnawed bones, blasphemous in His name." God, however, did not give up on humanity, but instead gave it the "new world" of America, "where a nation . . . could be founded in humility and pity and sufferance and pride of one to another." People like Carothers McCaslin, however, brought the sins of the old world into the new. Faulkner is concerned with two of these sins: their use of the land for their own ends instead of in the "communal anonymity of brotherhood," and their misuse of human beings over whom they had power through possession of the land.

Carothers McCaslin could no more "buy" the land from Ikkemotubbe, the Indian who had once "owned" it, than one of
Carothers' slaves could, because "on the instant when Ikkemotubbe discovered . . . that he could sell it for money, on that
instant it ceased ever to have been his forever . . . and the man
who bought it bought nothing." The only true possession is sharing.

Nothing, however, could be further from "brotherhood" than
"ownership" of human beings. But Faulkner makes it clear that
the white man's sin against the Negro is more than just that of
keeping the black man as his vassal. His introduction of miscegenation and incest into the McCaslin history is a direct statement that whenever the race problem is considered these sins must
be taken into account.

God, however, observing these misdeeds, did not give up attempting to shape the land and its inhabitants to His purposes.
Concluding that such men could evidently *"learn nothing save
through suffering,"* He laid on them a twofold curse: a curse of
physical poverty brought on by the Civil War, and a curse of
spiritual poverty brought on by the very nature of the sin itself.

With the rehabilitation of the plantation, the curse of war has
lessened, but the blight on men's souls remains. Each generation
is obscured from the truth because it inherits the lies that its
fathers have told themselves about their own sins. The conflict
between these inherited lies and a basic goodness of heart which
instinctively seeks the truth causes spiritual suffering, which in
turn motivates each generation to try to break through its inherited prejudices. Thus Ike can say in "Delta Autumn" that
"most men are a little better than their circumstances give them a
chance to be."

From this standpoint, Ike is able to look back on his grandfather as having been deliberately chosen for his role; in Ike's
words, perhaps God "chose Grandfather out of all of them He
might have picked. Maybe He knew that Grandfather himself
would not serve His purpose [as Ike later did] . . . but that
Grandfather would have descendants, the right descendants;
maybe He had foreseen already the descendants Grandfather
would have." Thus Ike's father and uncle could not be expected to

understand their heritage completely. By its very essence, God's method is evolutionary, not revolutionary, and the cleansing of a bloodline in one generation is virtually impossible, no matter how sincere the misguided efforts of such people as his father and uncle to "fumble-heed," as Ike puts it, the truth. And in Ike's own case, God had to introduce certain circumstances apart from his family heritage: his contact with the wilderness. This contact with the wilderness enables Ike, because he accepts the moral responsibility that it implies, to understand and therefore largely to escape the family curse.

The evolutionary nature of this vision, however, is not to be taken to mean that Faulkner makes no place for free will. Although all men are conditioned largely by their "circumstances," the outstanding man will be one whom "even the circumstances . . . [can't] stop." "Circumstances" may be a reason *why* a man fails to transcend his heritage; but reasons *why* will not change the circumstances; these can only be changed by will power. For those who fail to transcend their heritage, God continues to compound the curse so that they may learn through suffering.

The operation of this curse may be plainly seen in Faulkner's characterization of the five descendants of Carothers with whom he has dealt most thoroughly: in the order of their birth, Uncle Buck and Uncle Buddy McCaslin, Cass Edmonds, Ike McCaslin, and Roth Edmonds.

Practically all of the various phases of the curse are embodied in the presentation of Uncle Buck and Uncle Buddy, only one generation from old Carothers. Its most obvious manifestations are in their relations with their slaves. Their attitude, in particular, toward the nearly white Turl—who through incest and miscegenation is three quarters their brother—is a hopeless mixture of the good and the cruel.

Buck and Buddy place themselves, first of all, in opposition to slavery; they favor a gradual type of emancipation. Immediately after Carothers' death, the twins move out of the still-unfinished hulk of Carothers' projected manor house, and build a modest log house with their own hands, refusing to let any Negro help them, save with work that two men cannot do alone. Faulkner then has them symbolically move the Negroes into the old mansion. The meaning of this seems clear: the land now belongs in some degree at least to the Negroes—though they are still slaves—in the "communal anonymity of brotherhood." Buck and Buddy are also, Faulkner states in "The Fire and the Hearth," the authors of a "scheme for the manumission of their father's slaves." Although this scheme is never elaborated in *Go Down, Moses,* it has received a clear statement in the story "Retreat" in *The Unvanquished* (1934). In this story, the twins are stated to be the authors of a system under which their slaves are "freed, not given freedom but earning it, buying it not in money from Uncle Buck and Buddy, but in work from the plantation." In addition to this scheme, Buck and Buddy make a special arrangement for Turl, granting him his freedom and making financial provisions for his children.

Such acts reveal Buck and Buddy as tremendously advanced, morally, over old Carothers. But the twins fail to make the ultimate sacrifice. Turl is never publicly acknowledged as their brother except "by inference" from the grant of the money to his children; and he is not allowed to take the name of McCaslin; he goes through life as "Tomey's Turl," and his children take the name of Beauchamp, after his wife's former master.

This lack of formal recognition, however, is the least of the cruelties done to Turl. In the story "Was," Buck considers him simply as "my nigger," and in passages laden with appallingly humorous irony, Faulkner shows how very far Buck and Buddy are from being able to conceive Turl even as a human being. Turl, before his future wife Tennie is won for him by Buddy in a poker game, runs away frequently to the neighboring Beauchamp plantation to see her; but Buck and Buddy will not buy Tennie because they have "so many niggers already that they . . . [can] hardly walk around their own land for them," and Hubert Beauchamp will not buy Turl because he refuses to "have that damn white half-McCaslin" on his land "even as a free gift."

This is not, however, the ultimate of their disregard for Turl. When Turl escapes, the only reason Buck and Buddy have for catching him immediately is to keep Miss Sophonsiba Beauchamp and her brother, Mr. Hubert, from using the capture and return of Turl as an excuse for visiting them. The two brothers are con-

stantly afraid Mr. Hubert will pull some trick like going off at
night while everyone is sleeping and leaving Miss Sophonsiba
alone in the house with them. This, according to their code, would
compromise Miss Sophonsiba and force one of them to marry her.

But far from merely catching Turl quickly to avoid Miss Sophonsiba, Buck launches himself on the chase with all the joy of a
man on a fox hunt, running Turl with dogs and treating him with
the objectivity with which a hunter stalks game. With Turl "treed"
in Tennie's house, Buck stands in front of the door while Cass
Edmonds makes a big noise at the back. Hearing the noise, Turl
explodes out the front door, knocking Buck flat. But Buck is mad
only at himself. He admits, as Faulkner puts it, "that it was his
own [Buck's] mistake, that he had forgotten when even a little
child should have known: not ever to stand right in front of or
right behind a nigger when you scare him; but always to stand to
one side of him."

There may be some question as to whether or not Faulkner's
contrast of this vein of light-hearted frontier humor with the bitter
irony that underlies it is successful artistically. There can be no
doubt, however, that it effectively points up Buck's and Buddy's
complete inability to understand their heritage clearly, a failure
which ultimately, they share with their sister's son, Cass Edmonds.
A far more intelligent man than Buck and Buddy, Cass nevertheless accepts old Carothers' ideas at face value, and more completely than the twins had done; Carothers, Cass tells Ike in "The
Bear," had "translated . . . [the land] into something to bequeath to his children, worthy of bequeathment for his descendants' ease and security and pride and to perpetuate his name and
accomplishments." The Civil War was in Cass's opinion no blessing to teach the people truth by suffering; it was simple tragedy in
which God had turned his back on the South. And the Negro is
to him an inferior race characterized by such evils as "Promiscuity.
Violence. Instability and lack of control. Inability to distinguish between mine and thine."

Faulkner seems, however, to approve in some degree the re-
enslavement of the Negroes during the Reconstruction by the
sharecropping system which McCaslin represents. Ike, who usually enunciates Faulkner's viewpoint, remembers the Negroes dur-

ing this time as a people who "misused" their freedom "as human beings always misuse freedom." And such memories lead Ike to reflect that evidently *"there is a wisdom beyond even that learned through suffering necessary for a man to distinguish between liberty and license."* Faulkner leaves no doubt, however, about Cass's methods with the Negroes in his running of the plantation; they amounted to what was frequently "downright savagery."

Perhaps a more important fact about Cass, however, is that he is a man who might, like Ike, have escaped from the family curse. Well read and intelligent, he can understand Ike's reasons for repudiating the plantation; but, like the "rich young ruler" of the gospels, he is unable to resign his worldly goods and follow the calling of truth. He denies vehemently that leaving the plantation will solve anything. He would deny it, as he says to Ike in "The Bear," "even if I knew it were true." He goes on: "I would have to. Even you can see that I could do no else. I am what I am; I will be always what I was born and have always been." And what he has been Faulkner makes quite plain; under his guidance, the plantation "enlarged and increased and would continue to do so," primarily for the benefit of the Edmonds family.

Such strong men as McCaslin Edmonds, then, had their place in bringing the South through the Reconstruction; but there is no doubt about Cass's failure to transcend his heritage; because he failed to understand the truth shown him through Ike's repudiation, he was doomed to repeat in some degree the sins of old Carothers, and through him God lays the old curse of Carothers on Cass's progeny.

In Ike McCaslin, as has been noted, the curse of the McCaslin heritage is countered by the primitive virtues of the Negro and Indian which he learned in the wilderness. In Ike's eyes, the whole structure of the plantation was "founded upon injustice and erected by ruthless rapacity." Similarly, he does not turn away from what he considers to be the ultimate truth about the Negroes: "They are better than we are. Stronger than we are"; even their very vices are "vices aped from white men or that white men and bondage have taught them."

True to the visionary nature of Faulkner's presentation of Ike's heritage, Ike's rejection of it is no simple act of conscience but a many-sided thing which he himself finds tremendously difficult to explain or even to understand. Although his own recent activities perhaps belie it, Faulkner, judging from the nature of Ike's actions in "The Bear" after his repudiation, does not seem to have faith in any kind of active crusading, either to free the Negroes from bondage or the white people from their curse; Ike fulfills all financial obligations to his Negro cousins to the best of his ability, but the remainder of his actions are negative only; he settles in Jefferson and maintains little or no contact with the McCaslin plantation. Such actions imply that Faulkner believes the problem is too large for one man to have any hope of prevailing against it. And in "Delta Autumn" he adds a more explicit statement. Although at fourteen Ike had believed that he could "cure the wrong and eradicate the shame" of his heritage, at twenty-one he "knew that he could do neither," he could only "repudiate the wrong and shame . . . in principle, and . . . the land itself in fact." Ike, indeed, in his long dialogue with Cass over the repudiation, seems happy enough that he himself will be able to "escape," and this is the note on which the dialogue ends; referring to the lessons he learned from Sam Fathers in the wilderness, he tells Cass, "Sam Fathers *set me free* [Italics mine]." This escape, furthermore, was evidently made fully as much for any descendants that Ike might have as for Ike himself. In the latter parts of "The Bear" Ike's desire for a son is brought out, and in "Delta Autumn" it is clear that the repudiation was made in part "for his son." The inference is clear. Faulkner had conceived Ike as the product of "the three generations He [God] saw it would take to set at least some of His lowly people free." In keeping with the historical nature of the vision, then, the people meant to benefit from Ike's repudiation are his descendants.

Ike, however, is childless, and so it must be assumed that the curse is to continue. It continues in the person of Carothers (Roth) Edmonds, of whom Ike's son would have been a contemporary. A constitutionally grumpy individual who cannot believe in himself or others, Roth is comparable to such other Faulkner moderns as Quentin Compson in *The Sound and the Fury* (1929), who, having lost the faith that men like Cass Edmonds had in the old traditions, have found nothing to take its place.

Roth's troubles stem from the family sin, failure to understand the proper value of the land. "You spoiled him," Roth's Negro mistress tells Ike, by giving to his grandfather, Cass, "that land which didn't belong to him." Like his grandfather, Roth has the opportunity of seeing, in Ike McCaslin, an example of a man who has transcended his heritage. But unlike Cass, Roth does not even take the trouble to listen to Ike; his comment on what Ike believes is ". . . where have you been all the time you were dead?"

As the plantation's head, Roth lives in an atmosphere of complete compromise. He is, in the first place, its owner only by right of the color of his skin; the owner by right of inheritance from the male line should be Lucas Beauchamp, son of Tomey's Turl. To add to the complexity of Roth's position, the only mother Roth can remember is Lucas' wife, Molly. Roth's own mother died at his birth, and Molly raised him with her own son Henry as a part of the family. He has thus learned his very virtues from the Negroes; it was Molly who, when he was a child, had cared "for his spirit . . . teaching him his manners, behavior."

In those childhood days, however, Roth had accepted Lucas' family without question; but as he grew older, "the old curse of his fathers, the old haughty ancestral pride . . . descended to him." He and Henry had always slept in the same pallet; but one night Roth refused to let Henry sleep with him. The next day, furious with himself, Roth knew he had been a fool; but the relationship was never the same again, no matter how he tried to breathe the old life into it.

Lucas, furthermore, never at any time treats him in the servile manner Roth expects from Negroes, but simply as an older man would treat a younger one. Nor does Lucas pay any attention to Roth's supposed authority. They have a little meaningless routine which they both observe with complete seriousness; in past years perhaps once during the summer, Roth would come to give Lucas advice about his crops, advice "which he completely ignored, ignoring not only the advice but the very voice which gave it, . . . whereupon Edmonds would ride on and he would continue with

whatever he had been doing, the incident already forgotten condoned and forgiven, the necessity and the time having been
served."

By false ownership of the land, then, Roth is caught in the old
curse he inherited from his family. But true to Ike's comment that
"most men are a little better than their circumstances give them a
chance to be," Roth usually makes an intense effort to do what he
thinks is right. In spite of his feelings of outrage and embarrass-
ment, he forces himself to put up with all kinds of "indignities"
from Lucas, and patiently looks after the aging couple when the
strong-willed Lucas nearly breaks up their marriage.

With Roth, then, the curse of the McCaslin family reaches the
present time, and the five descendants of old Carothers whom
Faulkner has characterized most thoroughly have all been viewed
in terms of it. Because of their misunderstanding of God's purpose
for the land ("communal anonymity of brotherhood"), and their
consequent use of it for their own aggrandizement under the code
of social caste into which they have been born, they have with the
exception of Ike frequently shown themselves as blind and selfish.
Each of them, however, has made some effort to transcend the
life to which the curse has doomed him. In Ike McCaslin, furthermore, Faulkner has shown how God has used contact with primitive peoples to evolve a man who could escape from the curse.

The wilderness, at the end of *Go Down, Moses,* has all but
vanished, but Ike is living evidence of the fact that in the old
days, God planted in the midst of the land He cursed a means of
escape from the curse. The inference is that Faulkner is optimistic
on the subject: the curse itself was an effort by God to help man
transcend his sins; and if God could evolve one Ike, he can evolve
another one.

It is significant that, with Ike childless, the only living male heir
of the McCaslin line mentioned in the book is the illegitimate son
of Roth by the granddaughter of Tennie's Jim. Faulkner has made
it plain in the *Harper's* article that he believes that the future of
the South lies with the Negro; these sentiments are clearly stated in
"The Bear," when Ike says to the husband of Lucas' sister:
"Granted that my people brought the curse onto the land: maybe
for that reason their descendants alone can—not resist it, not com-

bat it—maybe just endure and outlast it until the curse is lifted. Then your people's turn will come because we have forfeited ours." In the Negro's heritage, the primitive virtues still exist; and it is therefore fitting when Ike gives the hunter's horn, symbol of his wilderness heritage, to Roth's part-Negro child. . . .

Because of his heritage of the primitive virtues, it is with the Negro that the future resides. But for Negroes like Butch Beauchamp, meanwhile, whose lives have been destroyed by these "vices aped from white men or that white men and bondage have taught them," this future is of little value. And it is on the white man, because of his failures to transcend his own heritage, that the blame must ultimately rest.

The Heart's Driving Complexity: An Unromantic Reading of Faulkner's The Bear

HERBERT A. PERLUCK

🌣

Instead of a romantic Christian pastoral of redemption, in which the repudiation of the land and earlier the apparently selfless rescue of the fyce from under the erect bear are seen as almost sanctifying gestures of renunciation, a searing tragedy of human desire and human limitation evolves, chiefly through ironic means. From McCaslin's scornful skepticism as he listens to Ike's account of God's circuitous providence, and the "lip-lift" of contempt when he realizes that even Ike does not wholly believe in his "freedom," to the almost hysterical laughter with which Part IV concludes, the principal effects are ironic.

The central thematic irony, however, upon which these effects are grounded, is slowly constructed of larger elements. The repudiation in the commissary *is* prefigured in the hunt-narrative; something of a parallel does develop between the selfless non-possession of Ike's gesture at twenty-one and the repudiation of

FROM *Accent*, XX:1 (Winter, 1960), 23-25, 42. Reprinted by permission of *Accent*.

passion earlier—that effort to preserve the idyll of the Big Woods, in the reluctance of both Ike and Sam Fathers to slay Old Ben. But the point of the parallel is not merely to provide background and extension to the "story-proper"; it is drawn and pressed home by McCaslin Edmonds on Ike because in both gestures there is weakness and something even sinister which cannot become clear to McCaslin, or to the reader, until the dense and complex drama of the debate in the commissary is enacted.

The terrible irony of Part IV develops in the growing awareness in the reader, as well as in the characters, of the discrepancy between what we and Ike supposed him to have achieved, to have attained to, and what in fact his repudiations actually represent. The whole inner section of "The Bear" reflects back on the hunt-narrative and forward into the last sequence: Ike's return at eighteen to the woods, which are being destroyed by the lumber company; his vague, troubled guilt at the sight of the nearly demented, grieving Boon. Coming where it does in the story structure, Part IV has the effect of making the reader, as it makes Ike and McCaslin, remember and painfully reinterpret the earlier events as of some dream-idyll of human perfection, of perhaps a kind of angelic pre-existence, now dissipated in the wakeful glare of the human reality. Slowly and relentlessly, Faulkner's intention takes hold in Part IV, in the tragic incompleteness of man, as the gulf is drawn between action, life as lived, and the memory of action and events, in which our dreams of life, our poems, are created.

"The Bear" is no Saint's Life; on the contrary, what it expresses ultimately is that there is no "freedom" in renunciation, no sanctity through repudiation—that actually there is no such thing as human sainthood as we have conceived it. If Isaac McCaslin is a saint at all, it is not in the traditional ascetic sense of a successful renunciation of the world and the flesh in atonement and expiation; it is rather a "sainthood" of *un*success, an unwitting, unwilled elevation produced in the tragic *defeat* of spirit and soul in the "uncontrollable mystery" of the world which men and "saints" must live in perforce. . . . Isaac McCaslin ascends without comprehending wherein that only "sainthood" man is allowed resides:

in the anguished, complex heart. "The Bear" is a story of a renunciation that fails, as they all must. It is also the story of man's ineluctable fate of being only man. And on another level, it is a parable of man's pride, in his trying to be more than man, and of the evil this pride accomplishes in its condescending ascription of all that man does not want to see in himself to a certain few untouchables, the Boons of the world. . . .

Faulkner's meaning in "The Bear" is that if man would live, he must be prepared for the dying too; if he would love, he must also grieve for the spilled life that loving and living require. Simply to repudiate the spilling, to relinquish the grief, by relinquishing the passion, is to remove oneself from life, and from love, which, like the hunt, necessarily involves us in blood. There is no renunciation of life and the world which we can choose to make, and there can be no "acceptance" of the inevitabilities; we may only choose life. What we may renounce is only renunciation itself, and what we may attain to is not a regenerate state, sainthood, being, but our humanity.

Ike McCaslin's Covenants

Irving Malin

❧

Faulkner uses the story of the "sacrifice" of Isaac by Abraham with subtlety. In the Old Testament [see Appendix, p. 402], Abraham, the first patriarch of the Hebrews, who had entered into a "mutually exclusive agreement with God, whereby he was to recognize and worship no other deity and God was to protect and seek the welfare of Abraham and his family . . ." is commanded one day by God to take his son, Isaac, to an altar and slay him. Actually this is to be a test of Isaac's obedience to Abraham and,

FROM *William Faulkner: An Interpretation*, pp. 70-73. Reprinted with the permission of the publishers, Stanford University Press. © Copyright 1957 by the Board of Trustees of the Leland Stanford Junior University.

in turn, of Abraham's obedience to the Father. The two prove their allegiance through the preparations for the ritual, and the son does not have to die. He and Abraham both learn that God is merciful and benevolent toward those who love Him. The Biblical ritual ends: "And Abraham lifted up his eyes, and looked, and behold behind *him* a ram caught in a thicket by his horns: and Abraham went and took the ram, and offered him for a burnt offering in the stead of his son." . . . It is quite evident that Faulkner chooses the name Isaac to suggest religious associations . . . "The Bear" stresses the submission of the son (Isaac) to the priest (Sam-Abraham) and of both the priest and the sacrificial victim to the wilderness. The hunt for the bear, which is part of the wilderness, is dangerous because it involves conflict. It is true that Sam, as Abraham, prepares Isaac for the hunt, but it is Sam's *covenant* with Old Ben, and with the trees—in short, with the awe-inspiring wilderness about him—which is at the heart of the story. Unfortunately, Faulkner means to imply that the happy ending no longer exists. He realizes that the blood relationship of Sam Fathers and Isaac McCaslin cannot last in our times. The death of the spiritual father is intertwined with the murder of Old Ben by Boon Hogganbeck. Man and animal were one in the past. They were both representatives of the old order in which humility could be sought by this entry into strife. Old Ben taught Sam Fathers to search for the wildness of nature and to tame it, in order to gain a clear understanding of the potentialities of the human spirit. This is what Isaac was able to learn from his father; but he alone lives on in "The Bear" to see the total ruin of the wilderness which was their temple. He witnesses the arrival of the lumber company machines. He realizes that modern men of commerce are concerned not with the preparation for spiritual understanding but with material gain.

The idea of a covenant in Faulkner's work is, like his emphasis upon the father-son relationship, related to the Old Testament. Abraham's agreement with the Lord which I have just mentioned was renewed, in turn, by Isaac and Jacob—He became "the Kinsman of Isaac" and the "Champion of Jacob"—but the Covenant between all the Hebrews and God came into existence during the period of Moses. The exodus from Egypt into the Promised Land, Canaan, with the giving of the Ten Commandments on Mount Sinai, indicated that He was now on the side of the entire nation. The personal agreement developed, then, into a distinct social reality—the Hebrews became the Chosen People. Faulkner believes that the South must accept the significance of a mutual agreement or bond not only between particular Negroes and white men, but between the region and destiny (the North, the land, and the will of God). The idea of the covenant, both personal and social, is an important aspect of his work, giving much of it a legalistic tone. . . .

The covenant theme, with important variations, is repeated in "The Bear." Part Four, Isaac's rhetorical conversation with his cousin, stresses the idea that the entire South, not merely a Buck or Buddy, is bound to the land; the isolated covenant in *The Unvanquished* is expanded here until it assumes cosmic proportions. Isaac realizes the nature of the agreement (because of his ritual with Sam-Abraham) and provokes the anger of his cousin (a believer in the design). Isaac believes that He entered into a covenant with Southerners, teaching them the necessity of reorientation after the War, the need to abide by freedom for the slaves and for the earth itself. His countrymen did not heed the warnings, the Commandments, and they are now suffering the wrath of God. But the Negroes, who have understood the goodness of the land and the higher teachings of the Bible, can help them to lift this "curse." Isaac McCaslin believes, therefore, in the recognition of a universal Covenant, a set of laws, to which all men, black and white, must aspire in order to save their land, their country, and themselves. His own strength is evident when he says, "I am free." McCaslin Edmonds, his cousin, senses that this is not pure talk, that Isaac is truly a believer in the equality of men. He says,

'Chosen, I suppose (I will concede it) out of all your time by Him as you say Buck and Buddy were from theirs. And it took Him a bear and an old man and four years just for you. And it took you fourteen years to reach that point and about that many, maybe more for Old Ben, and more than seventy

for Sam Fathers. And you are just one. How long then? How
long?' and he
    'It will be long. I have never said otherwise.'

The Hero in the New World:
William Faulkner's The Bear

R. W. B. LEWIS

❧

If, as several of Faulkner's most enlightened observers have suggested, the novels and stories preceding *Go Down, Moses* possess
an atmosphere like that of the Old Testament, then *The Bear* may
be regarded as Faulkner's first sustained venture towards the more
hopeful and liberated world after the Incarnation. It is also of
course a story about the South in the 1880's, when the frontier was
rapidly disappearing. And it is another American *bildungsroman,*
another tale of a boy growing up in America, with all the special
obstacles to moral maturity which our culture has erected and
which comprise the drama for many another sad or lucky protagonist of fiction. We must not forget that *The Bear* is grounded in
these historic and locally traditional elements. But we should say
at the outset that in it we meet Faulkner's first full-fledged hero—
and that he is a young man who quite deliberately takes up carpentering because

> if the Nazarene had found carpentering good for the life and
> ends He had assumed and elected to serve, it would be all
> right too for Isaac McCaslin.

The Bear is a canticle or chant relating the birth, the baptism and
the early trials of Isaac McCaslin; it is ceremonious in style, and
it is not lacking in dimly seen miraculous events. We get moreover *an* incarnation, if not *the* Incarnation: or at least we get a re-

FROM the *Kenyon Review,* XIII:4 (Autumn, 1951), 641-660. Reprinted by
permission of the author and the *Kenyon Review.*

incarnation; and we witness an act of atonement which may con-
ceivably flower into a redemption.

Consequently *The Bear* is a pivotal work. Change is of its essence. Our notion about it is reinforced when we encounter the
same reanimated human will at work and a still larger conviction
of human freedom in the novel which followed it, *Intruder in the
Dust.* In both stories, but much more spectacularly and indeed
much more visibly in *The Bear,* what is positive in human nature
and in the moral structure of the world envelops and surrounds
what is evil; which is to say, more significantly, that the corrupt-
ing and the destructive and the desperate in human experience become known to us in their opposition and even their subordination
to the creative and the soul-preserving. This presents us with just
the sort of dramatic clarity that seems otherwise denied to writers
for almost a century. The highest reaches of modern literature, in
fact, have taken the form of an ultimate and vibrant duplicity, the
best account of our times that honest genius has been empowered
to construct—with every virtue and every value rendered instantly
suspect by the ironic co-existence of its opposite: Ahab and Star-
buck, and all their fellows, in a never-ending exchange of the
reader's allegiance. We have known these splendid discords and
artful confusions in the early novels of William Faulkner: which
is why *The Bear* appears as pivotal; although it is as likely to
appear merely old-fashioned, and to be regretted—the way *Billy
Budd* is sometimes regretted—as a regression to lucidity.

It is true, and worth pausing over for a moment, that in those
earlier novels as well a not entirely dissimilar ethical distribution
can be alleged. *As I Lay Dying,* for example, and *Light in August*
have been compared to Jacobean drama; presumably with the
thought that they are projections of worlds wherein what is human
or decent or pure flickers uncertainly in a darkness charged with
violence and horror; the horror and the darkness being the norm,
and the measure of such pitiful virtue as stirs feebly to combat
them. But even there, something more ancient and enduring,
something more substantial than the central tragic characters and
their wicked propensities flows through them and reaffirms itself
at the end as it flows on into the future. And this is what, with a
wry face, we have to call life itself. The grimace is due to the form

in which life re-exerts itself: a new set of false teeth, in *As I Lay Dying,* a new wife for Anse Bundren: "a kind of duck-shaped woman all dressed up, with them kind of hard-looking pop eyes like she was daring ere a man to say nothing"; an illegitimate child, which Dewey Dell has not found the medical means to get rid of. Life in *Light in August* is personified on the first and the last pages by Lena Grove, moving calmly and with animal obstinacy across a stage littered elsewhere with depravity and death, carrying in her womb her own bastard child, to be born on the other side of town. But it would scarcely be honest to describe either novel as a drama of the triumph of life: the design in each case is, if anything, a tension between creative and destructive possibilities.

In *The Bear,* however, the balance is tipped. What we discover first, along with young Ike McCaslin, and what determines his and our subsequent judgments is an archetypal or ideal human personality. It is something composed of a cluster of virtues unambiguously present from the beginning, as qualities to be striven for, prizes to be won: proving their efficacy in the mastery of self and the conquest of temptation—pity and humility and courage and pride and the will to endure and the rest. Their names recur with musical regularity, like the burden of a song. And together they are what we may call the honorable: something Roman and a trifle stiff, but independent of the fluctuation of moral fashions in the city. It is the honorable which permeates the wilderness, scene of the main action and home of the main actors in the story. And like Old Ben, the bear, patriarch of the wilderness, embodying the virtues in some undefined and magical way, the honorable exists as an ethical reality before the story opens, "before the boy was born": as a glimpse of immortality. It is an ideal prior to civilization, but it is not an uncivilized ideal and has nothing to do with noble savagery; it is prior exactly insofar as it is ideal, not so much older as timeless; and taking the humanly recognizable shape of a ritual pattern of behavior. The narrative image of that pattern is "the yearly rendez-vous," "the yearly pageant-rite of the old bear's furious immortality": the annual duel between the skilled hunters and the shaggy, tremendous, indomitable Old Ben. It is a duel enacted within a solid set of conventions and rules, faultlessly observed on both sides. This is the ritual by participation in which the young hero, Isaac McCaslin, becomes reborn and baptized, receives the sacramental blessing and accomplishes his moral liberation. It is the substance of the first half of the story; in a sense I will suggest later, it is the whole of the story; the rest of the book tells us how a properly baptized and educated hero may act when confronted with evil.

But it is evident that in order to explain these remarks and to see more deeply into the total experience, we must examine the experience in its only exact and living form. We must, that is, look more closely at the story's structure.

II

The difficulty of any Faulkner story lies in the order of its telling. He has always provided us with lots of action; and if his unconventional arrangement of incidents sometimes suggests an antic shuffle through a fateful crazy-house, it does at least avoid the other extreme in modern fiction: it never dissolves into atmosphere and "situation." What *happens* in a Faulkner story is more important than anything else; but it is the last thing we understand —we are let in on it gradually, from many different viewpoints and at different times. *The Bear* has a plot relatively simpler than, say, *The Sound and the Fury:* but here also Faulkner has played weird tricks with chronology. In particular, he has concluded his narrative with an episode that occurs at a moment earlier in conventional time than one of the chief episodes which precede it in the telling. If we follow the events in the life of Isaac McCaslin rather than the numerical sequence of the sections, we discover this personal history:

(Sections One, Two, Three) A boy named Ike McCaslin grows up in Mississippi, during the years after the Civil War. Every year from the time he is ten, he goes bear-hunting in the still untracked wilderness north of the town, along with his cousin Cass and some of the town's leading citizens—all highly skilled hunters. He gradually acquires some of the skill of the older men, and the virtues that are the product of so severe and masculine a life. There is one bear, greater and older than any of the others, who engages the hunters in an annual duel. He is called Old Ben. When the

boy is sixteen, Old Ben is killed by one of the men and a huge
mongrel dog.

(Section Five) After Old Ben's death, the boy, now eighteen,
comes back once to the wilderness, but the old hunting-lodge is
gone, the group of hunters broken up, and tourists have begun to
invade and transform the forest. He encounters Boon Hogganbeck,
the man who had killed Old Ben, and finds him reduced to hysteria.

(Section Four) At the age of twenty-one, Ike inherits the land
and money that have been passed down through his father (known
as Uncle Buck) from his grandfather, Carothers McCaslin. Ike
decides to give up this inheritance, since he had previously discovered that it is tainted at the source by the misdeeds of his
grandfather. The latter had seduced and had a child by a negress
slave, Tomasina, who may well have been his own daughter also.
Such a combination of incest and miscegenation represents for Ike
an image of the evil condition of the South—and of humanity in
general from the beginning of time. Ike determines not to compromise with this condition. He continues to live a simple, somewhat Christ-like existence. He takes up carpentering and marries
the daughter of his partner. He has no children.

Thus the "real life" equivalent of the career of Ike McCaslin;
but we must keep in mind, during the remarks that follow, that
we come upon the incidents of his twenty-first year and of his later
years *before* we are told about the return to the woods, at eighteen,
in the fifth section.

André Gide, when he was writing *The Counterfeiters*, confided
to his journal an ambition to render the events of his novel *légère-
ment déformés*, so that the reader's interest might be aroused in
the effort to restore the originals: the reader becoming thereby the
author's collaborator. Faulkner's motive may be much the same;
his so-called contempt for the reader (and others have made the
point) has the effect anyhow of involving the reader nearly to the
extent of devouring him. Certainly no other American writer engages his readers so strenuously; and there is no doubt that, except
for those who fear and resent him on quite other grounds, the
readers of Faulkner do or can derive immense aesthetic pleasure

in that participation with him that verges on the creative. Homer and Virgil (not to mention Conrad, or the Russians) ask no less of us. *The Odyssey,* for example, indicates importance by the chronological order of presentation, and we can only assess the famous wanderings of Odysseus when we notice that they are not given us directly but as they issue much later from the memory of a gifted liar: much, though Ike is no liar, as the revelations of evil exist primarily in the young man's memory. And in the *Aeneid* of Virgil (a poet much closer to Faulkner), the last event in the poem occurs many centuries before some of the events already described in it. Here of course the grandiose history of the ages to come appears explicitly as a prophecy, and almost as a dream: but I am willing to suggest that such may also be the nature of the fourth section in *The Bear.*

Before we get that far, however, a few mechanical observations may be helpful. It is worth seeing that the fourth section has the same purely formal organization and is roughly the same in length as the first three combined: this suggests, rightly, that it has the function of counter-weight. Both of these two large parts begin at a certain moment in Ike's life (16 and 21 respectively), retreat to an earlier period and circle back through their starting-points. The recurring insistence of Faulkner upon his hero's age is too striking to be overlooked: a whispering connivance, like a plea: "He was sixteen then . . . then he was sixteen." Ike's age is the chief structural element; and his sixteenth year was the *annus mirabilis:* the story flows through that year on three distinct occasions, as though only by this means could the contradictory richness of its experience be made apparent.

This aspect of the structure can be presented graphically, while not forgetting the many warnings against draining away Faulkner's vitality in cold schemas. [See the figure on page 312.]. The graph suggests, at least, the very considerable artfulness that governs Faulkner's temporal re-arrangements; if we have survived the shock of the initial disorder, we can admire the elegance and symmetry in the redistribution. The solid lines are of course the sustained narrative, and the broken lines the more rapid shifts in time: even these, however, not so much sudden leaps across the

Ike's age ... 0   10   12   14   16   18   21   35

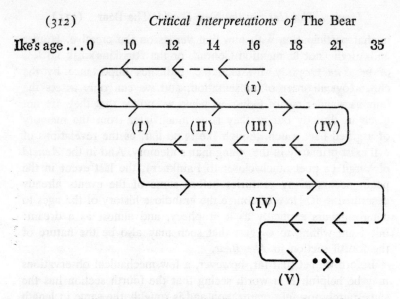

years as a fading backward of memory or a surge forward of imagination. But while we are aware of strong currents carrying us forward and backward in *The Bear,* we must also acknowledge the corollary impression that time is motionless, and everything is occurring simultaneously. This effect Faulkner achieves by bringing in past events as they are returned to in present memory: by parentheses, and by parentheses within those parentheses, like one memory jogging another. He achieves it too, in his narrative order, by the triple journey through the sixteenth year. *The Bear* thus constitutes (as the graph may dimly show) a unique conjunction of time and eternity: if we accept the word of Boethius, who distinguished between them as between a flowing-away and a standing-still.

The story begins in Ike's sixteenth year. It would have to, because it is Ike's story, and it is only then that his history ceases to be mysterious; it is only then that he completes the ritual of his initiation. Till that moment he had grasped the importance but not fully the meaning of the experience.

It seemed to him there was a fatality in it. It seemed to him that something, he didn't know what, was beginning;

had already begun. It was like the last act on a set stage. It was the beginning of the end of something, he didn't know what except that he would not grieve. He would be humble and proud that he had been found worthy to be a part of it or even just to see it too.

The drama he is engaged in is the drama of death and birth, and this is what he is disciplined to perceive as the story returns, in part three, to the great year: the death of Old Ben, of Sam Fathers, of Lion—and of the wilderness as wilderness and the companionship Ike had known there; and the birth of Isaac McCaslin as the reincarnation of those dead and the witness of that world. We might almost say that Old Ben dies in child-birth; he has many features in common with the "terrible mother" of many heroic myths; and the name of Sam Fathers is in no way accidental. It requires only the slightest twist of the tongue to convert the story's title into "The Birth."

Then, finally, we find out in the fourth section, if we submit ourselves to its spell, that it is in his sixteenth year also, on a December night after the last bear-hunt, that Ike solves the riddle of his family's history. That section begins with the sentence, ominously uncapitalized: "then he was twenty-one"; and the defining occasion of most of it is a conversation between Ike and his cousin Cass Edmonds in the plantation commissary on what appears to be Ike's twenty-first birthday; but, while the entire span of Ike's eighty-year-long life is touched on, it is specifically the discoveries of his sixteenth year that account for the intensity of Ike's speech and the resoluteness of his decision to give up his inheritance. With the conversation as foreground, those discoveries pass through Ike's memory like shadows on the wall behind— shadows themselves engaged in ghostly conversation; for they appear as remembered entries in the commissary ledgers, written in a question-and-answer manner. The very language of the entries —made several decades earlier by Ike's uncle and father, and agonizingly pieced together by Ike five years before the present moment—has the sparseness and the foreshortened quality of a memory.

Uncle Buck: "Eunice Bought by Father in New Orleans 1807 650 dolars. Marrid to Thucydus 1809 Drowned in Crick Cristmas Day 1832."

Uncle Buddy: "June 21th 1833 Drowned herself."

Uncle Buck: "23 Jun 1833 Who in hell ever heard of a niger drownding herself."

Uncle Buddy: "Aug. 13th Drownd herself."

The motivation for Eunice's suicide is revealed to us through its implications, in the shape it assumes in Ike's oddly mythopoetic imagination. It is up to us, participants in the hunt, to discover that Eunice had been the mistress of the grandfather, Carothers McCaslin, and bought by him and married to "Thucydus" when she was pregnant with the child Tomasina; and that Eunice drowned herself when she realized that her daughter was pregnant by her lover. For Ike, the tragic event has the fixed formality of legend:

> He seemed to see her actually walking into the icy creek on that Christmas day six months before her daughter's and her lover's (*Her first lover's,* he thought. *Her first*) child was born, solitary, inflexible, griefless, ceremonial, in formal and succinct repudiation of grief and despair, who had already had to repudiate belief and hope.

The first essential link between the first three and the fourth sections is the literal near-simultaneity of the death of Old Ben and the discovery of mixed blood in the McCaslin clan. But the relationship is a good deal more organic than that; the fourth section of *The Bear* ought not to be taken (as I am afraid it sometimes is taken) as merely the further adventures of Isaac McCaslin. We appreciate the harmony of the parts when we begin to describe the two different moments in ancient formulae: the birth into virtue and the vision of evil. For only a person adequately baptized is capable of having the vision at all; and only the grace bestowed at the baptism enables the initiate to withstand the evil when it is encountered. The action in Section Four is made possible by the experience preceding it: the ritual in the wilderness *contains* the decision in the commissary.

And this leads us into a somewhat more complex view of the relationship. For it is quite exact to say that the whole of the fourth section is contained within the sections which have the wilderness as their setting: this is the unmistakable effect accomplished when Faulkner concludes the story with a short section which returns to the forest, returns to the life of Ike before he is twenty-one, returns to the atmosphere and the rhythms of the hunting world. The fifth section reverts too to the style—relatively straightforward, though highly orchestrated and charged with autumnal splendor—of the first, second and third: picking up that style where it had been left almost sixty pages before, and so enveloping and containing the style in between. The difference is shown by quoting the last lines of section four and the first of section five—breaking in anywhere on the endlessly flowing sentence of the former:

> and on their wedding night she had cried and he thought she was crying now at first, into the tossed and wadded pillow, the voice coming from somewhere between the pillow and the cachinnation: 'And that's all. That's all from me. If this don't get you that son you talk about, it won't be mine': lying on her side, her back to the empty rented room, laughing and laughing

> He went back to the camp one more time before the lumber company moved in and began to cut the timber. Major de Spain himself never saw it again.

Faulkner has even gone to the extreme of employing the single inverted comma in the conversations of the fourth section: the conventional sign of the speech contained within the speech—as against the double comma elsewhere. It is the sort of device that is peculiarly trying for those not already persuaded by Faulkner; but it is another instance of his anxiety that we should recognize the mode of existence of this moment in the experience.

For what we are given in the fourth section is essentially not a narrative of past events, but a vision of the future. We can justify its appearance between the third and the fifth sections—between, that is, episodes of Ike's sixteenth and his eighteenth years—by thinking of it as a dream; perhaps, though this is not necessary, a dream in the year between. It is a true dream to be sure, issuing securely from the gate of horn, but passing before our eyes events which, at this moment of perception, exist only in a state of possibility. A condition of potentiality, as of something not yet fully realized, is carried in the prose itself. We are struck at once by the decrease in visibility: on an immeasurably vast setting, actions and dialogue have curiously hazy outlines; sentences spray out in all directions, rarely reaching (within our hearing) their probable periods. Everything is unfinished, incomplete. But the experience is not a *mere* possibility, in the sense that its opposite is equally possible; for we have to reckon here with Faulkner's implicit theories of time and destiny, according to which all events are predetermined and so can be said to exist and to be seen as taking place simultaneously. To see them this way is to assume the divine viewpoint, as Mme. Magny has observed; divine also, as she does not go on to say, because Faulkner manages—in *The Bear* anyhow—to detect a modicum of human liberty within the grand design: as though not discontent with the ancient and irresolvable paradox of fixity and freedom. Thus the events are certain, but they are not yet; and so they are not clearly to be distinguished by a human perception fully competent only with the past.

Something like this fourth section is probably as close as contemporary fiction can come to that moment in the traditional career of the hero when he descends into the dark underworld, encounters his ancestry and has a vision of the future. We have become skeptical of prophecy; we no longer project spiritual darkness in such simple geographic terms. But here, as Ike sees his inevitable moral decision and its determination in the vast sweep of human history, we partake again of that transfiguring moment narrated already by Homer in *Odyssey* XI and by Virgil in *Aeneid* VI.

III

It is a very long way from Mississippi to ancient Rome and Greece, and no doubt it is time now to remember the national and provincial boundaries within which Ike's initiation is undertaken. For like *Moby Dick, The Bear* is most in tune with primary and perennial rhythms of experience when it is most explicitly American. The content of its story is drawn from that imaginary world inhabited also by many of the heroes of Hawthorne and Melville, and much more recently of F. Scott Fitzgerald. And if we close in more sharply on the particular portion of America that provides the image for its dramatic scene (as, in *The Divine Comedy,* we must remember Florence as well as Italy in general), we recognize the most significant prototype of *The Bear* in *Huckleberry Finn.* Both are narratives of boys growing up in the 19th Century southwest; but the essence of the analogy lies, of course, in their common sense of the kinship between white and black, in their common identification of slavery as a kind of original sin, in their common reversal of the conventional morality that legitimizes social injustice. Faulkner, characteristically, carries the inter-racial kinship literally into the blood streams: Ike and Tennie's Jim are cousins in fact as well as brothers in the spirit of humanity; and also characteristically, Faulkner intrudes a lecture on social legislation, with a warning to the national government up north to keep its hands off the problems of the south—while Mark Twain never exposes Huck Finn to the danger of a pretentious awareness of his own virtue. But both novelists, while telling again the most familiar of stories, confront their heroes with the trials peculiar to the southerner before and just after the Civil War: especially, the challenge of negro slavery.

The central poetic insight, however, which Faulkner shares with Mark Twain and many another American writer is something larger: it is an insight into the fertile and ambiguous possibility of moral freedom in the new world. In the Mississippi wilderness of the eighteen-seventies and -eighties, Faulkner has projected another compelling image, so striking elsewhere in American fiction, of the ethically undefined: undefined, that is—like the river in *Huckleberry Finn* and the sea in *Moby Dick*—only in the sense of not yet fixed in the implicitly hypocritical conventions of "civilized" life. The frontier, as Turner and Constance Rourke were the first to make clear, was the major physical source of this uniquely American idea: the idea, I mean, of a new, unspoiled area in which a genuine and radical moral freedom could once again be exercised—as once, long ago, it had been, in the garden of Eden; and Faulkner locates his image in time at the very moment when the frontier was disappearing. Insofar as *The Bear* is a story about death, it is about the death of the frontier-world; and to a very limited degree it may be regarded as a narrative enactment of the historic development elaborated in Turner's famous essay. But to say so without qualification would be to ascribe to Faulkner a view of innocence quite the opposite of that finally revealed in *The Bear;* and it would be to forget how often Faulkner, like Hawthorne and Melville, has engaged in the ritual slaughter of the animal innocent.

A part of the history Ike McCaslin rehearses for Cass Edmonds seems to echo the comfortable story optimistic Americans were telling each other a century ago.

> [God] made the earth first and peopled it with dumb creatures, and then He created man to be His overseer on the earth and to hold suzerainty over the earth and the animals on it in His name, not to hold for himself and his descendants inviolable title forever. . . . and all the fee He asked was pity and humility and endurance. . . . He watched it. And let me say it. Dispossessed of Eden. Dispossessed of Canaan and those who . . . devoured their ravished substance ravished in turn again and then snarled in what you call the old world's worthless twilight over the old world's gnawed bones, blasphemous in His name until He used a simple egg to discover to them a new world where a nation of people could be founded in humility and pity and sufferance and pride of one to another.

Such an identification of the new world as a divinely offered second chance for humanity, after the first opportunity had been so thoroughly muffed, can be matched in countless editorials and orations: especially during the generation before the Civil War. But Faulkner's hero is examining the myth to see where it went wrong; and he concludes, not that the new world is devoid of evil, but that evil was brought into it with the first settlers, "as though in the sailfuls of the old world's tainted wind which drove the ships." It was the evil of slavery; and beneath it and responsible for it, the sin of spiritual pride. Ike McCaslin is the first of Faulkner's characters to understand American history.

He can do so because he is free—or rather, because he has achieved freedom. He is even, we may say, innocent: but in a crucially new sense. For the quality of innocence undergoes a profound dialectical transformation in *The Bear*. The nature of the dialectic is indicated very forcefully in the opening sentences:

> There was a man and a dog too this time. Two beasts counting Old Ben, the bear, and two men, counting Boon Hogganbeck, in whom some of the same blood ran which ran in Sam Fathers, even though Boon's was a plebeian strain of it and only Sam and Old Ben and the mongrel Lion were taintless and incorruptible.

Taintless, in a new sense, for Lion is a mongrel and Sam (we know this also from "A Justice") is the half-breed offspring of a negress slave and a Chickasaw Indian. But in the moral world of *The Bear* a primary purity, fundamentally materialistic and suggested by the physical purity of the land, is transcended as a dangerous illusion; and for it there is substituted a purity and a freedom much tougher and far more durable. This innocence is an achievement, not merely a gift; it is gained through discipline and submission, it is announced in a ritual. This innocence is nothing else than conscience itself.

Now conscience is the mark of maturity; and, exactly because of the historical illusion so tenaciously clung to, conscience has been something not often reached without the intervention of tragedy, in the American literature of education: consider Donatello and Billy Budd and Jay Gatsby. Isaac's achievement is the achievement of his creator, working an astonishing alchemical change on specifically American materials: converting not only history into art, but illusion into reality, and converting qualities like innocence from a lower to a higher order of value. In order to see the magnitude of this change—of the transmutation of values on which the story rests—we must move into a somewhat more expansive vocabulary than we have employed so far.

Faulkner himself is most willing, too willing perhaps, that we should recognize the universal design into which his southern saga fits; he plants, if anything, too many clues to his wider ranges of meaning. Nonetheless *The Bear* is his masterpiece in this respect: it is his most successful attempt to accommodate to each other in a single narrative the various accounts of themselves that the world and man can give. The fusion has been strained and uneven heretofore; but now it is as though Faulkner, the artist, had like his hero Ike discovered the unity of meaning. And so, while grounded historically and built out of the moral dilemmas which the history gave rise to, *The Bear* no less impressively reflects a timeless psychic drama. It is indeed a treasure-chest for psychologists in criticism (among whom I do not very warmly count myself), for object after object that are known to be recurring symbols in the dream legends of the unconscious are scattered throughout the story: the forest, the tree, the rifle, the bear, and a score of others. The great adventure in which these objects play such a prominent part is quite plainly that transformation of character which is like a second birth, and which some psychologists refer to as the return to the womb; as Faulkner is careful we should see: "It seemed to [Ike] that at the age of ten he was witnessing his own birth." "The birth of the hero," Carl Jung concludes from his survey of world-mythology, "is not that of an ordinary mortal, but is a rebirth from the mother-spouse . . . because only through her does he share in immortality." The second mother is often an animal, Jung assures us, and may be one normally thought of as male: like Hiawatha's mother who first appeared as the Great Bear of the Mountains. Ike first shares in Old Ben's "furious immortality" during that extraordinary episode, like a dream in color, when he penetrates the heart of the forest, finds the (sacred) tree, manifests his submission by abandoning first his gun and then his watch and his compass: until, stripped of hostility and outside of time, he stands in the presence of the wilderness god. It is a liberating experience, as the return to the womb (or any well-organized education) is supposed to be. But final freedom comes only with the death of the parents: for Ike, of Sam Fathers and Old Ben; and then he is prepared to meet the challenge of maturity. Traditionally in this phase of the psychic journey, the hero moves, in the words of Joseph Campbell, "in a dream landscape of curiously fluid, ambiguous forms, where he must survive a succession of trials." It is an apt description of the fourth section.

Yet if Old Ben does have some of the qualities of the "terrible mother" in the myth of the hero, he is at the same time the embodiment of the courage and chivalry and the will to endure which are shaping elements in the honorable. He is "not malevolent, just big"; and if in one of the most extraordinary verbal achievements in modern literature we hear of "the legend" about him: "corncribs broken . . . shoats and grown pigs and even calves carried bodily into the woods and devoured . . . dogs mangled and slain . . . a corridor of wreckage and destruction"—still, Old Ben emerges from this epic portrait by way of a comparison with Priam, King of Troy. Priam, we remember, was the ruler of the old citadel and was destroyed with it; but one warrior survived him, Aeneas, his nephew and we may say his foster-child, who after many trials established a new kingdom in a new country. I do not say that all this is packed into Faulkner's single allusion; but I suggest that we are closer to the archetypal image reproduced in *The Bear* if we think of it as a pattern of redemption in terms of the ultimate forces in the world (like the *Aeneid*), rather than a dream projection mirroring interior psychic conflicts. And in identifying the pattern, we do well to look carefully at the nature and use of *power* within it.

Power is often symbolized, in the heroic myth, by the character of the hero's "magic weapon," and the use to which he puts it: and we can contemplate a significant range from the great bow of Odysseus, with which he ruthlessly slays a houseful of political and domestic rivals, to St. Martin of Tours, telling the pagan Emperor that "Armed only with the Cross, in the forefront of the enemy, I will fear no evil." Aeneas enters his supreme battle wearing a shield on which is engraved the histories and the triumphs to come of the Roman people; it is a recorded destiny which renders him invulnerable to the mightiest of the Latins. In *Moby Dick*, Ahab forges a tremendous harpoon for the final hunt (in a scene consciously modelled on similar moments in Homer and Virgil), and he baptizes it "Not in the name of the father, but in the name of the devil"—the book's secret motto, Melville said later: the secret source of Ahab's strength; and the harpoon is the instrument of his own violent death. For Isaac McCaslin there is the rifle, and much is made of it. First, a rifle too large for him, a man's weapon in a boy's hands, which he can no more handle than can Telemachus his father's bow; and then at ten years, the year of his first communion with Old Ben, he receives "his own gun . . . a new breech-loader, a Christmas gift." "He would own it and shoot it for almost seventy years." The imagery of the gun is diffused through the story; it becomes one of the central unifying symbols. Ike has two occasions on which he might use his rifle against Old Ben: the first time, he abandons it in order to present himself in evident humility to the bear; the second time, he throws it away and risks his life in the charitable act of rescuing the little fyce.

This, I believe, is the essential symbolic movement of the story (it was the conclusion, in the original short version of *The Bear*), and it is not surprising that this, of all incidents, is remembered and re-examined in the fourth section when Ike is expressing his insight into history and his own historic role. For what we comprehend at last in *The Bear* is the transmutation of power into charity. No loss of power is effected; but it suffers a rich seachange, it comes under the control of moral understanding; grace enters into it. More concretely: Ike does not give up his gun altogether; on the contrary, we have swift previews of him in later years as the greatest hunter in Yoknapatawpha County; but he uses his power with restraint and fidelity, and for a life lived as closely as possible to the source of his moral energy. It is what he gains from that source that makes the life possible and makes Ike what he is: a Christ-like person with some ineradicable southern biases. It is a dimensional increase of perception, and through this also Ike is uniquely capable of reading the past correctly. The total change at work in *The Bear* may thus, in these various respects, be compared to the transition from the pagan to the Christian era, if not from the Old to the New Testament.

History became readable, according to most apologists, when meaning was put into it at the moment of the Incarnation. Now what has been most striking in Faulkner's earlier novels has been just that endless, hopeless fumbling in the past, that obsessive struggle for its meaning by constant re-arrangements of its content: which seem the only resource of a person or a people from whom the gift of illumination has been so far withheld. From this point of view, the repeated attacks of Quentin Compson on the history of his country may be fruitfully contrasted with the disciplined exposition of Isaac McCaslin, and Quentin's suicide with Ike's honorable long career. This is not to say that Ike is intended to represent Christ in a second coming, but only that Ike moves in a world of light—a light still meagre but definite; a new world in which values have been confirmed by being raised to a higher power; not the new world beyond the frontier—that is precisely what is transcended—but a world so perpetually new that Ike sometimes seems to be its only living inhabitant. It is worth insisting that the life of Christ is not under any circumstances a subject for fiction: not at all because it would be irreverent, but because within the limits of literature it would be impossible. But *The Bear* does as much as literature may with propriety try to do: it enacts for us, by means of human individuals in a local habitation, the miracle of moral regeneration.

God's Moral Order and the Problem of Ike's Redemption

Olga W. Vickery

❧

Of central importance . . . is the significance of Isaac's renunciation. On one side of him is Cass Edmonds representing the plantation world and its tradition. On the other is Sam Fathers, scion of a "vanished and forgotten people," who is linked to the plantation only through that drop of blood which had been the blood of slaves. For Isaac, it is scarcely a matter of choosing between the two traditions as represented by Sam and Cass. His

FROM *The Novels of William Faulkner: A Critical Interpretation* (Baton Rouge: Louisiana State University Press, 1959), pp. 130-134. Reprinted by permission of the publisher.

long midnight conversation with Cass in the commissary represents his effort to explain a decision already made inevitable by and encompassed in the ritual of the hunt. Significantly enough, his explanation of the eternal consists of juxtaposing the McCaslin ledger, symbol of the history of the South, against the Bible and its expression of the eternal verities of the heart.

Isaac's interpretation of history is Biblical and, more specifically, Miltonic in its poetic emphasis on the hierarchy and the contractual agreement between man and God: "He made the earth first and peopled it with dumb creatures, and then He created man to be His overseer on the earth and to hold suzerainty over the earth and the animals on it in His name." Man's happiness consists in recognizing the greatness and the limitations of his position in the divine order. By forgetting, even momentarily, that he is at once the ruler and the ruled, man destroys that order and with it his proper relationship to God and to nature. Nor does it matter whether he sinks below or attempts to rise above his divinely ordained position. Since animal and demi-god are both foreign to his nature, both constitute a threat to his distinctive humanity. It is only by recognizing and accepting his place in the hierarchy that man fully realizes his moral nature.

The fact that men will destroy the hierarchy and deny God is foreknown though not foredoomed: "'I will give him his chance. I will give him warning and foreknowledge too, along with the desire to follow and the power to slay.'" Since man is created sufficient to stand, though free to fall, the responsibility for the destruction of the moral order and the consequent corruption of his own nature, must be his alone. His sin is pride and the lust for power, the one perverting his relationship to God, the other to nature and other men. In either case, the overseer becomes the tyrant, seeing himself as the measure of all things and replacing God's laws with his own. His punishment is increasing blindness to his own corruption until the game he hunts and kills becomes human.

The original sin, repeated by each successive generation, spreads through time and place. Even the new world with its promise of a new beginning serves only to confirm the old error. Out of it, however, there slowly emerges the reverse pattern of redemption. The actual enslavement of man by man marks the final horrifying destruction of the moral order. But ironically, his bondage prevents the Negro from learning how to forget God. Barred from possessing land or exercising authority over other men, he is forced into " 'the communal anonymity of brotherhood' " where he pays God's fee of " 'pity and humility and sufferance and endurance and the sweat of his face for bread.' " In his chains lies the assurance of his salvation. And he is not alone. In the midst of the fallen world there is still the individual who can resist the way of the world and say " *'I am just against the weak because they are niggers being held in bondage by the strong just because they are white.'* " This gesture of protest prepares the way for Isaac's repudiation of his patrimony and the more active engagement of Chick Mallison. That such gestures are made indicates God's continued presence in the fallen world and gives earnest of His final forgiveness. Each is a preparation for and an anticipation of the triumph of Christ as a man. Thus, what begins as an explanation of Isaac's decision to relinquish the land becomes an impassioned poetic effort to "justify God's ways to man."

Isaac's repudiation of the wrong and the shame, symbolized for him by Eunice's suicide, is made possible by the fact that Sam Fathers has provided him with the wilderness and the code of the hunter as an alternative to the plantation world. In the forest Isaac can be one of a group of men "not white nor black nor red but men, hunters, with the will and hardihood to endure and the humility and skill to survive." From this vantage point Isaac can examine the history of his people and although he cannot change it, he can at least refuse to condone it and to contribute to it. The gesture of protest too can become part of recorded time. His rejection of the McCaslin tradition and his subsequent life together constitute a transcendence of public morality. But the significance of that rejection depends on whether it is juxtaposed against the wilderness or the tamed land. Isaac's moral and spiritual stature is not only derived from but, in a sense, dependent on the existence of the wilderness and the ritual of the hunt. He becomes literally one of the "Old People" who have vanished and been forgotten by invoking the past until "those old times would cease to be old times and would become a part of the boy's present, not only as if they had happened yesterday but as if they were still happening." What is an annual vacation for Major de Spain and his friends becomes Isaac's life.

This pastoral form of existence in which the hunter and the hunted share immortality and eternal youth constitutes Isaac's dream of escape from the McCaslin world. Because it is an escape and a desire to find personal salvation, his gesture of relinquishment is only superficially an atonement for the sin of his forefathers. He shows his own awareness of this when he calls himself " 'an Isaac born into a later life than Abraham's and repudiating immolation: fatherless and therefore safe declining the altar because maybe this time the exasperated Hand might not supply the kid.' " Accordingly, Isaac's withdrawal is in reality an attempt to evade both the guilt of his forefathers and his own responsibilities. Thus, while his daily life is a humble imitation of Christ's, it also denies the spirit of Christ who did not hesitate to share in the life of men, to accept guilt, and to suffer immolation. In rejecting sin, Isaac also rejects humanity. Significantly, he holds himself aloof from close human ties; though he is uncle to half the county, he is father to no-one and husband solely to the wilderness. Having confused the wilderness with the Garden of Eden, he not only dedicates but sacrifices his life to it. Man must leave the Garden in order to discover his humanity and whatever the reason, Isaac does not do so; his knowledge stops just short of the paradox of the fortunate fall.

When he is outside the wilderness, Isaac is virtuous but ineffective. His is essentially "a fugitive and cloistered virtue, unexercised and unbreathed." The measure of this lies in the fact that nothing happens to him between his twenty-first and seventieth year. We know that he married and that his wife failed to draw him back into history, failed even to give him a son who might have provided the crucial test of his withdrawal from life. And we know that he retreated into his dream while excluding his wife from it. The magnificent ritual of the hunt holds a promise which is never fulfilled by Isaac's life. The significance of any ritual must lie in its power to create order and to establish a sense of continuity with the past for the individual. Isaac, however, confuses the ritual with the life it orders. The qualities he learned under the tutelage of Sam Fathers, the fyce, and Old Ben should have been asserted within the context of civilization, whereas he forever applies them solely to the hunt itself, until he finally presides over a group of city vacationers who find sport in slaying a doe. Thus, as the wilderness retreats and shrinks in size, Isaac seems to lose stature even as his gesture of dissent loses significance.

The Purpose of Faulkner's Ike

DAVID H. STEWART

❦

I propose to re-examine the one Faulkner character, Isaac McCaslin, who has been most favorably and generously received by the critics, and to examine him as briefly as possible both within the larger context of Faulkner's Southern cycle and within the largest context of all, the social and ideological world outside Faulkner's fiction which Ike was evidently devised to influence. I shall try to describe what Ike's life and thought actually mean once the fine patina, provided by the critics, is removed.

Of the many aristocratic families whose chronicles Faulkner has detailed, the McCaslins, except for their founder, appear to follow a path quite different from those of the others, though as I shall show this is only the surface impression. What is striking about the McCaslins is that from the day of old Carothers' death in 1837, the second generation set out in a curious direction. The twin brothers, Buck and Buddy, conceived a sort of rural cooperative, a Mississippian New Harmony, slaveless yet solvent because it could compete with big planters. It was to be so constituted that the coercive features of patriarchal aristocracy could be avoided as easily as the equally coercive features of the radical Yankee alternative which meant black insurrection and, later on,

FROM *Criticism*, III:4 (Fall, 1961), 333-342. Reprinted by permission of the Wayne State University Press.

carpetbag domination. But the entire program vanished over the precipice of civil war.

Then comes Isaac, the most fascinating McCaslin of all—and perhaps Faulkner's most fascinating character for the simple reason that he seems to be his creator's favorite standard-bearer, a forthright "positive hero." This is not to call him unique in the Faulkner canon. He is, indeed, a spiritual brother to the gentlemen who function as central consciousnesses in Faulkner's earlier novels: Quentin Compson, Gail Hightower, Bayard Sartoris (narrator of *The Unvanquished*), and Vladimir Ratliff. Like Quentin and Bayard, he is acutely conscious of the overriding importance of social form, evidenced by his formal gesture of repudiating his patrimony when he cannot actually "cure the wrong and eradicate the shame" of his heritage. Similarly, he denies that his young fourth cousin, Roth, would actually promise to contract a legal marriage with a woman whom he loved illicitly. More important, he too believes in the efficacy of that abiding Faulknerian virtue, announced already in *Sartoris,* "spitting in deestruction's [sic] face"; he learned it first from a mongrel and later from the great bear. It is supposed to explain not only the Southern performance in the Civil War but human behavior in general.

Ike's trouble with time is exactly like that of his precursors: they all desire to elude it, to resist distinguishing what actually happened from what they had been told, hence to prolong or postpone things past into the present or even the future. In addition, the impulse which seems to animate Ike and give him direction— as it does Quentin and Bayard and Gail Hightower—is a need for peace and escape. He shares even the superficial characteristic of shaking and trembling when excited or confronted with difficulty.

The only differences between him and every other Faulknerian central consciousness are first, his freedom from feminine influence, though even he had to struggle against an Amazonian wife comparable in some ways to Drusilla, who disturbed Bayard so violently, or Eula Varner Snopes and her daughter, who confounded Gavin Stevens. Ike had no grandmother to mold his character nor a mother or sister to betray the old sacred code for him. Instead he has Sam Fathers who, of course, seems comparable to

Teiresias, hence probably combines female qualities with his primitive masculinity. The second difference is his singular inheritance from his father and uncle, who were not cavaliers like Colonel John Sartoris or generals and governors like Quentin's forbears. Slightly similar to the first Ratliff (Ratcliffe), Uncle Buck and Buddy disapproved slavery and hence alleviated for their progeny the burden imposed by this social crime.

Differences notwithstanding, Ike is a creation essentially similar to Faulkner's earlier central consciousnesses: he feels what they feel, fails where they fail. Born after the Civil War (1867), he has escaped exposure to its violence, which helps explain the estrangement, emphasized frequently by Faulkner, between him and his substitute-father, cousin McCaslin Edmonds. It is the period in which he lives, together with his heritage, which defines the problems he must confront and delimits the range and manner in which he responds. He seems to be involved in three things: reaching maturity, expiating the original sin of miscegenation and incest committed by Carothers, and reconciling or achieving a viable position with regard to the dilemmas of property ownership. Restitution for inherited guilt plus self-justification are fundamental, the latter taking precedence as Ike lives further into the twentieth century.

Ike's approaches to his problems are as varied and devious as they are revealing. As we learn in "The Old People" and "The Bear," he comes to maturity in three stages. After a belated infant baptism in the blood of the deer he killed as a nine-year-old boy, he reaches age twelve (the Protestant "age of responsibility") and under Sam's tutelage passes through a ritual, comparable perhaps to the confirmation. The rite is curious: his task is to go forth into the wilderness, like the Indian boys of an earlier age, and to see a vision, vouchsafed only after he has stripped off all the accoutrements of civilization and reduced himself to the level of an animal. Then he sees Old Ben, the wilderness symbol, and returns home purified. More than this, he is ostensibly prepared to face the world on its own terms so that when he realizes the next year that Old Ben must die, he knows "that he would not grieve." Of course, he cannot play the role of priestly executioner. Twice he had the opportunity but, like his mentor, declined it despite his eminent worthiness. For him decisive action is difficult; and he waits until the plebeian, Boon Hogganbeck, who is as much animal as man (Faulkner's plebeians often are), commits the final deed and thus absolves Ike of responsibility so that he can assist with pure hands at Sam Fathers' funeral. What Ike achieves through this sequence of events is not only a degree of maturity but sanctity: he emerges incorruptible, a kind of consecrated altar boy, who can in time develop into the wise prophet and judge which he is destined to become, without losing the "young boy's high and selfless innocence."

But before his position is secure, he must pass through another ritual, comparable to the venerable Protestant practice of making an adult Decision for Christ, a mature reaffirmation of the childhood commitment. This Ike does when he is twenty-one by renouncing the things of this world, adopting the kenotic idea, becoming a carpenter "because if the Nazarene had found carpentering good for the life and ends He had assumed and elected to serve, it would be all right too for Isaac McCaslin. . . ." Thus he becomes a man.

The solution of Ike's second problem, expiating the old sin of his heritage, is not very imaginative. His grandfather's will has imposed upon him the legal duty of transferring a cash forfeit to the colored descendants of the McCaslin line. The thousand dollars, bequeathed for this purpose by Carothers, has been increased by Buck and Buddy to three thousand, one for each of the children of the black man begot incestuously by the old patriarch.

Now the "pay-off," softened and rendered a little more palatable by Ike's kindly ruminations and the clouds of rhetoric in which he and his cousin love to indulge, stands before Ike as a solemn obligation, harsh, mechanical, and brutal. And he discharges his duty. Bearing up nobly beneath the weight of his white burden, he arranges for Fonsiba's security, protecting her from her own silly illusion of freedom and from her ridiculous negro husband whose very skin exuded "that rank stink of baseless and imbecile delusion, that boundless rapacity and folly, of the carpet-bagger followers of victorious armies." The youngest son, Lucas, claims his own third: the oldest, Jim, vanishes in 1885 so that Ike has to wait forty-five years until he can pay the final third to Jim's grand-daughter whom he rewards additionally with the old hunting horn given him by General Compson and with the consoling admonition that *"We* will have to wait" for racial equality. Although Ike might disagree, one may fairly consider that his solution was a good bargain: three thousand dollars of someone else's money and a horn discharge a century of guilt.

His solution to the land problem is also easy—indeed almost pathetic beside Buck's and Buddy's earlier attempt. In the first place Ike ponders the ingenious possibility that he personally does not own any land at all, on the ground that buying or bequeathing land is impossible by divine edict. Cousin McCaslin Edmonds puts an end to this notion by insisting that in practice at any rate old Carothers did own land and did hand it on to his descendants. Later on, McCaslin suggests that even if Carothers never owned the land, it must then have passed from Ikkemotubbe to Sam Fathers, and "who inherited from Sam Fathers if not you? co-heir perhaps with Boon . . . ?" Whichever way Ike may try to look at it, he does own or "hold suzerainty" over the family plantation fifteen miles from Jefferson, and he is obsessed with the desire to free himself from this land which he believes contaminates him morally (because of Carothers' wickedness) and spiritually (because property-owning is unchristian or at least un-Christ-like).

What he does is simple: after all the talk and theorizing, he gives all of his property to his cousin, fastidiously and successfully evading the entire problem of social position and power. He remains inviolable and pure—and is on two occasions judged rather severely for it: Faulkner, thinking about such rugged individuals as Lucas Beauchamp, Buck and Buddy, says that "old Isaac . . . in a sense, say what a man would, had turned apostate to his name and lineage by weakly relinquishing the land which was rightfully his. . . ." Later on, when Ike is an old man, the colored girl, remotely his kin and pregnant with Roth Edmonds' child, tells him that she could have made a man of Roth, but Isaac had spoiled him before birth by transferring the McCaslin land to the Edmonds family, hence weakening or emasculating them just to save himself.

So much for Ike's attempts to solve his problems. What he

achieves is little more than cheap self-satisfaction, cheap because his basic urge is to gain peace and to escape, which prevents him from finding solutions that really satisfy or that are really meaningful. To reach a clear estimate of his character and behavior is, therefore, difficult. What is one to say of a person presented by his creator as a Christ-figure, yet whose entire performance is negative? He repudiates land, writes off the guilt of slavery with three thousand dollars and a horn, proclaims for the black race a theory of "wait and endure," constantly evades responsibility to his fellow men, lives alone, isolated, impotent, ineffectual, and childless, and appears finally to have more in common with the pathetic Reverend Hightower than with Christ. He is a mere passive consciousness whose meager gestures at activity, far from contradicting, serve to emphasize his passivity.

Yet he is portrayed for the most part so sympathetically that instead of judging him immediately, one is inclined to attempt a closer examination in order to ascertain exactly what his habitual attitudes are, what he stands for. His mind focuses again and again on three things, the nature and role of mankind, the "ways of God," and the nature and meaning of the Southern order. His view of man seems to rest on a pair of complementary theorems: that man is "puny" and that total irrationality is man's proper condition. His insignificance is seen in relation to the wilderness which, in the seventies of the nineteenth century, appeared to scorn the traces "of man's puny gnawing at the immemorial flank." The wilderness was "a phantom, epitome and apotheosis of the old wild life which the little puny humans swarmed and hacked at in a fury of abhorrence and fear like pygmies about the ankles of a drowsy elephant." Even as an old man nearing eighty when, in order to reach the receding remnant of wilderness, Ike had to travel two hundred miles, he still thought it a "tremendous, primeval, looming" thing looking down upon the camp (and perhaps every human habitation) and considering it "the puny evanescent clutter of human sojourn which after a single brief week would vanish and in another week would be completely healed, traceless in the unmarked solitude."

This would be an unpleasant or at least uncomfortable judgment against man if it were true. But man in time triumphed over

the wilderness, hacked the "drowsy elephant" to pieces, an exas-
perating fact which Ike cannot ignore. He must extricate himself
from a curious predicament. Ike, after all, is a man whose theory
ought to have led him to join the local conservation club in order
to preserve his beloved forests. Instead, all his life he has been a
member of rich men's hunting parties which can afford to penetrate deeper and deeper into the virgin lands and leave a "clutter"
each time which, despite Ike's assurance, is not "healed" or "traceless" in two weeks (a bottle, for example, does not decay quickly).
Thus Ike feels at last a need to justify himself and tells us that
"suddenly he knew why he had never wanted to own any of it,
arrest at least that much of what people called progress, measure
his longevity at least against that much of its ultimate fate. It was
because there was just exactly enough of it." That is, there is just
enough wilderness to last out Ike's lifetime. With extraordinary
selfishness he explains that the "two spans"—he himself and the
wilderness—will run out together, "not toward oblivion, nothingness, but into a dimension free of both time and space." In short,
Ike and the virgin land will be born again in heaven. And the
moral of the story seems to be: man may live out his years doing
what he pleases with no sense of responsibility, but with the assurance that he is doing only and always what fate has destined
him to do, and with the guarantee that paradise is a comfortable
Eldorado where everything is restored to its happy youthful state.

The natural corollary to this is Ike's other theorem about man,
namely that he is irrational. When cousin McCaslin objects to
Ike's highly subjective interpretation of the Bible, Ike silences him
with the explanation that there is no possibility of contradictory
interpretations because "the heart already knows." Biblical scribes
themselves sometimes lied because they could not make truth simple enough, but this does not matter because the pure-in-heart
know truth instinctively. Ike's truth is *the* truth, if only men would
stop using their minds long enough to recognize it.

This brings Ike to confront the deity and to answer the obvious
question about how he managed to establish direct contact with
Him. Ike's God is a predestinator who first gave men Europe and
then, when they spoiled it, He gave them America "founded in
humility and pity and sufferance and pride. . . ." But then (Ike's

dialectic is a little obscure here) He found that even in the New World there was corrupt blood because the Indians too tried to possess and bequeath land; hence, to accomplish His purpose, He "voided" the Indian blood with White blood, which in turn raised "the white man's curse," that is, Black blood. God did all this and more: He created the beautiful South, watched wicked men destroy it, collaborated with John Brown though disapproving his methods, kept His blessed face turned toward His special people because the Southern ladies fed jelly to niggers and nursed them, and finally made the Rebels unite and fight against hopeless odds, which was far more significant than their having somehow lost the war. God, in short, "must accept responsibility for what He Himself had done in order to live with Himself in His lonely and paramount heaven." But in Ike's view, God does not mind this responsibility at all for He has already appointed a Divine Emissary whose duty it is to begin the long task of leading mankind away from the path of darkness. Who is this Emissary? Ike! "Chosen," says McCaslin Edmonds, "out of all your time by Him. . . ."

God is a great comfort to Isaac, who has lived directly under His sanctifying hand since he was twelve—whence, I suppose, his confidence in the future. Guided by God Almighty, he has done nothing to protect his beloved wilderness, nothing to save Old Ben. But this is all right, since the divine powers "would give [Old Ben] his paw back even, certainly they would give him his paw back." Here, then, is Ike's Calvinist God, a private and personal friend who doubtless has a special salvation prepared for Isaac just as He had a special reason for creating him.

Ike's handling of the Southern order stems logically from his view of God and man. If men (except Ike) are puny runts, and if Ike's beneficent Creator alone is responsible for what happens, then the South, past, present, or future, is the best of all possible worlds because it is the only possible world. "Submit!" becomes the catchword. And the world to which one is invited to submit is really no worse than any other. The true Southern lady is, after all, an angel. The ugliest features of Southern life, for example the Ku Klux Klan lynchings, are not, after all, authentically Southern but direct products of vile Yankee abolitionist or carpet-bagger meddling. The racial problem, while at times vexing, is at least bearable. Witness Isaac himself who became as vexed as he could be but learned to bear up at the cost of three thousand dollars—which he had not earned. He treats the black race exactly as he treats the wilderness, perhaps a little less kindly. The woods will last until Ike is gone, and he is satisfied; the colored people will keep their subordinate place until Ike is gone, but he is not quite satisfied and suggests that they stay down for an additional thousand years or two which of course is no time at all, a mere wink to God's benevolent eye, especially for people who above all else love to be patient and to endure. In the last analysis, the one thing Ike, like his grandfather before him, cannot tolerate is recognition of racial cross-breeds. To acknowledge the product of miscegenation is the ultimate outrage as Ike explicitly says: "No wonder the ruined woods I used to know don't cry for retribution! . . . The people have destroyed it and will accomplish its revenge." And who are the people? Precisely *"Chinese and African and Aryan and Jew,* [who] *all breed and spawn together until no man has time to say which one is which nor cares."*

Although he has stirred many American critics to sympathy, Isaac is in many ways an unattractive creature. Whether his creator willed it or not, he turns out to be a more eloquent and persuasive apologist for the Old Order than the Vardamans and Bilbos whom Faulkner at times detests so much. Like Hightower's personality, Ike's is so perfectly divided between the will to preserve and perpetuate intact his heritage and the will to escape responsibility for the iniquities which his heritage places upon him that he continually approaches a futile and agonized passivity. His acts are usually inconclusive, his ideas always autocathartic.

Just as Faulkner twice registered objections against Ike's ineffectuality, so at the end of "The Bear," Ike's biggest story, Faulkner relates an incident which may be taken as his final negative judgment upon Ike. Clearly imitating his Indian-negro preceptor, Sam Fathers, Ike salutes a child of the wilderness in Sam's own tongue. But Sam's salutation was addressed to a handsome deer, Ike's to a rattlesnake—the one a symbol of life, the other a symbol of death. Thus it appears that Faulkner recognizes the failure of Ike to achieve a vision of reality in any way more profound or satisfying than Quentin's or Bayard's. His subjective effusions bring a viable conclusion no closer. He remains selfish, self-satisfied, and alone, retaining nevertheless a certain seductive charm.

Ike McCaslin surpasses his earlier spiritual brethren in three ways. His unique heritage of purity permits him to walk safely the thin line between guilt and expiation, and it prepares him for his special role as savior, while his predecessors were only executors of the regional conscience. His supreme egotism saves him from the evil consequences of isolation which destroyed Quentin and Hightower because it insulates him against the sense of futility and defeat which beset them. He survives as old Bayard survived, though his abdication from the office of "The McCaslin" preserves him from active engagement in the social organism and permits him to play the kindly sage like Will Fall in *Sartoris*. As a central consciousness, therefore, he is admirably equipped to tell us (or rather refract for us) the Southern story. Indeed, he is a far more persuasive narrator than the Stevens-Mallison team in *Intruder in the Dust* or than Faulkner himself in the entr'actes of *Requiem for a Nun*, though the argument remains the same. Even the shrewd tale-teller, V. K. Ratliff, who informs us in *The Hamlet* that the color-line still exists beyond the grave, is no match for Ike. Like William Jennings Bryan at the monkey trial, Ike can readily evoke in the jurors a kindly disposition toward himself because he is the authentic, sterling example and product (impurities notwithstanding) of the righteous Cause which he advocates.

To conclude with the assertion that Faulkner is echoing Yeats's famous lines in "The Second Coming" would be attractive but unjustified:

> The best lack all conviction, while the worst
> Are full of passionate intensity.

By refusing to decide the issue, by declining Yeats's aristocratic solution, Faulkner induces a condition of paralysis and in this way perpetuates the status quo. It is his frenzied meditations that many critics have mistaken for actual commitment, negative or positive, when in fact Mr. Faulkner provides little more than consolation for the suspended intellect.

The Relation of Style
and Meaning in
Faulkner's Work

Faulkner's Concepts of Time

FREDERICK J. HOFFMAN

✤

[One of the major thematic concerns in Faulkner's work is his]
treatment of time (including historical time, tradition, as well as
narrative rhythm and pace) . . . it is probably the most important approach one may make to Faulkner. While a literal, lineal
time has no place of appreciable significance in Faulkner's work,
the pressure of past upon present is seen in a variety of complex
and interesting ways as affecting the psychology and morality of
individual actions.

I shall begin by offering a diagram of the several time patterns
in Faulkner's work. It is an oversimplification, but it should
help. . . .

FROM *William Faulkner* by Frederick J. Hoffman, Twayne's United States
Authors Series (TUSAS #1), pp. 24-31. Reprinted by permission of
Twayne Publishers, Inc., copyright 1961.

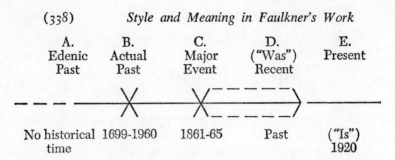

A.	B.	C.	D.	E.
Edenic	Actual	Major	("Was")	Present
Past	Past	Event	Recent	

No historical 1699-1960   1861-65   Past   ("Is")
time   1920

This sketch demands several preliminary observations. The "Edenic time" (A) is a pre-historical or a non-historical time, or a non-temporal existence, a point before or beyond time, when active moral criteria either have not yet entered human history or are not really contained within the human consciousness. The "actual past" (B) means the beginning of recorded history—that is, within Faulkner's record; the earliest specific date mentioned by him is 1699, a date given in the 1946 appendix of *The Sound and the Fury.* But the developing time is largely emphasized as within the nineteenth century, leading toward and away from the Major Event (C), the Civil War, in which the accumulated tensions and moral crises received a catastrophic and a significantly violent expression. This does not mean that Faulkner is an "historical novelist," nor that he gives the Civil War much specific attention. . . . The most important use of time in Faulkner is the pattern or movement of it—largely in the consciousness of his characters, not in terms of narrative exposition—from this major event through the Recent Past (D) to the Present (E). This movement is reciprocal, and it alternates in terms of symbol and forms of psychological reaction. . . .

There is, of course, an historical pattern in Faulkner's work, but it has to be picked up from here and there in the novels and stories; it is not presented as a straightforward chronology. . . .

Faulkner sees time in a complex of human tensions and as fully absorbed in and integrated with rhetoric, style, and narrative pace and rhythm. The reader is almost never aware of a pure present . . . nor is a *specific past* very often exclusively given. There are two important, typical uses of time in the novels: the slow, gradual, painstaking reconstruction of the past by narrators who exist in the present or existed in the recent past (as in *Absalom*); and the pattern of movement from past to present to past, or within points in the past (*The Sound and the Fury* is a good example). In either case, one almost never sees the present as a pure or separate time; it is infused with the past, it has meaning only in terms of it, and its complex nature results from the fusion of the two.

One may describe Faulknerian time as a continuum time flowing from past into present and from present into past. Reality is not so much objective existence but what past and present have made of an object or an event within a given set of psychological conditions. . . .

Besides this very important view of time, there is the idea of an "Edenic past" (A of the above diagram). This may be called pure stasis or a timeless vision or an unhistorical condition existing before and transcending human complication. In various ways it is described (and glimpsed briefly) in "The Bear," *Absalom, Light in August, Requiem for a Nun,* and in numerous brief images elsewhere. Irving Howe calls it "a past removed from historical time, an Eden coexisting with society yet never mistaken for society by those who come to it for refreshment and purification." . . .

The vision of an Edenic past is one of the more substantial in American literature. The "state of innocence" which ante-dates or ignores or avoids experience is in one way or another expressed as a point of reference for a major journey of the American personality from innocence to experience. As Henry Nash Smith has abundantly proved in *The Virgin Land* (1950), it was one of the most frequently employed images on the frontier. Its many literary variations include James Fenimore Cooper's Leather-Stocking tales, Mark Twain's *The Adventures of Huckleberry Finn,* the Nick Adams of Hemingway's *In Our Time* and stories of other volumes, and such cruder uses of it as Sherwood Anderson's *Dark Laughter* and Waldo Frank's *Holiday*.

In Faulkner's novels, the figure of the Edenic past is symbolized variously in the wilderness of "The Bear"; in the state of pre-historical innocence described in *Absalom*; and in the vision of the arrested, static, still reality of the road to Jefferson in the first chapter of *Light in August* and of the landscape of the farm beyond Jefferson in *Intruder in the Dust*.

Faulkner's language also has an especial relevance to this kind of "still moment": the words *motionless, arrested, frozen, suspended, immobile, soporific,* and others define the condition of static innocence. The following passage, from *Intruder in the Dust*, illustrates the effect upon Faulkner's rhetoric:

> . . . there should have been fixed in monotonous repetition the land's living symbol—a formal group of ritual almost mystic significance identical and monotonous as milestones tying the county-seat to the county's ultimate rim as milestones would: the beast the plow and the man integrated in one foundationed into the frozen wave of their furrow tremendous with effort yet at the same same [sic] vacant of progress, ponderable immovable and immobile like groups of wrestling statuary set against the land's immensity . . .

This rhetoric, and many figures like it, is used to define an arrest of consciousness, a state of suspension; in many cases it also suggests an "ideal" state of nature which precedes the onrushing of time, the beginning of "progress" and decay in human affairs. In most examples, there is an implicit criticism of the nature of human evil or vileness or sheer moral insensibility. But it would be a serious mistake to assume from this that Faulkner is a "primitivist": that he counsels a retreat from the present to an ideal, undefiled state of nature.

In many respects, the quality of Edenic stillness is also a matter of characterization and description; the hero in Faulkner frequently matches stillness against violence. He is sometimes badly mistaken in so doing. . . . The Edenic past is a form of representing a state of nature, both a descriptive and a normative means of defining the role and the effect of man's effect upon it and upon history.

Gavin Stevens says at one point in *Intruder in the Dust* that time is "all man had, . . . all that stood between him and the death he feared and abhorred . . ." There is much in Faulkner's novels of this kind of tension. His characters are intense creatures, obsessed with their isolation in the world, abnormally puzzled over the character and degree of the burdens they must assume, and desperate to assert themselves before death closes in on them. In this respect, the complex of past and present, assuming both the "burdens" of history and the struggle of self-definition, becomes a means of classifying Faulkner's characters. A not uncommon type of struggle in his novels is, therefore, that against the threat and menace of time—a struggle to put a stop to time and to prevent it from defiling an ideal.

. . . perhaps the most obvious [of the human attempts to fix time] is the cliché reaction or stock response to human event. Men and women give labels to events unthinkingly and irresponsibly, and this tendency is an example of meeting evasively the moral burden of the past. Faulkner most successfully contrasts this cliché with the problem of man himself: the abstraction "nigger" is forced to meet the test of the vitality of "man." . . .

Besides [this manipulation] of time as abstract versus time as "real," there are five other ways in which Faulkner describes the relationship of the individual to the past. On occasions, the Faulkner character assumes the burden of the past in an obsessive way. . . .

In another example, the Faulkner hero drives relentlessly toward the accomplishment of an abstract "design." . . .

In a third example of the individual's reaction to time, we have the hero who is "trapped in history"—immobilized because of a fixation in the past. . . .

The fourth kind of available reaction to time is to deny that the past exists. The reverse of assuming that only it exists, it is a psychological variant upon the obsessed figure who tries to order the world in his own image. . . .

Finally, the Faulkner character may adopt a simple vision of the past, setting aside its extreme aberrations and resting trustfully upon its promise of stability and endurance. This fifth class of response to time is truly complex, and it involves many variants. There is the "Edenic vision," discussed above; there is the steady, balanced "acceptance" of time and its erosive effect upon man . . . There are many such characters in Faulkner's works who often seem his "reserve" of stability: . . . Sam Fathers and

Ike McCaslin of "The Bear"; and many of the Negroes throughout his fiction.

Rhetoric in Southern Writing: Faulkner

WILLIAM VAN O'CONNOR

Faulkner's rhetoric has several sources: it is indebted to Tennyson and to Swinburne, to the elegance of *la fin de siècle,* to the Ciceronian periods of Southern oratory, and to a Southern folk tradition that is anti-grammatical and colorful. Perhaps his major styles can be classified as "high rhetoric" and as "folk language." The two styles meet in *The Hamlet,* and there are varieties of the folk language in most of his books. When people speak of Faulkner's rhetoric, however, they commonly mean the "high rhetoric."

Millar MacLure, writing in the *Queen's Quarterly* (Autumn, 1956), says: "Faulkner's prose has an archaic sound, like a hunter's horn." This is the best characterization of it I have read. Faulkner's prose has a nineteenth century quality, it belongs to a different world from the present.

Perhaps the simplest way of examining the high rhetoric is to read and then analyze a characteristic sentence. The sentence is from "The Bear":

> It was as if the boy had already divined what his senses and intellect had not encompassed yet: that doomed wilderness whose edges were being constantly and punily gnawed at by men with plows and axes who feared it because it was wilderness, men myriad and nameless even to one another in the land where the old bear had earned a name, and through which ran not even a mortal beast but an anachronism indomitable and invincible out of an old dead time, a phantom, epitome and apotheosis of the old life which the little puny humans swarmed and hacked at in fury of abhorrence and

FROM the *Georgia Review,* XII:1 (Spring, 1958), 83-86. Reprinted by permission of the *Georgia Review.*

fear like pygmies about the ankles of a drowsing elephant;—
the old bear, solitary, indomitable, and alone; widowered,
childless and absolved of mortality—old Priam reft of his old
wife and outlived all his sons.

First, there is the suspension of meaning in the long sentence,
there are colons, semicolons, and dashes (sometimes there are
parentheses); the sentence is a small self-contained world. Second,
there is the now famous vocabulary: *divined, encompassed,
doomed, myriad, nameless, anachronism, indomitable, invincible,
phantom, apotheosis, abhorrence, absolved*—words that evoke
an older morality and recall an older order. Third, there is a
reference to a tragic or noble event in an older romantic literature
—"old Priam." Fourth, there is the negative followed by a positive, usually, not this nor this but this; in this sentence it is "and
through which ran *not* even a mortal beast *but* an anachronism indomitable and invincible . . ." Fifth, there is repetition: "*solitary,*
indomitable, and *alone.*" Sixth, there is poetic extension of meaning brought about by an unexpected word, "absolved of mortality," whereas one expected "freed from" or "escaped from."
Seventh, there is the metaphor the vehicle of which is foreign to
the subject under discussion, but which sheds a light on that subject: thus the relationship of the man to the bear is likened to
pygmies troubling a drowsy elephant. And lastly, there is Faulkner's indifference to standard structures—"reft of his old wife and
outlived all his sons."

There are several other characteristic devices which are not
found in this passage; the use of paradox, as in the oxymoron
"roaring silence"; the piling up of adjectives as in the phrase "passionate tragic ephemeral loves of adolescence" (leaving out of
commas of course adds to the dream-like quality, the being above
time and space that the true work of art sometimes achieves); the
running of two words together (after the manner of Joyce and
Cummings), such as "allembracing" and "eunuchmountebank";
and the liking for hyphenated words, as with "rodent-scavengered
tomb," "smoke-colored twilight," or better, this sentence: "It (the
talking, the telling) seemed (to him, to Quentin) to partake of
that logic- and reason-flouting quality upon which it must depend
to move the dreamer (verisimilitude) to credulity—horror or

pleasure or amazement—depends as completely upon a formal recognition of an acceptance of elapsed and yet-elapsing time as music or a printed tale."

What do we have thus far in the way of devices? We have

1. the long sentence, with colons, semicolons, dashes, and parentheses
2. the vocabulary that evokes an older morality and a realm of high romance
3. the allusions to romantic episodes in history and in literature
4. the sentence that employs a negative or series of negatives followed by a positive
5. the use of synonyms for the purpose of repetition
6. a symbolist or poetic extension of the meaning of words
7. the reaching out for a metaphor or a simile the "vehicle" of which is foreign to the subject being discussed
8. breaking with standard grammatical forms; sometimes solecisms
9. the use of paradox
10. the piling up of adjectives
11. the merging of two words into one word
12. the use of hyphenated words

For many writers the paragraph, or the chapter, or even the over-all argument or thesis is the chief unit of composition. For Faulkner the chief unit is the sentence. His ideal, as certain sections in *Requiem for a Nun* suggest, would be a booklength sentence. His public statements and short speeches show that Faulkner is not a gifted expository writer, and he seems incapable of developing a thesis slowly or subtly. Faulkner's sentences evoke, they do not state. Perhaps I should qualify this argument to the extent of saying the sentence is the chief unit in those books that most depend upon the high style. The parallel phrases, the repetitions, the circling of the subject, or the piling up of adjectives— everything contributes to a self-contained and static world. Faulkner's sentences are spatial rather than analytical.

One is likely to think of Faulkner as having a "voice," just as one thinks of James as having a voice. Faulkner's world lives because the voice evokes it for us, just as James' world lives in the Master's polite, intelligent telling. There is, of course, a distinction. All of James' characters talk Jamesian English. Faulkner's characters have identities apart from as well as in relation to the "voice." Sometimes the "voice" takes over or heightens a character's speech, and sometimes it is a "chorus" saying what the events at the front of the stage signify. We may look at the following example, the close of Chapter IV of *Absalom, Absalom!*. Quentin is imagining the final encounter between Henry Sutpen and his brother Charles Bon:

> They faced one another on the two gaunt horses, two men, young, not yet in the world, not yet breathed over it long enough, to be old but with old eyes, with unkempt hair and faces gaunt and weathered as if cast by some spartan and even niggard hand from bronze, in worn and patched gray weathered now to the color of dead leaves, the one with the tarnished braid of an officer, the other plain of cuff, the pistol lying yet across the saddle bow unaimed, the two faces calm, the voices not even raised: *Don't you pass the shadow of this post, this branch, Charles;* and *I am going to pass it, Henry.*

Almost all of the characteristics of Faulkner's high rhetoric are here. It is Faulkner's "voice," not Quentin's. It is Faulkner's evocation over the shoulder on Quentin. The passage that immediately follows, however, the speech of Mr. Compson recalling Wash Jones' reporting the murder, comes as an electrifying contrast:

> . . . and then Wash Jones sitting that saddleless mule before Miss Rosa's gate, shouting her name into the sunny and peaceful quiet of the street, saying, "Air you Rosie Coldfield? Then you better come on out yon. Henry has done shot that durn French feller. Kilt him dead as a beef."

Compson's idiom is his own, and Wash Jones' idiom is decidedly his—and they release the reader from the hypnotic world created by the "voice." Or perhaps one should say they enlarge or extend the world created by the "voice."

Ratliff's speech is probably the purest example of the folk style. This is a passage from *The Hamlet*:

> I did, that is, because Ab was laying out in the wagin bed by then, flat on his back with the rain popping him in the face and me on this slat driving now and watchin' the whiny black horse just turning into a bay horse. Because I was just eight then, and me and Ab had done all our horse trading up and down that lane that run past his lot. So I just drove under the first roof I come to and shaken Ab awake.

Many of Faulkner's characters talk a variety of folk language, including some, like Gavin Stevens, with university degrees. Sometimes they shift from standard to folk usages and back again in a single conversation.

Although they are far from fully accounting for Faulkner's success as a fiction writer, these styles, the high style and the folk style, do account for much of his greatness. There are innumerable passages that would serve very well as set pieces for anthologies. He has always been able to use language as a virtuoso—but if this helps to account for his genius it also helps to account for his failures, especially his more recent failures, *The Fable* and *The Town*. In the former, the high style creates a world out of words, a world that seems hypnotized and bemused by the sounds that went into its making. In the latter, each of the narrators is a cracker-barrel philosopher, pleased as all hell with his shrewd and comic folk idiom. In each book character and dramatized incident have been sacrificed to Faulkner's style, to the voice of high rhetoric, and to the color of the folk language.

Faulkner's Uses of Imagery and Humor

HARRY MODEAN CAMPBELL AND RUEL E. FOSTER

❧

Except for his Freudian symbolism, which requires special treatment, Faulkner's imagery . . . is fairly well limited to the following uses, which may be summarized thus: (1) for developing tone through ironical contrasts, and atmosphere through a pathetic fallacy coloring of the natural background; (2) for introducing flashbacks and antecedent exposition; (3) for describing characters; (4) for carrying significant parts of the main narrative itself; (5) for unifying the main narrative through structural refrains; (6) for relating the chaotic world of appearances to what Faulkner considers the equally chaotic cosmic realm; and, finally (7) for embodying the very bitter satire which seems inspired by his comprehensive pessimistic philosophy. Some parts of his imagery, to be sure, fail to perform any of these functions well, but far more frequent are the metaphorical passages which have contributed in a significant way to his becoming, not a great poet, but a great poetic artist in prose fiction.

. . . we must consider the atmospheric function of Faulkner's humor, the use of humor to give an emotional ambivalence to a scene—the guarded style. A classic example of this is contained in what is probably Faulkner's most important long short story, "The Bear." This story is a rather complicated one concerning the consciousness of Isaac McCaslin as he matures and learns the primitive mysticism of the wilderness and the ancient guilt which lies upon the bloodline of his family. One of the important—and for the boy, tragic—scenes of the book is the one in which he learns that his grandfather, old Carothers McCaslin, has been guilty of both incest and miscegenation. He has fathered a child by a slave and then has had incestuous relations with his own

FROM *William Faulkner: A Critical Appraisal* (Norman: University of Oklahoma Press, 1951), pp. 40, 111. Reprinted by permission of the publisher.

mulatto daughter. The boy learns this indirectly through the crudely humorous and laconic entries in an old plantation ledger which dates back before the Civil War. Here is the entry (in his father's hand):

> *Eunice Bought by Father in New Orleans 1807 $650. dolars.*
> *Marrid to Thucydus 1809 Drownd in Crick Cristmas Day*
> *1832*

and then the other hand appeared . . . his uncle's . . . :

> *June 21th 1833 Drownd herself*

and the first:

> *23 Jun 1833 Who in hell ever heard of a niger drownding*
> *him self*

and the second hand, unhurried with a complete finality . . . :

> *Aug 13th 1833 Drownd herself*

Eunice, who drowned herself, was Old McCaslin's first Negro mistress and it was her daughter (by McCaslin) who was involved in the incest. This knowledge, disclosed with Olympian casualness by the ledger entries, is tremendously unsettling for the boy. But the involved ledger entries, odd spelling, and the laconic dialect humor help underplay and protect the scene from open emotionalism. Thus the horror of incest and miscegenation is presented, and presented realistically and skillfully by tempering it in the fashion noted above. At the same time, as the scene is finished, a delayed reaction comes, in which, for some people, the horror may be increased by the very casualness of the humorous contrast offered.

Faulkner, then, we see, is a writer who conceives his stories in a complicated mood—a mood for the most part generously salted with humor. His humor may be cruel and sadistic, or it may be genial and anecdotal, or it may, and often does, mingle both the cruel and the genial. In his best work, the humor is almost always an integral part of the experiential context of the narrative—it is very seldom exploited for its own sake. Faulkner is not primarily, however, a humorous writer, but he is a writer with a unique sense of humor which is used to give new perspectives into the meaning of the human experience he is portraying.

The Relationship Between Part IV and the Rest of The Bear

IRVING HOWE

❧

Without ado let us turn to the most problematic aspect of Faulkner's long story, "The Bear." What is the relation between its two halves?—between the sections devoted to the hunt and the counterbalancing Section IV in which Isaac McCaslin, parrying the conventional views of his cousin Edmonds, decides to forego his heritage?

In earlier pages something has been said of the significance of this story, both as a solitary work and with regard to its place in Faulkner's development. Several interpretations are possible. Finding in Faulkner's preceding books "an atmosphere like that of the Old Testament," R. W. B. Lewis describes "The Bear" as Faulkner's "first sustained venture toward the more hopeful and liberated world after the Incarnation." It may also be read as a story about the disappearance of the Southern frontier in the 1880's, or as "another American *bildungsroman* of a boy growing up in America, with all the special obstacles to moral maturity which our culture has erected . . ."

Such a variety of readings is entirely desirable, but it must be remembered that they take one (the figure is a matter of choice) very deeply into the work or very far from its surface of narrative. In its more important half, "The Bear" is primarily a story about hunting. For having said as much, Malcolm Cowley has been berated by several critics interested in the story's symbolic dimensions—mythic, anthropological, psychological. That such dimen-

FROM *William Faulkner: A Critical Study* (New York: Random House, 1952), pp. 186–189. Copyright 1952 by Irving Howe. Reprinted by permission of Random House, Inc.

sions are present in "The Bear" is obvious, Faulkner himself referring to its events as a "pageant-rite." But the sophisticated reader, he more than others, is in danger of neglecting the literal aspect, of forgetting that the bear, like the white whale, is a real animal, and in this case an animal with fur and four legs.

This point is of some importance in trying to solve the problem of the story's structure. For once "The Bear" is considered primarily in thematic terms, it is easy enough to establish the necessity for Isaac McCaslin's long debate with Edmonds and the spray of memory that accompanies it. If Isaac's earlier experience with Sam Fathers is a kind of baptism or initiation, then his gesture at twenty-one is a fulfillment of the vow to virtue which constituted the ceremony. The decision in the commissary is foreshadowed, made inevitable by the ritual in the wilderness. And if we accept the suggestion that Section IV be regarded as Isaac's dream of what his vow will entail for later life, then its place in the story seems all the more secure.

These claims for Section IV have considerable appeal, but it is in the nature of the literary experience that they *cannot* be conclusive. What finally matters is not our ability to connect the two halves of the story by logical ties, but their dramatic relation within the story. If Section IV were omitted, "The Bear" would profit in several ways: the narrative would flow more evenly toward its climax; there would be a superior tonal unity; and the meaning, never reduced to the brittle terms of Isaac's politics, would be allowed to rest in a fine implication. Since Section IV is "contained" in the previous three sections, it might be desirable for the story to resolve itself on the plane of the implicit, with the ritual in the wilderness suggesting, but no more than suggesting, its relation to the life of Yoknapatawpha. The loss, however, would be considerable. What Section IV now does is to give the story social and historical density, the ceremony in the forest reverberating through the town, and thus it keeps Faulkner's meaning from the confinement of abstract morality.

Whatever the justification for the presence of Section IV, there can hardly be any doubt that as a piece of writing it is much inferior to the other parts. The first three sections, a changed recital of the "pageant-rite" in the wilderness, comprise one of Faulkner's major achievements in style, a style at once richly chromatic and singularly direct. Of Faulkner's more important literary tech-niques—the stream-of-consciousness in which the character's voice takes over and the stream-of-eloquence in which an anonymous voice, of Faulkner's own, assumes control—"The Bear" is second only to "Red Leaves" as a happy example of the latter. The voice in "The Bear" is that of an observer who knows all the actors, Isaac McCaslin and Sam Fathers and Major de Spain; more important, it is the voice not so much of an individual as of the community itself, the collective conscience of Yoknapatawpha. First heard in *Light in August* it pervades most of Faulkner's later books, its very pitch and inflection conveying moral judgment.

Section IV represents a sharp drop in both composition and content. Its style is also a style of eloquence, but one that is often inflated to Confederate rhetoric. The dialogue between McCaslin and Edmonds, fanciful, flowery and pretentious, is of a kind seldom heard on heaven or earth. As sheer narrative, the section breaks down several times, forcing the reader to fumble his way through cryptic references and opaque prose. It may be urged that similar demands are made by other works of literature, and this is true; the only question, here as elsewhere, is whether the reward is worth the labor. Whenever Faulkner troubles to drama-tize Section IV, as in Isaac's visit to the freed slave Fonsiba, the writing is unforgettably strong; but the bulk of the section is merely an exchange of rhetorical sentiments, frequently interesting but slowed and stopped by passages of turgidity. The hunt sections present an image and the commissary section records a discourse. The two are related somewhat like poem and paraphrase; and while there is no need to suppose that in literature discourse is always inferior to image, something of the sort is usually true for the work of Faulkner. At the end "The Bear" returns to its open-ing style: "He went back to the camp once more . . ." Just as the story began with a majestic image of the bear prowling through the wilderness, so it ends with an equally powerful image: Boon Hogganbeck, the man who killed the bear, sitting beneath a tree, his gun dismembered and his mind shriveled by hysteria. Nothing in Section IV—neither the entries in the family record-book nor the eloquence of Isaac McCaslin as he castigates the sins of the

South and praises the virtues of the Negroes—nothing can equal these images: the bear in the forest, the man beneath the tree.

Faulkner's Stylistic Failings

SEAN O'FAOLAIN

✤

It is always provoking when a writer has more genius than talent. Sean O'Casey, with whom Faulkner might be compared, is this sort of writer. Gorki was another; so was Whitman. You never know what is going to come out of their mouths, golden wisdom or the most abysmal folly, and they, least of all, know it because one of the great gifts that God gave them is their unself-consciousness. When they are really writing, that is, speaking out of their natural genius, the Holy Ghost talks through their mouths; when the divine current is not working they talk through their hats.

We are very familiar with this type of genius in Ireland, and from what little I have seen of Mississippi and all I have read about it, life there sounds very much like life in County Cork. There is the same passionate provincialism, the same local patriotism; the same southern nationalism—those long explicit speeches of Gavin Stevens in *Intruder in the Dust* might, *mutatis mutandis,* be uttered by a southern Irishman; the same feeling that whatever happens in Ballydehob or in Jefferson has never happened anywhere else before, and is more important than anything that happened in any period of history in any part of the cosmos; there is the same vanity of an old race; the same gnawing sense of old defeat; the same capacity for intense hatred; a good deal of the same harsh folk-humour; the same acidity; the same oscillation between unbounded self-confidence and total despair; the same escape through sport and drink. There are, of course, differences.

FROM *The Vanishing Hero* (London: Eyre and Spottiswoode, 1956), pp. 101-103, 111-112, 133-134. Reprinted by permission of Little, Brown and Co.—Atlantic Monthly Press, and by permission of Eyre & Spottiswoode (Publishers) Ltd. Copyright © 1956, 1957 by Sean O'Faolain.

There is, for example, no escape in Ireland through sex. But there are enough similarities to make one sympathize profoundly with any writer born into such a community, and admire any writer who, as Faulkner has not been, is not silenced by the disadvantages of birth, education and tradition.

To read Faulkner is to invite a mixed and troubling pleasure. He is an ingenuous man, of strong feelings, a dedicated sincerity and poor equipment: a maimed genius. By no means the least of his handicaps—and from the point of view of mere pleasure as a Common Reader it is one of his greatest—is the fact that he cannot write plain English; not because he is untutored but because his psyche is completely out of his control. In this, again, he is strongly reminiscent of O'Casey. There are times when he seems to be writing with a blunt chisel on his grandfather's grave-stone alone at midnight by candlelight; and times when he seems to be babbling into a microphone as if he were addressing a crowd of twenty thousand people. This creates a strong and often wholly justifiable temptation in the reader to cease to pay attention; thereby, it may be, losing some of his best things when, quite without warning, the divine current is switched on again. The attentive listener nudges one awake with, "That was *good!*"; one pricks up one's ears; by the time one has caught his drift once more the divine current has probably been switched off again. . . .

I am sensitively aware that this is not the usual view taken of Faulkner's methods. It is more generally assumed that he writes as he does because he chooses to write that way. If one were at any point entirely satisfied that he was getting as close to his own purpose as he wished to get, this assumption would not be, as I think it is, an abnegation of the function of criticism. But one gets no such sense of security from his work: least of all from his groping style. Those sequences of possible words—"it was seeking, hunting . . ."; "he had invented, made it . . ."; "He would never have said this, put it into words himself . . ."—suggest only a man who does not know what he is about to say. So does the use of second-thought words: "He did not know why he had been compelled, or anyway needed, to claim it . . ."; "This, anyway, will, shall, must be invulnerable . . ."; "He kept the style pure and intact and unchanged and inviolate . . ."; "a willingness to

surrender, relinquish himself . . ." Most disconcerting is his way
of saying, "I mean . . .", whose corollary is that he often does
not know what he means. The fustian language he uses is of the
same order and origin. He is a writer not swimming along on the
river of his intention but drowning in it. So, when he writes about
"the gasoline-roar of apotheosis" he is relying on sound rather than
sense. It is a common romantic habit. Is he using, with care, the
artist's meaningful language or the demagogue's careless, rhetorical and often meaningless language when he writes of an "unbelievable quantity", or of an "incredible height"? The sounds of
words intoxicate him. "A thunderous and silent solitude." "The
oblivious and arch-adultress." "The apotheosis of his youth assumed a thousand avatars." I must, however, insist that my purpose here is not to find fault with Faulkner for using this type of
English—though I think it tedious, ineffective and, at times, bogus.
My point is single—to draw attention to the dissociation from
what, for short, we may here call common realities, indicated by
this romantic style. It is an outward mark of an inward failure to
focus clearly. . . .

One of the truest things said about him was said by Mr. Henry
Nash Smith in that tiny periodical devoted to his work, called
Faulkner Studies [Summer 1953, II, 2, "William Faulkner and
Reality"]. "He seems often to be battling publicly with something
deep and hostile within himself which he cannot see or define. It
is this struggle which causes readers to turn again to books which
repel and attract them almost indistinguishably." With which I
put the shrewd remark of one of my American students: that I am
unfitted to speak about this man, because my approach to literature is too like that of French critics, through the intelligence,
seeking an intelligence—and this man is without an intelligence.
He is devoured by a daemon and it is this daemon which is his subject.

I find that I can admire Faulkner better as a man than as a
writer; except when he is being a humorous writer. He *has* felt
those inescapable urges through pit, and passion, towards ideals
that he can vaguely feel but never express. His Nobel Prize Speech,
his Commencement Address at Pine Manor College, in Wellesley,
were eloquent of this in the nobility of their aspirations combined

with the total unintelligibility of their ideas. It is his great spirit that pulls him through, and it is, I think, for this spirit that he is to be most admired. If one is insistent on asking for something more, one will always leave him deeply dissatisfied, as I always do.

The Saxon Beauty and the Three Black Bears

MARTHA BENNETT STILES

Once in the middle, center of the Okeyouchokee Forest lived three black bears where Father Bear (a tall, silent, but not overly silent, either; speaking up when Mother Bear had the porridge too hot or someone had rumpled the cushions on his pet chair: chair made by his grandfather who had been part red bear, part black zoo captive, in those days when the black bear's position had been less desirable perhaps, perhaps more circumscribed but possibly not, but less equivocal too than now, now that a bear was free but had to keep to the woods or get shot by men; bear) had built them a house, with window boxes and such; where they could be bears and never see any men to remind them that they were, after all, bears, not men.

It (the sanctuary) housed (sheltered) in addition to this tall proud male bear Mother Bear and Baby Bear, tall too, for his years, but not so tall as his father; black, too, as all black bears are in some degree, but not so black as his mother, who was (she, Mother Bear, was) blacker. Mother Bear had not been born in captivity but her mother had, whose mother had danced for gypsies, or rather for the audiences these gypsies gathered but were not well paid by, or appreciated by, indeed were even feared, loathed, looked down upon by.

One day Mother Bear made porridge, a kind of pottage but they didn't know that, had forgotten that; had forgotten it came from *pot* a pot, lost it from their memories before they were born

FROM *Generation* (Spring, 1958), pp. 29-30. Reprinted by permission of the author.

even; boiling the (some) leguminous or perhaps farinaceous substance in water, or milk (in a liquid, then) stirring and waiting waiting and watching watching and stirring until it was done, finished, ready to eat

but not quite ready either, it (the porridge) being still steaming, exhalation of warm hot (milk, liquid) vapor curling reaching winding groping wriggling toward the ceiling when Mother Bear took it from the stove which was electric now, now that even the bears themselves no longer chopped wood, carried ashes, stirred the fire, Montgomery Ward having become, one might almost say, handyman to the whole bear community, who named their sons Gomry or Ward, or even Roebuck if some forgotten taint of *droit du seigneur* left in them some nonconformist streak, ability, tendency, pride.

Steaming then it (the porridge) was placed on the table—oh, yes, there was a table too, in the bear's (Father Bear's) house to cool until it was edible, could be eaten without burning the tongue throat gullet gut of Father Bear, and Mother Bear and Baby Bear too, who all picked up malacca canes (they had those too, even then) and went for a walk in the Forest, immemorial, static, immemorial.

That was when Goldy Snocks, like her tribe tow headed blue eyed fair skinned (Goldy Snocks) not very bright came tripping or wandering or blundering or anyhow coming up the path to the bear's house even though she had been told by Missis Snocks, Uncle Sickly Snocks' distant cousin by marriage with the Jukes (Kalikaks?) and married to his nephew too, so there was a double relationship, not to go into the Forest, immemorial, timeless, immemorial. "What uh purty house" said Little Goldy Snocks, scratching, or not so much scratching as currying, her head and went inside without knocking because that too was like her tribe and saw there the table with the steaming, but not steaming so much now since time—time that had brought Goldy Snocks into the world as surely as it would take her out or at least would help and who would miss her?—had passed and the porridge was cooler; bowls of porridge, and she

decided to taste some whom by her appearance and, yes, behaviour, no Snocks could say was not a true Snocks, although paternities were not their surest points, and grabbed a spoon (Little Goldy Snocks never picked up something without seeming to seize, capture, it) grabbed a spoon and tasted the first bowlful. "Crawlin Hawg Waller, thet porrdge is too hot" exclaimed (cried) Goldy Snocks, and moved to the next bowl, basin, tureen, or whatever Mother Bear liked to call it now that her bear talk was taking on a thin and sometimes treacherous (because deceptive) veneer of men's talk. "Phth-h-h-h-t" spit Goldy Snocks, "thet'n's too cole" and she took up the third bowl, who was determined to eat something since she was hungry, always—and why not Baby Bear's porridge, since she had as much right to it as anything she (the Snockses) ate? She was a Snocks (one of them) and she ate it all up.

Feeling full, replete, sated, packed, satiated, surfeited, glutted, gorged, surfeit-gorged, fed to the gills or neck, overfed, or some adverb the Thesaurus doesn't list, she—Goldy Snocks now—sat down in the nearest chair or even throne and leaned back, not tilting, for it was too big a chair or throne for that, but leaning until her back—Goldy Snocks'—touched its back, but not for long, because the chair (or throne) was too hard, not soft enough. Into the next one then, not knowing it was a bear's chair, a bear's house she had entered, she sat and, because it was she found too old, too sag-bottomed, like Mother Bear herself, got up once more, still seeking questing perfection finding it at last but for a brief moment only in Baby Bear's seat. Brief because, with scarcely a warning creak cry give crackle it, the baby bear's seat, split from under her, Goldy Snocks, dumping her, Goldy Snocks still, on the floor hard, harder than even Father Bear's—whose great-grandfather the red bear never sat in chairs—chair, or throne.

"Good Gawd Ah reckon!" shrieked, cried protesting, yelled Goldy Snocks—to express disapprobation, discontent—and leapt up, or anyhow got up, since those of her—large—family or clan or even race or nation were not noted for precipitate action, or even action, as a rule.

Rubbing not currying this time that portion of her which was (it was) bruised Little Goldy Snocks ascended muttering the stairs—

not knowing whither they led, but ascending nonetheless—who had been bruised—Goldy Snocks—and came at length (short or long) to the bedroom, sleeping quarters (they slept there) (the bears) of Father, Mother, and, not to hold anything back, Baby Bear. This time she was unable to sample the first, nearest, bed because it was too high, far off the ground for her (she was a Snocks) to reach and turning to the (relatively) lower one next to it she sank luxuriously but too luxuriously since she right away got up again, not liking it, into Mother Bear's bed.

No, she didn't like it, it was too yielding, not sufficiently rejecting of her (Snocks) weight, too immersing in bedclothes—quilts and sheets and coverlets and blankets, and yes, even a spread now, in a bear's house—so she, getting impatient now, wanting to go to bed, as what girl—what Snocks—in particular, what Snocks girl—didn't, she, who was a girl, and a Snocks, a Snocks girl even, transferred or shifted if you like herself to Baby Bear's bed. Who wasn't there then, any more than he had been when she busted up his chair.

There she slept (nor woke) finding perfection at last, in that form of narcosis, in oblivion, in peace or if you like simply in digestive processes. There she was sleeping, still, when the bears, all of them, came home and proud-silent, voluble-murmurous, eager-excited, according to their natures, ages, followed her trail, her spoor (for she *was* a Snocks) from porridge to chairs, upstairs, knowing all the time and fearing too maybe but without being afraid and she

what course would—could—dared Goldy Snocks take when awakening she beheld (not dreamt, beheld) Father Bear, and Mother Bear and Baby Bear too, coming in the door? Not saying anything, coming into the room; a bear's room, that she, a human, had entered, walked into, uninvited; though they could not have come into her, Snocks, home, and she knew that; knew that and leapt, this time leapt unequivocally, out of that bed, Baby Bear's bed, and fled through the window through the forest (immemorial, immutable, immemorial), called the Okeyouchokee Forest by the people who lived there, called it anything (nobody else ever called it anything, ever thought of it even) to her own home house dwelling domicile, nor did she tell the truth, whatever that is, about where she had been to Uncle Sickly Snocks' niece by marriage, who was, after all, her mother [and curiously enough that was by marriage too, but that (curiosity) is another story, tale, legend].

The Relationship Between "Delta Autumn" and *The Bear*

"Delta Autumn"

WILLIAM FAULKNER

❧

Soon now they would enter the Delta. The sensation was familiar to him. It had been renewed like this each last week in November for more than fifty years—the last hill, at the foot of which the rich unbroken alluvial flatness began as the sea began at the base of its cliffs, dissolving away beneath the unhurried November rain as the sea itself would dissolve away.

At first they had come in wagons: the guns, the bedding, the dogs, the food, the whisky, the keen heart-lifting anticipation of hunting; the young men who could drive all night and all the following day in the cold rain and pitch a camp in the rain and sleep in the wet blankets and rise at daylight the next morning and

FROM *Go Down, Moses* (New York: Random House, 1942), pp. 333-365. Copyright 1942 by William Faulkner. Reprinted by permission of Random House, Inc.

hunt. There had been bear then. A man shot a doe or a fawn as quickly as he did a buck, and in the afternoons they shot wild turkey with pistols to test their stalking skill and marksmanship, feeding all but the breast to the dogs. But that time was gone now. Now they went in cars, driving faster and faster each year because the roads were better and they had farther and farther to drive, the territory in which game still existed drawing yearly inward as his life was drawing inward, until now he was the last of those who had once made the journey in wagons without feeling it and now those who accompanied him were the sons and even grandsons of the men who had ridden for twenty-four hours in the rain or sleet behind the steaming mules. They called him 'Uncle Ike' now, and he no longer told anyone how near eighty he actually was because he knew as well as they did that he no longer had any business making such expeditions, even by car.

In fact, each time now, on that first night in camp, lying aching and sleepless in the harsh blankets, his blood only faintly warmed by the single thin whisky-and-water which he allowed himself, he would tell himself that this would be his last. But he would stand that trip—he still shot almost as well as he ever had, still killed almost as much of the game he saw as he ever killed; he no longer even knew how many deer had fallen before his gun—and the fierce long heat of the next summer would renew him. Then November would come again, and again in the car with two of the sons of his old companions, whom he had taught not only how to distinguish between the prints left by a buck or a doe but between the sound they made in moving, he would look ahead past the jerking arc of the windshield wiper and see the land flatten suddenly and swoop, dissolving away beneath the rain as the sea itself would dissolve, and he would say, "Well, boys, there it is again."

This time though, he didn't have time to speak. The driver of the car stopped it, slamming it to a skidding halt on the greasy pavement without warning, actually flinging the two passengers forward until they caught themselves with their braced hands against the dash. "What the hell, Roth!" the man in the middle said. "Cant you whistle first when you do that? Hurt you, Uncle Ike?"

"No," the old man said. "What's the matter?" The driver didn't answer. Still leaning forward, the old man looked sharply past the face of the man between them, at the face of his kinsman. It was the youngest face of them all, aquiline, saturnine, a little ruthless, the face of his ancestor too, tempered a little, altered a little, staring sombrely through the streaming windshield across which the twin wipers flicked and flicked.

"I didn't intend to come back in here this time," he said suddenly and harshly.

"You said that back in Jefferson last week," the old man said. "Then you changed your mind. Have you changed it again? This aint a very good time to ———"

"Oh, Roth's coming," the man in the middle said. His name was Legate. He seemed to be speaking to no one, as he was looking at neither of them. "If it was just a buck he was coming all this distance for, now. But he's got a doe in here. Of course a old man like Uncle Ike cant be interested in no doe, not one that walks on two legs—when she's standing up, that is. Pretty light-colored, too. The one he was after them nights last fall when he said he was coon-hunting, Uncle Ike. The one I figured maybe he was still running when he was gone all that month last January. But of course a old man like Uncle Ike aint got no interest in nothing like that." He chortled, still looking at no one, not completely jeering.

"What?" the old man said. "What's that?" But he had not even so much as glanced at Legate. He was still watching his kinsman's face. The eyes behind the spectacles were the blurred eyes of an old man, but they were quite sharp too; eyes which could still see a gun-barrel and what ran beyond it as well as any of them could. He was remembering himself now: how last year, during the final stage by motor boat in to where they camped, a box of food had been lost overboard and how on the next day his kinsman had gone back to the nearest town for supplies and had been gone overnight. And when he did return, something had happened to him. He would go into the woods with his rifle each dawn when the others went, but the old man, watching him, knew that he was not hunting. "All right," he said. "Take me and Will on to shelter where we can wait for the truck, and you can go on back."

"I'm going in," the other said harshly. "Dont worry. Because this will be the last of it."

"The last of deer hunting, or of doe hunting?" Legate said. This time the old man paid no attention to him even by speech. He still watched the young man's savage and brooding face.

"Why?" he said.

"After Hitler gets through with it? Or Smith or Jones or Roosevelt or Willkie or whatever he will call himself in this country?"

"We'll stop him in this country," Legate said. "Even if he calls himself George Washington."

"How?" Edmonds said. "By singing God bless America in bars at midnight and wearing dime-store flags in our lapels?"

"So that's what's worrying you," the old man said. "I aint noticed this country being short of defenders yet, when it needed them. You did some of it yourself twenty-odd years ago, before you were a grown man even. This country is a little mite stronger than any one man or group of men, outside of it or even inside of it either. I reckon, when the time comes and some of you have done got tired of hollering we are whipped if we dont go to war and some more are hollering we are whipped if we do, it will cope with one Austrian paper-hanger, no matter what he will be calling himself. My pappy and some other better men than any of them you named tried once to tear it in two with a war, and they failed."

"And what have you got left?" the other said. "Half the people without jobs and half the factories closed by strikes. Half the people on public dole that wont work and half that couldn't work even if they would. Too much cotton and corn and hogs, and not enough for people to eat and wear. The country full of people to tell a man how he cant raise his own cotton whether he will or wont, and Sally Rand with a sergeant's stripes and not even the fan couldn't fill the army rolls. Too much not-butter and not even the guns ——"

"We got a deer camp—if we ever get to it," Legate said. "Not to mention does."

"It's a good time to mention does," the old man said. "Does and fawns both. The only fighting anywhere that ever had anything of God's blessing on it has been when men fought to protect

does and fawns. If it's going to come to fighting, that's a good
thing to mention and remember too."

"Haven't you discovered in—how many years more than seventy is it?—that women and children are one thing there's never
any scarcity of?" Edmonds said.

"Maybe that's why all I am worrying about right now is that
ten miles of river we still have got to run before we can make
camp," the old man said. "So let's get on."

They went on. Soon they were going fast again, as Edmonds
always drove, consulting neither of them about the speed just as
he had given neither of them any warning when he slammed the
car to stop. The old man relaxed again. He watched, as he did
each recurrent November while more than sixty of them passed,
the land which he had seen change. At first there had been only
the old towns along the River and the old towns along the hills,
from each of which the planters with their gangs of slaves and
then of hired laborers had wrested from the impenetrable jungle
of water-standing cane and cypress, gum and holly and oak and
ash, cotton patches which as the years passed became fields and
then plantations. The paths made by deer and bear became roads
and then highways, with towns in turn springing up along them
and along the rivers Tallahatchie and Sunflower which joined and
became the Yazoo, the River of the Dead of the Choctaws—the
thick, slow, black, unsunned streams almost without current,
which once each year ceased to flow at all and then reversed,
spreading, drowning the rich land and subsiding again, leaving it
still richer.

Most of that was gone now. Now a man drove two hundred
miles from Jefferson before he found wilderness to hunt in. Now
the land lay open from the cradling hills on the East to the ram-
part of levee on the West, standing horseman-tall with cotton for
the world's looms—the rich black land, imponderable and vast,
fecund up to the very doorsteps of the negroes who worked it and
of the white men who owned it; which exhausted the hunting life
of a dog in one year, the working life of a mule in five and of a
man in twenty—the land in which neon flashed past them from
the little countless towns and countless shining this-year's auto-
mobiles sped past them on the broad plumb-ruled highways, yet in

which the only permanent mark of man's occupation seemed to
be the tremendous gins, constructed in sections of sheet iron and
in a week's time though they were, since no man, millionaire
though he be, would build more than a roof and walls to shelter
the camping equipment he lived from when he knew that once
each ten years or so his house would be flooded to the second
storey and all within it ruined;—the land across which there came
now no scream of panther but instead the long hooting of loco-
motives: trains of incredible length and drawn by a single engine,
since there was no gradient anywhere and no elevation save those
raised by forgotten aboriginal hands as refuges from the yearly
water and used by their Indian successors to sepulchre their fathers' bones, and all that remained of that old time were the
Indian names on the little towns and usually pertaining to water
—Aluschaskuna, Tillatoba, Homochitto, Yazoo.

By early afternoon, they were on water. At the last little Indian-
named town at the end of pavement they waited until the other
car and the two trucks—the one carrying the bedding and tents
and food, the other the horses—overtook them. They left the
concrete and, after another mile or so, the gravel too. In caravan
they ground on through the ceaselessly dissolving afternoon, with
skid-chains on the wheels now, lurching and splashing and sliding among the ruts, until presently it seemed to him that the
retrograde of his remembering had gained an inverse velocity
from their own slow progress, that the land had retreated not in
minutes from the last spread of gravel but in years, decades, back
toward what it had been when he first knew it: the road they now
followed once more the ancient pathway of bear and deer, the
diminishing fields they now passed once more scooped punily and
terrifically by axe and saw and mule-drawn plow from the wilderness' flank, out of the brooding and immemorial tangle, in place
of ruthless mile-wide parallelograms wrought by ditching the dyk-
ing machinery.

They reached the river landing and unloaded, the horses to go
overland down stream to a point opposite the camp and swim the
river, themselves and the bedding and food and dogs and guns
in the motor launch. It was himself, though no horseman, no
farmer, not even a countryman save by his distant birth and boy-

hood, who coaxed and soothed the two horses, drawing them by his own single frail hand until, backing, filling, trembling a little, they surged, halted, then sprang scrambling down from the truck, possessing no affinity for them as creatures, beasts, but being merely insulated by his years and time from the corruption of steel and oiled moving parts which tainted the others.

Then, his old hammer double gun which was only twelve years younger than he standing between his knees, he watched even the last puny marks of man—cabin, clearing, the small and irregular fields which a year ago were jungle and in which the skeleton stalks of this year's cotton stood almost as tall and rank as the old cane had stood, as if man had had to marry his planting to the wilderness in order to conquer it—fall away and vanish. The twin banks marched with wilderness as he remembered it—the tangle of brier and cane impenetrable even to sight twenty feet away, the tall tremendous soaring of oak and gum and ash and hickory which had rung to no axe save the hunter's, had echoed to no machinery save the beat of old-time steam boats traversing it or to the snarling of launches like their own of people going into it to dwell for a week or two weeks because it was still wilderness. There was some of it left, although now it was two hundred miles from Jefferson when once it had been thirty. He had watched it, not being conquered, destroyed, so much as retreating since its purpose was served now and its time an outmoded time, retreating southward through this inverted-apex, this ▽-shaped section of earth between hills and River until what was left of it seemed now to be gathered and for the time arrested in one tremendous density of brooding and inscrutable impenetrability at the ultimate funnelling tip.

They reached the site of their last-year's camp with still two hours left of light. "You go on over under that driest tree and set down," Legate told him. "—if you can find it. Me and these other young boys will do this." He did neither. He was not tired yet. That would come later. *Maybe it wont come at all this time,* he thought, as he had thought at this point each November for the last five or six of them. *Maybe I will go out on stand in the morning too;* knowing that he would not, not even if he took the advice and sat down under the driest shelter and did nothing until camp was made and supper cooked. Because it would not be the fatigue. It would be because he would not sleep tonight but would lie instead wakeful and peaceful on the cot amid the tent-filling snoring and the rain's whisper as he always did on the first night in camp; peaceful, without regret or fretting, telling himself that was all right too, who didn't have so many of them left as to waste one sleeping.

In his slicker he directed the unloading of the boat—the tents, the stove, the bedding, the food for themselves and the dogs until there should be meat in camp. He sent two of the negroes to cut firewood; he had the cook-tent raised and the stove up and a fire going and supper cooking while the big tent was still being staked down. Then in the beginning of dusk he crossed in the boat to where the horses waited, backing and snorting at the water. He took the lead-ropes and with no more weight than that and his voice, he drew them down into the water and held them beside the boat with only their heads above the surface, as though they actually were suspended from his frail and strengthless old man's hands, while the boat recrossed and each horse in turn lay prone in the shallows, panting and trembling, its eyes rolling in the dusk, until the same weightless hand and unraised voice gathered it surging upward, splashing and thrashing up the bank.

Then the meal was ready. The last of light was gone now save the thin stain of it snared somewhere between the river's surface and the rain. He had the single glass of thin whisky-and-water, then, standing in the churned mud beneath the stretched tarpaulin, he said grace over the fried slabs of pork, the hot soft shapeless bread, the canned beans and molasses and coffee in iron plates and cups,—the town food, brought along with them—then covered himself again, the others following. "Eat," he said. "Eat it all up. I dont want a piece of town meat in camp after breakfast tomorrow. Then you boys will hunt. You'll have to. When I first started hunting in this bottom sixty years ago with old General Compson and Major de Spain and Roth's grandfather and Will Legate's too, Major de Spain wouldn't allow but two pieces of foreign grub in his camp. That was one side of pork and one ham of beef. And not to eat for the first supper and breakfast neither. It was to save until along toward the end of camp when everybody was so sick of bear meat and coon and venison that we couldn't even look at it."

"I thought Uncle Ike was going to say the pork and beef was for the dogs," Legate said, chewing. "But that's right; I remember. You just shot the dogs a mess of wild turkey every evening when they got tired of deer guts."

"Times are different now," another said. "There was game here then."

"Yes," the old man said quietly. "There was game here then."

"Besides, they shot does then too," Legate said. "As it is now, we aint got but one doe-hunter in ——"

"And better men hunted it," Edmonds said. He stood at the end of the rough plank table, eating rapidly and steadily as the others ate. But again the old man looked sharply across at the sullen, handsome, brooding face which appeared now darker and more sullen still in the light of the smoky lantern. "Go on. Say it."

"I didn't say that," the old man said. "There are good men everywhere, at all times. Most men are. Some are just unlucky, because most men are a little better than their circumstances give them a chance to be. And I've known some that even the circumstances couldn't stop."

"Well, I wouldn't say—" Legate said.

"So you've lived almost eighty years," Edmonds said. "And that's what you finally learned about the other animals you lived among. I suppose the question to ask you is, where have you been all the time you were dead?"

There was a silence; for the instant even Legate's jaw stopped chewing while he gaped at Edmonds. "Well, by God, Roth—" the third speaker said. But it was the old man who spoke, his voice still peaceful and untroubled and merely grave:

"Maybe so," he said. "But if being what you call alive would have learned me any different, I reckon I'm satisfied, wherever it was I've been."

"Well, I wouldn't say that Roth—" Legate said.

The third speaker was still leaning forward a little over the table, looking at Edmonds. "Meaning that it's only because folks happen to be watching him that a man behaves at all," he said. "Is that it?"

"Yes," Edmonds said. "A man in a blue coat, with a badge on it watching him. Maybe just the badge."

"I deny that," the old man said. "I dont ——"

The other two paid no attention to him. Even Legate was listening to them for the moment, his mouth still full of food and still open a little, his knife with another lump of something balanced on the tip of the blade arrested halfway to his mouth. "I'm glad I dont have your opinion of folks," the third speaker said. "I take it you include yourself."

"I see," Edmonds said. "You prefer Uncle Ike's opinion of circumstances. All right. Who makes the circumstances?"

"Luck," the third said. "Chance. Happen-so. I see what you are getting at. But that's just what Uncle Ike said: that now and then, maybe most of the time, man is a little better than the net result of his and his neighbors' doings, when he gets the chance to be."

This time Legate swallowed first. He was not to be stopped this time. "Well, I wouldn't say that Roth Edmonds can hunt one doe every day and night for two weeks and was a poor hunter or a unlucky one neither. A man that still have the same doe left to hunt on again next year ——"

"Have some meat," the man next to him said.

"—aint no unlucky— What?" Legate said.

"Have some meat." The other offered the dish.

"I got some," Legate said.

"Have some more," the third speaker said. "You and Roth Edmonds both. Have a heap of it. Clapping your jaws together that way with nothing to break the shock." Someone chortled. Then they all laughed, with relief, the tension broken. But the old man was speaking, even into the laughter, in that peaceful and still untroubled voice:

"I still believe. I see proof everywhere. I grant that man made a heap of his circumstances, him and his living neighbors between them. He even inherited some of them already made, already almost ruined even. A while ago Henry Wyatt there said how there used to be more game here. There was. So much that we even killed does. I seem to remember Will Legate mentioning that too—" Someone laughed, a single guffaw, stillborn. It ceased and they all listened, gravely, looking down at their plates. Edmonds was drinking his coffee, sullen, brooding, inattentive.

"Some folks still kill does," Wyatt said. "There wont be just one buck hanging in this bottom tomorrow night without any head to fit it."

"I didn't say all men," the old man said. "I said most men. And not just because there is a man with a badge to watch us. We probably wont even see him unless maybe he will stop here about noon tomorrow and eat dinner with us and check our licenses ——"

"We dont kill does because if we did kill does in a few years there wouldn't even be any bucks left to kill, Uncle Ike," Wyatt said.

"According to Roth yonder, that's one thing we wont never have to worry about," the old man said. "He said on the way here this morning that does and fawns—I believe he said women and children—are two things this world aint ever lacked. But that aint all of it," he said. "That's just the mind's reason a man has to give himself because the heart dont always have time to bother with thinking up words that fit together. God created man and He created the world for him to live in and I reckon He created the kind of world He would have wanted to live in if He had been a man—the ground to walk on, the big woods, the trees and the water, and the game to live in it. And maybe He didn't put the desire to hunt and kill game in man but I reckon He knew it was going to be there, that man was going to teach it to himself, since he wasn't quite God himself yet ——"

"When will he be?" Wyatt said.

"I think that every man and woman, at the instant when it dont even matter whether they marry or not, I think that whether they marry then or afterward or dont never, at that instant the two of them together were God."

"Then there are some Gods in this world I wouldn't want to touch, and with a damn long stick," Edmonds said. He set his coffee cup down and looked at Wyatt. "And that includes myself, if that's what you want to know. I'm going to bed." He was gone. There was a general movement among the others. But it ceased and they stood again about the table, not looking at the old man, apparently held there yet by his quiet and peaceful voice as the heads of the swimming horses had been held above the water by his weightless hand. The three negroes—the cook and his helper and old Isham—were sitting quietly in the entrance of the kitchen tent, listening too, the three faces dark and motionless and musing.

"He put them both here: man, and the game he would follow and kill, foreknowing it. I believe He said, 'So be it.' I reckon He even foreknew the end. But He said, 'I will give him his chance. I will give him warning and foreknowledge too, along with the desire to follow and the power to slay. The woods and fields he ravages and the game he devastates will be the consequence and signature of his crime and guilt, and his punishment.'—Bedtime," he said. His voice and inflection did not change at all. "Breakfast at four oclock, Isham. We want meat on the ground by sunup time."

There was a good fire in the sheet-iron heater; the tent was warm and was beginning to dry out, except for the mud underfoot. Edmonds was already rolled into his blankets, motionless, his face to the wall. Isham had made up his bed too—the strong, battered iron cot, the stained mattress which was not quite soft enough, the worn, often-washed blankets which as the years passed were less and less warm enough. But the tent was warm; presently, when the kitchen was cleaned up and readied for breakfast, the young negro would come in to lie down before the heater, where he could be roused to put fresh wood into it from time to time. And then, he knew now he would not sleep tonight anyway; he no longer needed to tell himself that perhaps he would. But it was all right now. The day was ended now and night faced him, but alarmless, empty of fret. *Maybe I came for this,* he thought: *Not to hunt, but for this. I would come anyway, even if only to go back home tomorrow.* Wearing only his bagging woolen underwear, his spectacles folded away in the worn case beneath the pillow where he could reach them readily and his lean body fitted easily into the old worn groove of mattress and blankets, he lay on his back, his hands crossed on his breast and his eyes closed while the others undressed and went to bed and the last of the sporadic talking died into snoring. Then he opened his eyes and lay peaceful and quiet as a child, looking up at the motionless belly of rain-murmured canvas upon which the glow of the heater was dying slowly away and would fade still further until the young negro, lying on two planks before it, would sit up and stoke it and lie back down again.

They had a house once. That was sixty years ago, when the Big Bottom was only thirty miles from Jefferson and old Major de Spain, who had been his father's cavalry commander in '61 and '2 and '3 and '4, and his cousin (his older brother; his father too) had taken him into the woods for the first time. Old Sam Fathers was alive then, born in slavery, son of a Negro slave and a Chickasaw chief, who had taught him how to shoot, not only when to shoot but when not to; such a November dawn as tomorrow would be and the old man led him straight to the great cypress and he had known the buck would pass exactly there because there was something running in Sam Fathers' veins which ran in the veins of the buck too, and they stood there against the tremendous trunk, the old man of seventy and the boy of twelve, and there was nothing save the dawn until suddenly the buck was there, smoke-colored out of nothing, magnificent with speed: and Sam Fathers said, 'Now. Shoot quick and shoot slow:' and the gun levelled rapidly without haste and crashed and he walked to the buck lying still intact and still in the shape of that magnificent speed and bled it with Sam's knife and Sam dipped his hands into the hot blood and marked his face forever while he stood trying not to tremble, humbly and with pride too though the boy of twelve had been unable to phrase it then: *I slew you; my bearing must not shame your quitting life. My conduct forever onward must become your death;* marking him for that and for more than that: that day and himself and McCaslin juxtaposed not against the wilderness but against the tamed land, the old wrong and shame itself, in repudiation and denial at least of the land and the wrong and shame even if he couldn't cure the wrong and eradicate the shame, who at fourteen when he learned of it had believed he could do both when he became competent and when at twenty-one he became competent he knew that he could do neither but at least he could repudiate the wrong and shame, at least in principle, and at least the land itself in fact, for his son at least: and did, thought he had: then (married then) in a rented cubicle in a back-street stock-traders' boarding-house, the first and last time he ever saw her naked body, himself and his wife juxtaposed in their turn against that same land, that same wrong and shame from whose regret and grief he would at least save and free his son and, saving and freeing his son, lost him. They had the house then. That roof, the two weeks of each November which they spent under it, had become his home. Although since that time they had lived during the two fall weeks in tents and not always in the same place two years in succession and now his companions were the sons and even the grandsons of them with whom he had lived in the house and for almost fifty years now the house itself had not even existed, the conviction, the sense and feeling of home, had been merely transferred into the canvas. He owned a house in Jefferson, a good house though small, where he had had a wife and lived with her and lost her, ay, lost her even though he had lost her in the rented cubicle before he and his old clever dipsomaniac partner had finished the house for them to move into it: but lost her, because she loved him. But women hope for so much. They never live too long to still believe that anything within the scope of their passionate wanting is likewise within the range of their passionate hope: and it was still kept for him by his dead wife's widowed niece and her children and he was comfortable in it, his wants and needs and even the small trying harmless crochets of an old man looked after by blood at least related to the blood which he had elected out of all the earth to cherish. But he spent the time within those walls waiting for November, because even this tent with its muddy floor and the bed which was not wide enough nor soft enough nor even warm enough, was his home and these men, some of whom he only saw during these two November weeks and not one of whom even bore any name he used to know—De Spain and Compson and Ewell and Hogganbeck—were more his kin than any. Because this was his land ——

The shadow of the youngest negro loomed. It soared, blotting the heater's dying glow from the ceiling, the wood billets thumping into the iron maw until the glow, the flame, leaped high and bright across the canvas. But the negro's shadow still remained, by its length and breadth, standing, since it covered most of the ceiling, until after a moment he raised himself on one elbow to look. It was not the negro, it was his kinsman; when he spoke the other turned sharp against the red firelight the sullen and ruthless profile.

"Nothing," Edmonds said. "Go on back to sleep."

"Since Will Legate mentioned it," McCaslin said, "I remember you had some trouble sleeping in here last fall too. Only you called it coon-hunting then. Or was it Will Legate called it that?" The other didn't answer. Then he turned and went back to his bed. McCaslin, still propped on his elbow, watched until the other's shadow sank down the wall and vanished, became one with the mass of sleeping shadows. "That's right," he said. "Try to get some sleep. We must have meat in camp tomorrow. You can do all the setting up you want to after that." He lay down again, his hands crossed again on his breast, watching the glow of the heater on the canvas ceiling. It was steady again now, the fresh wood accepted, being assimilated; soon it would begin to fade again, taking with it the last echo of that sudden upflare of a young man's passion and unrest. Let him lie awake for a little while, he thought; He will lie still some day for a long time without even dissatisfaction to disturb him. And lying awake here, in these surroundings, would soothe him if anything could, if anything could soothe a man just forty years old. Yes, he thought; Forty years old or thirty, or even the trembling and sleepless ardor of a boy; already the tent, the rain-murmured canvas globe, was once more filled with it. He lay on his back, his eyes closed, his breathing quiet and peaceful as a child's, listening to it—that silence which was never silence but was myriad. He could almost see it, tremendous, primeval, looming, musing downward upon this puny evanescent clutter of human sojourn which after a single brief week would vanish and in another week would be completely healed, traceless in the unmarked solitude. Because it was his land, although he had never owned a foot of it. He had never wanted to, not even after he saw plain its ultimate doom, watching it retreat year by year before the onslaught of axe and saw and log-lines and then dynamite and tractor plows, because it belonged to no man. It belonged to all; they had only to use it well, humbly and with pride. Then suddenly he knew why he had never wanted to own any of it, arrest at least that much of what people called progress, measure his longevity at least against that much of its ultimate fate. It was because there was just exactly enough of it. He seemed to see the two of them—himself and the wilderness— as coevals, his own span as a hunter, a woodsman, not contemporary with his first breath but transmitted to him, assumed by him gladly, humbly, with joy and pride, from that old Major de Spain and that old Sam Fathers who had taught him to hunt, the two spans running out together, not toward oblivion, nothingness, but into a dimension free of both time and space where once more the untreed land warped and wrung to mathematical squares of rank cotton for the frantic old-world people to turn into shells to shoot at one another, would find ample room for both—the names, the faces of the old men he had known and loved and for a little while outlived, moving again among the shades of tall unaxed trees and sightless brakes where the wild strong immortal game ran forever before the tireless belling immortal hounds, falling and rising phoenix-like to the soundless guns.

He had been asleep. The lantern was lighted now. Outside in the darkness the oldest negro, Isham, was beating a spoon against the bottom of a tin pan and crying, "Raise up and get yo foa clock coffy. Raise up and get yo foa clock coffy," and the tent was full of low talk and of men dressing, and Legate's voice, repeating: "Get out of here now and let Uncle Ike sleep. If you wake him up, he'll go out with us. And he aint got any business in the woods this morning."

So he didn't move. He lay with his eyes closed, his breathing gentle and peaceful, and heard them one by one leave the tent. He listened to the breakfast sounds from the table beneath the tarpaulin and heard them depart—the horses, the dogs, the last voice until it died away and there was only the sounds of the negroes clearing breakfast away. After a while he might possibly even hear the first faint clear cry of the first hound ring through the wet woods from where the buck had bedded, then he would go back to sleep again—The tent-flap swung in and fell. Something jarred sharply against the end of the cot and a hand grasped his knee through the blanket before he could open his eyes. It was

Edmonds, carrying a shotgun in place of his rifle. He spoke in a harsh, rapid voice:

"Sorry to wake you. There will be a ———"

"I was awake," McCaslin said. "Are you going to shoot that shotgun today?"

"You just told me last night you want meat," Edmonds said. "There will be a ———"

"Since when did you start having trouble getting meat with your rifle?"

"All right," the other said, with that harsh, restrained, furious impatience. Then McCaslin saw in his hand a thick oblong: an envelope. "There will be a message here some time this morning, looking for me. Maybe it wont come. If it does, give the messenger this and tell h— say I said No."

"A what?" McCaslin said. "Tell who?" He half rose onto his elbow as Edmonds jerked the envelope onto the blanket, already turning toward the entrance, the envelope striking solid and heavy and without noise and already sliding from the bed until McCaslin caught it, divining by feel through the paper as instantaneously and conclusively as if he had opened the envelope and looked, the thick sheaf of banknotes. "Wait," he said. "Wait:"—more than the blood kinsman, more even than the senior in years, so that the other paused, the canvas lifted, looking back, and McCaslin saw that outside it was already day. "Tell her No," he said. "Tell her." They stared at one another—the old face, wan, sleep-raddled above the tumbled bed, the dark and sullen younger one at once furious and cold. "Will Legate was right. This is what you called coon-hunting. And now this." He didn't raise the envelope. He made no motion, no gesture to indicate it. "What did you promise her that you haven't the courage to face her and retract?"

"Nothing!" the other said. "Nothing! This is all of it. Tell her I said No." He was gone. The tent flap lifted on an in-waft of faint light and the constant murmur of rain, and fell again, leaving the old man still half-raised onto one elbow, the envelope clutched in the other shaking hand. Afterward it seemed to him that he had begun to hear the approaching boat almost immediately, before the other could have got out of sight even. It seemed

to him that there had been no interval whatever: the tent flap falling on the same out-waft of faint and rain-filled light like the
suspiration and expiration of the same breath and then in the next
second lifted again—the mounting snarl of the outboard engine,
increasing, nearer and nearer and louder and louder then cut
short off, ceasing with the absolute instantaneity of a blown-out
candle, into the lap and plop of water under the bows as the skiff
slid in to the bank, the youngest negro, the youth, raising the tent
flap beyond which for that instant he saw the boat—a small skiff
with a negro man sitting in the stern beside the up-slanted motor
—then the woman entering, in a man's hat and a man's slicker
and rubber boots, carrying the blanket-swaddled bundle on one
arm and holding the edge of the unbuttoned raincoat over it with
the other hand: and bringing something else, something intangi-
ble, an effluvium which he knew he would recognise in a moment
because Isham had already told him, warned him, by sending the
young negro to the tent to announce the visitor instead of coming
himself, the flap falling at last on the young negro and they were
alone—the face indistinct and as yet only young and with dark
eyes, queerly colorless but not ill and not that of a country woman
despite the garments she wore, looking down at him where he sat
upright on the cot now, clutching the envelope, the soiled under-
garment bagging about him and the twisted blankets huddled about
his hips.

"Is that his?" he cried. "Dont lie to me!"

"Yes," she said. "He's gone."

"Yes. He's gone. You wont jump him here. Not this time. I
dont reckon even you expected that. He left you this. Here." He
fumbled at the envelope. It was not to pick it up, because it was
still in his hand; he had never put it down. It was as if he had to
fumble somehow to co-ordinate physically his heretofore obedient
hand with what his brain was commanding of it, as if he had
never performed such an action before, extending the envelope at
last, saying again, "Here. Take it. Take it:" until he became
aware of her eyes, or not the eyes so much as the look, the regard
fixed now on his face with that immersed contemplation, that
bottomless and intent candor, of a child. If she had ever seen

either the envelope or his movement to extend it, she did not show it.

"You're Uncle Isaac," she said.

"Yes," he said. "But never mind that. Here. Take it. He said to tell you No." She looked at the envelope, then she took it. It was sealed and bore no superscription. Nevertheless, even after she glanced at the front of it, he watched her hold it in the one free hand and tear the corner off with her teeth and manage to rip it open and tilt the neat sheaf of bound notes onto the blanket without even glancing at them and look into the empty envelope and take the edge between her teeth and tear it completely open before she crumpled and dropped it.

"That's just money," she said.

"What did you expect? What else did you expect? You have known him long enough or at least often enough to have got that child, and you dont know him any better than that?"

"Not very often. Not very long. Just that week here last fall, and in January he sent for me and we went West, to New Mexico. We were there six weeks, where I could at least sleep in the same apartment where I cooked for him and looked after his clothes ——"

"But not marriage," he said. "Not marriage. He didn't promise you that. Dont lie to me. He didn't have to."

"No. He didn't have to. I didn't ask him to. I knew what I was doing. I knew that to begin with, long before honor I imagine he called it told him the time had come to tell me in so many words what his code I suppose he would call it would forbid him forever to do. And we agreed. Then we agreed again before he left New Mexico, to make sure. That that would be all of it. I believed him. No, I dont mean that; I mean I believed myself. I wasn't even listening to him anymore by then because by that time it had been a long time since he had had anything else to tell me for me to have to hear. By then I wasn't even listening enough to ask him to please stop talking. I was listening to myself. And I believed it. I must have believed it. I dont see how I could have helped but believe it, because he was gone then as we had agreed and he didn't write as we had agreed, just the money came to the bank in Vicksburg in my name but coming from nobody as we had agreed. So I must have believed it. I even wrote him last month to make sure again and the letter came back unopened and I was sure. So I left the hospital and rented myself a room to live in until the deer season opened so I could make sure myself and I was waiting beside the road yesterday when your car passed and he saw me and so I was sure."

"Then what do you want?" he said. "What do you want? What do you expect?"

"Yes," she said. And while he glared at her, his white hair awry from the pillow and his eyes, lacking the spectacles to focus them, blurred and irisless and apparently pupilless, he saw again that grave, intent, speculative and detached fixity like a child watching him. "His great great—Wait a minute.—great great *great* grandfather was your grandfather. McCaslin. Only it got to be Edmonds. Only it got to be more than that. Your cousin McCaslin was there that day when your father and Uncle Buddy won Tennie from Mr Beauchamp for the one that had no name but Terrel so you called him Tomey's Terrel, to marry. But after that it got to be Edmonds." She regarded him, almost peacefully, with that unwinking and heatless fixity—the dark wide bottomless eyes in the face's dead and toneless pallor which to the old man looked anything but dead, but young and incredibly and even ineradicably alive—as though she were not only not looking at anything, she was not even speaking to anyone but herself. "I would have made a man of him. He's not a man yet. You spoiled him. You, and Uncle Lucas and Aunt Mollie. But mostly you."

"Me?" he said. "Me?"

"Yes. When you gave to his grandfather that land which didn't belong to him, not even half of it by will or even law."

"And never mind that too," he said. "Never mind that too. You," he said. "You sound like you have been to college even. You sound almost like a Northerner even, not like the draggle-tailed women of these Delta peckerwoods. Yet you meet a man on the street one afternoon just because a box of groceries happened to fall out of a boat. And a month later you go off with him and live with him until he got a child on you: and then, by your own statement, you sat there while he took his hat and said

goodbye and walked out. Even a Delta peckerwood would look
after even a draggle-tail better than that. Haven't you got any
folks at all?"

"Yes," she said. "I was living with one of them. My aunt, in
Vicksburg. I came to live with her two years ago when my father
died; we lived in Indianapolis then. But I got a job, teaching
school here in Aluschaskuna, because my aunt was a widow, with
a big family, taking in washing to sup——"

"Took in what?" he said. "Took in washing?" He sprang, still
seated even, flinging himself backward onto one arm, awry-haired,
glaring. Now he understood what it was she had brought into the
tent with her, what old Isham had already told him by sending
the youth to bring her in to him—the pale lips, the skin pallid
and dead-looking yet not ill, the dark and tragic and foreknowing
eyes *Maybe in a thousand or two thousand years in America,* he
thought. *But not now! Not now!* He cried, not loud, in a voice of
amazement, pity, and outrage: "You're a nigger!"

"Yes," she said. "James Beauchamp—you called him Tennie's
Jim though he had a name—was my grandfather. I said you were
Uncle Isaac."

"And he knows?"

"No," she said. "What good would that have done?"

"But you did," he cried. "But you did. Then what do you expect here?"

"Nothing."

"Then why did you come here? You said you were waiting in
Aluschaskuna yesterday and he saw you. Why did you come this
morning?"

"I'm going back North. Back home. My cousin brought me up
the day before yesterday in his boat. He's going to take me on to
Leland to get the train."

"Then go," he said. Then he cried again in that thin not loud
and grieving voice: "Get out of here! I can do nothing for you!
Cant nobody do nothing for you!" She moved; she was not looking
at him again, toward the entrance. "Wait," he said. She paused
again, obediently still, turning. He took up the sheaf of banknotes
and laid it on the blanket at the foot of the cot and drew his hand
back beneath the blanket. "There," he said.

Now she looked at the money, for the first time, one brief blank glance, then away again. "I dont need it. He gave me money last winter. Besides the money he sent to Vicksburg. Provided. Honor and code too. That was all arranged."

"Take it," he said. His voice began to rise again, but he stopped it. "Take it out of my tent." She came back to the cot and took up the money; whereupon once more he said, "Wait:" although she had not turned, still stooping, and he put out his hand. But, sitting, he could not complete the reach until she moved her hand, the single hand which held the money, until he touched it. He didn't grasp it, he merely touched it—the gnarled, bloodless, bone-light bone-dry old man's fingers touching for a second the smooth young flesh where the strong old blood ran after its long lost journey back to home. "Tennie's Jim," he said. "Tennie's Jim." He drew the hand back beneath the blanket again: he said harshly now: "It's a boy, I reckon. They usually are, except that one that was its own mother too."

"Yes," she said. "It's a boy." She stood for a moment longer, looking at him. Just for an instant her free hand moved as though she were about to lift the edge of the raincoat away from the child's face. But she did not. She turned again when once more he said Wait and moved beneath the blanket.

"Turn your back," he said. "I am going to get up. I aint got my pants on." Then he could not get up. He sat in the huddled blanket, shaking, while again she turned and looked down at him in dark interrogation. "There," he said harshly, in the thin and shaking old man's voice. "On the nail there. The tent-pole."

"What?" she said.

"The horn!" he said harshly. "The horn." She went and got it, thrust the money into the slicker's side pocket as if it were a rag, a soiled handkerchief, and lifted down the horn, the one which General Compson had left him in his will, covered with the unbroken skin from a buck's shank and bound with silver.

"What?" she said.

"It's his. Take it."

"Oh," she said. "Yes. Thank you."

"Yes," he said, harshly, rapidly, but not so harsh now and soon not harsh at all but just rapid, urgent, until he knew that his voice was running away with him and he had neither intended it nor could stop it: "That's right. Go back North. Marry: a man in your own race. That's the only salvation for you—for a while yet, maybe a long while yet. We will have to wait. Marry a black man. You are young, handsome, almost white; you could find a black man who would see in you what it was you saw in him, who would ask nothing of you and expect less and get even still less than that, if it's revenge you want. Then you will forget all this, forget it ever happened, that he ever existed—" until he could stop it at last and did, sitting there in his huddle of blankets during the instant when, without moving at all, she blazed silently down at him. Then that was gone too. She stood in the gleaming and still dripping slicker, looking quietly down at him from under the sodden hat.

"Old man," she said, "have you lived so long and forgotten so much that you dont remember anything you ever knew or felt or even heard about love?"

Then she was gone too. The waft of light and the murmur of the constant rain flowed into the tent and then out again as the flap fell. Lying back once more, trembling, panting, the blanket huddled to his chin and his hands crossed on his breast, he listened to the pop and snarl, the mounting then fading whine of the motor until it died away and once again the tent held only silence and the sound of rain. And cold too: he lay shaking faintly and steadily in it, rigid save for the shaking. This Delta, he thought: This Delta. *This land which man has deswamped and denuded and deriverd in two generations so that white men can own plantations and commute every night to Memphis and black men own plantations and ride in jim crow cars to Chicago to live in millionaires' mansions on Lakeshore Drive, where white men rent farms and live like niggers and niggers crop on shares and live like animals, where cotton is planted and grows man-tall in the very cracks of the sidewalks, and usury and mortgage and bankruptcy and measureless wealth, Chinese and African and Aryan and Jew, all breed and spawn together until no man has time to say which one is which nor cares. . . .* No wonder the ruined woods I used to know dont cry for retribution! he thought: The people who have destroyed it will accomplish its revenge.

The tent flap jerked rapidly in and fell. He did not move save to turn his head and open his eyes. It was Legate. He went quickly to Edmonds' bed and stooped, rummaging hurriedly among the still-tumbled blankets.

"What is it?" he said.

"Looking for Roth's knife," Legate said. "I come back to get a horse. We got a deer on the ground." He rose, the knife in his hand, and hurried toward the entrance.

"Who killed it?" McCaslin said. "Was it Roth?"

"Yes," Legate said, raising the flap.

"Wait," McCaslin said. He moved, suddenly, onto his elbow. "What was it?" Legate paused for an instant beneath the lifted flap. He did not look back.

"Just a deer, Uncle Ike," he said impatiently. "Nothing extra." He was gone; again the flap fell behind him, wafting out of the tent again the faint light and the constant and grieving rain. McCaslin lay back down, the blanket once more drawn to his chin, his crossed hands once more weightless on his breast in the empty tent.

"It was a doe," he said.

"Delta Autumn": Postlude to The Bear

Arthur F. Kinney

❦

After one reads *The Bear,* change seems to permeate "Delta Autumn." More than a half-century has passed: it is November, 1940, now, and Ike is seventy-three. He is again on a hunting party, but no longer is he awed by the countryside, sensing the threshold of life in the man-smelling cabin or preparing for a sacrament of initiation and rebirth. Now he is simply old; "he no longer told anyone how near eighty he actually was." He is not now central figure of a puberty rite; he is retired teacher, titular

---

A slightly different version of this paper was read before the Annual Meeting of the Michigan Academy of Science, Arts, and Letters, March 22, 1963.

grandfather only, still accompanying men on the hunt out of their good graces, out of their sympathy but not out of their anticipation. No longer student and no longer mentor, he comes only to observe, to lie awake the first night and recall the past glories.

The change oppresses Ike. He comes not thirty miles, but more than two hundred—not to an inland "big woods" but to the delta, and not by horse and wagon, but by car. The quarry is no longer a great, transcendental bear, but deer. " 'The game was here then,' " Ike tells the younger men. But now the game is scarce; they can no longer shoot does. In great sadness, Ike must warn his fellow hunters to kill enough to feed the camp; he does so under the pressure of the change and with the awareness that the past is gone: " 'Eat it all up. I dont want a piece of town meat in camp after breakfast tomorrow. Then you boys will hunt. You'll have to. When I first started hunting in this bottom sixty years ago with old General Compson and Major de Spain and Roth's grandfather and Will Legate's too, Major de Spain wouldn't allow but two pieces of foreign grub in his camp. That was one side of pork and one ham of beef. And not to eat for the first supper and breakfast neither. It was to have until along toward the end of camp when everybody was so sick of bear meat and coon and venison that we couldn't even look at it.' "

That was, for Ike, the good time; the past often seems better, but Ike has had reasons. "Since that time they had lived during the two fall weeks in tents and not always in the same place two years in succession and now his companions were the sons and the grandsons of them with whom he had lived in the house and for almost fifty years now the house itself had not even existed." Major de Spain's cabin is gone, and so is the Major. What is left is a group of quarrelsome young men. There is Will Legate, who gets as much joy from baiting Roth as he does from stalking deer. There is Henry Wyatt, always on edge—not to see the break of dawn but to prevent the outbreak of fighting. There is Roth himself: always defensive, always self-deprecating, who, when he sees his mulatto mistress in the road on the way to the camp, has to slam on his brakes, "actually flinging [Uncle Ike and Will] forward until they caught themselves with their braced hands against the dash." There is no longer fraternity here, and the men condescend to Ike. They suffer his presence with silence, out of pity.

Yet warning came for Ike as early as his trip into the woods in the closing section of *The Bear:* "he had forewarning and had believed himself prepared." The sawmills and the railroad were destroying the woods, and slowly he had come to accept them, as the maddened Boon could not. But Kierkegaard has warned that "the specific character of despair is precisely this: it is unaware of being despair." So the sawmills were followed by dust and then by highways, and Ike had not seen that far ahead; not until "Delta Autumn" can he see that with the life of the woods being snuffed out, so too is his own. Now "he seemed to see the two of them— himself and the wilderness—as coevals." He makes "this land which man has deswamped and denuded and derivered in two generations" a concrete representation of himself, and thus he watches it, "not being conquered, destroyed, so much as retreating since its purpose was served now and its time an outmoded time."

The boy of *The Bear,* the boy that General Compson praises as the one who "was born knowing and fearing too maybe but without being afraid," the man who could turn his life into a life of renunciation "because if the Nazarene had found carpentering good for the life and ends He had assumed and elected to serve, it would be all right too for Isaac McCaslin" has become a withered old man, shivering on a cot which can never make his cold blood turn warm again. Ike is a man left with a single sharp image of horror: his "gnarled, bloodless, bone-light bone-dry old man's fingers touching for a second the smooth young flesh where the strong old blood ran." The blood is blood again guilty of miscegenation; the crime Ike has served a lifetime of penance for has come full circle upon him. Suddenly he is both old and ineffectual.

Ike McCaslin has apparently failed.

II

Ike has apparently failed because he cannot bridge romanticism and reality. Ike's failure is twofold: his theories are wrong, and so are his actions. One theory, although perhaps the least important in "Delta Autumn," is that of communal penance—a theory echoed from *The Bear.*

Faulkner himself has been interested in this idea. During World War II, Faulkner published some stories on Yoknapatawpha's reaction to Pearl Harbor. In one of them, "The Tall Men," the town marshal, Mr. Gombault, remarks that it is "honor and pride and discipline that make a man worth preserving, make him of any value. That's what we got to learn again. Maybe it takes trouble, bad trouble, to teach it back to us; maybe it was the walking to Virginia because that's where [Anse McCallum's] ma come from, and losing [the Civil War] and then walking back, that taught it to old Anse. Anyway, he seems to learned it, and to learned it good enough to bequeath it to his boys."

The marshal's theory—that lessons learned through trial, often by a whole population, result in the *bequest* of salvation—is Ike's theory, too. The idea first comes to Ike when he stands, at twenty-one, with McCaslin Edmonds among dirty and dusty journal-leaves. There Ike is confronted with a profound puzzle for man: if God is omnipotent, why does He allow His chosen people to pervert humanity with the sins of rape, of incest, of miscegenation? The only answer Ike can summon—searching through the corridors of his past and the scribblings of his forbears—is that the Civil War was a time of communal purgation. He likens the war to an earlier but similar trial—the War Between the States was "a harsher book and McCaslin, fourteen and fifteen and sixteen, had seen it and the boy himself had inherited it as Noah's grandchildren had inherited the flood although they had not been there to see the deluge." The implication that follows is that as the flood was not sufficient so the Civil War will not suffice, but if Ike sees this fallacy in his analogy, he does not admit it to McCaslin or to himself. For Ike must appease his conscience through a rational theory of history and this theory accounts for his two problems—God's failure and Lucius McCaslin's failing—and both frightening facts—the bloody war and the blood-mingling miscegenation.

So with Ike, theoretically at least, the penance can be wholly communal. And thus it is when Roth cynically defines patriotism as barroom singing and "dime-store flags in our lapels," that Ike counters with "This country is a little mite stronger than any one man or group of men, outside of it or even inside of it either. I

reckon, when the time comes and some of you have done got tired
of hollering we are whipped if we dont go to war and some more
are hollering we are whipped if we do, it will cope with one Austrian paper-hanger, no matter what he will be calling himself."
The conclusion is axiomatic given Ike's own premise: most men
are a little better than their circumstances give them a chance to
be. It is also consistent: war is welcome, because it is not only
tragedy as punishment, but trial for penance.

The other hunters counter Ike, for they are realists; they do not
see an Edenic past as Ike does. Wyatt tries again to torment Roth,
but he really answers Uncle Ike. " 'Meaning that it's only because
folks happen to be watching him that a man behaves at all,' "
and Roth, as realistic as anyone in the story, agrees and is not
annoyed: " 'Yes,' Edmonds said. 'A man in a blue coat, with a
badge on it watching him.' " The attack is on Ike; he argues con-
cisely, firmly, and yet all his lessons—from the day he has seen
the railroad and the day he has searched ledgers in the commissary—speak out supporting Wyatt and Roth.

For Ike sees too simply, forgets too easily. He cannot now accept what is established fact: that, in his oversimplified theory,
the Civil War sets a precedent. God may have allowed opportunity for communal atonement, but the process failed. World
War II can do no better by the Negro; it will not rub out the sins
of slavery and miscegenation too deeply imbedded in Southern
and personal historic fact. Like Thomas Sutpen in *Absalom, Absalom!*, Ike retreats to the comfort of an inflexible plan, a "grand
design." He continues to hope. But because his romantic day-
dreaming counters the world of the present—the world of Roth's
"doe-hunting," the world of denuded swamp land—Ike is seen by
the other hunters as a foolish old man bordering on senility.

III

Ike's answer involves more than a communal penance, however,
for that shifts onto a group the responsibility which, because he
has Lucius McCaslin's blood in his veins, Ike feels so deeply, so
personally. Ike might like to transfer the absolution of the sin
of slavery onto his fellow Southerners who fought in the Civil War,
and those who continued afterwards to hold the Negro in a con-

dition of servility, but the stark, cold ledgers show to him—as he insists they should show McCaslin Edmonds—his own inherited guilt for past sin. So Ike becomes a carpenter like Christ; like the sinless Nazarene who illustrated by example a way to pay for a sin committed by forbears, Ike plods through a life of renunciation and atonement for his family, for his people. Although the Christ imagery is not so overt in "Delta Autumn" as in *The Bear,* it still lurks in the postlude, where Ike continues to play the role of peacemaker, where he sleeps on "the old worn groove of mattress" with "his hands crossed on his breast." He is Olympian; removed from the action and the talk with a feigned sleep, he hears and looks upon the events of the dark; he stops the Roth who cannot sleep from anxiety over recent deeds of wrongdoing. If communal or social atonement fails, then (although Ike does not see the distinction) personal atonement may succeed.

For here there are specific precedents for Ike to follow. Sam Fathers had given up the comforts of the white man to pay respect to the wilderness and to Joe Baker by living year-round in Major de Spain's cabin. Boon denied himself and his injuries upon the death of Old Ben, lost as he was in Lion's pain. Closer to his own problem, Ike is aware that his father and uncle have attempted to atone for slavery by allowing their own slaves freedom of the night through an unlocked back door, and have tried to atone for the sin of miscegenation by bequests of a thousand dollars to each of *their* father's grandchildren through his affair with his mulatto daughter. So Ike takes upon himself the delivery of the bequests: he travels West through exhausting days and nights to leave money with the now-married Fonsiba and, at the end of "Delta Autumn," continues such a plan of redemption by paying James Beauchamp's granddaughter with money Roth has left for her support.

But Ike is guilty of the same innocence and ignorance that Uncle Buck and Uncle Buddy were: one cannot atone with blood money. In their feelings of guilt and responsibility—in their desire for repudiation—all the McCaslins, including Ike, forget the lesson of Ike's Nazarene in Gethsemane: the sins of the world are not easy to bear, and pain is the price.

In "Delta Autumn," Faulkner recalls Ike's repudiation of his

wife and home for a life of penance; Ike pleads for Roth to do the
same—to stay and present the envelope of cash himself. It is
Faulkner's own answer of individual responsibility—like the answer of Bayard Sartoris, and the newspaper reporter in *Pylon,*
and Gavin Stevens and Chick Mallison. But the McCaslins want
salvation too easily, and their concern turns into cowardice. Ike
doesn't spend a life of penance—he runs from the guilt-ridden
line of the McCaslins into a useless dream world of emulating
Christ. Both Ike and Roth cheapen penance by trying to pay it
in easy cash installments. They sublimate the evil, they sidestep
their guilt, proclaiming both but paying neither. This is because
they are unrealistic: Ike feels that cash is enough, that a role-
playing in imagined life can become a reality of life. Ike cannot
accept a situation—just as he cannot believe that his wife's naked-
ness is brought on by her desire to gain for herself the McCaslin
inheritance (in horror, he gives in momentarily, then runs), so he
cannot believe that the crime of the McCaslins has come full circle. He cannot accept another mulatto child in the blanket before
him; he gives the mother a tin horn (which she rightly recognizes
as a cheap payment) and, in horror, he brushes her aside and out
of the tent.

Because he is unrealistic, Ike refuses to acknowledge the fact
that his theory of communal atonement has not worked—and will
not, at least in his oversimplified statement of it. And because he
is unrealistic, the answer of personal atonement fails: he has not
the wisdom which, coupled with the desire, will allow him to
grasp the real situation. And so, actually, Ike runs.

IV

The beauty of "Delta Autumn" is not only that it shows Ike's
failings, but that it points the way for final repudiation despite
them. As the Negro servant Dilsey offers the only hope for the
degenerate and dying Compsons in *The Sound and the Fury,* here
the final hope is suggested by a Negro. The forewarning comes
with the only successful land; denuded by the white man, the
land is still "fecund up to the very doorsteps of the negroes." Ike
does see this, and he has the opportunity to see in Roth's mulatto
mistress exactly those saving prerequisites of the Negro he has

already listed for McCaslin Edmonds in the commissary: " 'Endurance . . . and pity and tolerance and fidelity and love of children.' "

Ike's naivete is sharply (even ironically) contrasted with the mulatto girl's knowing. For given the chance to see, Ike cannot; he fumbles for his glasses, but they are out of his reach. The girl, with the mixed blood running in her veins, is like Fonsiba's husband, who wears lenseless glasses but who, nevertheless, *can* see. She knows the money is a token payment; she knows the horn is useless. She has known all along—in the months of pregnancy, in the reunion in January—that she will not live her life out with Roth. It does not matter. Their love, momentary, transitory, has its own value—for her and for him, too. That does matter.

Her figure is one of silence and of suffering. She never compares herself with Christ—never thinks to—but her attitude is more His than Ike's, despite Ike's loud and hollow proclamations. Her knowledge is steeped in simplicity: " 'Not marriage,' " Ike rushes, betraying his real desire to be master, not redeemer. " 'Not marriage. He didn't promise you that.' " And " 'So,' " she answers, " 'He didn't have to. I didn't ask him to. I knew what I was doing.' " Roth did not—he must ease his conscience with money; he must duck out of the tent before she can leave the road where he first saw her and trail him to his bed. She does not expect him, but she will give him the chance. She will deny her pride; she will seek him out in humility. She will leave him if he asks it, but she will give him, too, the chance to personal atonement, to unburden his sin of miscegenation and rape. Nor will she, as other McCaslins might, hold over his head her heritage from the same family line; she will not hint at the crime of incest. She is wholly giving. Her action in seeking Roth is filled with humility, with self-abnegation, with selfless love to another. It is the Greek *agape,* the Latin *caritas*; she is not the Nazarene nor does she proclaim to be, yet *hers* is the real lesson of Christ.

V

As Faulkner has captured the central meaning of the hunt for Old Ben in two basic words—*pride* and *humility*—so the essence of "Delta Autumn" is held in the three key words. They all spring from the mulatto girl, the source of the story's real hope. With no betrayal of pride, but with the wellspring of wisdom, she tells Ike she did not expect marriage: " 'I knew what I was doing. I knew that to begin with, long before honor I imagine he called it told him the time had come to tell me in so many words what his code I suppose he would call it would forbid him forever to do. And we agreed. Then we agreed again before he left New Mexico, to make sure. That that would be all of it. I believed him. No, I dont mean that; I mean I believed myself. I wasn't even listening to him anymore by then because by that time it had been a long time since he had had anything else to tell me for me to have to hear.' "

The sins are clearly spelled out. The girl uses *code* and *honor* not in the proud, aristocratic sense where they are virtues, but with their new-found value; in the shapes into which Roth and Ike, too, have twisted them. For her, *code* has become the communal laws which fail to take into account the individual, and *honor* has been bent now into the personal sense of self that is buried in pride. Not only Roth, but also Ike, is guilty of them both. His theory of communal atonement has fallen to the *code* of the South that preaches the aristocracy of the white man and the purity of racial bloods. And the code has dictated to him as well as to Roth the meaning of *honor*—that cheapening of one's self because it destroys emphasis on responsibility for emphasis on respectability. It is the oldest fault of man, and part of the same pride that caused Lucius Quintus Carothers McCaslin one night to exercise his superiority and rape the Negro servant named Eunice. Not only Roth, but Ike, has brought the McCaslins full circle, back to the original evil. His story is a new retelling of the plight of Macbeth: "That we but teach / Bloody instructions, which, being taught, return / To plague the inventor."

No, the answer comes not from *code* nor from *honor,* which are too absolute, too selfish; the answer comes from *love,* from charity. With a useless envelope (useless because it has money, not a personal message of concern or love) in one hand and a cheap old horn in the other (cheap because it comes from the early days, the evil days of Lucius McCaslin), Roth's mulatto mistress again provides the key to Ike's atonement in the third word: " 'Old man,' " she asks him in simple clarity, because he needs simplicity and clarity now, " 'have you lived so long and forgotten so much that you dont remember anything you ever knew or felt or even heard about love?' "

This is the answer to the rigid proud *code* and the personal selfish *honor*. It is the *love* Ike thinks he knows when he tells the hunters of it so well: " 'that every man and woman, at the instant when it dont even matter whether they marry or not . . . at that instant the two of them together were God.' " It is the answer Ike thinks he knows, but does not.

VI

Yet what hope is there, really, if the hero of *The Bear* is as weak as this? If man has the will to atonement, he is also free to fall, and Ike has fallen. He has fallen too easily in love with a nonexistent wilderness, fallen to the spell of an Eden which is of the past, and therefore cannot be his. He is victim of too-easy theories of communal penance sent just in time by a God who wants to save those whom He created, so that he is not "all alone up there in his paramount Heaven." Ike has fallen too easily to the romantic role of repudiation.

In an interview with Cynthia Grenier, Faulkner has commented on Ike, "I think a man ought to do more than just repudiate. He should have been more affirmative instead of shunning people." Instead of service, Ike's method is one of shunning his family— he escapes his wife and work by allowing McCaslin Edmonds to support him with a monthly payment, into his bank account, of the money he has publicly disowned when he renounced the plantation. Ike shuns Roth's mistress, too—he uses Roth's money this time to pay her off. His relinquishment of the plantation was foreshadowed earlier in his relinquishment of the civilized watch and compass when he wished to see Old Ben. But then he had to show, subsequent to that relinquishment, the courage to stand in the woods alone and not run. That courage was left in the woods; Ike has shrunk now to the coward who lies on a bed, unable to reach his glasses, undressed with his pants far from him. He lies with the props of an envelope and a horn, his courage shrivelled into cowardice as he points the girl toward the door, and tells her to wait a thousand years. Where once he waited to see a bear, he now cannot bring himself to acknowledge and accept miscegenation. The stumbling block which caused him to start a new life of simple carpentry—his inability to accept miscegenation among the McCaslins—only underlines the present failure of his romantic plan, for he still stumbles.

But if the hero fails, is there no possibility of heroism for the next thousand or two thousand years? Faulkner, in his public addresses, has denied this. In his Nobel address, Faulkner said, "[Man] is immortal not because he alone among creatures has an inexhaustible voice, but because he has a soul, a spirit capable of compassion." In a speech to the high school graduating class of his daughter Jill, Faulkner remarked, "It is not man in the mass who can and will save Man. It is Man himself, created in the image of God so that he shall have the power and the will to choose right from wrong, and so be able to save himself because he is worth saving."

Ike's chief failure is that he has only reacted to his past, but not acted to determine the future. Ike has too easily accepted the fallen state of man; he has not questioned man's fallibilities so that he may more clearly see his own. Concentrating as he has on some dusty old ledgers and some boyhood experiences, his own view of man and his own pilgrimage has become ingrown; his mission stems from myopic observation, his vision is stillborn. He has depended on the solace of a stereotyped reaction, that of simple renunciation.

Dr. Johnson once said, "It ought to be the first endeavor of a writer to distinguish nature from custom, or that which is established because it is right from that which is right only because it is established." For Ike has only apparently failed; "Delta Autumn" holds a glimmer (though only a glimmer) of future possibilities for Ike. That Ike begins to perceive this at the end of "Delta Autumn" is shown by his own bony hand resting on the girl's: the moment of horror is also the moment of hope. "The old blood"—the Lucius McCaslin blood—has returned, but it is a strong blood and with it comes miscegenation. This is an answer which Ike cannot accept *now*, but he *does* accept it as the answer. Though it is repulsive, he recognizes it as saving; he is able to touch her hand, to give her a horn, to admit miscegenation in the future, to announce (even by circumvention) to Legate that the "doe" has come and Roth, in discovery and in despair, has shot it. So the crime is also its own solution. Salvation will come in the repetition of the sin, but when the sin is acceptable, and no longer, therefore, "sin." Ike recognizes at last—after a fruitless lifetime and an agonizing failure—that the time will come, but that it is "not yet."

Ike can become ruler with his new-won knowledge (from the girl), yet for a while he must still be ruled by his ancient, out-moded time and place. But he is neither the saint R. W. B. Lewis proposes, nor the sinner David Stewart has suggested. Rather, Ike is man—man weak, limited, lustful (as seen in the commissary); man destined to travel a long and lonely road to individual salvation at best, or an awareness of futility at worst. He is man with all the limitations of humanity—with both the sins of Lucius McCaslin and the wisdom of the mulatto. Yet he is also man with his awareness of responsibility, his need for liberation and deliverance.

No, "the time is not yet." But the man who is fallen is yet free to act. In one who can feel guilt and pain and understand responsibility and freedom, there is both sentience and reason; because of this, there is also the possibility of joy.

APPENDIXES

Included here are materials which provide additional information about Yoknapatawpha County, the McCaslin family tree, the Biblical significance of Isaac, and the critical reception of Go Down, Moses (1942) *upon its publication. The study guide questions, annotated bibliography, and Faulkner canon should enable the reader to further explore the selections included in this book as well as other materials relevant to* The Bear *and Faulkner's other writings.*

FROM *The World of William Faulkner*

WARD L. MINER

❦

[Yoknapatawpha County is really Lafayette County, Mississippi, where Faulkner lives, except for a few significant changes.] Perhaps a good start in our comparative study is with statistics. First as to size—Lafayette county has a land area of 679 square miles; Faulkner gives his county 2400 square miles. In population—the 1940 census gave the actual county 21,257, of whom 8,573 or 40.3% were Negroes; the fictitious county in 1936 was given a population of 15,611, of whom 9,313 or 59.6% were Negroes. . . . Faulkner has apparently made his county large enough to include within it everything he wanted to throw in, though he is quite careless with his size. . . . The population of Lafayette county has since 1870 varied between approximately 19,000 and 11,000. Faulkner gives his legendary county the number of people about half-way between the 1850 and 1860 figures. Why? Lafayette county in 1940 had 31.3 people per square mile, compared to a state of Mississippi average of 46.1 and a national average of 44.2 per square mile. Lafayette county is obviously a rural county. But Faulkner makes Yoknapatawpha county still more rural. His county averages 6.5 people per square mile—way below even the average for Lafayette county in its first census return, 1840, which showed about 9.0 per square mile. . . .

Yoknapatawpha county has, as was pointed out before, 59.6% Negroes. The highest percentage of Negroes for the actual county was 47.5% in 1880—always more whites than Negroes. In 1940 the actual figures just above reverse Faulkner's—59.7% whites. . . . In trying to make his legendary county count for more than Lafayette county, the novelist has used characteristics intermediate

FROM *The World of William Faulkner* (Duke University Press, 1952; Grove Press, 1959), pp. 88-90. Reprinted by permission of Duke University Press. For an opposing viewpoint, see G. T. Buckley, "Is Oxford the Original of Jefferson in William Faulkner's Novels?" *PMLA*, LXXVI:4, Part I (September. 1961).

between Lafayette county and the Delta. . . . This proportion in the fictitious county indicates a psychological awareness by the inhabitants. They are so aware of the Negro's presence that it is as though there were more of them than there actually are. So Faulkner has given a kind of psychological figure rather than a physical one. Last but not least, the novelist may be saying that the presence of the Negro is his county's, Mississippi's, the South's number one problem, and the why for the "split land" of Yoknapatawpha.

Descendants of L. Q. C. McCaslin ❧ Michael Millgate

DESCENDANTS OF L. Q. C. McCASLIN

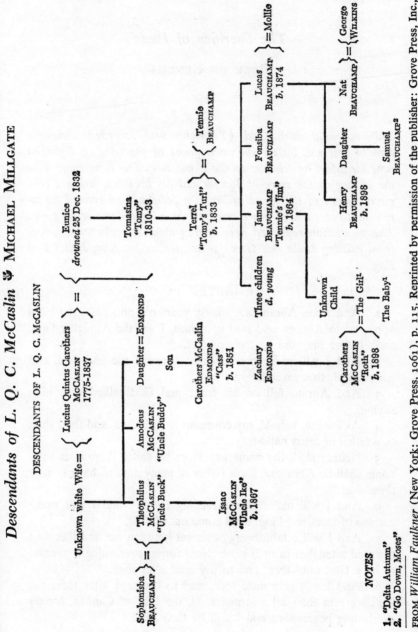

NOTES

1. "Delta Autumn"
2. "Go Down, Moses"

FROM *William Faulkner* (New York: Grove Press, 1961), p. 115. Reprinted by permission of the publisher: Grove Press, Inc., and Oliver & Boyd Ltd., Edinburgh. Copyright © 1961 by Michael Millgate.

The Sacrifice of Isaac

BOOK OF GENESIS

This covenant with God (Yahweh) was recorded sometime around 750 B.C. by an unknown priest of the tribe of Ephraim now identified by scholars as the E narrator. The E narrator, also the author of the story of Joseph and his brothers, wrote a religious history of the Israeli tribes in a polished and refined narrative that ran through other accounts in a logical but serial form. The translation reprinted here is that made by selected scholars from existing Latin and Greek texts in 1611 for King James I of England.

CHAPTER 17

1 And when Abram was ninety years old and nine, the Lord appeared to Abram, and said unto him, I am the Almighty God; walk before me, and be thou perfect.

2 And I will make my covenant between me and thee, and will multiply thee exceedingly.

3 And Abram fell on his face: and God talked with him, saying,

4 As for me, behold, my covenant is with thee, and thou shalt be a father of many nations.

5 Neither shall thy name any more be called Abram, but thy name shall be Abraham; for a father of many nations have I made thee.

6 And I will make thee exceeding fruitful, and I will make nations of thee, and kings shall come out of thee.

7 And I will establish my covenant between me and thee and thy seed after thee in their generations for an everlasting covenant, to be a God unto thee, and to thy seed after thee.

8 And I will give unto thee, and to thy seed after thee, the land wherein thou art a stranger, all the land of Canaan, for an everlasting possession; and I will be their God.

CHAPTER 22

1 And it came to pass after these things, that God did tempt Abraham, and said unto him, Abraham; and he said, Behold, here I am.

2 And he said, Take now thy son, thine only son Isaac, whom thou lovest, and get thee into the land of Moriah; and offer him there for a burnt offering upon one of the mountains which I will tell thee of.

3 And Abraham rose up early in the morning, and saddled his ass, and took two of his young men with him, and Isaac his son, and clave the wood for the burnt offering, and rose up, and went unto the place of which God had told him.

4 Then on the third day Abraham lifted up his eyes, and saw the place afar off.

5 And Abraham said unto his young men, Abide ye here with the ass; and I and the lad will go yonder and worship, and come again to you.

6 And Abraham took the wood of the burnt offering, and laid it upon Isaac his son; and he took the fire in his hand, and a knife; and they went both of them together.

7 And Isaac spake unto Abraham his father, and said, My father: and he said, Here am I, my son. And he said, Behold the fire and the wood: but where is the lamb for a burnt offering?

8 And Abraham said, My son, God will provide himself a lamb for a burnt offering: so they went both of them together.

9 And they came to the place which God had told him of; and Abraham built an altar there, and laid the wood in order, and bound Isaac his son, and laid him on the altar upon the wood.

10 And Abraham stretched forth his hand, and took the knife to slay his son.

11 And the angel of the Lord called unto him out of heaven, and said, Abraham, Abraham: and he said, Here am I.

12 And he said, Lay not thine hand upon the lad, neither do thou any thing unto him: for now I know that thou fearest God, seeing thou hast not withheld thy son, thine only son, from me.

13 And Abraham lifted up his eyes, and looked, and behold behind him a ram caught in a thicket by his horns: and Abraham

went and took the ram, and offered him up for a burnt offering in the stead of his son.

14 And Abraham called the name of that place Jehovah-jireh: as it is said to this day, In the mount of the Lord it shall be seen.

15 And the angel of the Lord called unto Abraham out of heaven the second time,

16 And said, By myself have I sworn, saith the Lord, for because thou hast done this thing, and hast not withheld thy son, thine only son,

17 That in blessing I will bless thee, and in multiplying I will multiply thy seed as the stars of the heaven, and as the sand which is upon the sea shore; and thy seed shall possess the gate of his enemies;

18 And in thy seed shall all the nations of the earth be blessed; because thou hast obeyed my voice.

The Immediate Critical Reception of Go Down, Moses

❦

William Abraham, book review, in the *Boston Globe* (May 6, 1942), p. 19.

. . . Here are seven stories that should be read by anyone who cares about the progress of American fiction. They represent William Faulkner at his best. Which is equivalent to saying the best we have.

J. D. Beresford, "New Novels," *Manchester* [England] *Guardian* (October 9, 1941), #29,963, p. 3, col. 1. Reproduced with permission of the "Guardian" and the author.

Mr. William Faulkner is one of those American writers who are as shy of direct narrative as some modern musicians are of harmony. There is no denying his gift for powerful writing, but some of the seven stories that make up *Go Down, Moses* . . . constitute a severe mental exercise rather than an entertainment. The longest of them, "The Bear," which fills a hundred pages, moves lucidly and interestingly during the first half and then plunges into a mass of irrelevant material that does not repay the pains necessary for its deciphering.

Milton Rugoff, "The Magic of William Faulkner," in *BOOKS, The New York Herald Tribune* (May 17, 1942), p. 2.

There is much in this collection of seven narratives that reveals all of William Faulkner's magic, his ability to weave strange spells, to re-create with a preternatural intensity the world as seen from the extraordinary perspective of his rural Mississippians. But there is also a kind of writing in it which must be described as perversely and eccentrically obscure. When Mr. Faulkner is at his best there is scarcely a novelist who can surpass him in exploring the submarine depths of consciousness, but when he rests his narrative on the stream-of-thought of unidentified characters and runs his sentences into hopelessly tangled skeins, the reader can only shake his head and sigh. These tendencies are fortunately not insistent enough to obscure his gifts. . . .

If we overlook several stretches of prose which gives the effect of tropical depths seen through a glass-bottomed boat, The Bear is no less impressive. It tells what fourteen-year-old Ike McCaslin learned from old Sam, in whom was merged the blood of Indian chiefs, African kings and white landlords. Sam taught Ike how to hunt, but beyond that he gave the boy a glimpse of a spirit that could not be humbled. The story itself revolves around the annual attempt to catch an almost legendary bear, and culminates when Sam finds a hunting-dog fierce enough to hunt Big Ben down. Before the story closes, the savage old bear and the huge blue mastiff have become symbols of the doomed yet untamable, of the mysterious teleology of nature such as was Moby Dick. Whether or not one accepts the implication that primitive ways are "purer" than our own, there is no denying the power of the tale. . . .

But one does get from this volume an acute sense of the social complexity of the New South, of the insidious roles played by class and family pride. Most subtle and most striking is Mr. Faulkner's development of the drama generated when a white landowner and his Negro sharecropper gaze at each other with the knowledge that the same blood runs in their veins. Peculiar to him, too (though we inevitably think of Joyce), is the steep plunging into the unplumbed depths of family memory, and those sprawling, word-intoxicated sentences which seem determined to include everything, just as it occurred, and as uninterruptedly as thought itself.

R.E.D., from "The Atlantic Bookshelf," in *The Atlantic Monthly* (September, 1942), p. 136.

This is Faulkner at his best and worst—perhaps not quite his worst, for no loonies, degenerates, or gentlemen who fall in love with cows figure as major characters in these stories. The same people, black and white, appear in all of them. The chronology is obscure, the characters are vague, the interrelationships demand closer study than the casual reader can afford, and there is a great deal of what—to all but Faulkner addicts—must seem to be merely maundering and verbiage. But there is enough magic, here and there, to justify this or any other book. Sometimes this splendid writer cannot help writing splendidly. "The Bear," from page 191 to page 254 in this volume, is a superb story, perhaps an immortal one, and then it falls to pieces and degenerates into drivel. One feels that to the author the drivel is the really important message, the thing he *has* to say, but there is a failure in his technique. His message does not come through. It bogs down in words and confusion. ". . . feeling again and as always the sharp shocking inrush from when Isaac McCaslin long yet was not . . ." is a slovenly way of expressing one's emotions on almost stepping on a rattler. Mr. Faulkner has always been, to this reviewer, an annoying writer. He has everything, a wealth of talents. But he lacks horse sense and discrimination. He can spoil his best work more thoroughly and quickly than any other man living. This book, I repeat, shows him at his best and his worst.

Unsigned, "Dark-Ride through Dawn," *Time*, XXXIX (May 11, 1942), 95. Courtesy *Time*; copyright Time Inc. 1942.

Reading the new Faulkner is like taking what carnival people call a "dark-ride": one of those slow Tunnels of Love which alternate blank darkness with suddenly illuminated views of dancing skeletons or Swiss lakes. *Go Down, Moses* is a dark-ride well worth taking. Stretches of it are blank enough but some of the views beat those of any other U.S. writer. . . .

Poetically rather than rationally, Faulkner manages to bulldoze the reader into believing that the South is indeed accursed, but he is never very clear why or how. On mixups of money and genealogy he constructs passages as intricate, but not as rewarding as a five-voiced fugue. On the pre-cotton Southern wilderness, he is superb. . . .

Faulkner knows his own country as few men do. His details of farming, hunting and folkways are as tangible as rusty nails and as tough as legal writ. . . .

Faulkner is perhaps the most gifted of living U.S. writers. He can be as funny as Mark Twain, as exalted as Melville, as solid as Joyce and as dull as Dreiser; but he has never done a book which has the sure, sound performance of any of these men. *Go Down, Moses,* like most Faulkner, is brilliant and uneven. Its special value is its evocative (though local) exploration of the U.S. national source and dawn. In it is a sometimes merely yeasty, sometimes 100-proof sense of those powers and mysteries of land and the people on it which make a nation.

Questions for Discussion and Writing

❦

1. Some literary critics contend that a work of fiction is a self-contained, self-explanatory unit which the perceptive reader can understand without reference to anything extrinsic to the work—such as knowledge about the author's life, opinions, other writings, and the times and culture in which he wrote. Do the selections by Millgate, Cullen, and Grenier, as well as Faulkner's Nobel Prize address, vitiate or validate this "new critical" position? Does a knowledge of the *Saturday Evening Post* version of *The Bear,* "Lion," "Delta Autumn," and the excerpts from *The Hamlet,* "A Justice," "Was," "The Old People," "Race at Morning," and *The Reivers* enhance your understanding of the content of *The Bear*? Of its literary techniques? Why? In what different ways do these various selections relate to *The Bear*?

2. Which of Faulkner's comments and writings in this book do you find most relevant to your own conception of *The Bear*? Why?

3. What concepts of audience might Faulkner have held in writing "Lion" and the *Saturday Evening Post* version of *The Bear*? How do they affect his writing?

4. Reprinted here is an entry from an exhibition of Faulkner's works, titled "The Literary Career of William Faulkner," and held at the Princeton University Library May 10–August 30, 1957 (see James B. Meriwether, *The Literary Career of William Faulkner: A Bibliographical Study*. Princeton: Princeton University Library, 1961). This is an early sketch of the genealogy of the McCaslin family, which differs in many ways from the chart by Millgate on p. 401 above, representing the final relationship of the McCaslins. One difference is that this early chart does not allow for repeated miscegenation; there are other major and minor differences as well. What are some of them? How might you account for them?

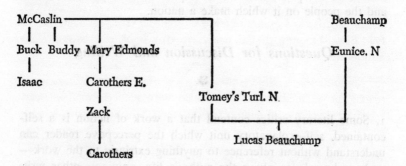

5. In her book on Faulkner, Mary Cooper Robb says that Faulkner's "animals are as real as his people. . . . Each of Faulkner's animals has his own personality; each is memorable for himself; and not because of the human character to whom he is attached." Do you find this to be so in "Lion"? In the *Saturday Evening Post* version of *The Bear*? In *The Bear* in Part I? Can you resolve this view with Utley's view, which equates some humans with their animal counterparts?

6. In Loïc Bouvard's "Conversation with William Faulkner" [*Modern Fiction Studies*, V:4 (Winter 1959-1960), 361-364], Faulkner said that the South is "the only really authentic region

in the United States because a deep indestructible bond still exists between man and his environment. In the South, above all, there is still a common acceptance of the world, a common view of life, and a common morality." In what ways does *The Bear* illustrate Faulkner's remarks? In what ways does it fail to support them?

7. If you agree that the Nobel Prize address is Faulkner's most nearly formal credo of his life's work, what of its principles does he exemplify in *The Bear*?

8. In the Nobel Prize address and in *The Bear* (for example, in the phrase "the heart's driving complexity"), Faulkner emphasizes the heart over all other parts of life. How does this affect writing, particularly Faulkner's? Does he neglect reason and intellect? Is he endangered by sentimentality?

9. Why are such words as "love," "honor," "pity," "pride," "compassion," and "sacrifice," taken from the Nobel Prize address, central words for Faulkner? Choose one and trace its definition in *The Bear*. Do any of the essays in this book aid you in your definition?

10. Some teachers object to excessive use of "myth criticism." Argue for or against such criticism, with respect to *The Bear*. What are the limits of such criticism?

11. Is Faulkner's story more credible than Twenyucis's dream? Why or why not?

12. What customs are common to Indian culture and the culture of Faulkner's Sam Fathers? What importance do they have?

13. Compare and contrast the initiation rituals of young Ike McCaslin and the Omaha and Bemba initiations.

14. Do any characters of *The Bear* transcend or differ significantly from the Southern characteristics described by Cash?

15. Do you find any characteristics common to *The Mind of the South*, *Adventures of Huckleberry Finn*, "Big Bear of Arkansas," and *The Bear*?

16. Compare and contrast the theme(s) and techniques of Thorpe's "Big Bear of Arkansas" and Faulkner's *The Bear*.

17. What are the epiphanies in *Huckleberry Finn* and in *The Bear*? (For the meaning of "epiphany," see "Pride and Humility: The Cultural Roots of Ike McCaslin," by Francis Lee Utley, p. 235.

18. What relations between the Negro and the white man are illustrated by Clemens and by *The Bear*?

19. Does Utley's interpretation allow for both Ike's heroism *and* Boon's near insanity when each of them fails to kill Old Ben?

20. Utley has said that Boon's trip to town "is not mere comedy." What are his reasons for this claim? Do you agree?

21. If Boon does not fire effectively at Old Ben and if Boon lives at the close of *The Bear,* is Utley correct in identifying him with Lion, who is effective and who dies?

22. What reasons would you give a publisher to justify including Part IV of *The Bear* when reprinting it? To justify excluding it?

23. The *Encyclopædia Britannica* states that "emphasizing the presence of the past, the power of doom, and the value of endurance, Faulkner transcended his region and his country to speak to the world." How appropriately does this apply to *The Bear*?

24. The Calvinist doctrine of predestination states that God determines a person's afterlife in heaven or hell at the moment of his birth. After reading *The Bear,* would you say Faulkner seems at times to be concerned with predestination? If so, where? How does it contribute to the story?

25. Apply the following quotation (from Faulkner's *The Sound and the Fury,* 1929), to *The Bear*: ". . . no battle is ever won . . . They are not even fought. The field only reveals to man his own folly and despair, and victory is an illusion of philosophers and fools."

26. In *Absalom, Absalom!* (1936), Faulkner has Judith Sutpen say: "You get born and you try this and you don't know why

only you keep on trying it and you are born at the same time with a lot of other people, all mixed up with them, same way like five or six people all trying to make a rug on the same loom only each one wants to weave his own pattern into the rug; and it can't matter, you know that, or the Ones that set up the loom would have arranged things a little better, and yet it must matter because you keep on trying." Apply Judith Sutpen's words to *The Bear* and "Delta Autumn."

27. In *Absalom, Absalom!* Faulkner says of Colonel Thomas Sutpen that he did "not what he wanted to do but what he just had to do, had to do it whether he wanted to or not, because if he did not do it he knew that he could never live with himself for the rest of his life." Show how this does or does not apply to Sam Fathers, Boon, Major de Spain, Lion.

28. Someone has said that "Lion" is essentially an adventure story which features action and *The Bear* is a piece of ritual embodying a set pattern of behavior. Is this true? If so, how well has Faulkner succeeded in combining these two antithetical treatments of a hunt in *The Bear*? Why?

29. In "The Fire and the Hearth" Lucas Beauchamp thinks the following of Ike: "He, Lucas Beauchamp, the oldest living McCaslin descendant, still living on the hereditary land . . . almost as old as old Isaac who in a sense, say what a man would, had turned apostate to his name and lineage by weakly relinquishing the land which was rightfully his to live in town on the charity of his great-nephew. . . ." Would Roth Edmonds agree? Is this view consistent with the picture of Ike given in *The Bear*? In "Delta Autumn"?

30. Identify and discuss the human equivalents of the fyce, Lion, and Old Ben.

31. In what ways does Faulkner use nature in *The Bear*? With what effects?

32. Malcolm Cowley has written of *Go Down, Moses* (and *The Bear*) that the "major theme is injustice to the Negroes, the minor theme is the destruction of the wilderness, and the two themes are

closely interwoven." Is this a correct summary of *The Bear* alone, out of the context of the other stories? Are the two themes compatible? Does Faulkner stress one consistently more than the other? How does he fuse them? How does he separate them for emphasis? Would the presentation be stronger if a separate story were devoted to each theme?

33. What explanations other than the one given in the story might account for Faulkner's having Ike accompany Boon on the trip for whiskey?

34. Compare the sacrifice of the bull in Keats's "Ode on a Grecian Urn" to the death of Old Ben.

35. In Part V of *The Bear,* Ike, Boon, and Major de Spain have different attitudes toward the hunt. Contrast these.

36. Why does Faulkner have Boon smash his rifle at the end of *The Bear?*

37. In "Faulkner's Mythology" [*The Kenyon Review,* I:3 (Summer 1939), 285-299], George Marion O'Donnell claims that "Mr. Faulkner is a traditional man in a modern South. All around him the antitraditional forces are at work. . . . It is not strange, then, that his novels are, primarily, a series of related myths (or aspects of a single myth) built around the conflict between traditionalism and [the] antitraditional modern world in which it is immersed." Although O'Donnell's remark antedates *The Bear,* can it be appropriately applied? If so, in what ways?

38. In "Wilderness and Civilization: A Note on William Faulkner" [*Partisan Review,* XXII (Summer 1955), 340-350], Ursula Brumm contends that Faulkner's "attachment to the South . . . is one of tormented love but not of admiration. . . . He always shows a tradition in the process of going to pieces, and probes into the past for the causes. In the causal complexity there is always at bottom the same thing: a guilt of rapacity and greediness which has corrupted the tradition right at its starting point, an inevitable sin in man's civilizing efforts." Apply this analysis to *The Bear* and to other Faulkner selections you have read.

39. Randall Stewart in *American Literature and Christian Doctrine* (Baton Rouge: Louisiana State University Press, 1958) says that Faulkner is not a sociological writer but a moral allegorist. Is Stewart's view defensible in connection with *The Bear*? With "Delta Autumn"? Why or why not?

40. In *The Tangled Fire of William Faulkner* (Minneapolis: University of Minnesota Press, 1954), William Van O'Connor remarks at length on *The Bear* and related writings. Comment on his assertion: "At the close of section two of the revised 'The Bear' there are these sentences about thirteen-year-old Ike's attitude toward Lion: 'So he should have hated and feared Lion. Yet he did not. It seemed to him that there was a fatality in it.' The sentences seem to be a plant, suggesting, but without explaining, to the reader that the apotheosis of Lion is not contradicting the apotheosis of Old Ben. But as a matter of fact, it does contradict it. If Ike is the voice of the wisdom to be learned from the wilderness, then indeed he should have been opposed to the spirit represented by Lion."

41. Comment on Irving Howe's opinion that "Clan [i.e., family] rather than class forms the basic social unit in Faulkner's world." If this is so, why should it be?

42. Resolve the apparent discrepancy between the fact that Ike, at twenty-one, actively takes up a new life of carpentering as an act of penance and repudiation and David Stewart's charge that Ike constantly postpones action.

43. What issues does David Stewart raise and use to prove his claim that Ike is a fraudulent hero? Does Lewis implicitly answer these charges? Does Utley, Perluck, or Kinney? In the final analysis does Ike become heroic or ridiculous?

44. It has been suggested that Utley has the idealist's view of Ike while Kinney holds the realist's position. Define these two terms and then defend or oppose such a charge.

45. In his Introduction to *The Portable Faulkner,* Malcolm Cowley writes: "Faulkner's novels are full of well-meaning and even

admirable persons, not only the grandsons of the cotton aristocracy, but also pine-hill farmers and storekeepers and sewing-
machine agents and Negro cooks and sharecroppers; but they are
almost all of them defeated by circumstances and they carry with
them a sense of their own doom." Show whether this generaliza-
tion applies to *The Bear*. Does "Delta Autumn" throw any new
light on the question?

46. Does *The Bear* illustrate Walter Slatoff's statement that
Faulkner's "world, in general, is to a very large extent a battle-
ground of individuals struggling with one another or with some
other adversary. Some of these struggles result in victory of a sort
for one of the antagonists, but the overwhelming emphasis is upon
the struggles themselves, upon the opposing forces in a protracted
balance, deadlock, or tension"?

47. Using examples from *The Bear,* comment on the following
statements by Malcolm Cowley in his Introduction to *The Portable
Faulkner:*
   a. [Faulkner] "has a brooding love for the land"
   b. "Faulkner's novels have the quality of being lived, ab-
      sorbed, remembered rather than merely observed"
   c. "the blood relationship is central"
   d. "Faulkner combines . . . the tradition of psychological
      horror . . . and the . . . tradition of frontier humor and
      realism"
   e. "he is an epic or bardic poet in prose"

48. Is Lewis's application of the Gide dictum to make the reader
a collaborator of the writer an apt one in Faulkner's case?

49. From whose point of view is *The Bear* told? How does it
affect the telling?

50. In an interview Faulkner said that one of his favorite books
for reading is the Old Testament. What evidence of this reading
do you find in the story, thought, and expression of *The Bear*?

51. In "Charactonyms in Faulkner's Novels" (*Bucknell Review,*
VIII:3, 189-201), Kelsie B. Harder writes that "Faulkner uses
names deliberately to illuminate important themes, and also to

structure the themes in the context of a story or a novel, or, as occasionally happens, in a continuing segment in the Yoknapataw-pha legend." What names are symbolic in *The Bear* and how? Is the symbolism handled consistently? Does it form a pattern?

52. Using *The Bear,* illustrate as many of O'Connor's twelve aspects of Faulkner's prose style as you can.

53. Comment on O'Connor's observations that
   a. Faulkner "seems incapable of developing a thesis slowly or subtly"
   b. "Faulkner's sentences evoke, they do not state"

54. Does *The Bear* manifest O'Connor's dichotomy of "high style" and "folk style"? Does Faulkner mix both? If so, what is the effect? Is it successful?

55. Harry Campbell suggests that Faulkner's style is the style of the future because he employs a unique and successful combination of outer incident and conflict (that is, among characters) and inner incident and conflict (within a given character's mind). Is this true in *The Bear*? Are both necessary for a good story? Contrast *The Bear* with a story by another author to support your claims.

56. What passages from *The Bear* would illustrate or disprove Irving Howe's observation that "Whereas a 'natural' story writer like Hemingway secretes his meaning in a few half-buried phrases, Faulkner allows his thought to spool its way through labyrinths of language"? What are the effects of such passages?

57. In "Faulkner in His Fury" (*The Inmost Leaf,* New York: Noonday Press, 1959), Alfred Kazin remarks that "the obscurities in [Faulkner's] work stem not from any particular profundity or complexity of ideas, but from the fact that his mind is so astonishingly energetic. . . . he is always leaping from one [issue] to the other in excited discovery. Faulkner writes like a man thinking aloud." Do you agree with Kazin's comment in whole or in part? Why?

58. How does Wertenbaker's concept of time in Faulkner agree or disagree with Hoffman's explanation?

59. Is Wertenbaker's elaborate chronology necessary? Should it be? Does it suggest a meaningful artist in Faulkner or a writer who is more obscure than is necessary?

60. In an interview with Jean Stein ["The Art of Fiction XII: William Faulkner," *The Paris Review*, XII (Spring 1956), 28-52], Faulkner said: "A writer is trying to create believable people in credible moving situations in the most moving way he can." Has he done so in *The Bear*? Consistently? Explain your answer. Do the writings of Faulkner with which you are familiar illustrate his claim in the Stein interview that "People between 20 and 40 are not sympathetic. . . . Between 20 and 40 the will of the child to do gets stronger, more dangerous, but it has not begun to learn to know yet"?

61. Of what value is it to read a parody, such as Mrs. Stiles's "The Saxon Beauty and the Three Black Bears," in connection with the specific work or author's writings in general which it caricatures?

62. Kinney's title calls "Delta Autumn" a "postlude" to *The Bear*, but he mentions that word only once in his essay. Does his argument justify the title? This interpretation rests on the assumption that Faulkner is consistent from work to work; for example, that Ike McCaslin is consistently developed in *The Bear* and "Delta Autumn." Is this assumption valid?

63. Rather than being wise as Kinney claims, isn't the girl of "Delta Autumn" really foolish to entangle herself with a white man if she knows there is little possibility of marrying him?

64. The Ike McCaslin of *The Bear* is proud and humble, courageous and meek. How would you describe the Ike of "Delta Autumn"?

65. What critical approaches presented in this book are used by any or all of the following: Utley, LaBudde, Breaden, Lewis, Taylor, Stewart, Kinney. Referring to Question #1 above, would you call any of these men "new critics"?

Bibliography

❦

Aiken, Conrad. "William Faulkner: The Novel as Form," *The Atlantic Monthly,* CLXIV (November 1939), 650-654. Aiken initiates the point, later common in Faulkner criticism, that a basic technique in Faulkner's style is "deliberately withheld meaning." In an easy, delightful style of his own, Aiken comments on the successes and failures in Faulkner's style.

Altenbernd, Lynn. "A Suspended Moment: The Irony of History in William Faulkner's 'The Bear,'" *Modern Language Notes,* LXXV:7 (November 1960), 572-582. A detailed and thorough explication of *The Bear,* which interprets Part IV as Ike's résumé of American and world history from the Creation onward. Altenbernd also shows how Faulkner develops the profound paradox that those who most love the land destroy it in their love for it.

Arthos, John. "Ritual and Humor in the Writing of William Faulkner," *Accent* (Autumn 1948), 17-30. Arthos sees Faulkner's concern with man's corrupt nature symbolized by the ghost-like figures and sense of the past which haunt his characters of the present. They try to expiate this sense of evil, guilt and foreboding through a formalized ritual, and Faulkner attempts to treat it both by ritual and by comic scenes and incidents. But his heart-driving emotions are at odds with his basic nature (that of a gifted comic writer) and his comedy usually does not succeed well. But when it does balance with pathos, as in *As I Lay Dying,* "the writing is merely simply true."

Backman, Melvin. "The Wilderness and the Negro in Faulkner's 'The Bear,'" *PMLA,* LXXVI (December 1961), 595-600. Backman cogently demonstrates that Faulkner, through his treatment of the Negro and the wilderness in *The Bear,* has shown how "mankind, driven by rapacity, has destroyed God's wilderness and enslaved His black creatures." The burden of guilt is on the South and on mankind, and is reflected in Ike McCaslin's behavior; for

Ike tries to "atone for the sin against the Negro" and attempts to escape the Southern dilemma. In "Delta Autumn" Faulkner again emphasizes Ike's behavior.

Beck, Warren. "Faulkner and the South," *The Antioch Review,* I:1 (March 1941), 82-94. An early attempt to recognize Faulkner's stature and genius. Beck disagrees with O'Donnell's opinion that Faulkner is overly romantic about the aristocratic past; rather, Beck maintains that Faulkner is melancholic in his concern for man as sinning and in need of redemption. Faulkner's melancholy was born through his service in the violence of World War I; it is epitomized by the lengendary past of Southern aristocrats (such as the Sartorises). Man as sinner and sinning is combatted by the patience and endurance of the Negro; the battleground for recognition of sin and of the need for redemption is in those of mixed blood.

Beck, Warren. "William Faulkner's Style," *American Prefaces,* IV (Spring 1941), 195-211. Beck amply illustrates his thesis that Faulkner's style is "progressive" because it synthesizes many past styles.

Bell, Jr., H. H. "A Footnote to Faulkner's 'The Bear,' " *College English,* XXIV:3 (December 1962), 179-183. Bell clarifies some of the problems of genealogy and chronology in *The Bear,* and says "By having Boon kill Old Ben, [Faulkner] manages to keep Ike unsullied to take part in the burial of Sam Fathers . . . and to become the caretaker and guardian of the ideals represented by Sam, and Old Ben, and the wilderness. . . ."

Blum, Irving D. "The Parallel Philosophy of Emerson's 'Nature' and Faulkner's 'The Bear,' " *Emerson Society Quarterly,* No. 13, 22-25. Blum shows how Ike's thoughts and actions illustrate Emerson's philosophy as expressed in *Nature,* "Self-Reliance," and the Phi Beta Kappa Address.

Buckley, G. T. "Is Oxford the Original of Jefferson in William Faulkner's Novels?" *PMLA,* LXXVI:4, Part 1 (September 1961), 447-454. It is an oversimplification to identify Oxford, Mississippi, with Jefferson in Faulkner's works. More likely, Faulkner's fictional locales are "a composite or abstraction of a half dozen small county seat towns of North Mississippi," such as Ripley, New Albany, and Holly Springs.

Cantwell, Robert. "The Faulkners: Recollections of a Gifted Family," *New World Writing,* 1952, pp. 300-315. A *Time* reporter's visit to Faulkner's home, with a description of the author, his conversation, and visits to the family home. Much of the emphasis is on Faulkner's great-grandfather, the model of Col. Sartoris of Yoknapatawpha.

Carter, Hodding. "Faulkner and His Folk." (An address delivered at the annual dinner of the Friends of the Princeton Library, May 10, 1957.) Reprinted in the *Princeton University Library Chronicle,* XVIII:3 (Spring 1957), 95-107. Faulkner has pricked the Southern conscience by his advocacy of integration, "not as an unforgiving castigator, as does the impatient outsider . . . but as one [of the South], feeling more strongly than most the ancient pull between our love and our anger at our region." Nevertheless, the Southern majority condemns Faulkner for his liberal views, despite the fact that Faulkner "is Southern in his pride in the past . . . in his clannishness; in his unposed love of the land; and in the ambivalent love and outrage with which he confronts the South."

Collins, Carvel. "Faulkner and Certain Earlier Southern Fiction," *College English,* XVI (November 1954), 92-97. Flamboyant humor, violence and various folklore traditions are characteristic of Southern regional literature, and are manifested in Thorpe's "Big Bear of Arkansas" and Faulkner's *The Bear.*

Collins, Carvel. "A Note on the Conclusion of 'The Bear,' " *Faulkner Studies,* II:4 (Winter 1954), 58-60. Whether or not Faulkner is aware of it, the final scene of *The Bear* represents Jung's "mandala" dream of release and assurance with its symbolic fourness (the posts of the grave), enclosed space, central point, and circular motion. (Ruel E. Foster answers Collins in the following issue of *Faulkner Studies,* pp. 4-5.)

Coughlan, Robert. *The Private World of William Faulkner* (New York: Harper and Brothers, 1954). A biography which emphasizes Faulkner's Southern culture and environment as related to his life, personality, and writings. Next to *Old Times in the Faulkner Country,* this is the most anecdotal of the books on Faulkner. Much of Coughlan's material first appeared in *Life* magazine.

Faulkner, William. *Big Woods* (New York: Random House, 1955). Reprints *The Bear* (without Part IV), "The Old People," and "A Bear Hunt" [a tall tale from *The Saturday Evening Post,* CCVI (Feb, 10, 1934), 8ff.]. "Race at Morning" is new to this volume. The interchapters tell the history of the wilderness, much of it rewritten from portions of "Red Leaves," "Delta Autumn," and Part IV of *The Bear.*

Faulkner, William. "A Courtship," from *Collected Stories* (New York: Random House, 1950), pp. 361-380. The most comic of Faulkner's wilderness tales, this is in the tradition of the frontier tall tale. Boon Hogganbeck's father, Dave, a captain of a steamboat used in the slave trade, and Doom (before he becomes the Chief) compete in many extravagant contests for the hand of the Indian Herman Basket's sister, who is lazy but lovely. An opening passage discusses at some length the white's apportionment of land to the Indians, and how the Indians came to possess what Ike, in *The Bear,* will say is unpossessable.

Faulkner, William. "The Fire and the Hearth," *Go Down, Moses* (New York: Random House, 1942). The first story of Lucas Beauchamp, modern Negro survivor of the McCaslin miscegenation, and his defense of mixed blood as well as his crafty and foolish hunt for gold. Important for the flashbacks, which reveal in more detail some of the heritage Ike reads in the commissary ledgers in *The Bear.* See particularly Chapter III, Part 1.

Faulkner, William. "Red Leaves," *These Thirteen* (New York: J. Cape and H. Smith, 1931), pp. 127-166. This story tells how Sam Fathers' ancestor, the Choctaw Indian chief Doom, was corrupted through miscegenation and slavery. He had a child by a French quadroon and he bought Negroes from the French explorers to raise and sell to the whites as slaves. Hence early the Indians attained ownership of land and became "burgher-like." In comparison with the Negro slave, who was "gaunt, lean, hard, tireless and desperate," the Indian became "thick, soft-looking, the apparent embodiment of the ultimate and the supreme reluctance and inertia." Already slavery breeds indolence in the slave owner.

Glicksberg, Charles I. "The World of William Faulkner," *Arizona Quarterly*, V:1 (Spring 1949), 46-58, 85-88. Faulkner's works are nihilistic, nightmarish representations of Faulkner's philosophy of naturalistic pessimism: "No Faulkner novel is complete without its compounded plot of horror, its ingredients of rape, seduction, prostitution, illegitimate children, incest, perversion, miscegenation. . . ." Although written in 1949, Glicksberg's essay is far more typical of the pre-1940s Faulkner criticism than of the more recent critical views.

Green, A. Wigfall. "William Faulkner at Home," *The Sewanee Review*, XL (Summer 1932), 294-306. A detailed description of the city and country on which Faulkner bases his work, and a highly personal summary of his early novels.

Guerard, Albert. "Justice in Yoknapatawpha County: Some Symbolic Motifs in Faulkner's Later Writing," *Faulkner Studies*, II:4 (Winter 1954), 49-57. In examining Faulkner's particular emphasis on interest in justice, Guerard counters the critically popular notion that the early Faulkner works present an apocalyptic doom while the later ones treat salvation. He shows that in some of the late works the Northern Snopeses reinforce Faulkner's earlier concern with the South as the scene of crime (slavery) and punishment (exploitation by the Snopeses).

Gwynn, Frederick L., and Joseph L. Blotner, eds. *Faulkner in the University: Class Conferences at the University of Virginia 1957-1958* (Charlottesville: University of Virginia Press, 1959). The most comprehensive publication of Faulkner's spontaneous opinions and recollections about his life, his writings, and the writings of others. Directly from tapes of Faulkner's interviews by students in advanced literature classes.

Hoffman, Frederick J., and Olga W. Vickery. *William Faulkner: Three Decades of Criticism* (East Lansing: Michigan State University Press, 1960). A compendium of significant critical essays on various Faulkner works, prefaced by a concise survey of Faulkner criticism since the publication of his first novel in 1926. [This is a revision of Hoffman and Vickery's *William Faulkner: Two Decades of Criticism* (East Lansing: Michigan State College Press, 1951).]

Jackson, James Turner. "Delta Cycle: A Study of William Faulkner," *Chimera,* V:1 (Autumn 1946), 3-14. A somewhat personal description of Faulkner's Mississippi fiction as illustrative of a seasonal and a historical cycle.

Jelliffe, Robert A., ed. *Faulkner at Nagano* (Tokyo: Kenkyusha, Ltd., 1956). The transcription of a series of fascinating discussions between Faulkner and Japanese teachers of literature in Japan in August 1955. Recurring topics are Faulkner's opinions of his own craftsmanship and works, and his impressions of Japanese literature and character.

Leaver, Florence. "Faulkner: The Word as Principle and Power," *The South Atlantic Quarterly,* LVII:4 (Autumn 1958), 464-476. Faulkner's key mood of intensity comes from making words serve dual and polar purposes, rather than from long, involuted sentences. His characteristic literary techniques involve use of abstract words, coined compound words, word repetition, and special "un-" or "-ness" words.

Litz, Walton. "Genealogy as Symbol in *Go Down, Moses,*" *Faulkner Studies,* I:4 (Winter 1952), 49-53. Litz presents a genealogy and shows how it is thematic in the novel.

Litz, Walton. "William Faulkner's Moral Vision," *Southwest Review,* XXXVII (Summer 1952), 200-209. Litz contends that a single moral vision pervades Faulkner's works from 1929 to 1952. He says that Faulkner views man as having the inner moral freedom "to endure and expatiate the evils which he inherits from the past," as having received the earth in trust but having "of his own free will . . . violated the conditions of stewardship." Thus Faulkner's man has broken "the foreordained pattern of respect between man and nature" in the South and left "a fragmented and loveless society suffering under the curse of its past history."

MacLean, Hugh. "Conservatism in Modern American Fiction," *College English,* XV:6 (March 1954), 315-325. With Fitzgerald, Marquand, and Salinger, Faulkner in his fiction upholds conservatism as a way of life. *The Bear* particularly represents conservatism in its approval of order, tradition, ritual, and class, and in its primary concern with God's purpose and grace for man.

Mayoux, Jean-Jacques. "The Creation of the Real in William Faulkner," *Études Anglaises* (February 1952), 25-39; trans. Frederick Hoffman in F. J. Hoffman and O. W. Vickery, *William Faulkner: Three Decades of Criticism,* pp. 156-172. An examination of Faulkner's style of immediacy, through the observing, narrating character and the listener character, which allows him to juxtapose the interior consciousness against the exterior action and to approach reality as the materialization of events, the "psychodrama of the present," the Platonic symbol for the eternal truth.

Meriwether, James B. *The Literary Career of William Faulkner: A Bibliographic Study* (Princeton: Princeton University Library, 1961). A bibliography whose comprehensiveness should delight the scholar and whose bibliographic descriptions should please the bibliographer. It contains a descriptive catalogue of the Faulkner exhibition held at the Princeton University Library in 1957 and of the Faulkner manuscript and typescript papers now at the University of Virginia; descriptions of the English editions and a checklist of the translations of Faulkner's works; a list of motion pictures on which Faulkner worked or which were adapted from Faulkner's writings; and a record of Faulkner's schedule of sending his early short stories to publishers. Meriwether also provides a good index.

Moses, W. R. "Where History Crosses Myth: Another Reading of 'The Bear,' " *Accent,* XIII:1 (Winter 1953), 21-33. Moses explores in detail the thesis that " 'The Bear' is an account of a person who as a child was able to participate in life under the conditions of myth [as expressed in the ritualistic circumstances of the hunt], but early saw those conditions smashed; who then examined the historical reality [of ancestral miscegenation and slavery] . . . and found it bad; who consequently refused to go with the historical drift of things and remained a myth-man all his life."

Robb, Mary Cooper. *William Faulkner: An Estimate of His Con-
tribution to the American Novel* (Pittsburgh: University of Pittsburgh Press, 1957). In this eclectic study of Faulkner, Miss Robb
counters charges of malice in his work with allusions to the Nobel
Prize address. She asserts that by means of his unusual style, Faulkner is merely extending the province of reality: "Because Faulkner's thesis is deceptively simple he has chosen to go beyond simplicity in illustrating it" (p. 217). Miss Robb sees Faulkner as a
writer concerned with nature (what is right) opposed to custom
(what is done). In Faulkner's works, as man reacts to nature, so
that man reacts to man. She also notes that "although Faulkner
never gives the reader any religious ideas through authorial comment, the ethical choices with which he presents his characters are
essentially Christian ones" (p. 35). If he insists there is evil, he
also insists man can save himself.

Sartre, Jean-Paul. "American Novelists in French Eyes," *Atlantic
Monthly,* CLXXVIII (August 1946), 114-118. Sartre maintains
that Europeans are much more responsive to Hemingway, Faulkner, Caldwell, and Steinbeck than are Americans. He believes that
the Europeans interpret the works of these authors as typical of
universal conditions, rather than as indictments of America, and
see them as "manifestations of American liberty." The literary
techniques of these American authors have inspired the techniques
of Camus, Simone de Beauvoir, and other French writers.

Sherwood, John C. "The Traditional Element in Faulkner," *Faulkner Studies,* III:2 (Summer-Autumn 1954), 17-23. A list and discussion of traditional literary situations which Faulkner uses, and
his curious mixture of naturalism and romanticism in treating them.

Slatoff, Walter J. "The Edge of Order: The Pattern of Faulkner's
Rhetoric," *Twentieth Century Literature,* III (October 1957), 107-
127. Slatoff discusses thoroughly the "number and variety of
things" which Faulkner presents in "conflicting terms." For example, Faulkner writes of events in ways which simultaneously
"suggest motion and immobility."

Sleeth, Irene Lynn. "William Faulkner: A Bibliography of Criticism," *Twentieth Century Literature,* VIII:1 (April 1962), 18-43.

A comprehensive bibliography of American criticism of Faulkner, from the 1920s to early 1961, and selected foreign criticism.

Stonesifer, Richard J. "Faulkner's 'The Bear': A Note on Structure," *College English,* XXIII (December 1961), 219-223. Stonesifer contends that in each section of *The Bear* Faulkner, "whether consciously or unconsciously, created by a consistent [sevenfold] pattern in his narration some significant clue to his meaning." Stonesifer then imposes this alleged pattern onto Parts I, II, III, and V of *The Bear.*

Sultan, Stanley. "Call Me Ishmael: The Hagiography of Isaac McCaslin," *Texas Studies in Literature and Language,* III:1 (Spring 1961), 50-66. This essay treats *Go Down, Moses* as an integrated single unit, not as a series of juxtaposed short stories. The tale of Ike McCaslin, as told in "The Old People," *The Bear,* and "Delta Autumn" is the paradigm of Faulkner's indictment of civilization. Ike's redemption is a principal question in *The Bear,* but "Delta Autumn" reveals that although "the wilderness had given him spiritual guidance and a way of life . . . [it] had not become his own heritage." Both the story "Go Down, Moses" and the book as a whole are "a plea for a deliverer."

Swiggart, Peter. *The Art of Faulkner's Novels* (Austin: University of Texas Press, 1962). Swiggart first examines Faulkner's "stylized characterization" and isolates "various techniques by which he establishes moral and social themes without sacrificing crucial elements of narrative realism"; Faulkner's "social mythology" and contrasts between rational-"puritan" and primitive-natural characters; and Faulkner's point-of-view techniques. In the rest of the book he analyzes Faulkner's canon in detail, emphasizing language, structure, theme, and characterization. He concentrates on *The Sound and the Fury, As I Lay Dying, Light in August,* and *Absalom, Absalom!*

Tate, Allen. "William Faulkner: 1897-1962," *The Sewanee Review,* LXXI:1 (Winter 1963), 160-164. [Reprinted from *New Statesman,* London.] An obituary. In assessing Faulkner's canon, Tate denies the importance of race relations and the land, which some critics believe are central to Faulkner's work.

Tick, Stanley. "The Unity of *Go Down, Moses,*" *Twentieth Century Literature,* VIII:2 (July 1962), 67-73. Except for "Pantaloon in Black," *Go Down, Moses* is a "six-part novel [whose architecture] is so compelling that no single section is fully explicable out of its context." Unity is provided by "the continuum of time and the consequent growth of moral consciousness," and by the theme of hunter—hunted—hunted-brought-home.

Tritschler, Donald. "The Unity of Faulkner's Shaping Vision," *Modern Fiction Studies,* V:4 (Winter 1959-1960), 337-343. In trying to discover the essence of any moment, Faulkner approaches it from past, present, and future, often mixed and submerged; he sacrifices chronological time to do so. The reader fights this by naturally superimposing chronological time. Hence Faulkner develops strategy to guarantee reader involvement at the same moment that he explores time in the Bergsonian sense of the past continually reshaping the present to plan anew the future.

Vickery, Olga W. *The Novels of William Faulkner: A Critical Interpretation* (Baton Rouge: Louisiana State University Press, 1959). Part II is a perceptive and philosophically oriented attempt to summarize many of Faulkner's views after the exhaustive examination of each of his novels in Part I. Mrs. Vickery discusses Faulkner's use of memory, legend, and point of view for an attempt at truth; his use of past, present, and future, and manipulation of time to achieve a sense of reality; the difficulty of exact communication in life, and the use of language as both technique and theme. She also considers Faulkner's view of man as a social being who has been disappointed by law and religion and finds salvation in his individual consciousness.

Waggoner, Hyatt H. *William Faulkner: From Jefferson to the World* (Lexington: University of Kentucky Press, 1959). Waggoner's discussion convincingly places Faulkner in the mainstream of American literature. Although Faulkner takes the position of a humanist and moralist in interviews, his fiction from *The Bear* onward proves that artistically, and perhaps basically, he is profoundly Christian in his philosophy.

Watkins, Floyd C. "The Gentle Reader and Mr. Faulkner's Morals," *The Georgia Review,* XIII:1 (Spring 1959), 68-75. Watkins answers the critics' charges that Faulkner's characters are too depraved and immoral: Watkins sees them as lifelike and as a part of life. He regards Faulkner's artistic achievement as honest and complete, like Shakespeare's and Chaucer's, but too immediate and realistic to be as easily accepted as that of the classical authors.

Williams, Cecil B. "William Faulkner and the Nobel Prize Awards," *Faulkner Studies,* I:2 (Summer 1952), 17-19. Americans generally reacted favorably to the awarding of the Nobel Prize to Faulkner, contrary to their attitudes when it went to Sinclair Lewis, Eugene O'Neill, and Pearl Buck. Williams attributes this acceptance of Faulkner in his own country "partly to the fact that his works have shown an evolution in the direction of patriotic acceptance and a hope for racial understanding and betterment at a time when his fellow Americans have especially wanted such affirmation."

Woodruff, Jr., Neal. " 'The Bear' and Faulkner's Moral Vision," *Studies in Faulkner,* Carnegie Series in English VI (Pittsburgh: Department of English, Carnegie Institute of Technology, 1961), 43-67. Woodruff's insightful essay takes issue with other accounts of Faulkner's moral vision as Christian, or primitivistic, or a rejection of "modernism." For Woodruff, Faulkner's moral vision is expressed in "the opposition between men and nature as ends" and as means. Faulkner's fiction contains many polarities of situation, theme, and character—the latter are principally "the self-contained," "victims of circumstances or exploitation," "the self-enslaved," and the exploiters. Such polarities "invite [the] reader to find human frustration or failure where men and nature are exploited as means to find human fulfillment where they become ends in themselves."

William Faulkner's Canon

❧

This is a listing of published volumes only; all books are novels unless otherwise indicated. For a listing of articles by and interviews of Faulkner, as well as foreign editions of his books, see reference to Meriwether, p. 423.

THE MARBLE FAUN (Poetry). Boston, 1924.

SOLDIERS' PAY. New York, 1926. London, 1930, 1931.

MOSQUITOES. New York, 1927.

SARTORIS. New York, 1929, 1951. London, 1932, 1954.

THE SOUND AND THE FURY. New York, 1929; with *As I Lay Dying*, in Modern Library, 1946.

AS I LAY DYING. New York, 1930; Modern Library, 1946.

THESE THIRTEEN. New York, 1930. See also *The Collected Stories of William Faulkner.*

SANCTUARY. New York, 1931.

SALMAGUNDI (Newspaper sketches), ed. (with intro.) Paul Romaine. Milwaukee, 1932.

LIGHT IN AUGUST. New York, 1932; Norfolk, Conn., 1947.

A GREEN BOUGH (Poetry). New York, 1933.

DOCTOR MARTINO AND OTHER STORIES. New York, 1934. See also *The Collected Stories of William Faulkner.*

PYLON. New York, 1935, 1951.

ABSALOM, ABSALOM! New York, 1936, 1951.

THE UNVANQUISHED. New York, 1938, 1952.

THE WILD PALMS (with OLD MAN). New York, 1939.

THE HAMLET. New York, 1940, 1956.

GO DOWN, MOSES. New York, 1942, 1945.

INTRUDER IN THE DUST. New York, 1948.

KNIGHT'S GAMBIT (Short stories). New York, 1949.

COLLECTED STORIES OF WILLIAM FAULKNER. New York, 1950.

NOTES ON A HORSETHIEF. Greenville, Miss., 1951.

REQUIEM FOR A NUN. New York, 1951.

A FABLE. New York, 1954.

BIG WOODS. New York, 1955.
THE TOWN. New York, 1957.
NEW ORLEANS SKETCHES (Newspaper sketches from *Salmagundi*),
  ed. (with intro.) Carvel Collins. New Brunswick, N.J., 1958.
THE MANSION. New York, 1959.
THE REIVERS. New York, 1962.

A NOTE ON THE TYPE

The text of this book was set on the Linotype in a face called TIMES ROMAN, designed by Stanley Morison for *The Times* (London), and first introduced by that newspaper in 1932.

Among typographers and designers of the twentieth century, Stanley Morison has been a strong forming influence, as typographical advisor to the English Monotype Corporation, as a director of two distinguished English publishing houses, and as a writer of sensibility, erudition, and keen practical sense.

A NOTE ON THE TYPE

The text of this book was set on the Linotype in a face called TIMES ROMAN, designed by Stanley Morison for The Times (London), and first introduced by that newspaper in 1932. Among typographers and designers of the twentieth century, Stanley Morison has been a strong forming influence, as typographical adviser to the English Monotype Corporation, as a director of two distinguished English publishing houses, and as a writer of sensibility, erudition, and keen practical sense.